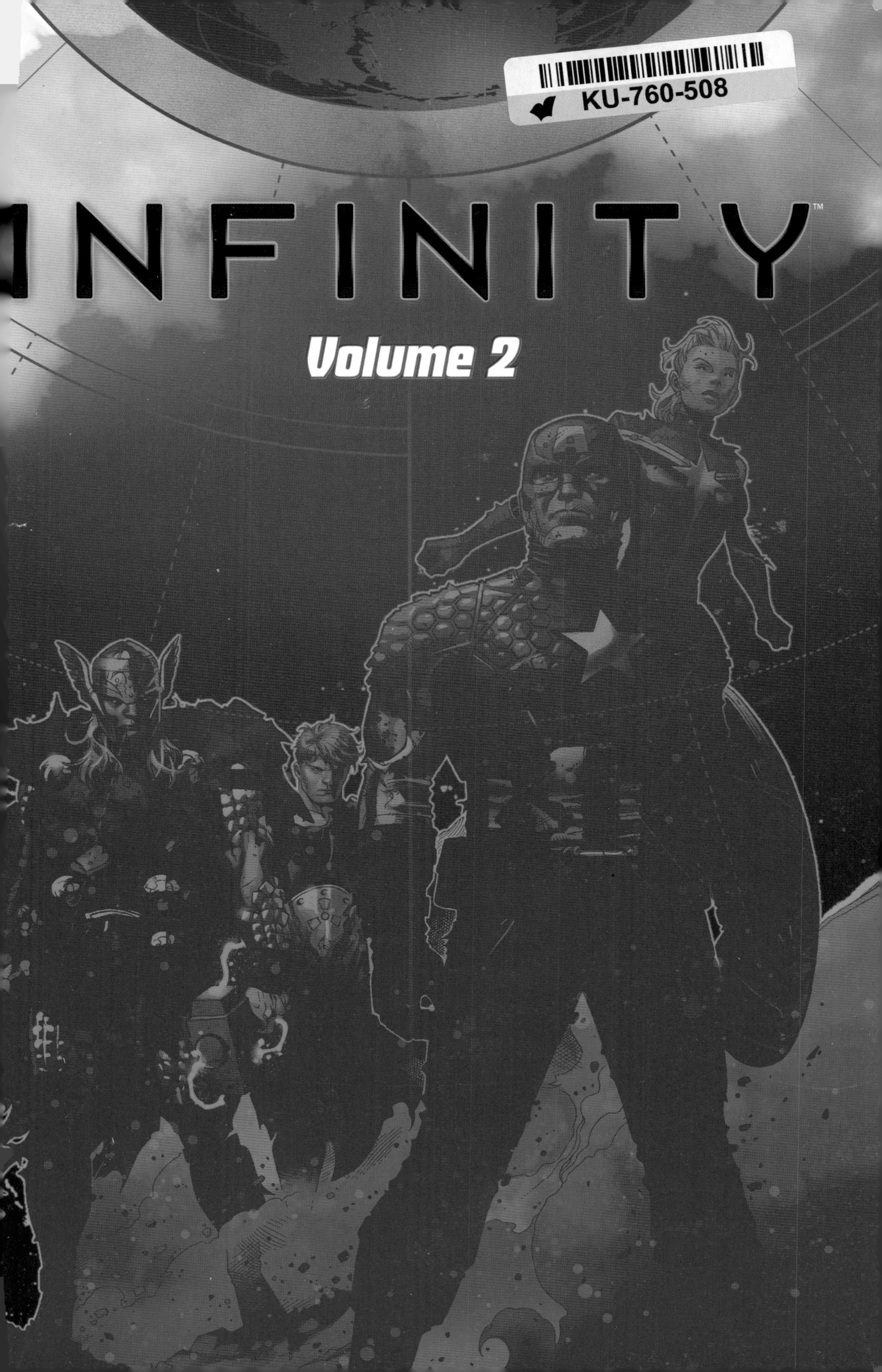
INFINITY™
Volume 2

INFINITY

Volume 2

WRITER: JONATHAN HICKMAN

INFINITY

PENCILERS: JIM CHEUNG, JEROME OPEÑA & DUSTIN WEAVER

INKERS: MARK MORALES, JOHN LIVESAY, DAVID MEIKIS, JEROME OPEÑA & DUSTIN WEAVER

LETTERS: VIRTUAL CALLIGRAPHY'S JOE CARAMAGNA & CHRIS ELIOPOULOS

COLOURIST: JUSTIN PONSOR

AVENGERS

PENCILERS: LEINIL FRANCIS YU

INKERS: GERRY ALANGUILAN & LEINIL FRANCIS YU

LETTERS: VIRTUAL CALLIGRAPHY'S CORY PETIT

COLOURIST: SUNNY GHO

NEW AVENGERS

ART: MIKE DEODATO JR.

LETTERS: VIRTUAL CALLIGRAPHY'S JOE CARAMAGNA

COLOURIST: FRANK MARTIN

ASSISTANT EDITOR: JAKE THOMAS

EDITORS: TOM BREVOORT & LAUREN SANKOVITCH

EDITOR IN CHIEF: AXEL ALONSO

CHIEF CREATIVE OFFICER: JOE QUESADA

PUBLISHER: ALAN FINE

EXECUTIVE PRODUCER: DAN BUCKLEY

COVER: ADAM KUBERT

Do you have any comments or queries about this graphic novel? Email us at graphicnovels@panini.co.uk
Find us on Facebook at Panini/Marvel Graphic Novels.

MARVEL
marvel.com

TM & © 2013 and 2014 Marvel & Subs. Licensed by Marvel Characters B.V. through Panini S.p.A., Italy. All Rights Reserved. First printing 2014. Published by Panini Publishing, a division of Panini UK Limited. Mike Riddell, Managing Director. Alan O'Keefe, Managing Editor. Mark Irvine, Production Manager. Marco M. Lupoi, Publishing Director Europe. Brady Webb, Reprint Editor. Angela Hart and Caroline Dunk, Designers. Office of publication: Brockbourne House, 77 Mount Ephraim, Tunbridge Wells, Kent TN4 8BS. This publication may not be sold, except by authorised dealers, and is sold subject to the condition that it shall not be sold or distributed with any part of its cover or markings removed, nor in a mutilated condition. Printed in Italy by SIZ. ISBN: 978-1-84653-587-1
LEGO and the Minifigure figurine are trademarks or copyrights of the LEGO Group of Companies. © 2013 and 2014 The LEGO Group

FSC www.fsc.org MIX Paper f… responsible… FSC® C0…

CAST

THE ILLUMINATI

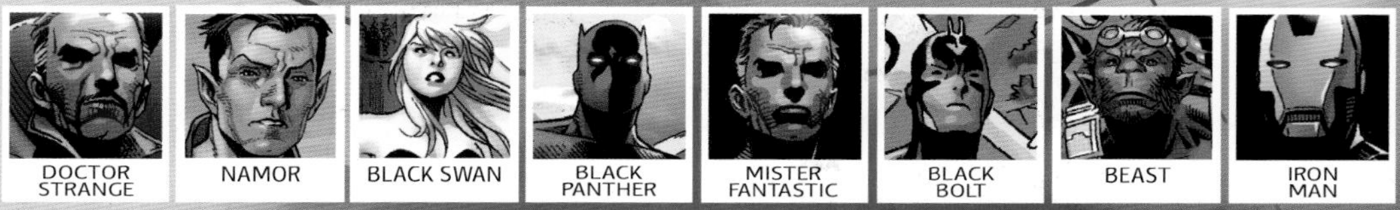

DOCTOR STRANGE · NAMOR · BLACK SWAN · BLACK PANTHER · MISTER FANTASTIC · BLACK BOLT · BEAST · IRON MAN

X-MEN

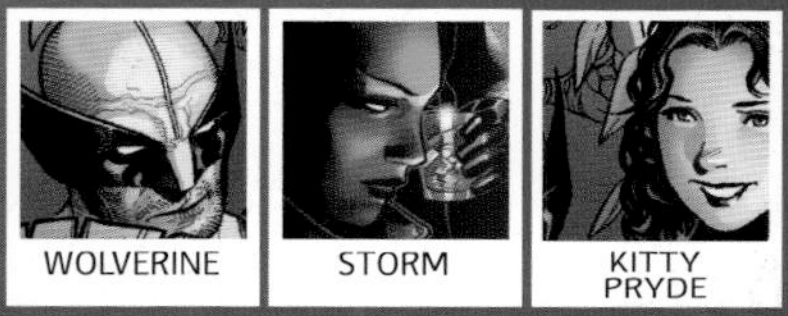

WOLVERINE · STORM · KITTY PRYDE

THE BUILDERS

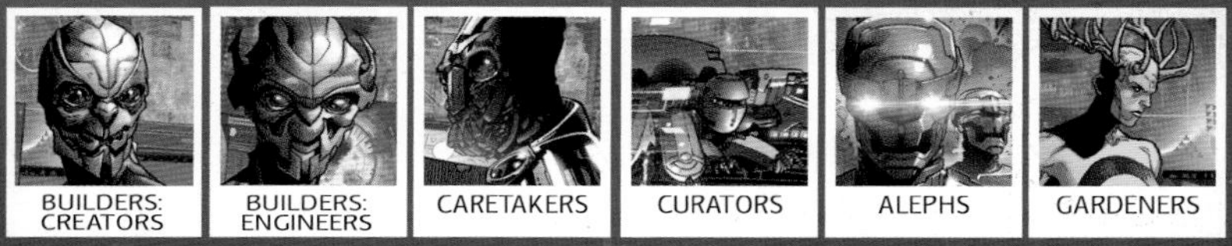

BUILDERS: CREATORS · BUILDERS: ENGINEERS · CARETAKERS · CURATORS · ALEPHS · GARDENERS

SPACEKNIGHTS

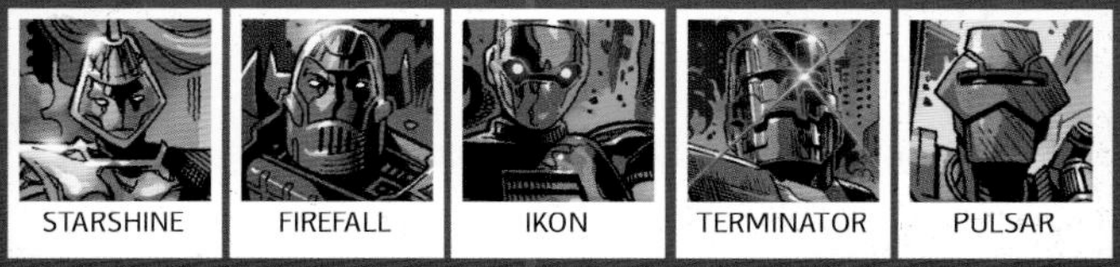

STARSHINE · FIREFALL · IKON · TERMINATOR · PULSAR

THE AVENGERS

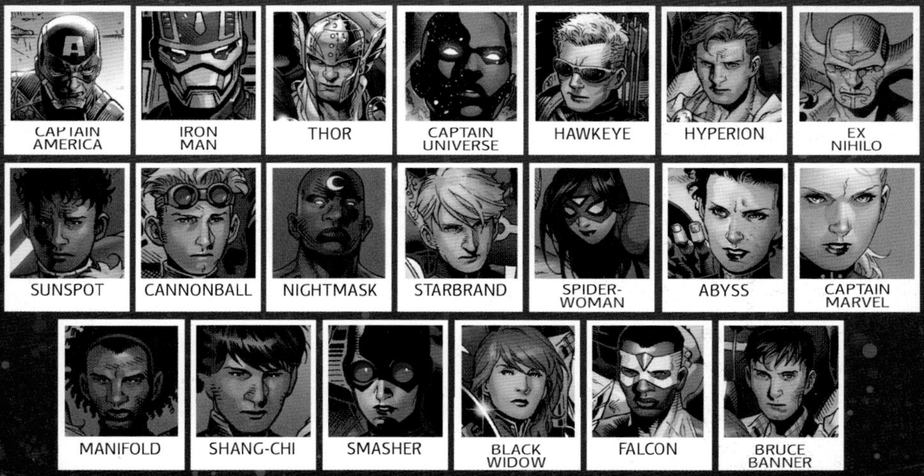

CAPTAIN AMERICA · IRON MAN · THOR · CAPTAIN UNIVERSE · HAWKEYE · HYPERION · EX NIHILO

SUNSPOT · CANNONBALL · NIGHTMASK · STARBRAND · SPIDER-WOMAN · ABYSS · CAPTAIN MARVEL

MANIFOLD · SHANG-CHI · SMASHER · BLACK WIDOW · FALCON · BRUCE BANNER

INHUMANS

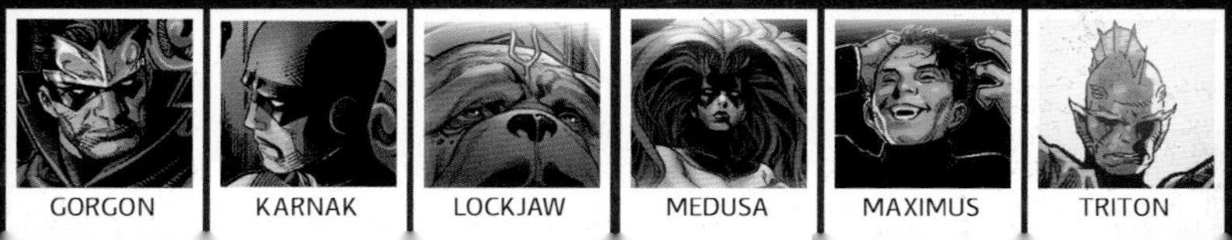

GORGON · KARNAK · LOCKJAW · MEDUSA · MAXIMUS · TRITON

PREVIOUSLY IN INFINITY

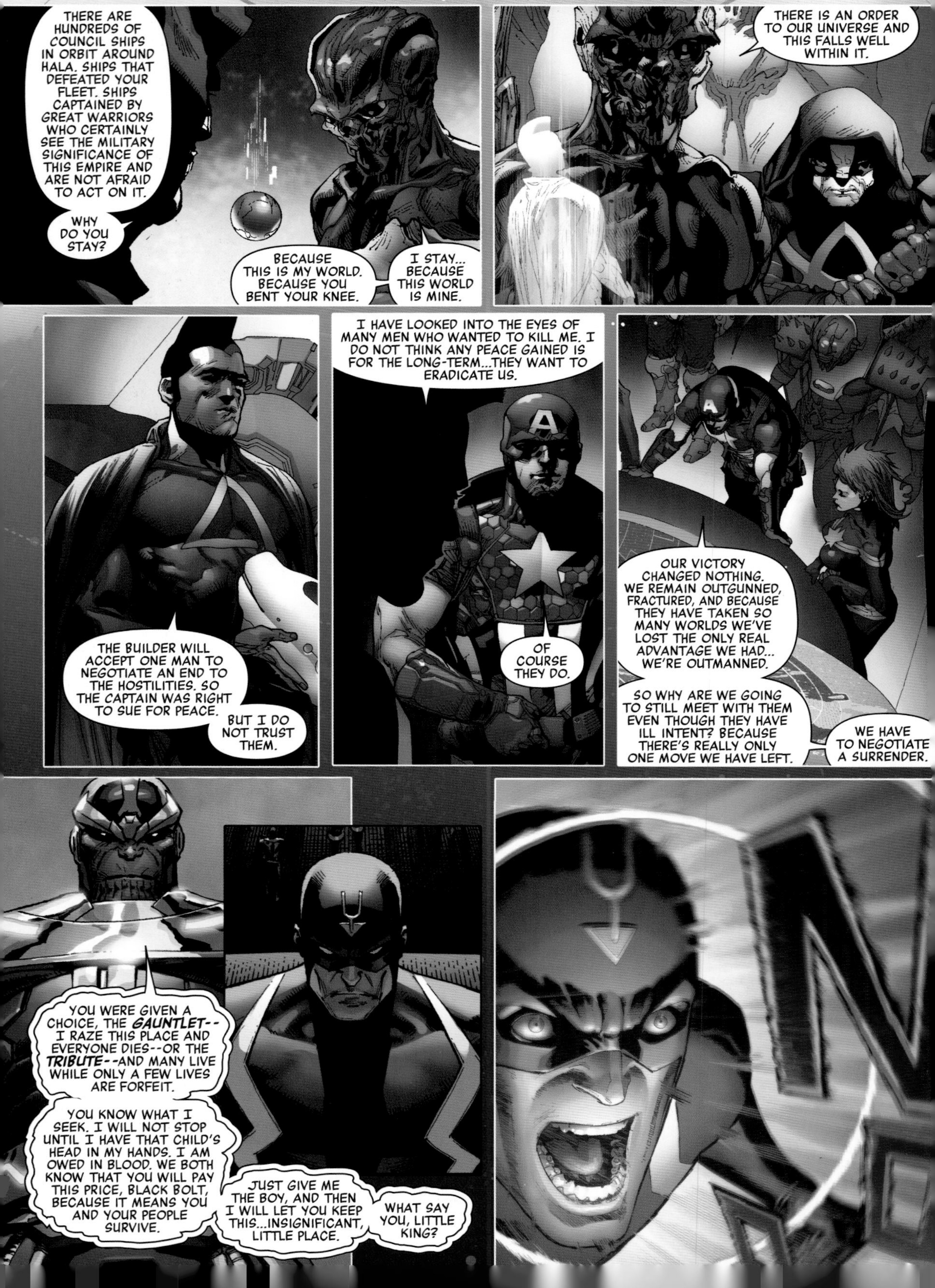

THERE ARE HUNDREDS OF COUNCIL SHIPS IN ORBIT AROUND HALA. SHIPS THAT DEFEATED YOUR FLEET. SHIPS CAPTAINED BY GREAT WARRIORS WHO CERTAINLY SEE THE MILITARY SIGNIFICANCE OF THIS EMPIRE AND ARE NOT AFRAID TO ACT ON IT.
WHY DO YOU STAY?
I STAY... BECAUSE THIS WORLD IS MINE.
BECAUSE THIS IS MY WORLD. BECAUSE YOU BENT YOUR KNEE.
THERE IS AN ORDER TO OUR UNIVERSE AND THIS FALLS WELL WITHIN IT.
THE BUILDER WILL ACCEPT ONE MAN TO NEGOTIATE AN END TO THE HOSTILITIES. SO THE CAPTAIN WAS RIGHT TO SUE FOR PEACE.
BUT I DO NOT TRUST THEM.
I HAVE LOOKED INTO THE EYES OF MANY MEN WHO WANTED TO KILL ME. I DO NOT THINK ANY PEACE GAINED IS FOR THE LONG-TERM...THEY WANT TO ERADICATE US.
OF COURSE THEY DO.
OUR VICTORY CHANGED NOTHING. WE REMAIN OUTGUNNED, FRACTURED, AND BECAUSE THEY HAVE TAKEN SO MANY WORLDS WE'VE LOST THE ONLY REAL ADVANTAGE WE HAD... WE'RE OUTMANNED.
SO WHY ARE WE GOING TO STILL MEET WITH THEM EVEN THOUGH THEY HAVE ILL INTENT? BECAUSE THERE'S REALLY ONLY ONE MOVE WE HAVE LEFT.
WE HAVE TO NEGOTIATE A SURRENDER.
YOU WERE GIVEN A CHOICE, THE GAUNTLET--I RAZE THIS PLACE AND EVERYONE DIES--OR THE TRIBUTE--AND MANY LIVE WHILE ONLY A FEW LIVES ARE FORFEIT.
YOU KNOW WHAT I SEEK. I WILL NOT STOP UNTIL I HAVE THAT CHILD'S HEAD IN MY HANDS. I AM OWED IN BLOOD. WE BOTH KNOW THAT YOU WILL PAY THIS PRICE, BLACK BOLT, BECAUSE IT MEANS YOU AND YOUR PEOPLE SURVIVE.
JUST GIVE ME THE BOY, AND THEN I WILL LET YOU KEEP THIS...INSIGNIFICANT, LITTLE PLACE.
WHAT SAY YOU, LITTLE KING?

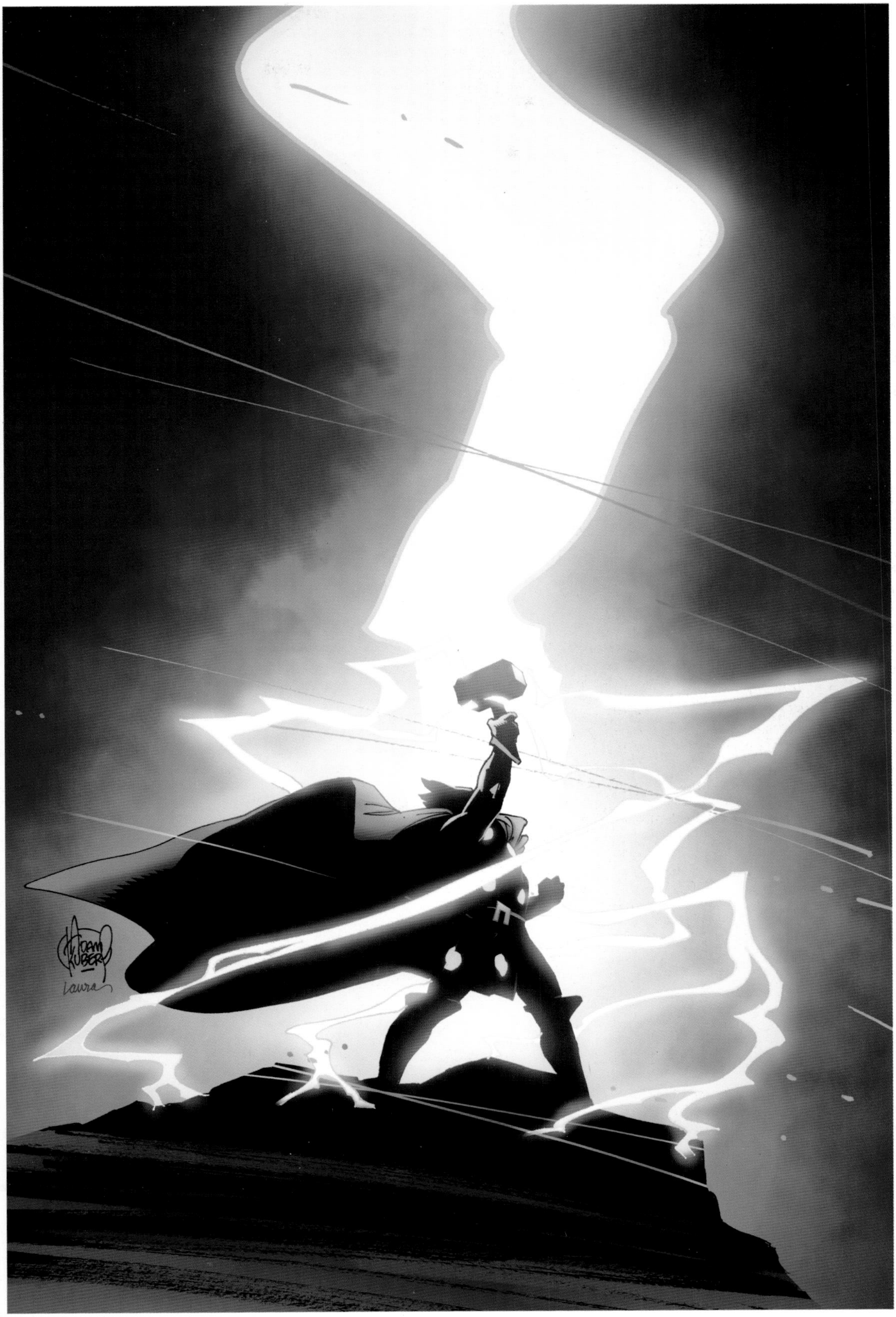
Adam Kubert
Laura

THE LAST LESSON

◆

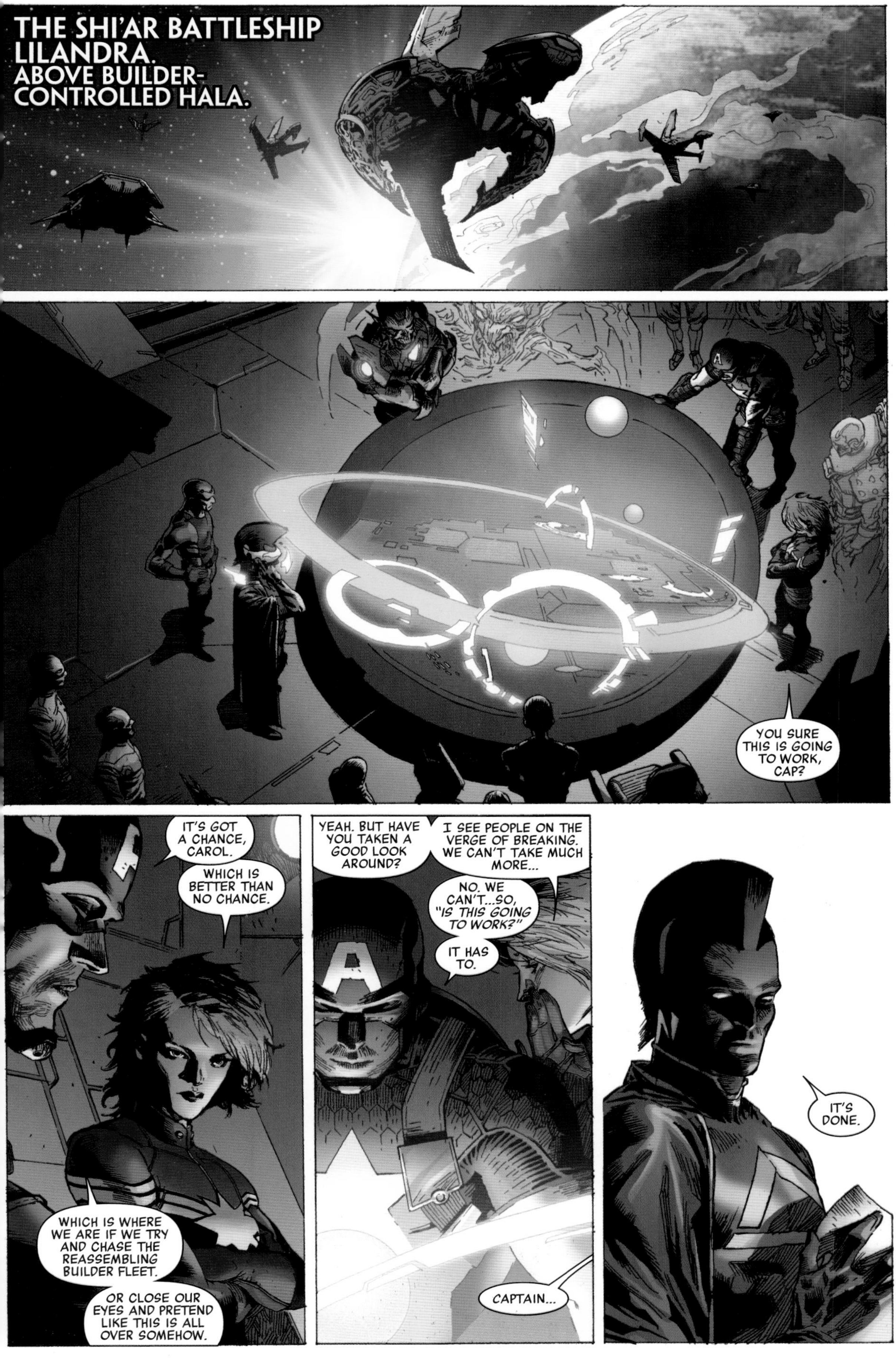
THE SHI'AR BATTLESHIP LILANDRA.
ABOVE BUILDER-CONTROLLED HALA.
YOU SURE THIS IS GOING TO WORK, CAP?
IT'S GOT A CHANCE, CAROL.
WHICH IS BETTER THAN NO CHANCE.
WHICH IS WHERE WE ARE IF WE TRY AND CHASE THE REASSEMBLING BUILDER FLEET.
OR CLOSE OUR EYES AND PRETEND LIKE THIS IS ALL OVER SOMEHOW.
YEAH. BUT HAVE YOU TAKEN A GOOD LOOK AROUND?
I SEE PEOPLE ON THE VERGE OF BREAKING. WE CAN'T TAKE MUCH MORE...
NO. WE CAN'T...SO, "IS THIS GOING TO WORK?"
IT HAS TO.
CAPTAIN...
IT'S DONE.

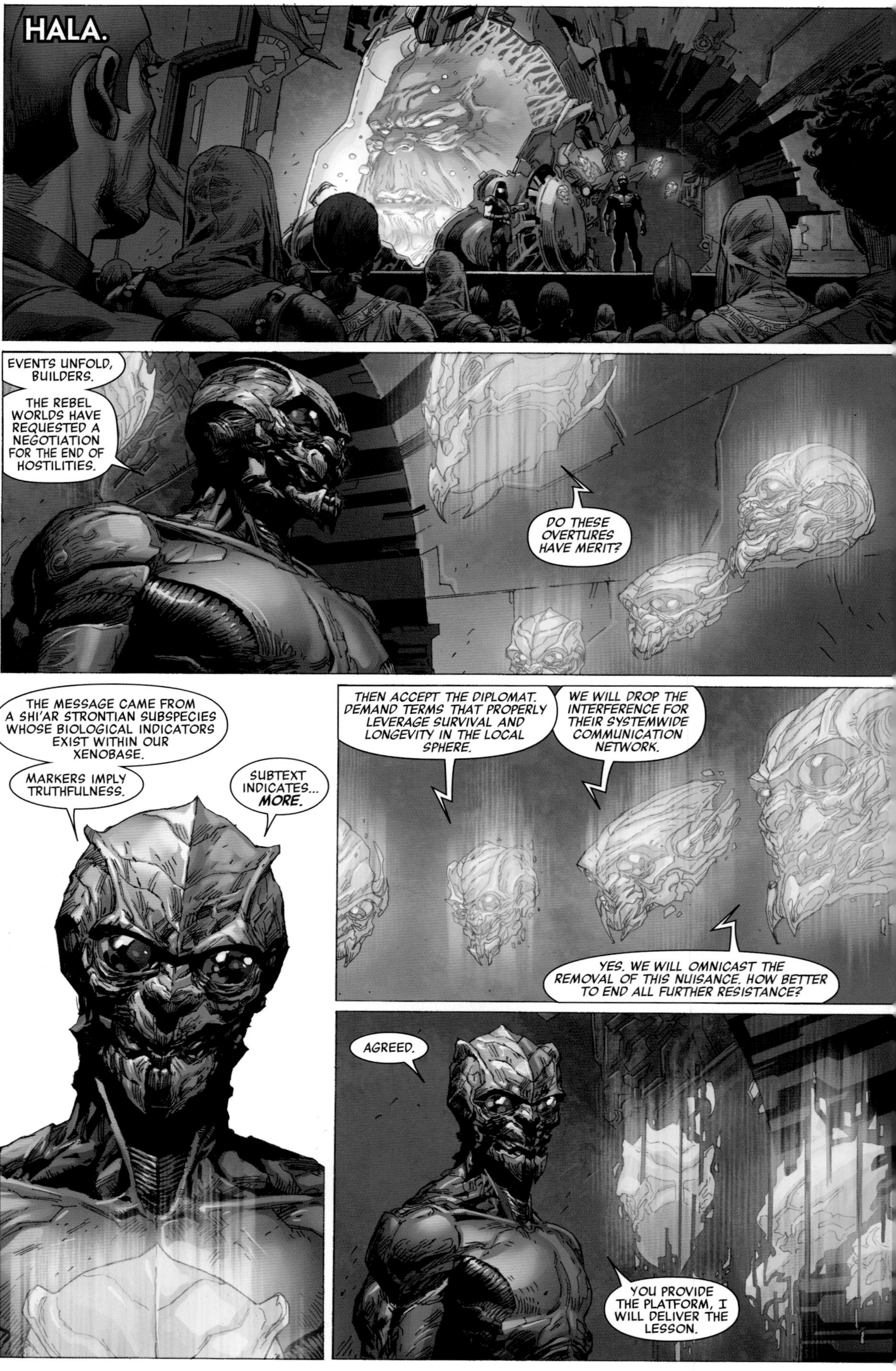
HALA.
EVENTS UNFOLD, BUILDERS.
THE REBEL WORLDS HAVE REQUESTED A NEGOTIATION FOR THE END OF HOSTILITIES.
DO THESE OVERTURES HAVE MERIT?
THE MESSAGE CAME FROM A SHI'AR STRONTIAN SUBSPECIES WHOSE BIOLOGICAL INDICATORS EXIST WITHIN OUR XENOBASE.
MARKERS IMPLY TRUTHFULNESS.
SUBTEXT INDICATES... MORE.
THEN ACCEPT THE DIPLOMAT. DEMAND TERMS THAT PROPERLY LEVERAGE SURVIVAL AND LONGEVITY IN THE LOCAL SPHERE.
WE WILL DROP THE INTERFERENCE FOR THEIR SYSTEMWIDE COMMUNICATION NETWORK.
YES. WE WILL OMNICAST THE REMOVAL OF THIS NUISANCE. HOW BETTER TO END ALL FURTHER RESISTANCE?
AGREED.
YOU PROVIDE THE PLATFORM, I WILL DELIVER THE LESSON.

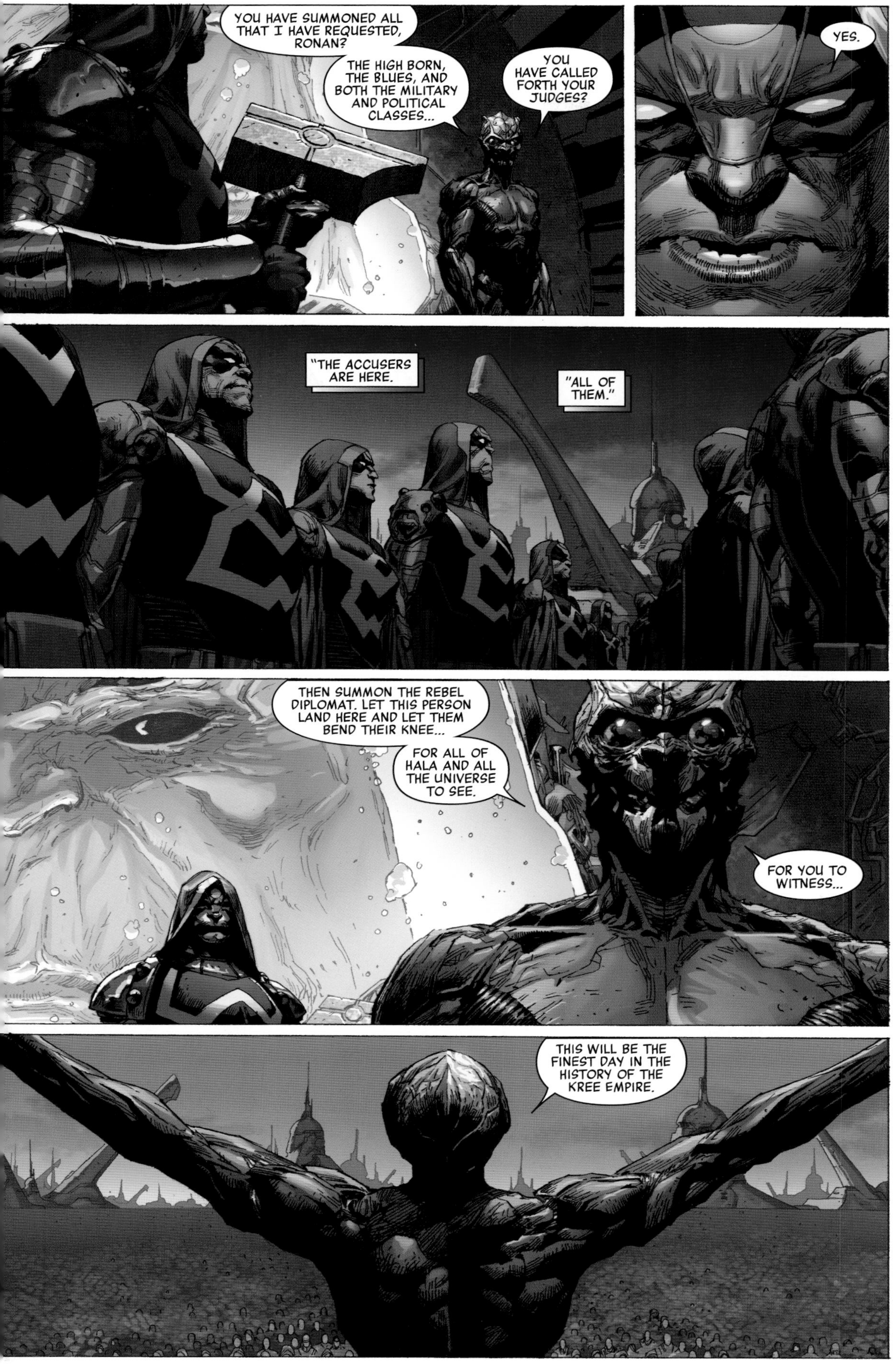
YOU HAVE SUMMONED ALL THAT I HAVE REQUESTED, RONAN?
THE HIGH BORN, THE BLUES, AND BOTH THE MILITARY AND POLITICAL CLASSES...
YOU HAVE CALLED FORTH YOUR JUDGES?
YES.
"THE ACCUSERS ARE HERE.
"ALL OF THEM."
THEN SUMMON THE REBEL DIPLOMAT. LET THIS PERSON LAND HERE AND LET THEM BEND THEIR KNEE...
FOR ALL OF HALA AND ALL THE UNIVERSE TO SEE.
FOR YOU TO WITNESS...
THIS WILL BE THE FINEST DAY IN THE HISTORY OF THE KREE EMPIRE.

THE CHANGE

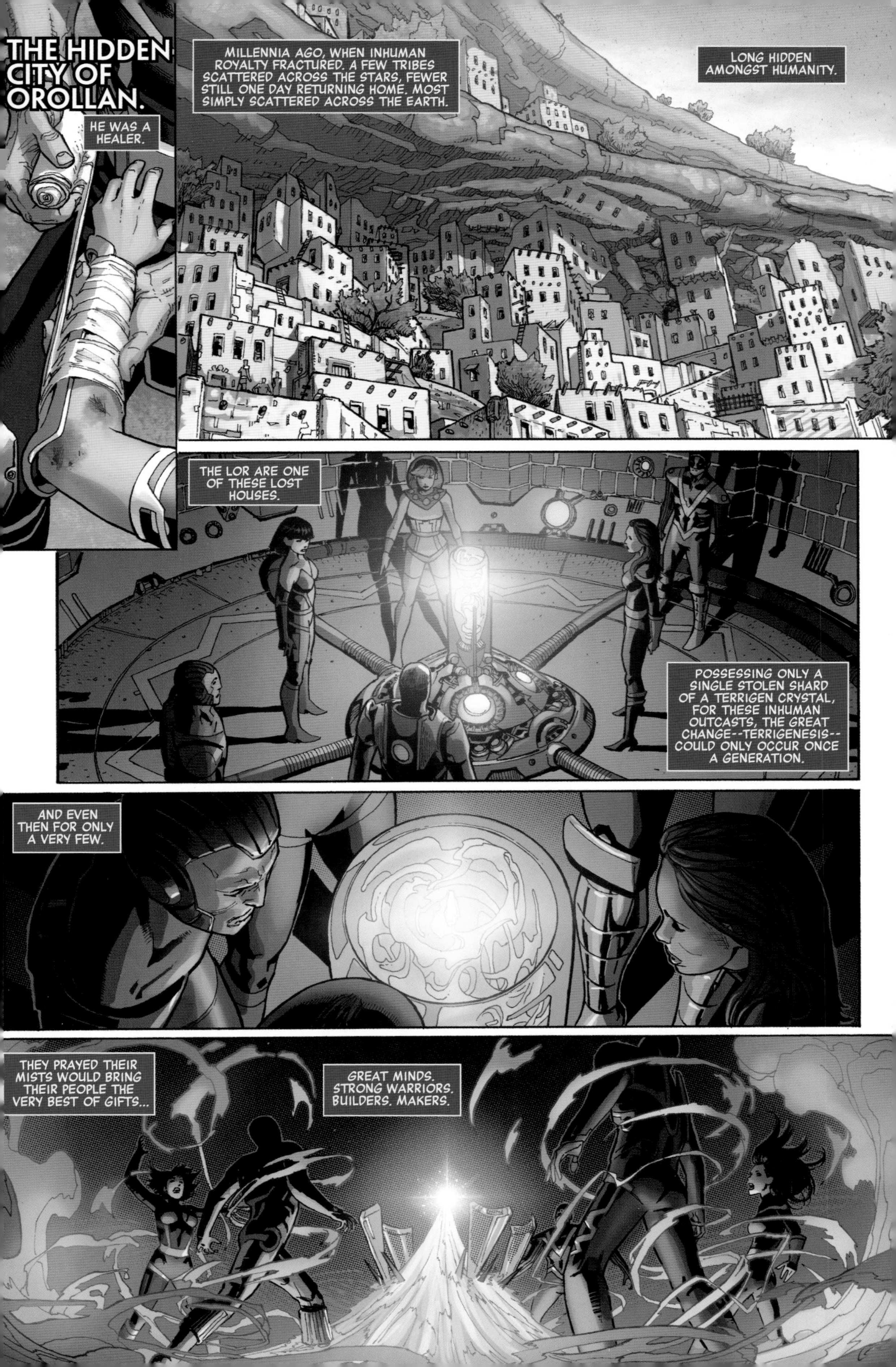
THE HIDDEN CITY OF OROLLAN.
HE WAS A HEALER.
MILLENNIA AGO, WHEN INHUMAN ROYALTY FRACTURED. A FEW TRIBES SCATTERED ACROSS THE STARS, FEWER STILL ONE DAY RETURNING HOME. MOST SIMPLY SCATTERED ACROSS THE EARTH.
LONG HIDDEN AMONGST HUMANITY.
THE LOR ARE ONE OF THESE LOST HOUSES.
POSSESSING ONLY A SINGLE STOLEN SHARD OF A TERRIGEN CRYSTAL, FOR THESE INHUMAN OUTCASTS, THE GREAT CHANGE--TERRIGENESIS--COULD ONLY OCCUR ONCE A GENERATION.
AND EVEN THEN FOR ONLY A VERY FEW.
THEY PRAYED THEIR MISTS WOULD BRING THEIR PEOPLE THE VERY BEST OF GIFTS...
GREAT MINDS. STRONG WARRIORS. BUILDERS. MAKERS.

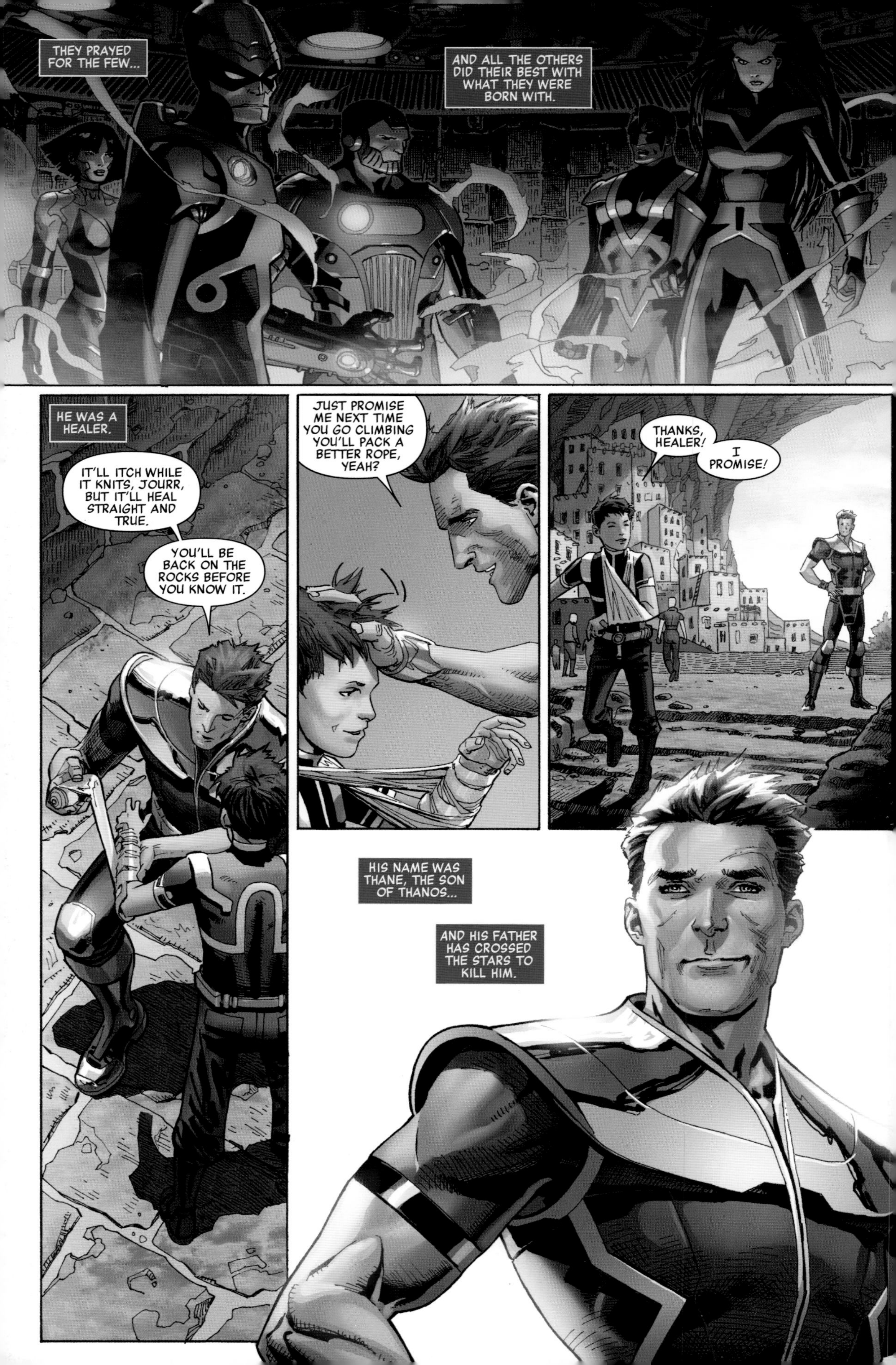

THEY PRAYED FOR THE FEW...
AND ALL THE OTHERS DID THEIR BEST WITH WHAT THEY WERE BORN WITH.
HE WAS A HEALER.
IT'LL ITCH WHILE IT KNITS, JOURR, BUT IT'LL HEAL STRAIGHT AND TRUE.
YOU'LL BE BACK ON THE ROCKS BEFORE YOU KNOW IT.
JUST PROMISE ME NEXT TIME YOU GO CLIMBING YOU'LL PACK A BETTER ROPE, YEAH?
THANKS, HEALER!
I PROMISE!
HIS NAME WAS THANE, THE SON OF THANOS...
AND HIS FATHER HAS CROSSED THE STARS TO KILL HIM.

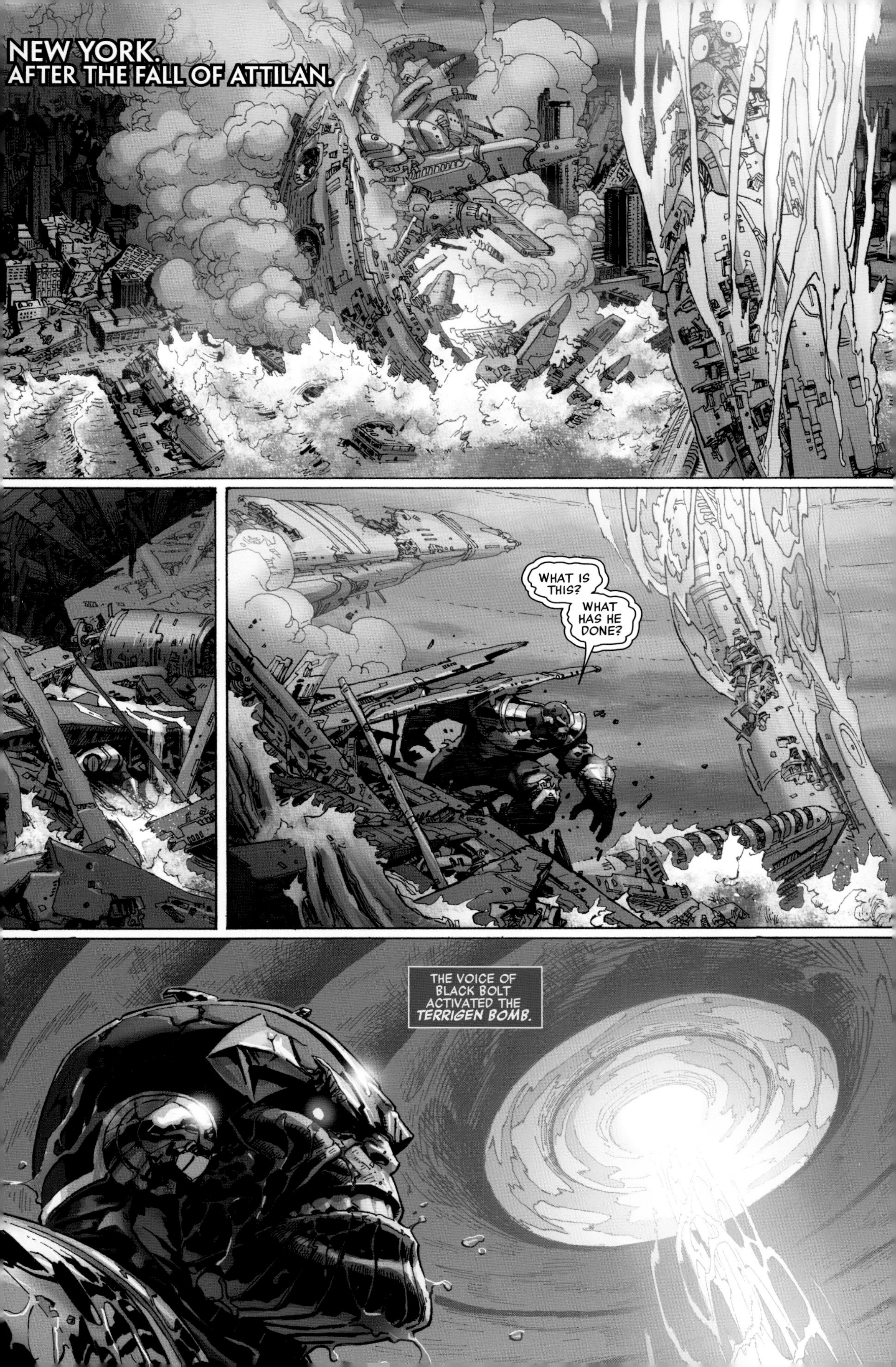
NEW YORK.
AFTER THE FALL OF ATTILAN.
WHAT IS THIS?
WHAT HAS HE DONE?
THE VOICE OF BLACK BOLT ACTIVATED THE TERRIGEN BOMB.

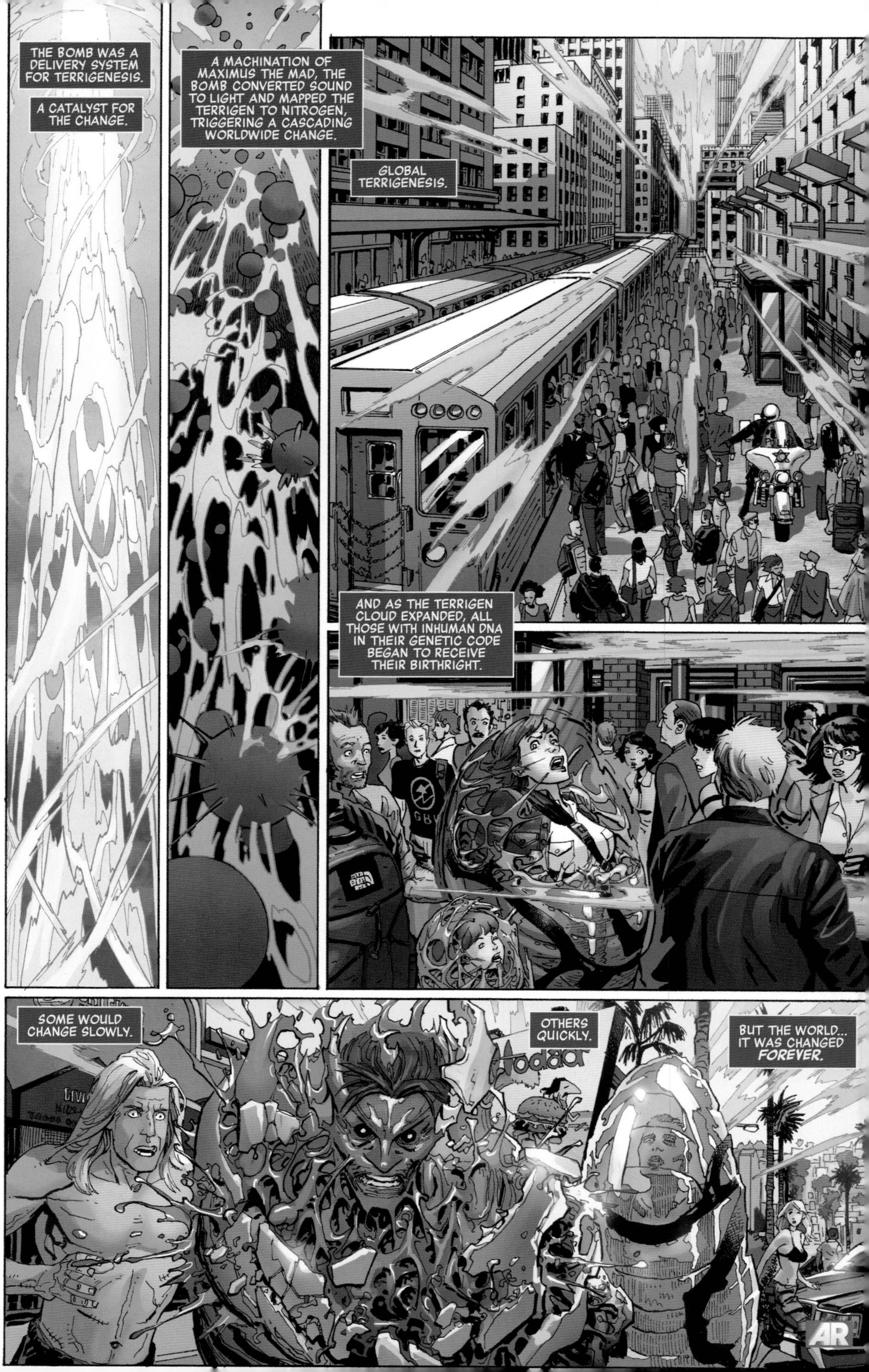
THE BOMB WAS A DELIVERY SYSTEM FOR TERRIGENESIS.
A CATALYST FOR THE CHANGE.
A MACHINATION OF MAXIMUS THE MAD, THE BOMB CONVERTED SOUND TO LIGHT AND MAPPED THE TERRIGEN TO NITROGEN, TRIGGERING A CASCADING WORLDWIDE CHANGE.
GLOBAL TERRIGENESIS.
AND AS THE TERRIGEN CLOUD EXPANDED, ALL THOSE WITH INHUMAN DNA IN THEIR GENETIC CODE BEGAN TO RECEIVE THEIR BIRTHRIGHT.
SOME WOULD CHANGE SLOWLY.
OTHERS QUICKLY.
BUT THE WORLD... IT WAS CHANGED *FOREVER.*

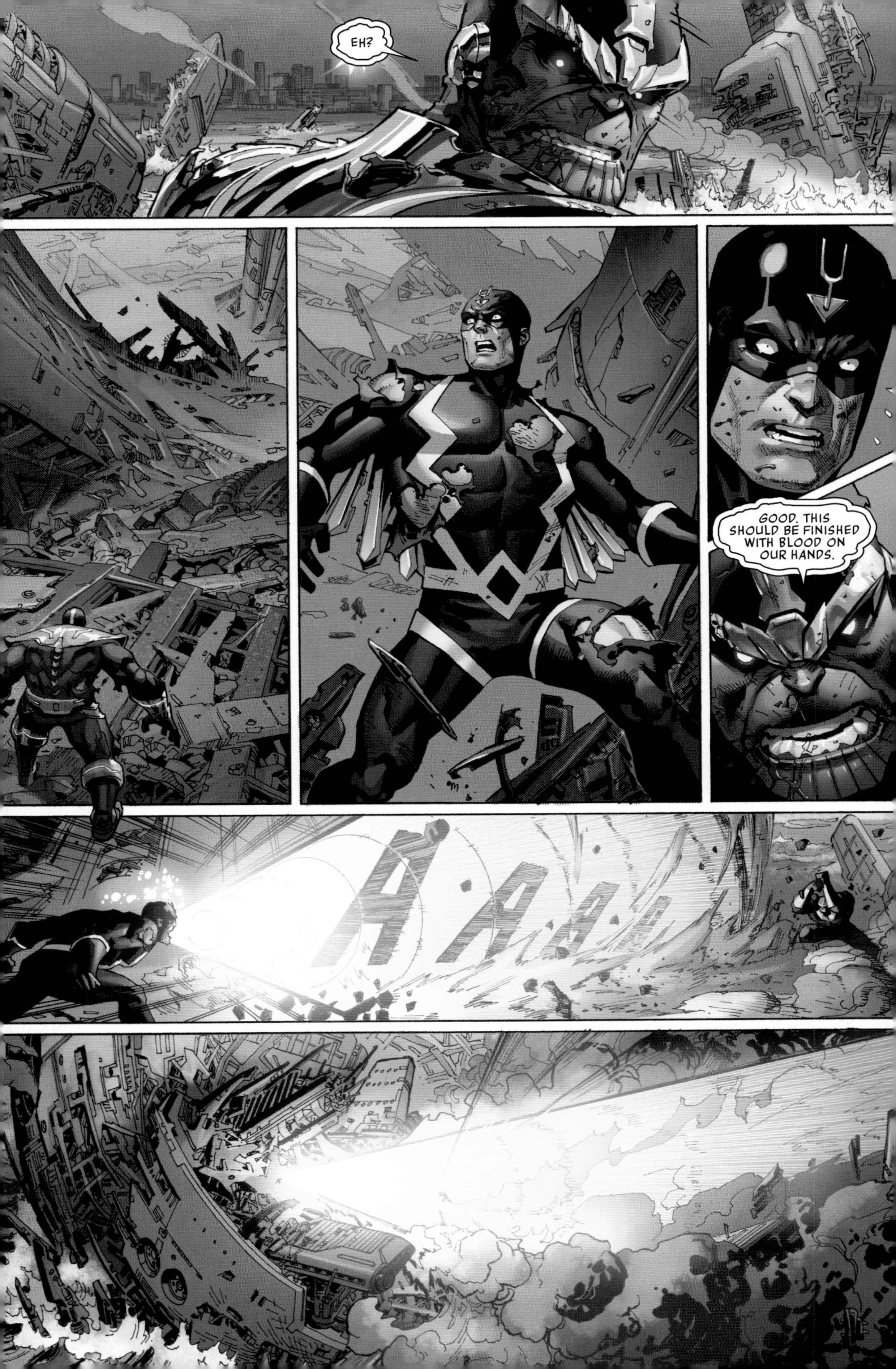
EH?
GOOD. THIS SHOULD BE FINISHED WITH BLOOD ON OUR HANDS.
AAAA

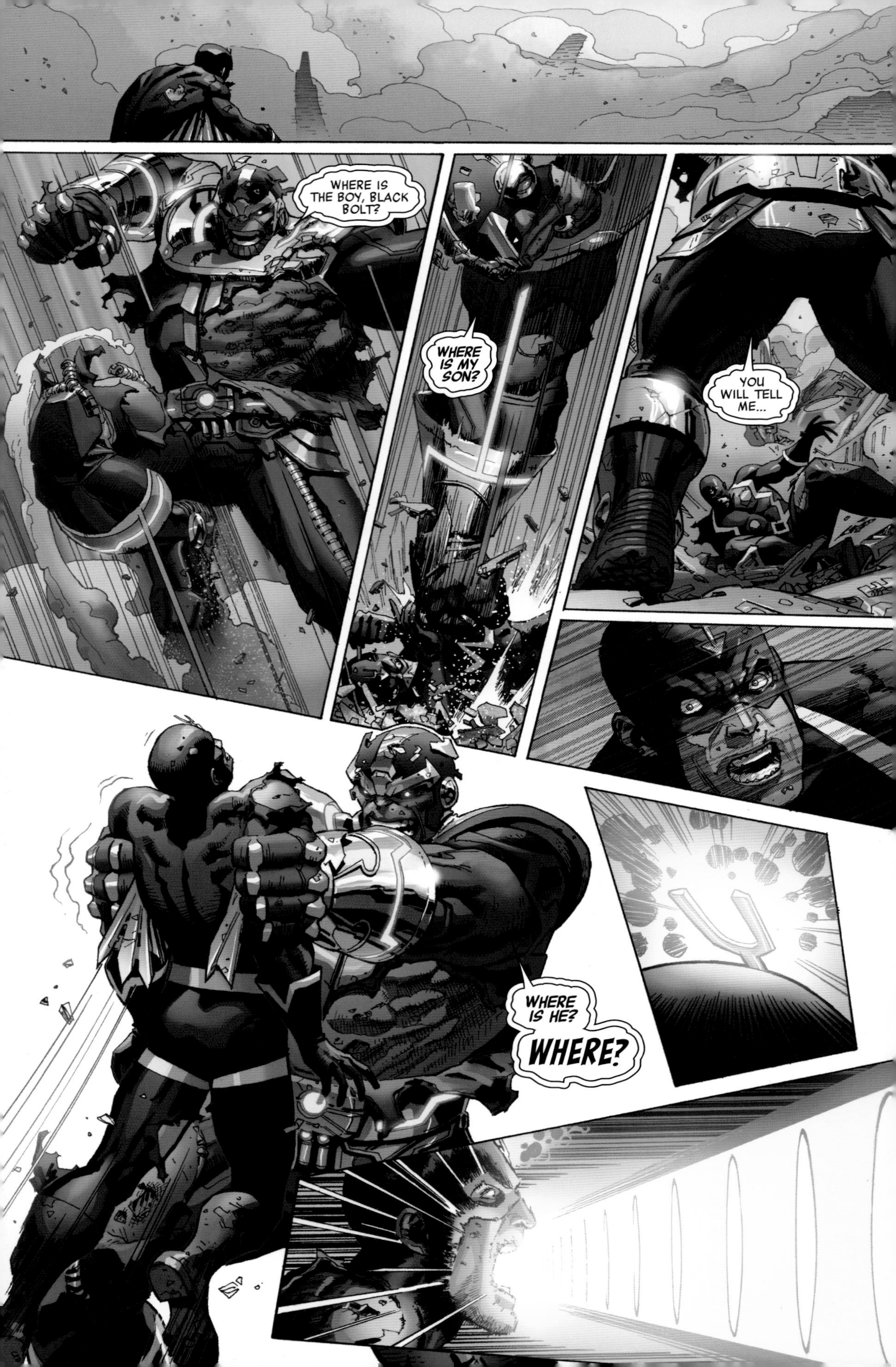
WHERE IS THE BOY, BLACK BOLT?
WHERE IS MY SON?
YOU WILL TELL ME...
WHERE IS HE?
WHERE?

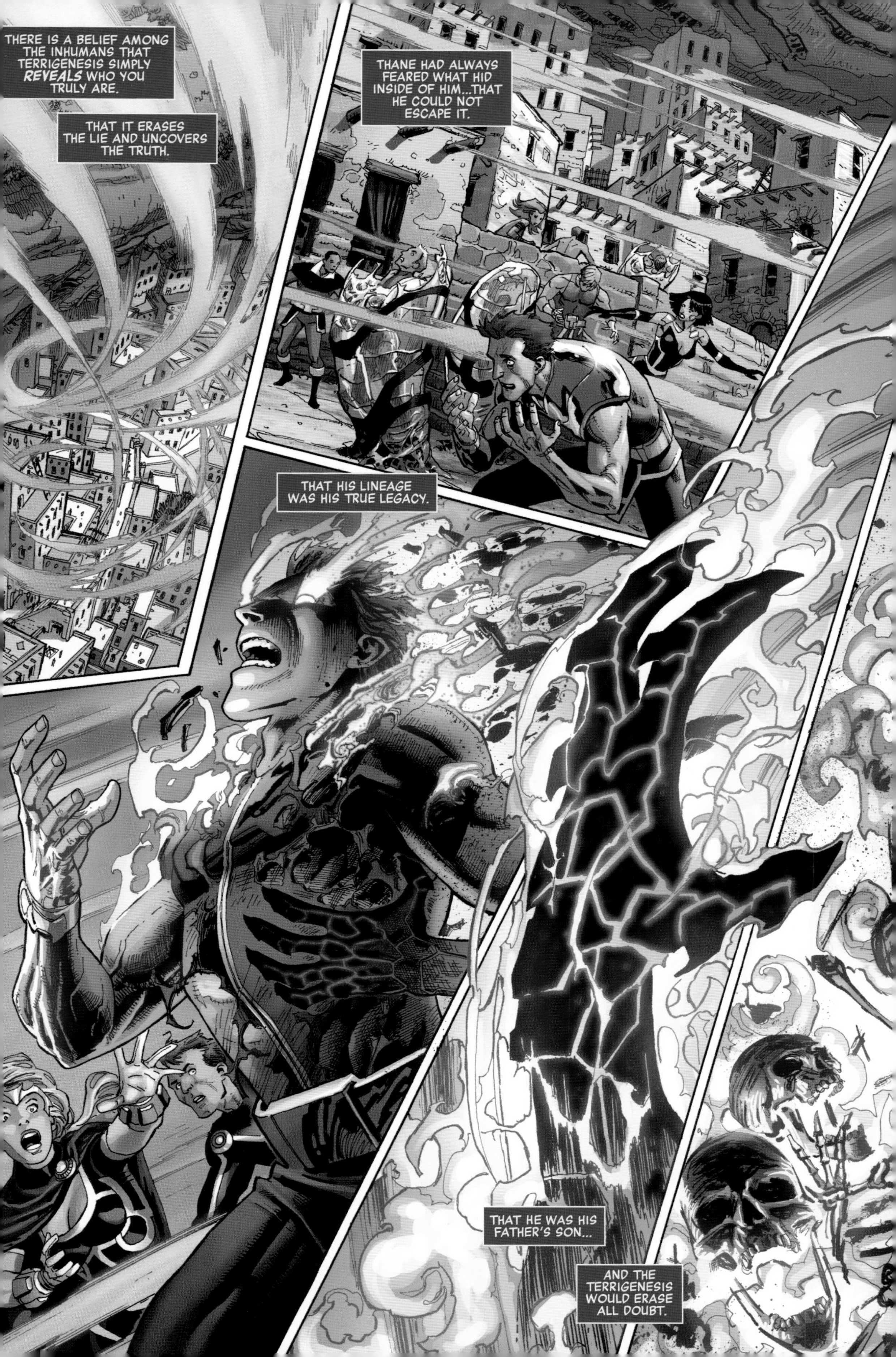
THERE IS A BELIEF AMONG THE INHUMANS THAT TERRIGENESIS SIMPLY *REVEALS* WHO YOU TRULY ARE.
THAT IT ERASES THE LIE AND UNCOVERS THE TRUTH.
THANE HAD ALWAYS FEARED WHAT HID INSIDE OF HIM...THAT HE COULD NOT ESCAPE IT.
THAT HIS LINEAGE WAS HIS TRUE LEGACY.
THAT HE WAS HIS FATHER'S SON...
AND THE TERRIGENESIS WOULD ERASE ALL DOUBT.

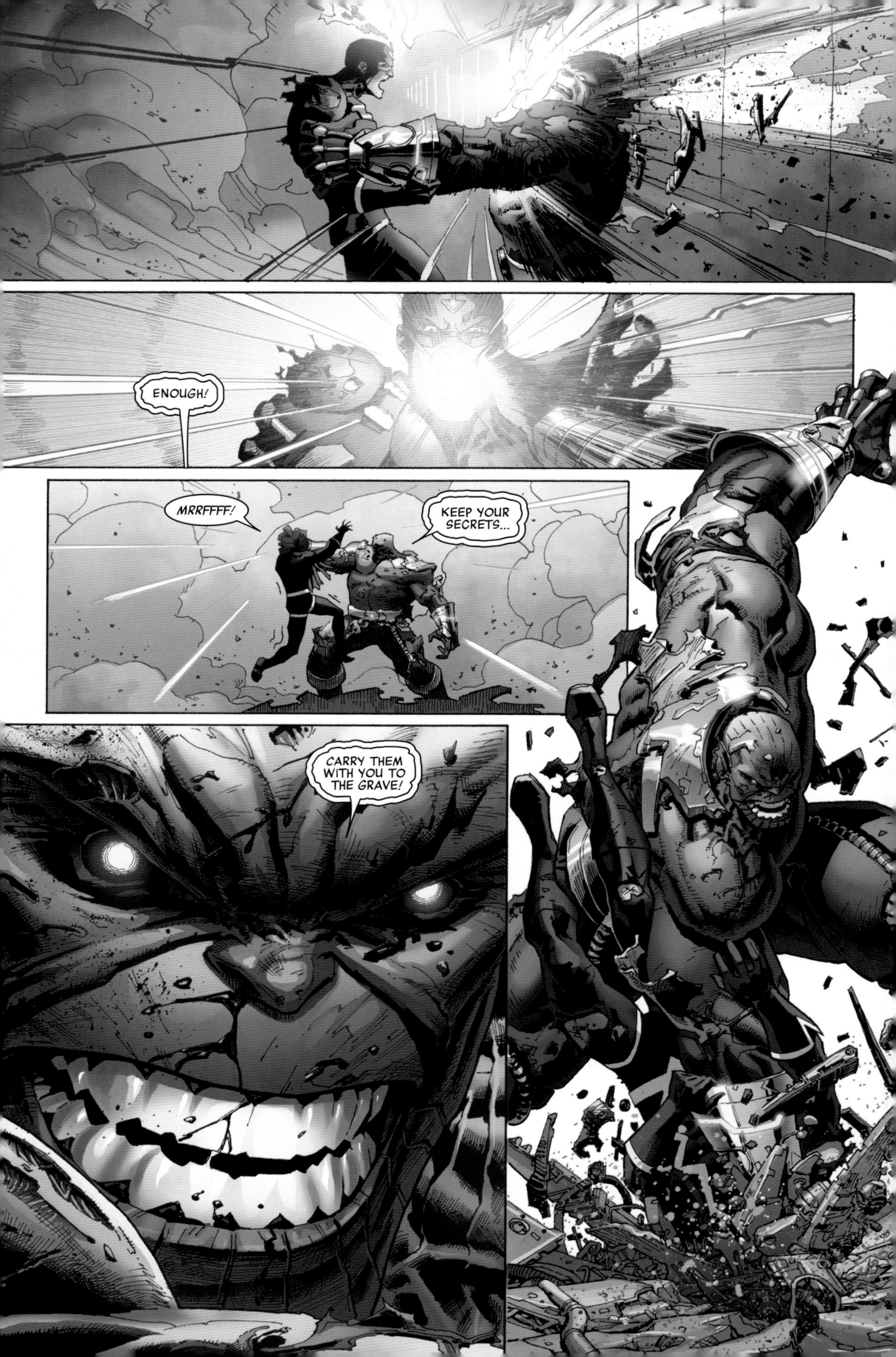

ENOUGH!
MRRFFFF!
KEEP YOUR SECRETS...
CARRY THEM WITH YOU TO THE GRAVE!

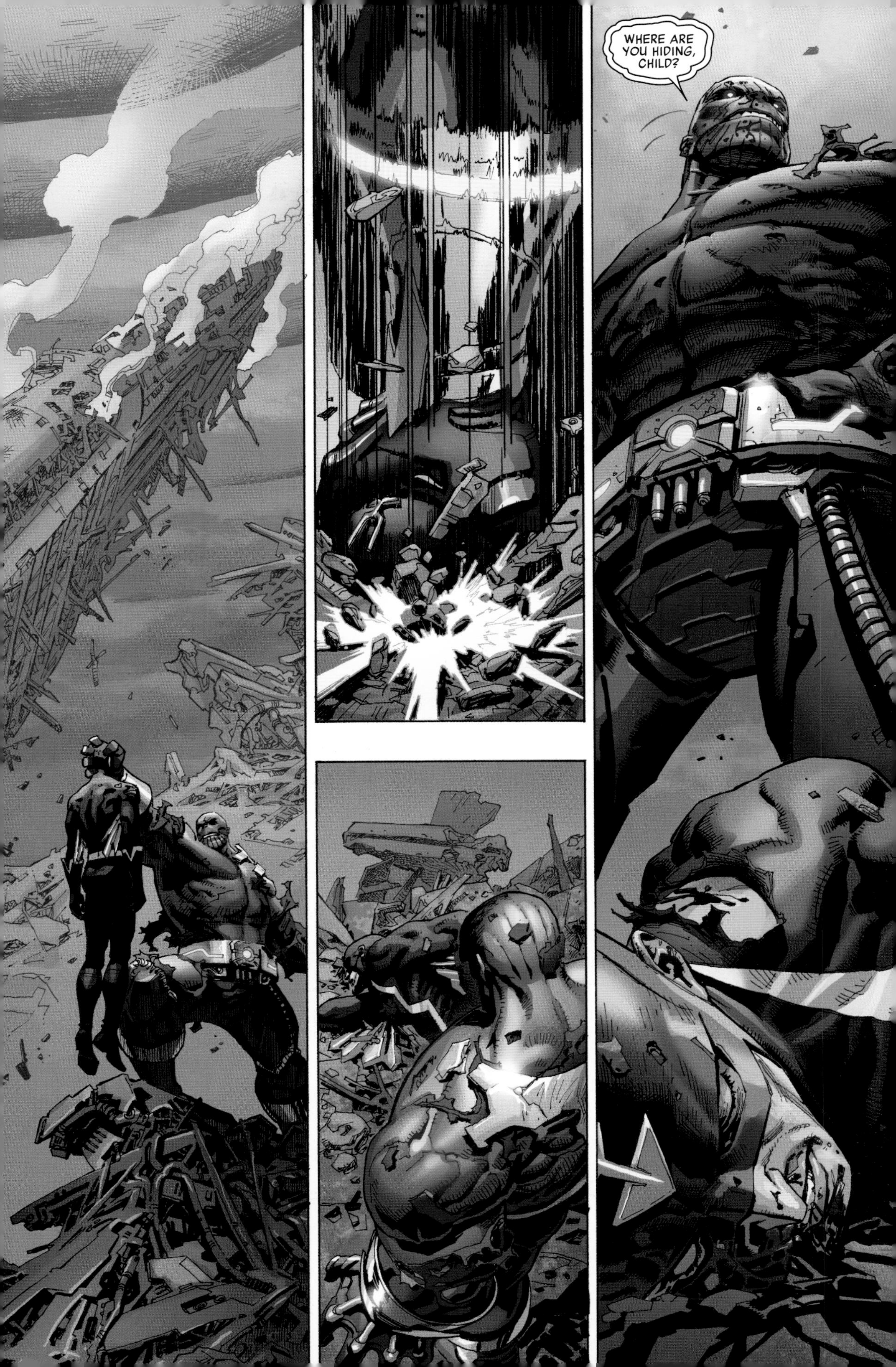

WHERE ARE YOU HIDING, CHILD?

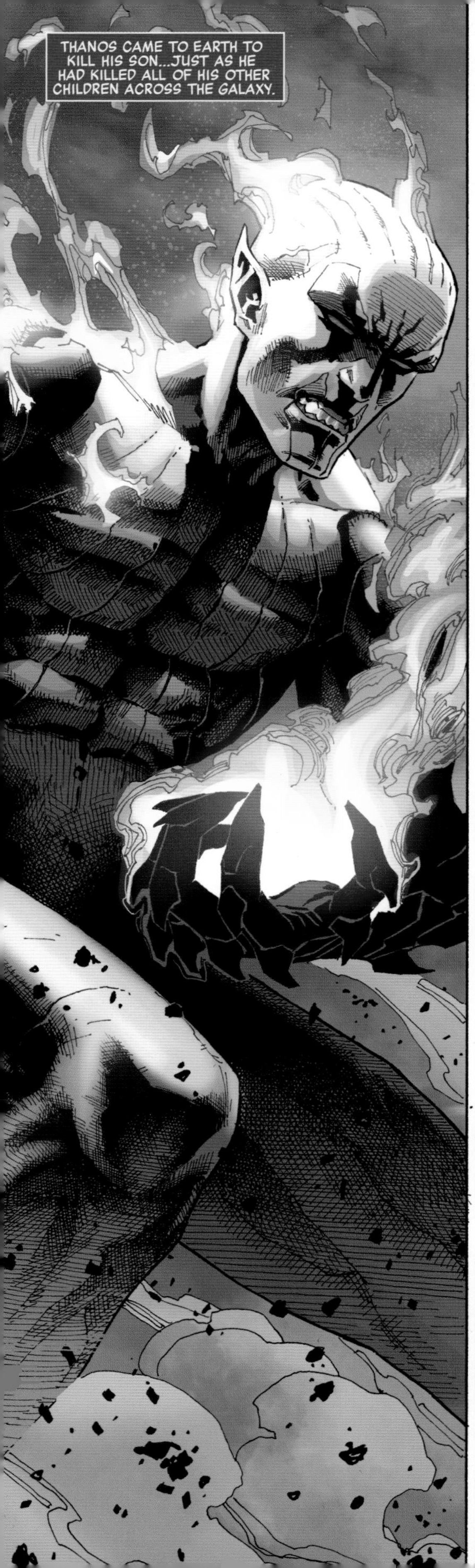
THANOS CAME TO EARTH TO KILL HIS SON...JUST AS HE HAD KILLED ALL OF HIS OTHER CHILDREN ACROSS THE GALAXY.
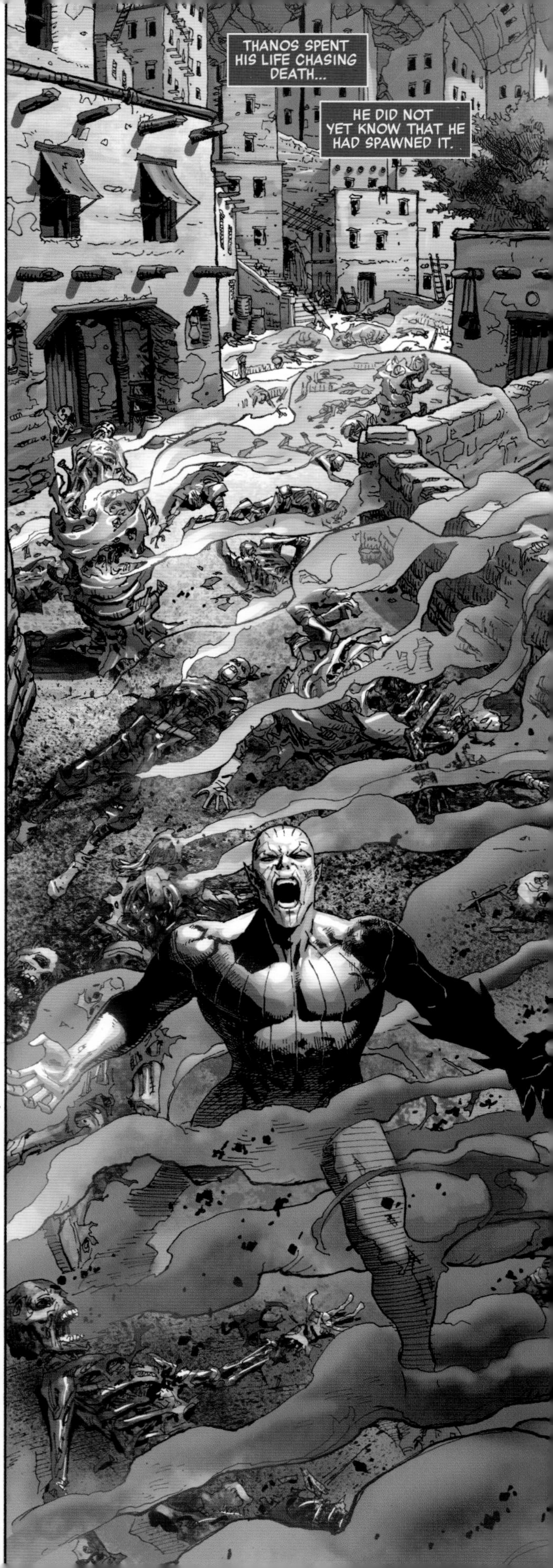
THANOS SPENT HIS LIFE CHASING DEATH...
HE DID NOT YET KNOW THAT HE HAD SPAWNED IT.

A PRAYER

◆

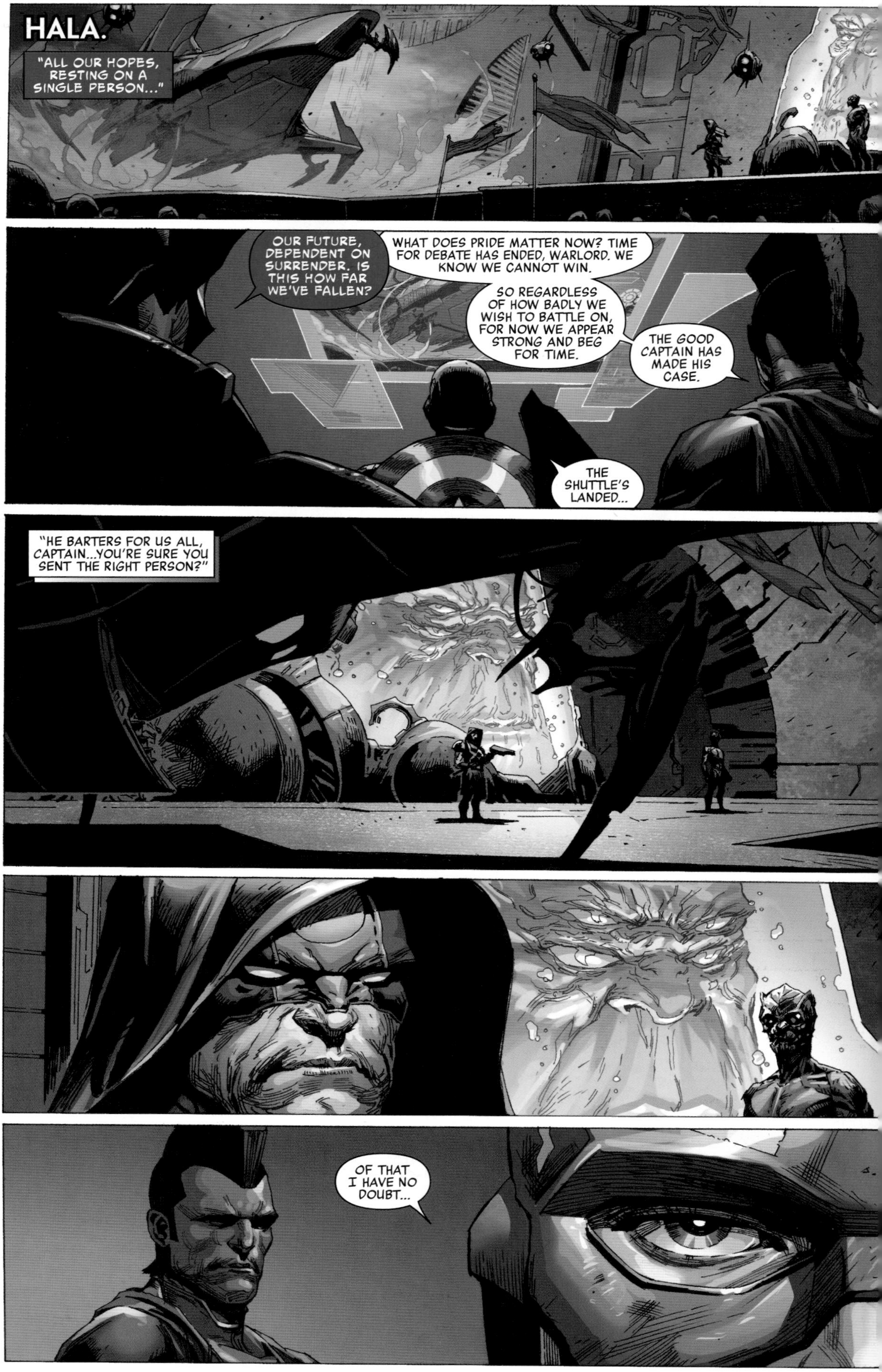
HALA.
"ALL OUR HOPES, RESTING ON A SINGLE PERSON..."
OUR FUTURE, DEPENDENT ON SURRENDER. IS THIS HOW FAR WE'VE FALLEN?
WHAT DOES PRIDE MATTER NOW? TIME FOR DEBATE HAS ENDED, WARLORD. WE KNOW WE CANNOT WIN.
SO REGARDLESS OF HOW BADLY WE WISH TO BATTLE ON, FOR NOW WE APPEAR STRONG AND BEG FOR TIME.
THE GOOD CAPTAIN HAS MADE HIS CASE.
THE SHUTTLE'S LANDED...
"HE BARTERS FOR US ALL, CAPTAIN...YOU'RE SURE YOU SENT THE RIGHT PERSON?"
OF THAT I HAVE NO DOUBT...

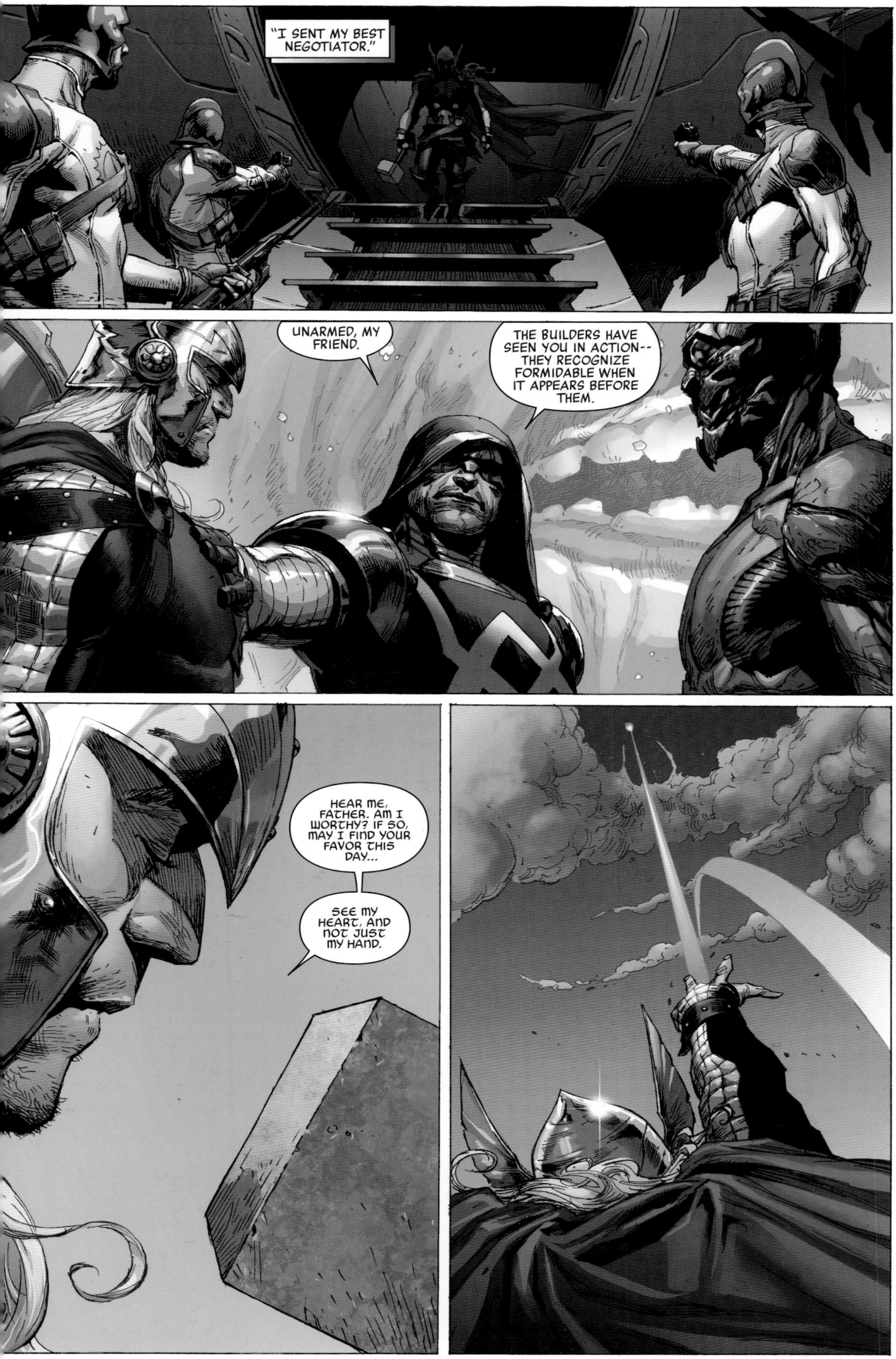

"I SENT MY BEST NEGOTIATOR."
UNARMED, MY FRIEND.
THE BUILDERS HAVE SEEN YOU IN ACTION-- THEY RECOGNIZE FORMIDABLE WHEN IT APPEARS BEFORE THEM.
HEAR ME, FATHER. AM I WORTHY? IF SO, MAY I FIND YOUR FAVOR THIS DAY...
SEE MY HEART, AND NOT JUST MY HAND.

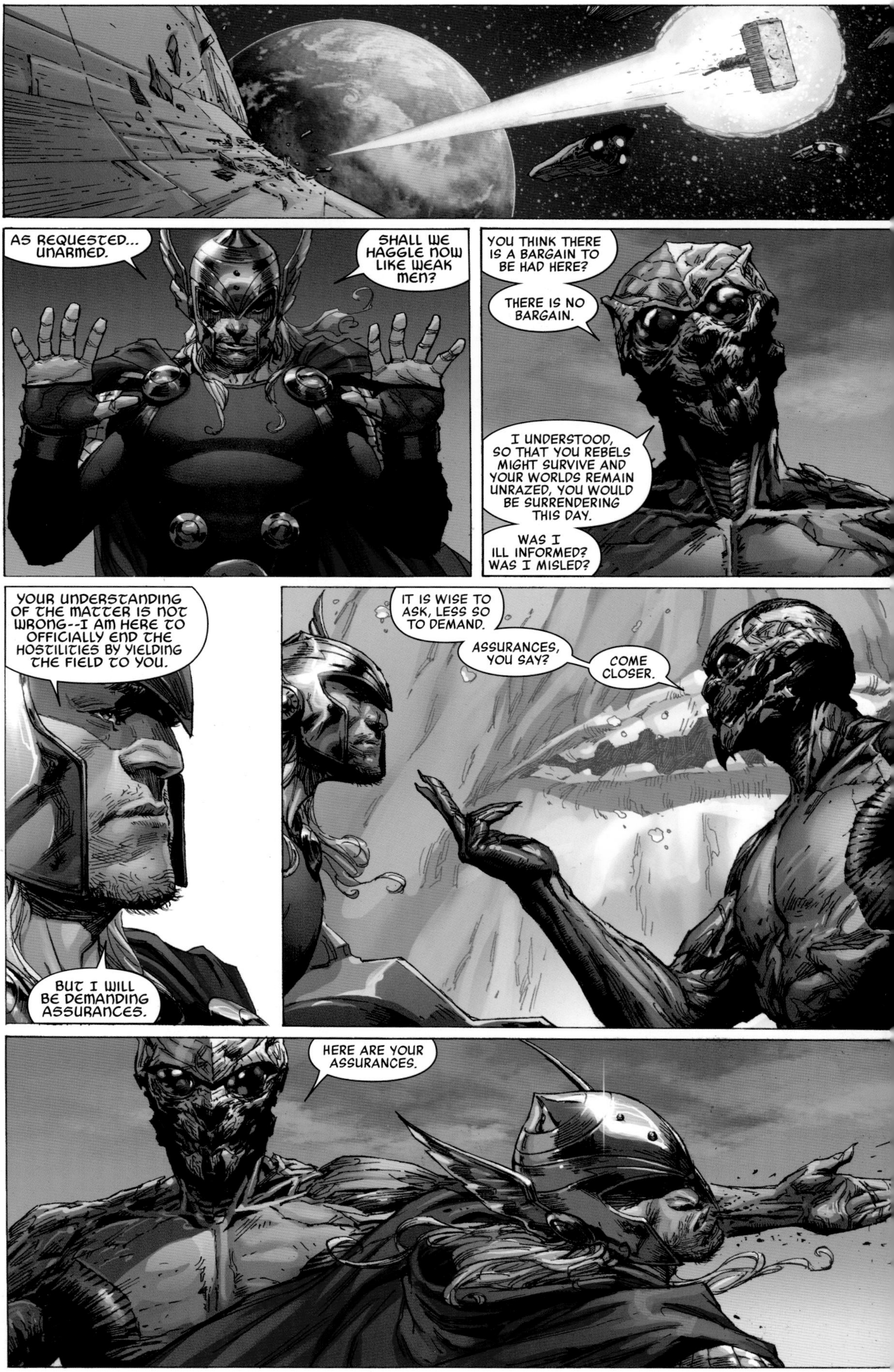

AS REQUESTED... UNARMED.
SHALL WE HAGGLE NOW LIKE WEAK MEN?
YOU THINK THERE IS A BARGAIN TO BE HAD HERE?
THERE IS NO BARGAIN.
I UNDERSTOOD, SO THAT YOU REBELS MIGHT SURVIVE AND YOUR WORLDS REMAIN UNRAZED, YOU WOULD BE SURRENDERING THIS DAY.
WAS I ILL INFORMED? WAS I MISLED?
YOUR UNDERSTANDING OF THE MATTER IS NOT WRONG--I AM HERE TO OFFICIALLY END THE HOSTILITIES BY YIELDING THE FIELD TO YOU.
BUT I WILL BE DEMANDING ASSURANCES.
IT IS WISE TO ASK, LESS SO TO DEMAND.
ASSURANCES, YOU SAY?
COME CLOSER.
HERE ARE YOUR ASSURANCES.

YOU WILL SUBMIT OR PERISH. YOU WILL KNEEL OR YOUR FELLOW WARRIORS WILL LOSE EVERYTHING THEY HOLD DEAR.

ALL THAT IS LEFT IS SURRENDER.

ON...YOUR... KNEES.

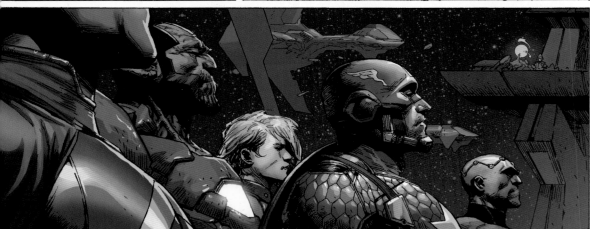

THIS IS GOOD...

DOES IT NOT SUIT YOU BETTER?

IS THIS NOT YOUR NATURAL STATE?

YOU HAVE SAVED SO VERY MANY BY YIELDING HERE TODAY...BUT YOU SHOULD KNOW, YOU HAVE NOT SAVED YOUR EARTH.

THERE IS NO SAVING THAT WORLD.

"WE WILL REDUCE IT TO ATOMS...BURNT TO NOTHING WITH THE POWER OF A THOUSAND SUNS.

"AND DO YOU KNOW WHY?"

HUMANITY IS A PLAGUE NOT JUST TO THIS GALAXY OR EVEN THIS UNIVERSE...

IT IS A SICKNESS THAT EXISTS IN EVERY UNIVERSE THAT HAS BEEN OR EVER WILL BE.

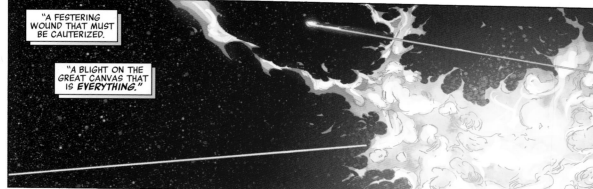

"A FESTERING WOUND THAT MUST BE CAUTERIZED.

"A BLIGHT ON THE GREAT CANVAS THAT IS *EVERYTHING*."

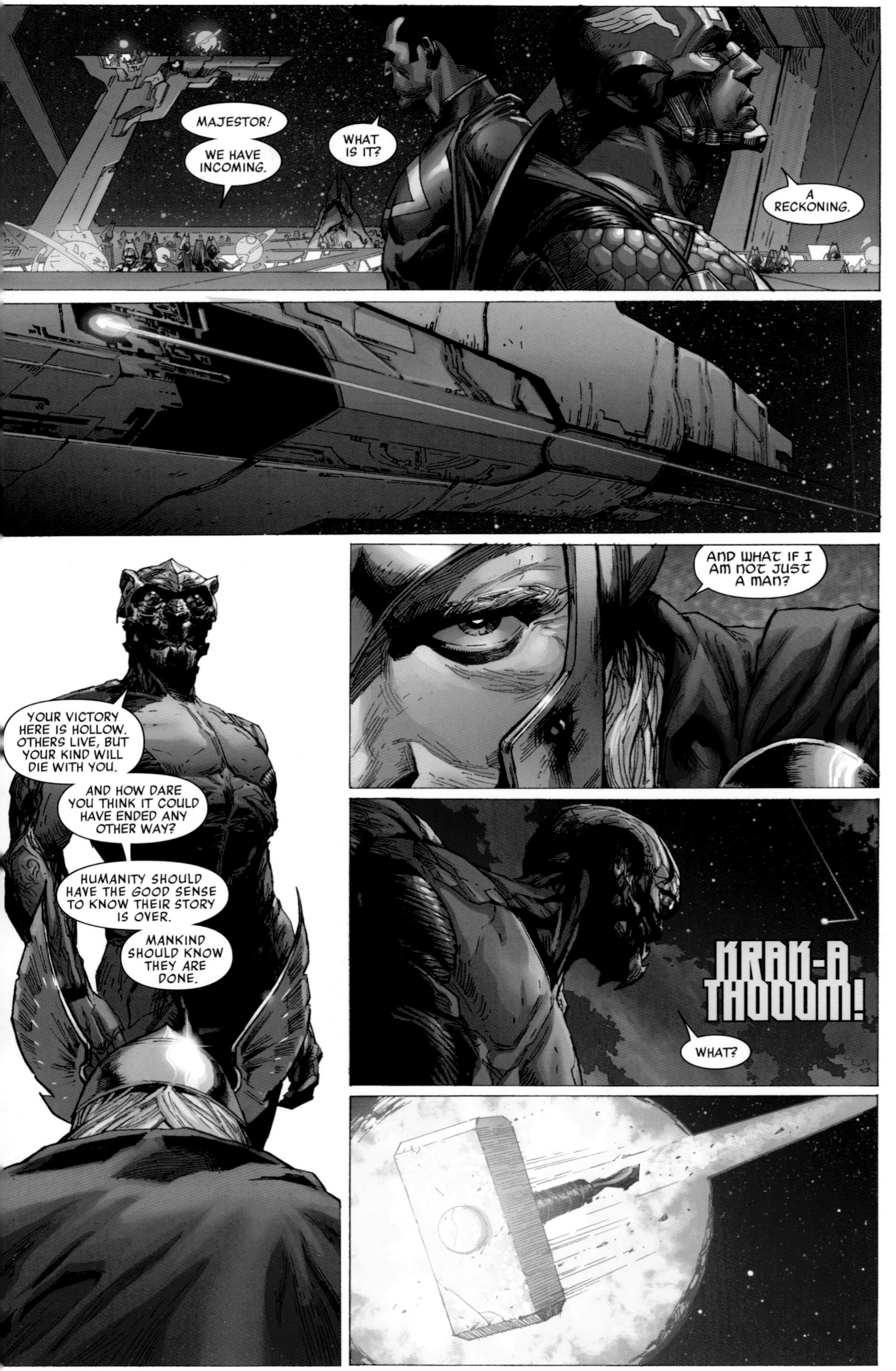
MAJESTOR!
WE HAVE INCOMING.
WHAT IS IT?
A RECKONING.
YOUR VICTORY HERE IS HOLLOW. OTHERS LIVE, BUT YOUR KIND WILL DIE WITH YOU.
AND HOW DARE YOU THINK IT COULD HAVE ENDED ANY OTHER WAY?
HUMANITY SHOULD HAVE THE GOOD SENSE TO KNOW THEIR STORY IS OVER.
MANKIND SHOULD KNOW THEY ARE DONE.
AND WHAT IF I AM NOT JUST A MAN?
KRAK-A THOOOM!
WHAT?

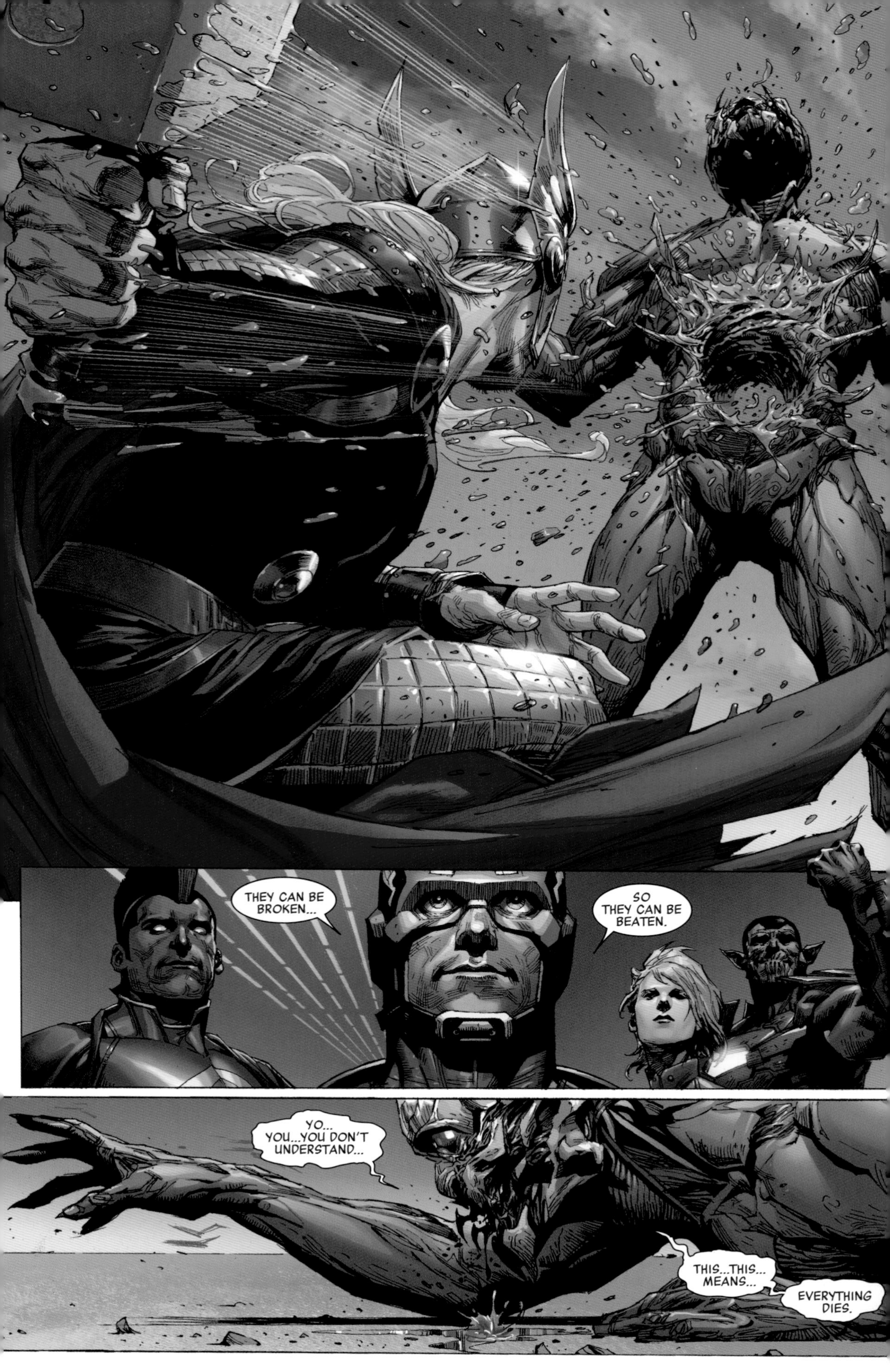
THEY CAN BE BROKEN...
SO THEY CAN BE BEATEN.
YO... YOU...YOU DON'T UNDERSTAND...
THIS...THIS... MEANS...
EVERYTHING DIES.

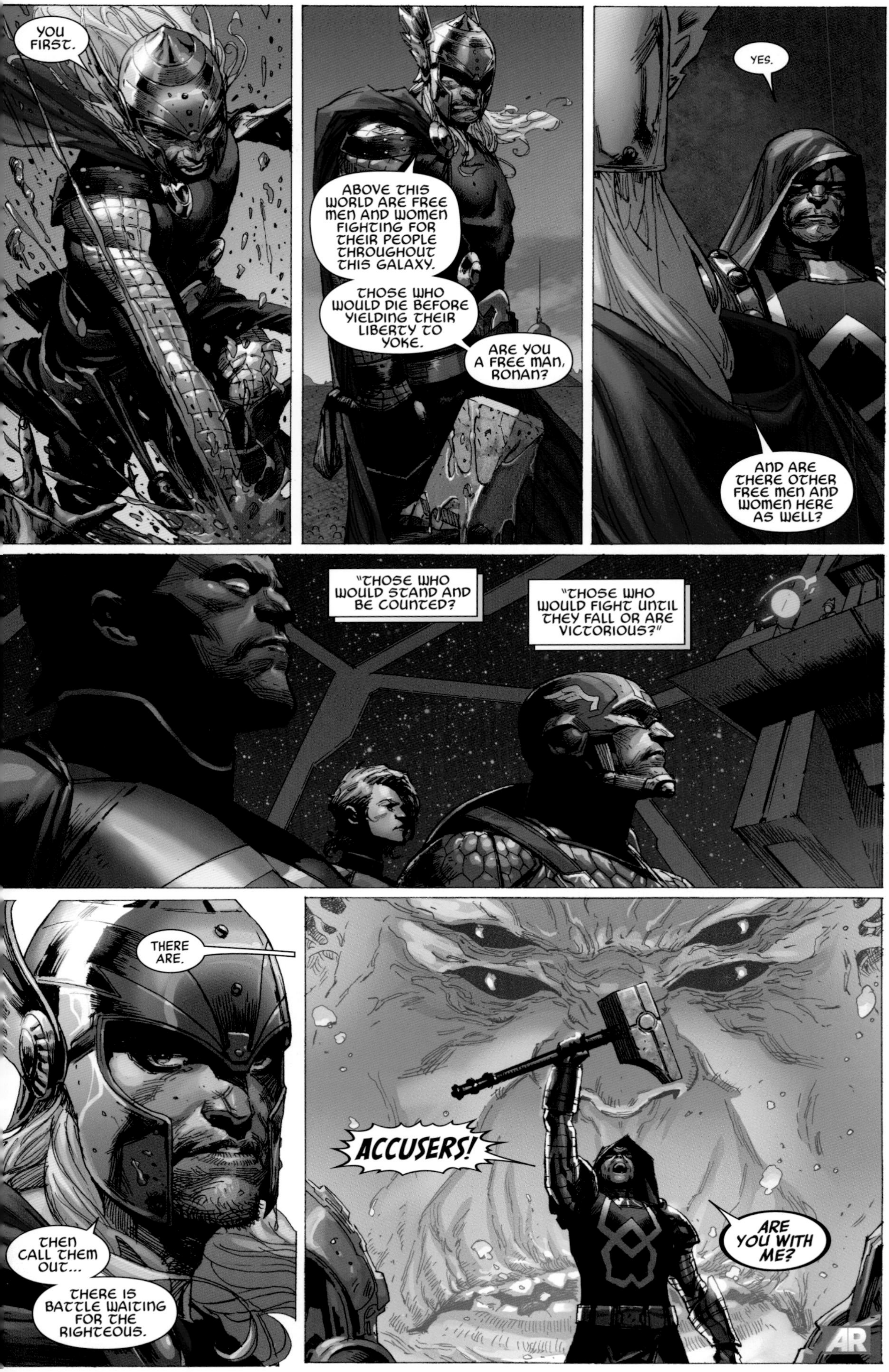
YOU FIRST.
ABOVE THIS WORLD ARE FREE MEN AND WOMEN FIGHTING FOR THEIR PEOPLE THROUGHOUT THIS GALAXY.
THOSE WHO WOULD DIE BEFORE YIELDING THEIR LIBERTY TO YOKE.
ARE YOU A FREE MAN, RONAN?
YES.
AND ARE THERE OTHER FREE MEN AND WOMEN HERE AS WELL?
"THOSE WHO WOULD STAND AND BE COUNTED?
"THOSE WHO WOULD FIGHT UNTIL THEY FALL OR ARE VICTORIOUS?"
THERE ARE.
THEN CALL THEM OUT...
THERE IS BATTLE WAITING FOR THE RIGHTEOUS.
ACCUSERS!
ARE YOU WITH ME?

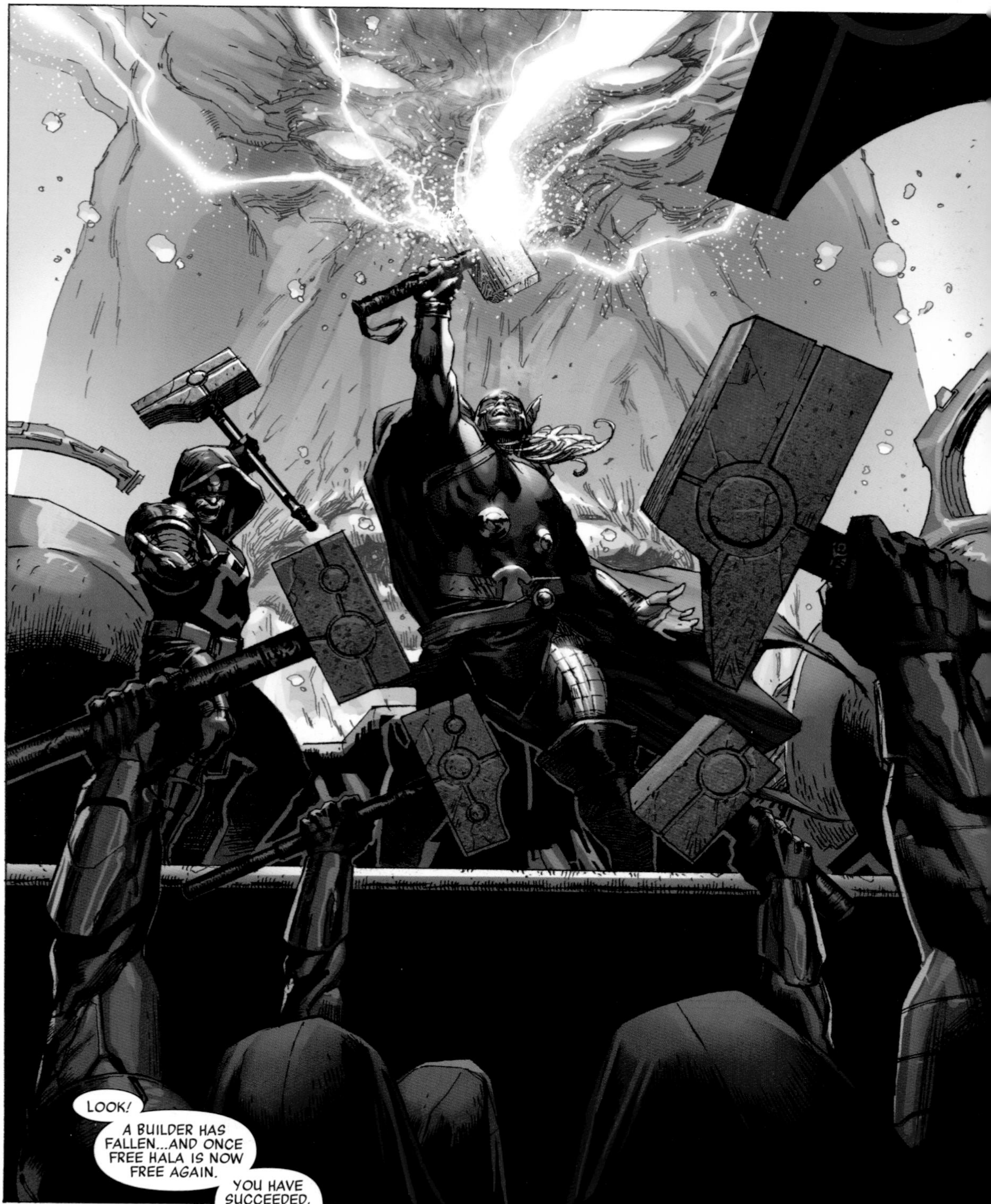
LOOK!
A BUILDER HAS FALLEN...AND ONCE FREE HALA IS NOW FREE AGAIN.
YOU HAVE SUCCEEDED, AVENGER... AGAIN.

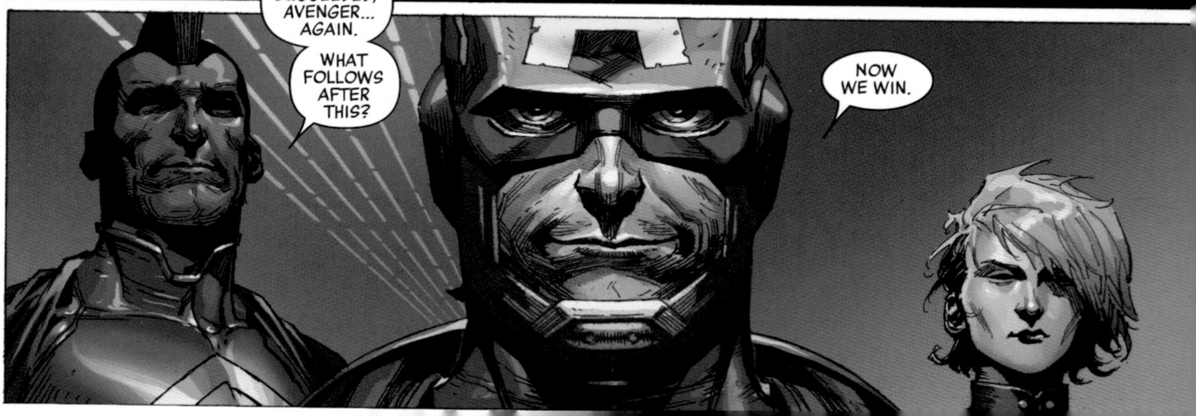
WHAT FOLLOWS AFTER THIS?
NOW WE WIN.

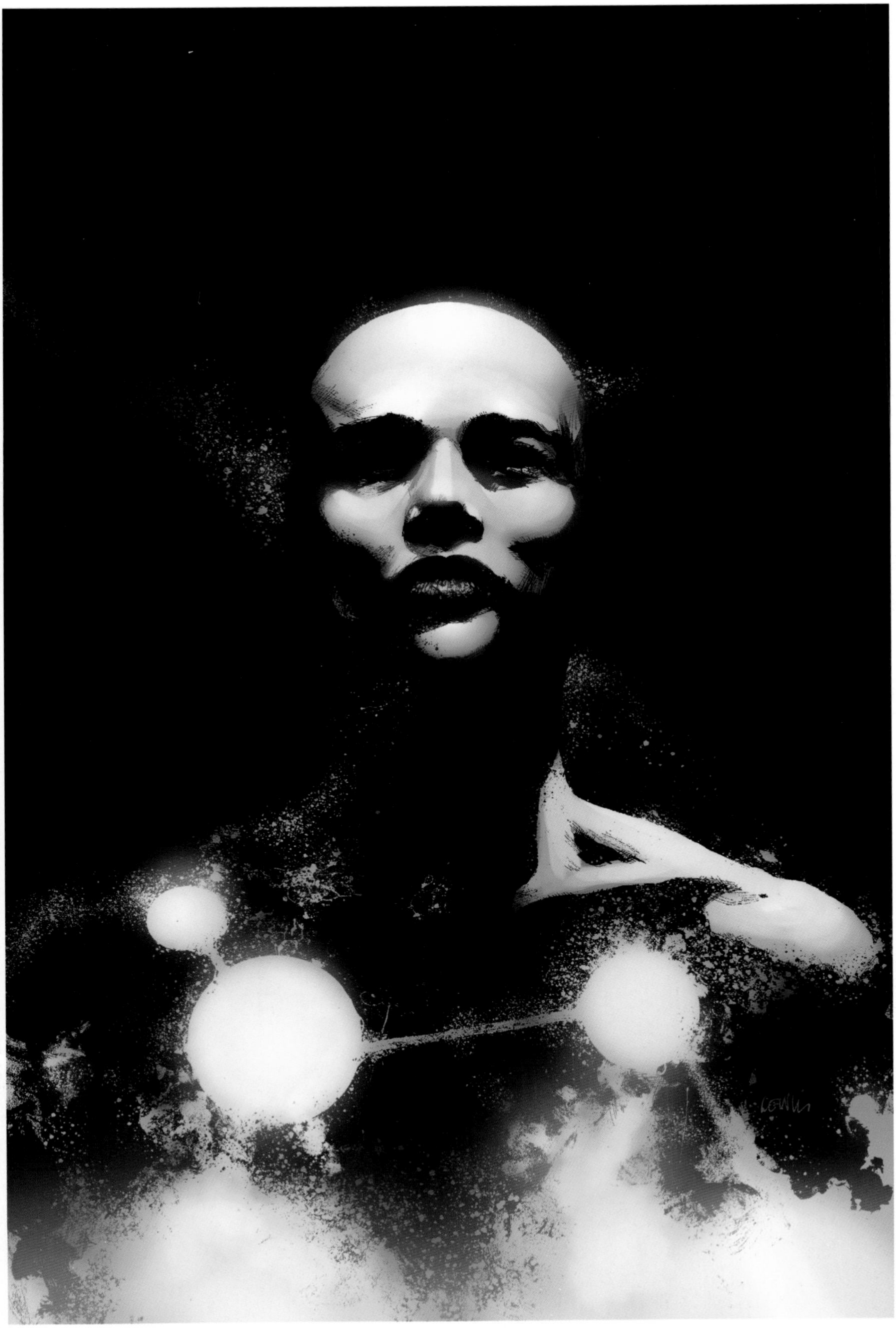

THE PROMISE OF
THE UNIVERSE

◆

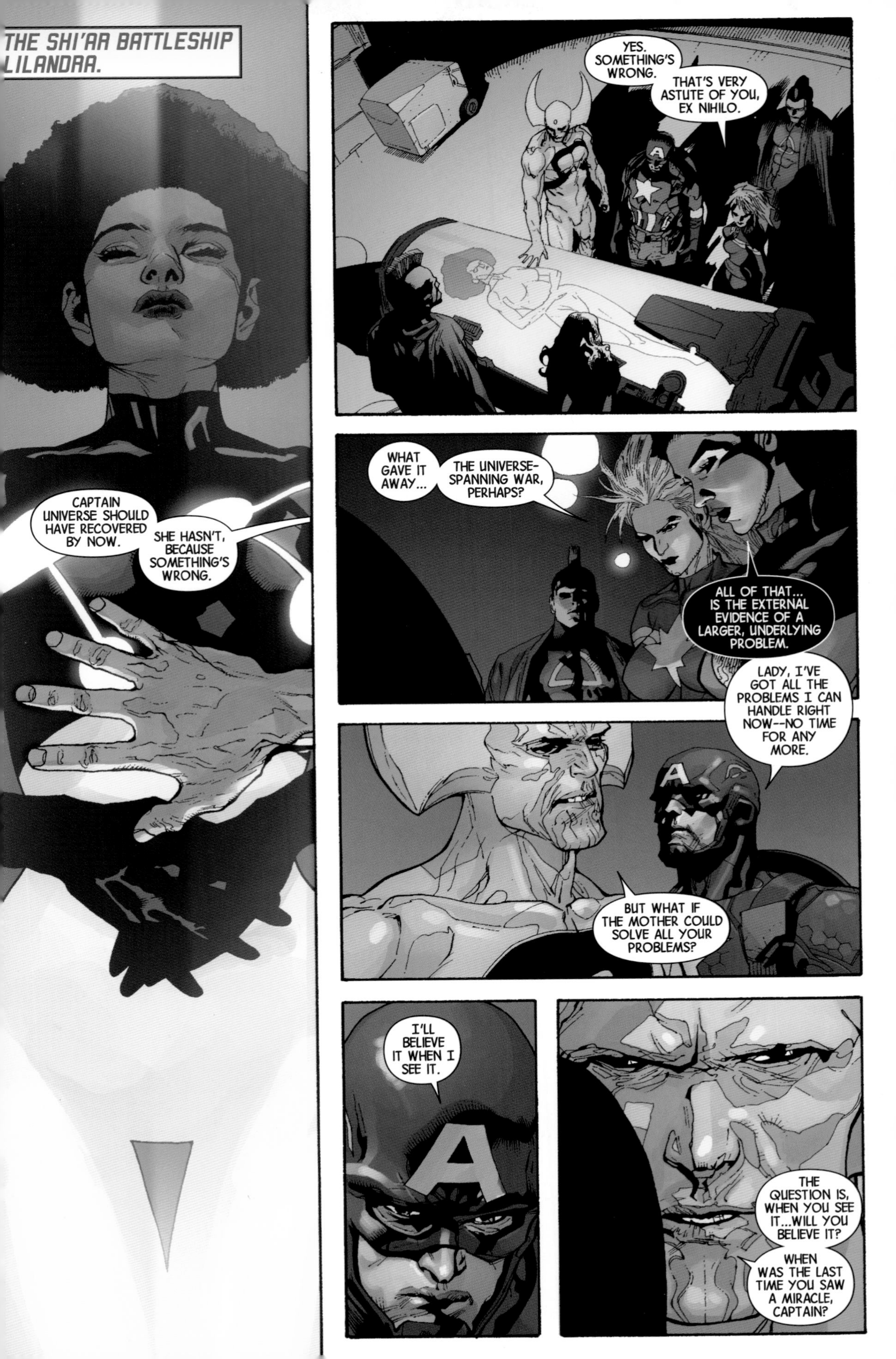

THE SHI'AR BATTLESHIP LILANDRA.
CAPTAIN UNIVERSE SHOULD HAVE RECOVERED BY NOW.
SHE HASN'T, BECAUSE SOMETHING'S WRONG.
YES. SOMETHING'S WRONG.
THAT'S VERY ASTUTE OF YOU, EX NIHILO.
WHAT GAVE IT AWAY...
THE UNIVERSE-SPANNING WAR, PERHAPS?
ALL OF THAT... IS THE EXTERNAL EVIDENCE OF A LARGER, UNDERLYING PROBLEM.
LADY, I'VE GOT ALL THE PROBLEMS I CAN HANDLE RIGHT NOW--NO TIME FOR ANY MORE.
BUT WHAT IF THE MOTHER COULD SOLVE ALL YOUR PROBLEMS?
I'LL BELIEVE IT WHEN I SEE IT.
THE QUESTION IS, WHEN YOU SEE IT...WILL YOU BELIEVE IT?
WHEN WAS THE LAST TIME YOU SAW A MIRACLE, CAPTAIN?

THE SECOND WAVE

◆

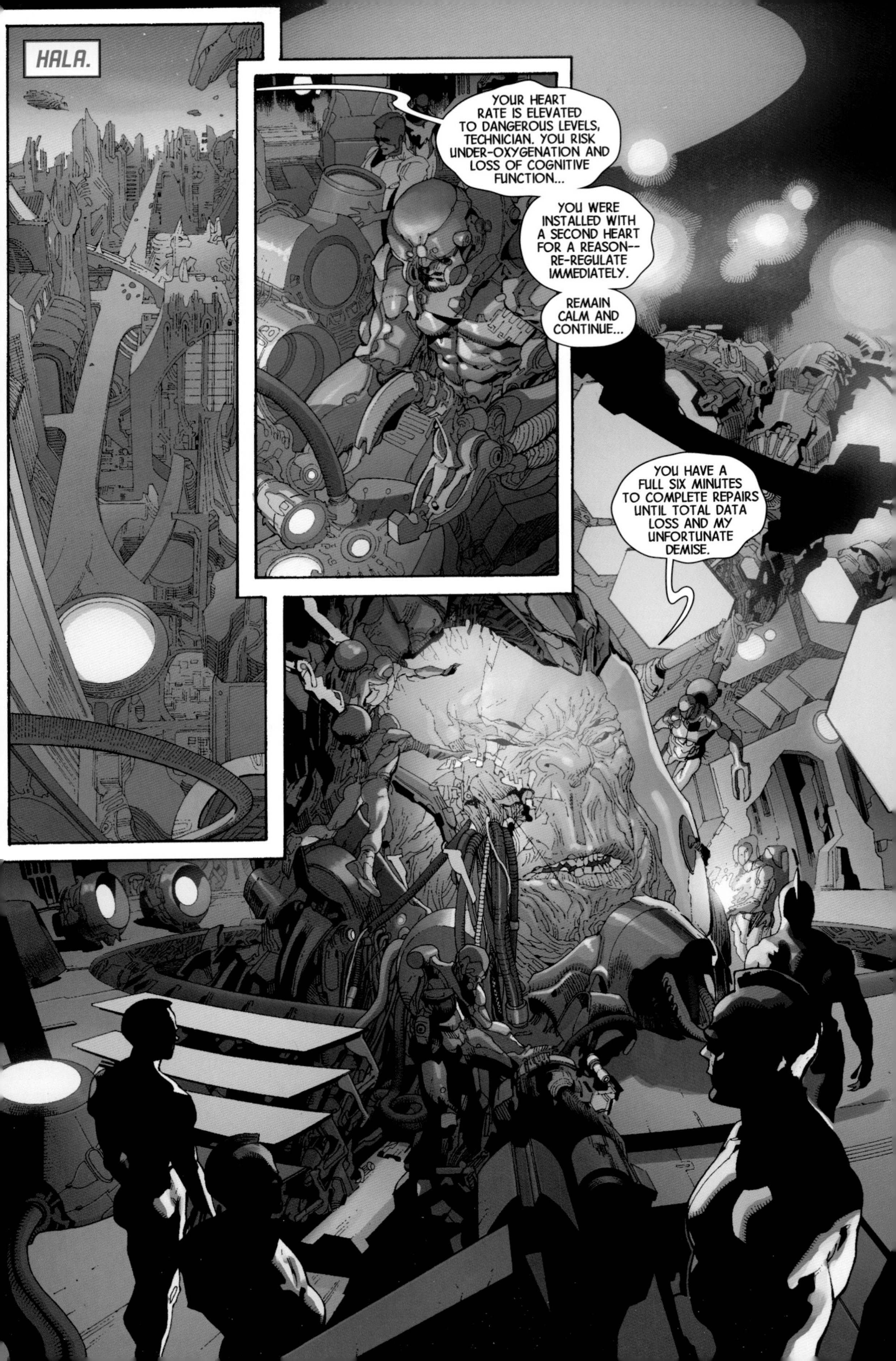
HALA.
YOUR HEART RATE IS ELEVATED TO DANGEROUS LEVELS, TECHNICIAN. YOU RISK UNDER-OXYGENATION AND LOSS OF COGNITIVE FUNCTION...
YOU WERE INSTALLED WITH A SECOND HEART FOR A REASON-- RE-REGULATE IMMEDIATELY.
REMAIN CALM AND CONTINUE...
YOU HAVE A FULL SIX MINUTES TO COMPLETE REPAIRS UNTIL TOTAL DATA LOSS AND MY UNFORTUNATE DEMISE.

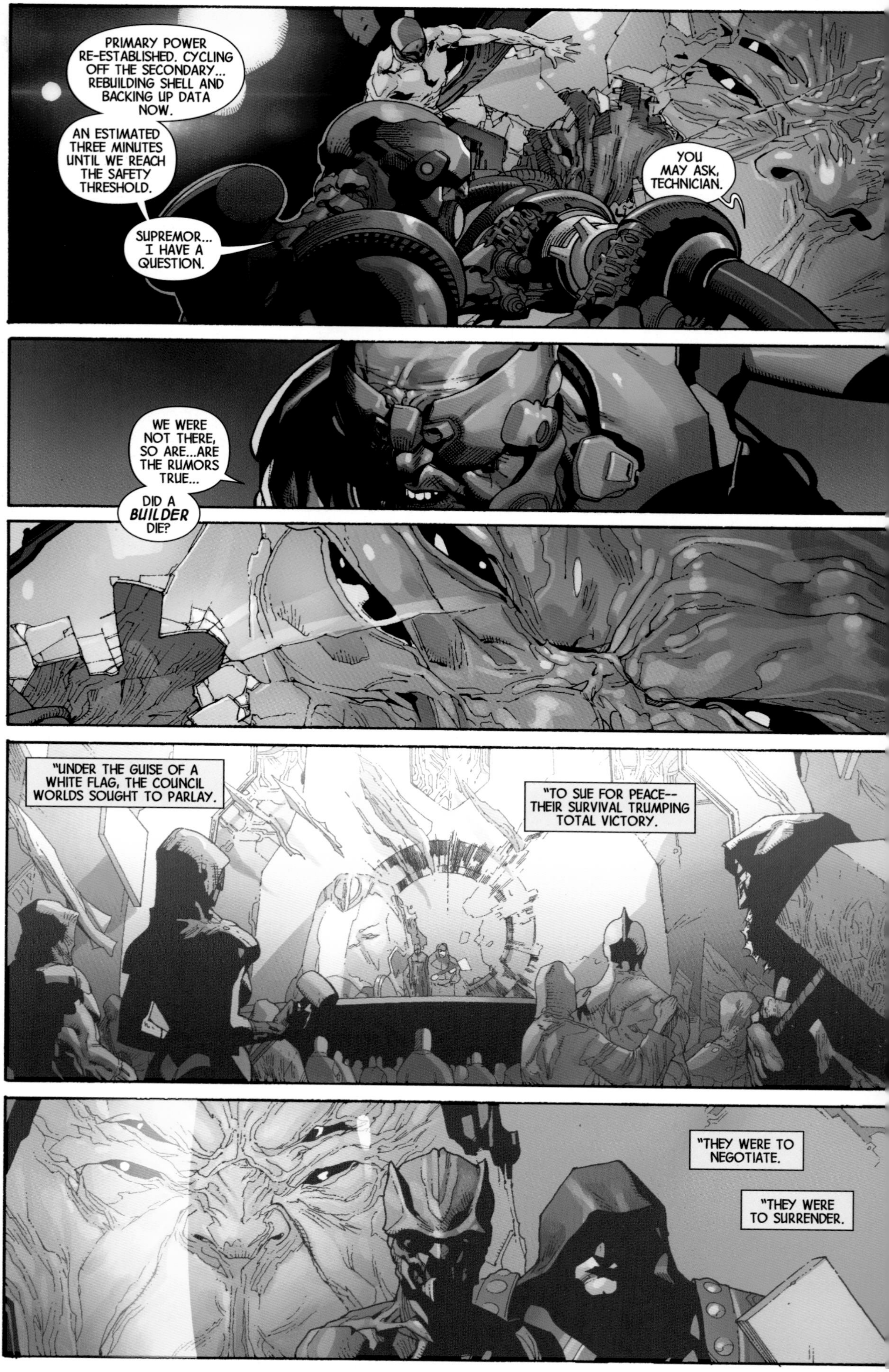
PRIMARY POWER RE-ESTABLISHED. CYCLING OFF THE SECONDARY... REBUILDING SHELL AND BACKING UP DATA NOW.
AN ESTIMATED THREE MINUTES UNTIL WE REACH THE SAFETY THRESHOLD.
SUPREMOR... I HAVE A QUESTION.
YOU MAY ASK, TECHNICIAN.
WE WERE NOT THERE, SO ARE...ARE THE RUMORS TRUE...
DID A BUILDER DIE?
"UNDER THE GUISE OF A WHITE FLAG, THE COUNCIL WORLDS SOUGHT TO PARLAY.
"TO SUE FOR PEACE-- THEIR SURVIVAL TRUMPING TOTAL VICTORY.
"THEY WERE TO NEGOTIATE.
"THEY WERE TO SURRENDER.

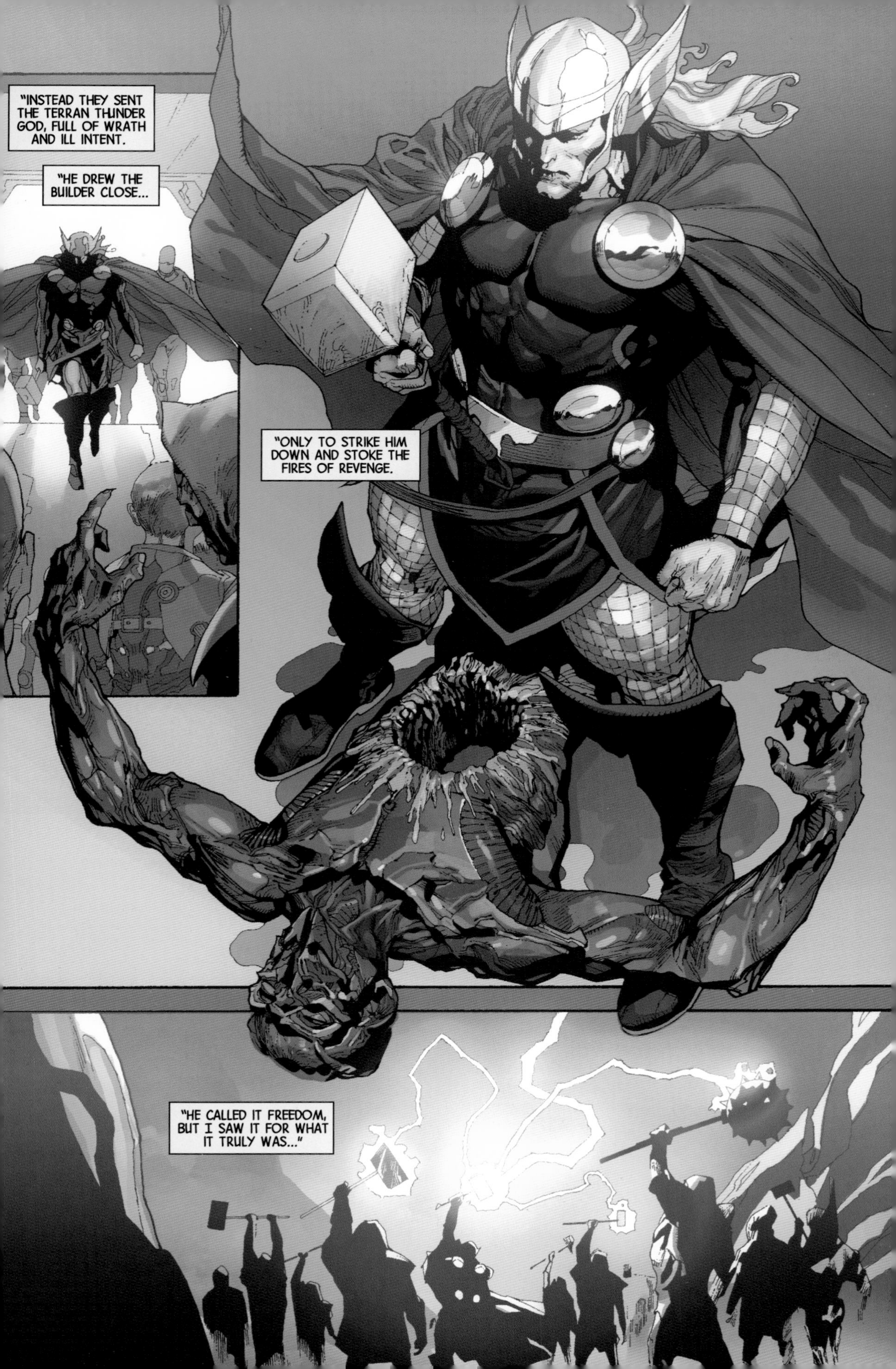
"INSTEAD THEY SENT THE TERRAN THUNDER GOD, FULL OF WRATH AND ILL INTENT.
"HE DREW THE BUILDER CLOSE...
"ONLY TO STRIKE HIM DOWN AND STOKE THE FIRES OF REVENGE.
"HE CALLED IT FREEDOM, BUT I SAW IT FOR WHAT IT TRULY WAS..."

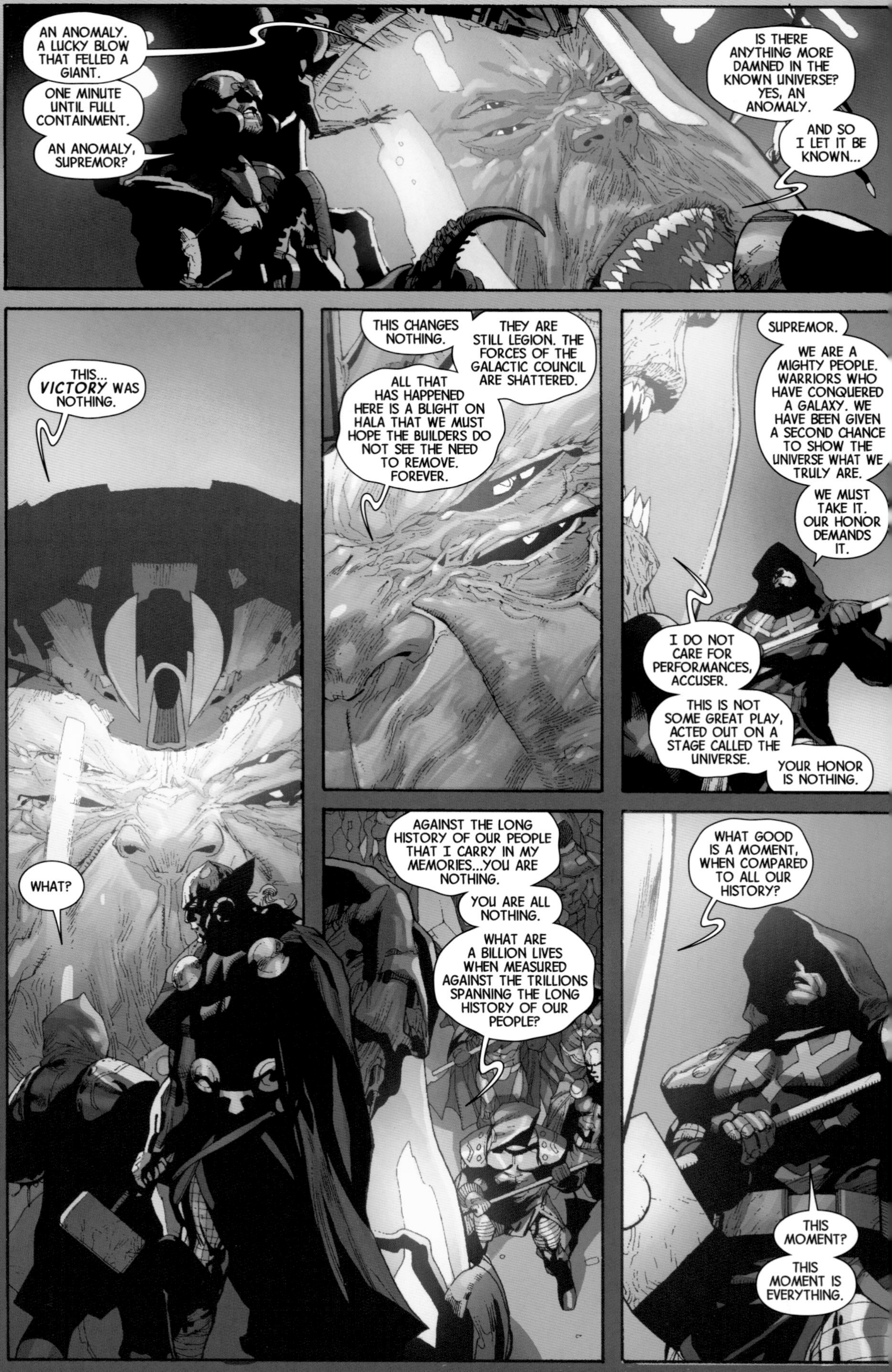
AN ANOMALY. A LUCKY BLOW THAT FELLED A GIANT.
ONE MINUTE UNTIL FULL CONTAINMENT.
AN ANOMALY, SUPREMOR?
IS THERE ANYTHING MORE DAMNED IN THE KNOWN UNIVERSE? YES, AN ANOMALY.
AND SO I LET IT BE KNOWN...
THIS... *VICTORY* WAS NOTHING.
WHAT?
THIS CHANGES NOTHING.
THEY ARE STILL LEGION. THE FORCES OF THE GALACTIC COUNCIL ARE SHATTERED.
ALL THAT HAS HAPPENED HERE IS A BLIGHT ON HALA THAT WE MUST HOPE THE BUILDERS DO NOT SEE THE NEED TO REMOVE. FOREVER.
SUPREMOR.
WE ARE A MIGHTY PEOPLE. WARRIORS WHO HAVE CONQUERED A GALAXY. WE HAVE BEEN GIVEN A SECOND CHANCE TO SHOW THE UNIVERSE WHAT WE TRULY ARE.
WE MUST TAKE IT. OUR HONOR DEMANDS IT.
I DO NOT CARE FOR PERFORMANCES, ACCUSER.
THIS IS NOT SOME GREAT PLAY, ACTED OUT ON A STAGE CALLED THE UNIVERSE.
YOUR HONOR IS NOTHING.
AGAINST THE LONG HISTORY OF OUR PEOPLE THAT I CARRY IN MY MEMORIES...YOU ARE NOTHING.
YOU ARE ALL NOTHING.
WHAT ARE A BILLION LIVES WHEN MEASURED AGAINST THE TRILLIONS SPANNING THE LONG HISTORY OF OUR PEOPLE?
WHAT GOOD IS A MOMENT, WHEN COMPARED TO ALL OUR HISTORY?
THIS MOMENT?
THIS MOMENT IS EVERYTHING.

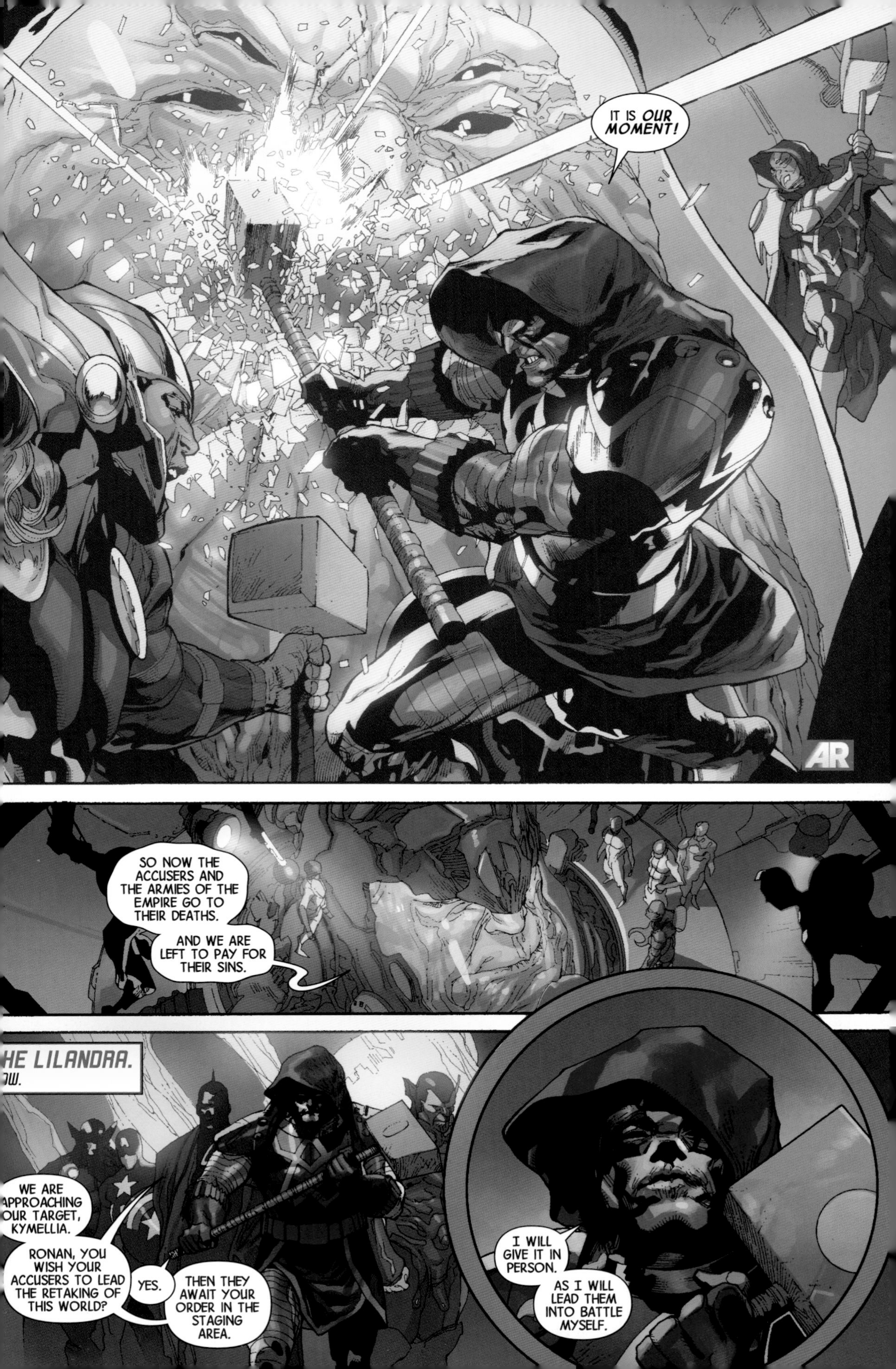
IT IS OUR MOMENT!
SO NOW THE ACCUSERS AND THE ARMIES OF THE EMPIRE GO TO THEIR DEATHS.
AND WE ARE LEFT TO PAY FOR THEIR SINS.
HE LILANDRA.
OW.
WE ARE APPROACHING OUR TARGET, KYMELLIA.
RONAN, YOU WISH YOUR ACCUSERS TO LEAD THE RETAKING OF THIS WORLD?
YES.
THEN THEY AWAIT YOUR ORDER IN THE STAGING AREA.
I WILL GIVE IT IN PERSON.
AS I WILL LEAD THEM INTO BATTLE MYSELF.

ON KYMELLIA III, THE ACCUSERS CATCH THE BUILDERS BY SURPRISE, OVERRUNNING THEIR ARMY OF ALEPHS AND FREEING THE WORLD.

THE KYMELLIAN CAVALRY REJOIN THE WAR.

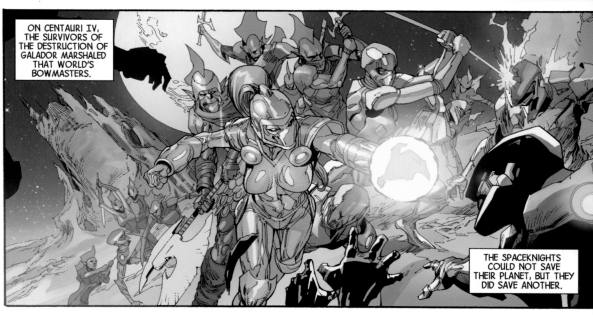

ON CENTAURI IV, THE SURVIVORS OF THE DESTRUCTION OF GALADOR MARSHALED THAT WORLD'S BOWMASTERS.

THE SPACEKNIGHTS COULD NOT SAVE THEIR PLANET, BUT THEY DID SAVE ANOTHER.

THE SKRULL WARLORDS WON ON KORM PRIME, BUT WITH A HEAVY COST...

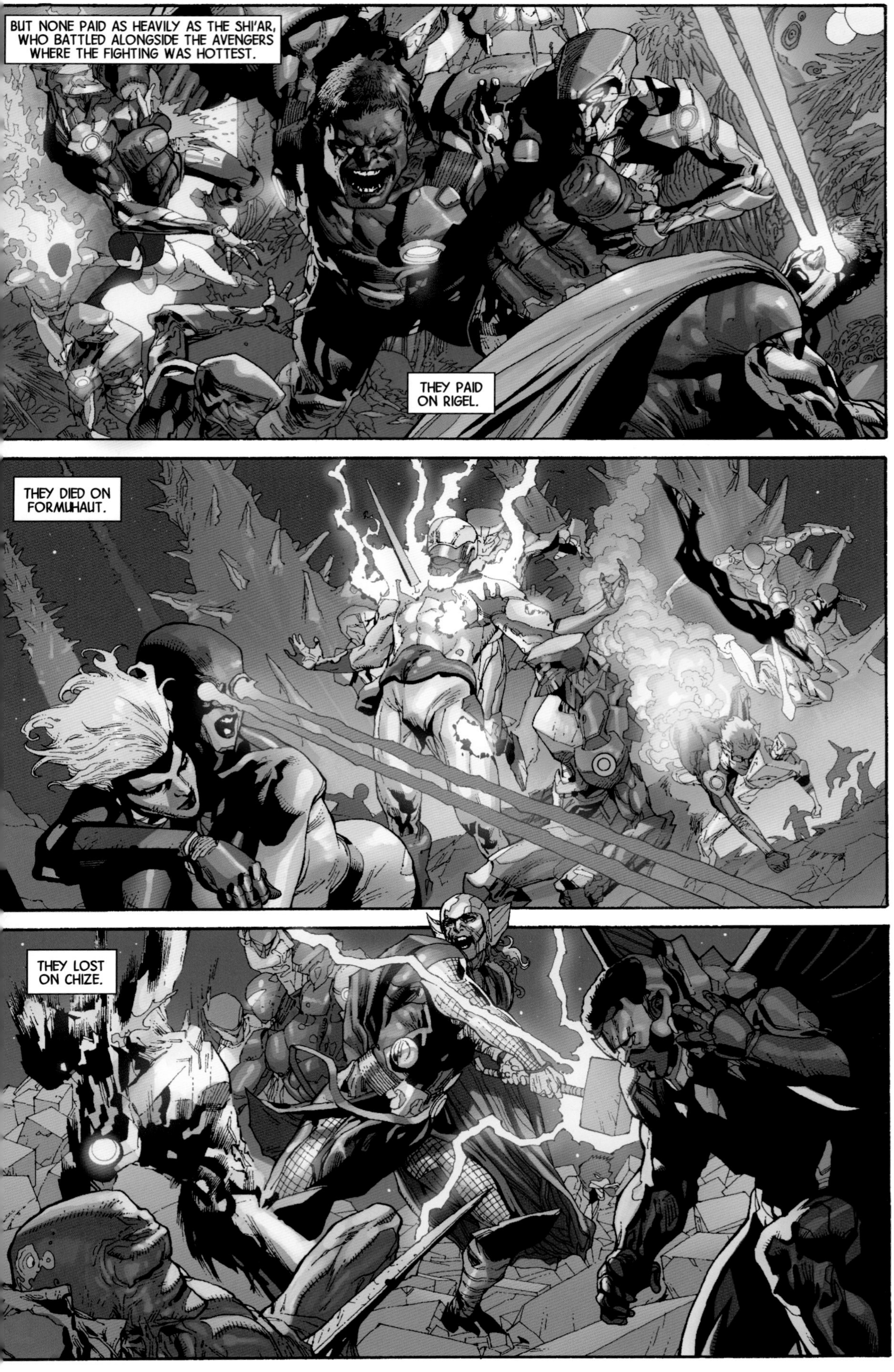
BUT NONE PAID AS HEAVILY AS THE SHI'AR, WHO BATTLED ALONGSIDE THE AVENGERS WHERE THE FIGHTING WAS HOTTEST.
THEY PAID ON RIGEL.
THEY DIED ON FORMUHAUT.
THEY LOST ON CHIZE.

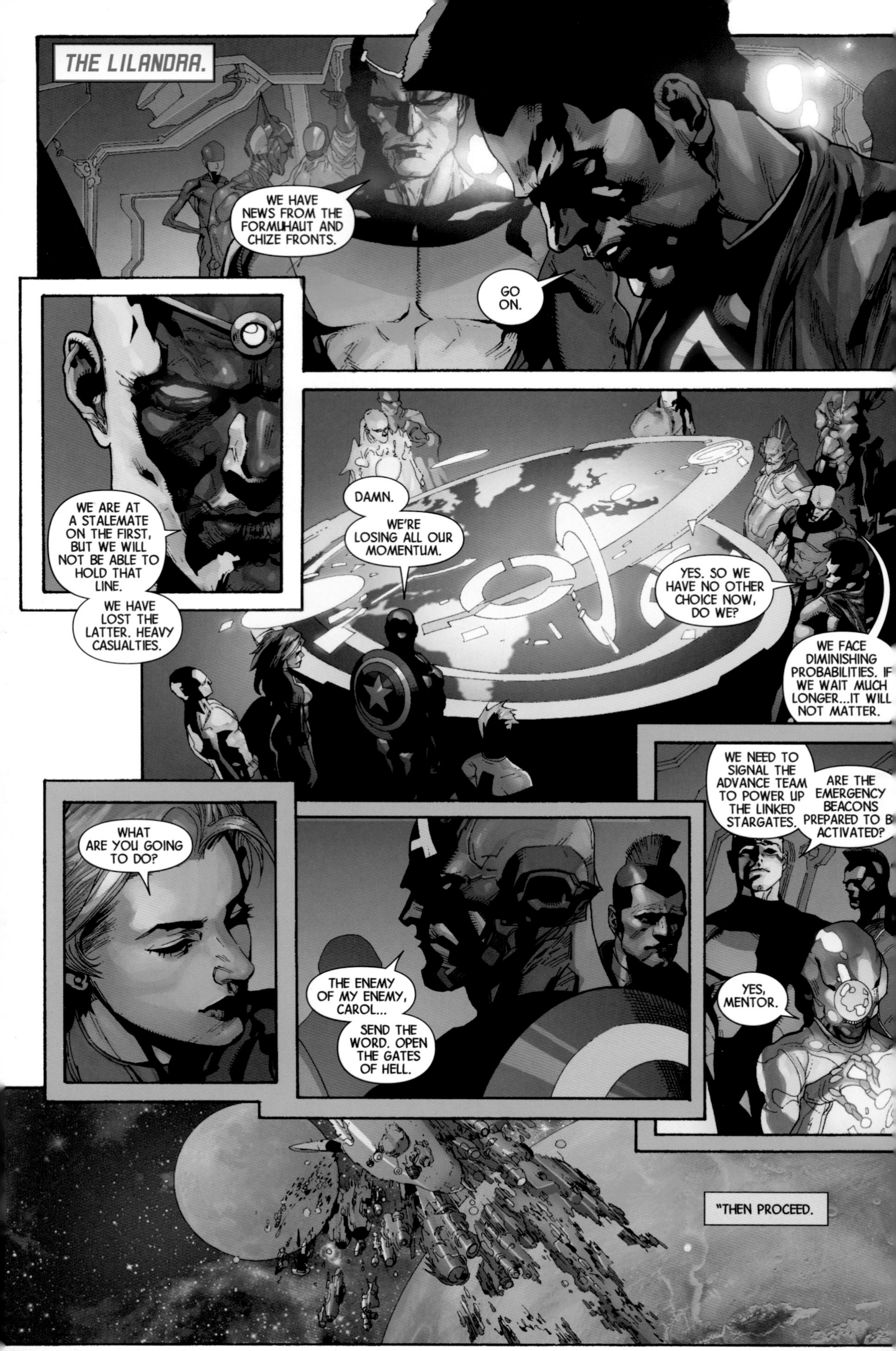
THE LILANDRA.
WE HAVE NEWS FROM THE FORMUHAUT AND CHIZE FRONTS.
GO ON.
WE ARE AT A STALEMATE ON THE FIRST, BUT WE WILL NOT BE ABLE TO HOLD THAT LINE.
WE HAVE LOST THE LATTER. HEAVY CASUALTIES.
DAMN.
WE'RE LOSING ALL OUR MOMENTUM.
YES. SO WE HAVE NO OTHER CHOICE NOW, DO WE?
WE FACE DIMINISHING PROBABILITIES. IF WE WAIT MUCH LONGER...IT WILL NOT MATTER.
WHAT ARE YOU GOING TO DO?
THE ENEMY OF MY ENEMY, CAROL...
SEND THE WORD. OPEN THE GATES OF HELL.
WE NEED TO SIGNAL THE ADVANCE TEAM TO POWER UP THE LINKED STARGATES.
ARE THE EMERGENCY BEACONS PREPARED TO B ACTIVATED?
YES, MENTOR.
"THEN PROCEED.

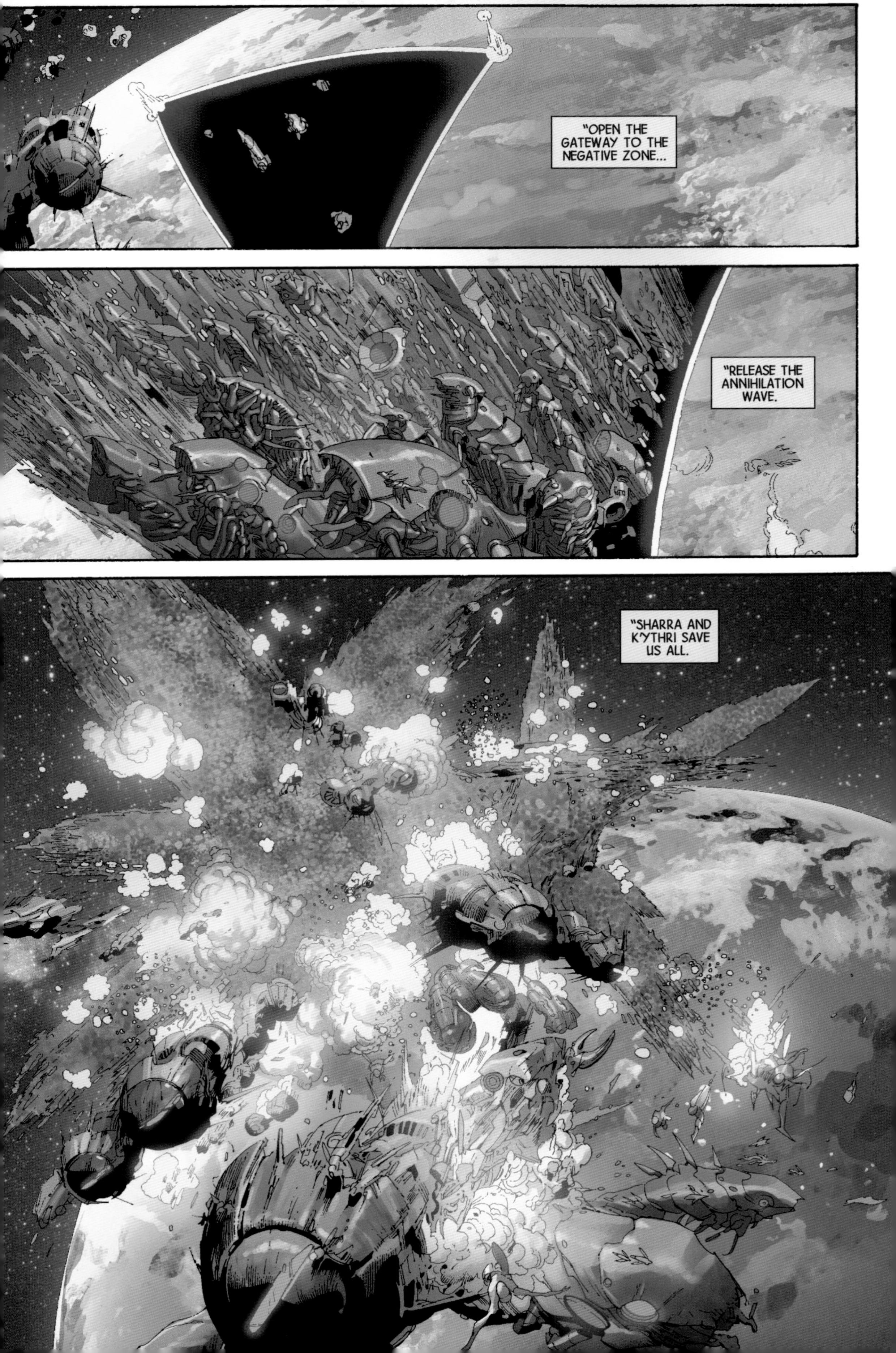
"OPEN THE GATEWAY TO THE NEGATIVE ZONE...
"RELEASE THE ANNIHILATION WAVE.
"SHARRA AND K'YTHRI SAVE US ALL.

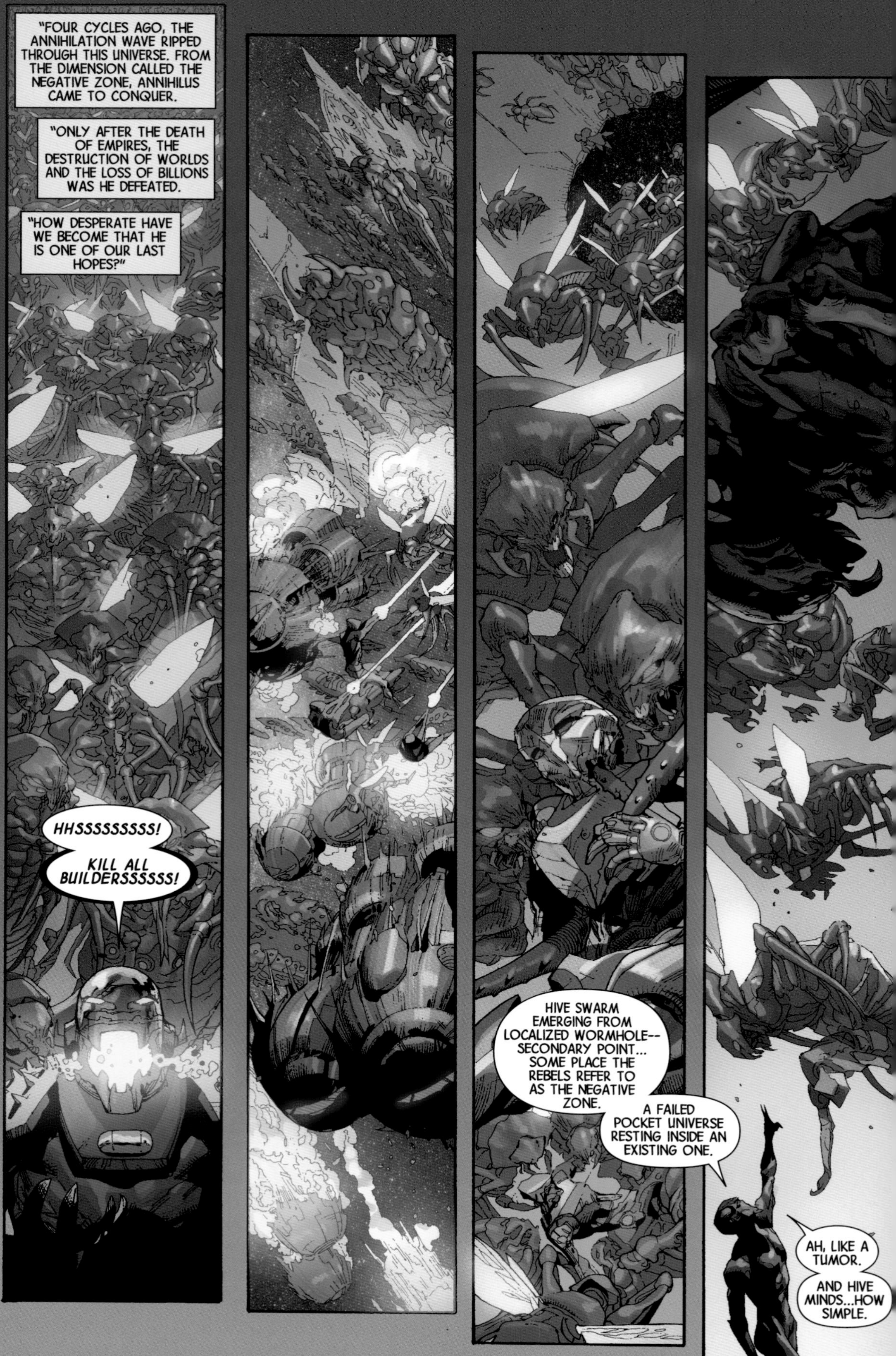
"FOUR CYCLES AGO, THE ANNIHILATION WAVE RIPPED THROUGH THIS UNIVERSE. FROM THE DIMENSION CALLED THE NEGATIVE ZONE, ANNIHILUS CAME TO CONQUER.
"ONLY AFTER THE DEATH OF EMPIRES, THE DESTRUCTION OF WORLDS AND THE LOSS OF BILLIONS WAS HE DEFEATED.
"HOW DESPERATE HAVE WE BECOME THAT HE IS ONE OF OUR LAST HOPES?"
HHSSSSSSSSS!
KILL ALL BUILDERSSSSSS!
HIVE SWARM EMERGING FROM LOCALIZED WORMHOLE--SECONDARY POINT... SOME PLACE THE REBELS REFER TO AS THE NEGATIVE ZONE.
A FAILED POCKET UNIVERSE RESTING INSIDE AN EXISTING ONE.
AH, LIKE A TUMOR.
AND HIVE MINDS...HOW SIMPLE.

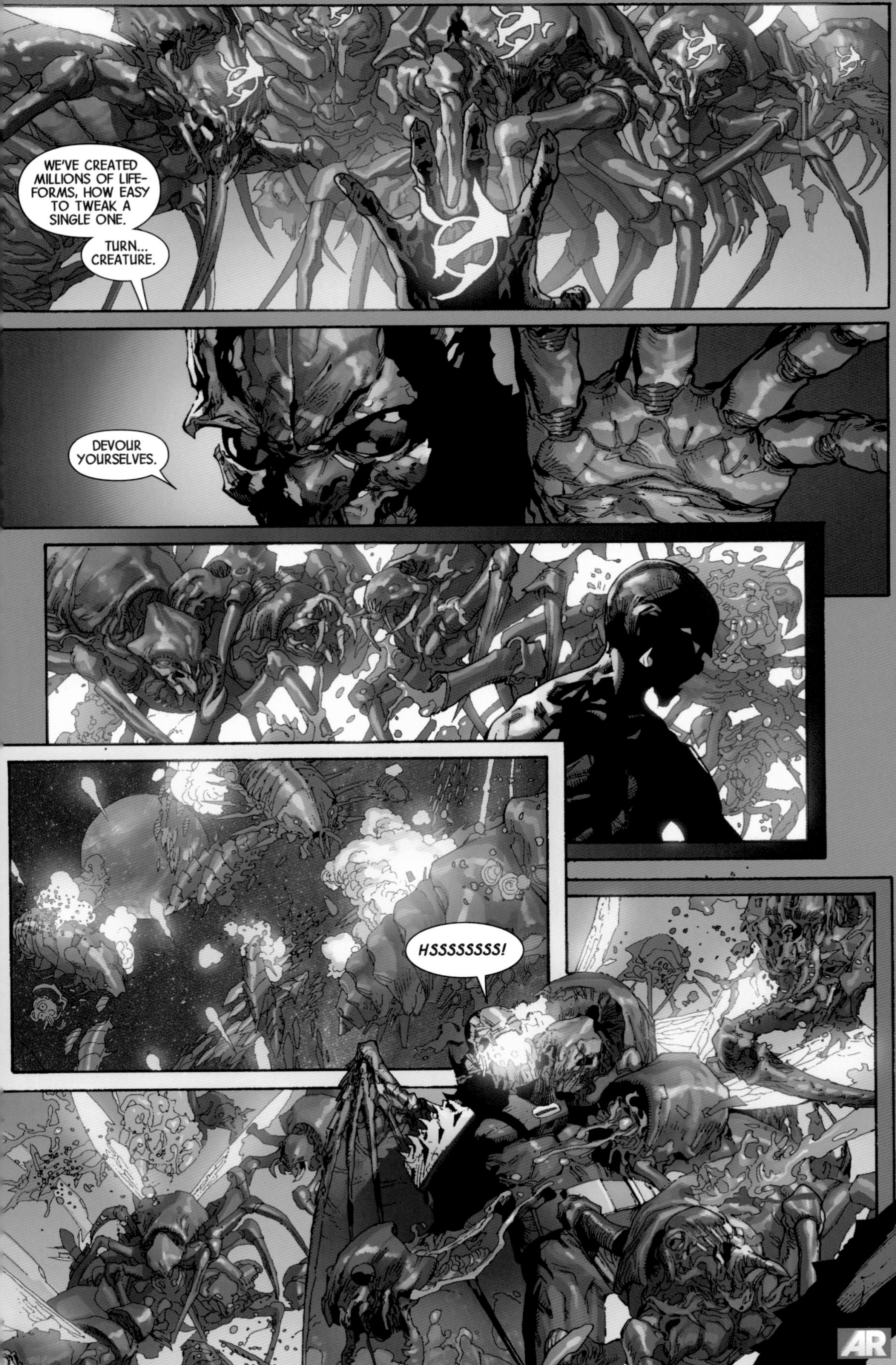
WE'VE CREATED MILLIONS OF LIFE-FORMS, HOW EASY TO TWEAK A SINGLE ONE.
TURN... CREATURE.
DEVOUR YOURSELVES.
HSSSSSSSS!
AR

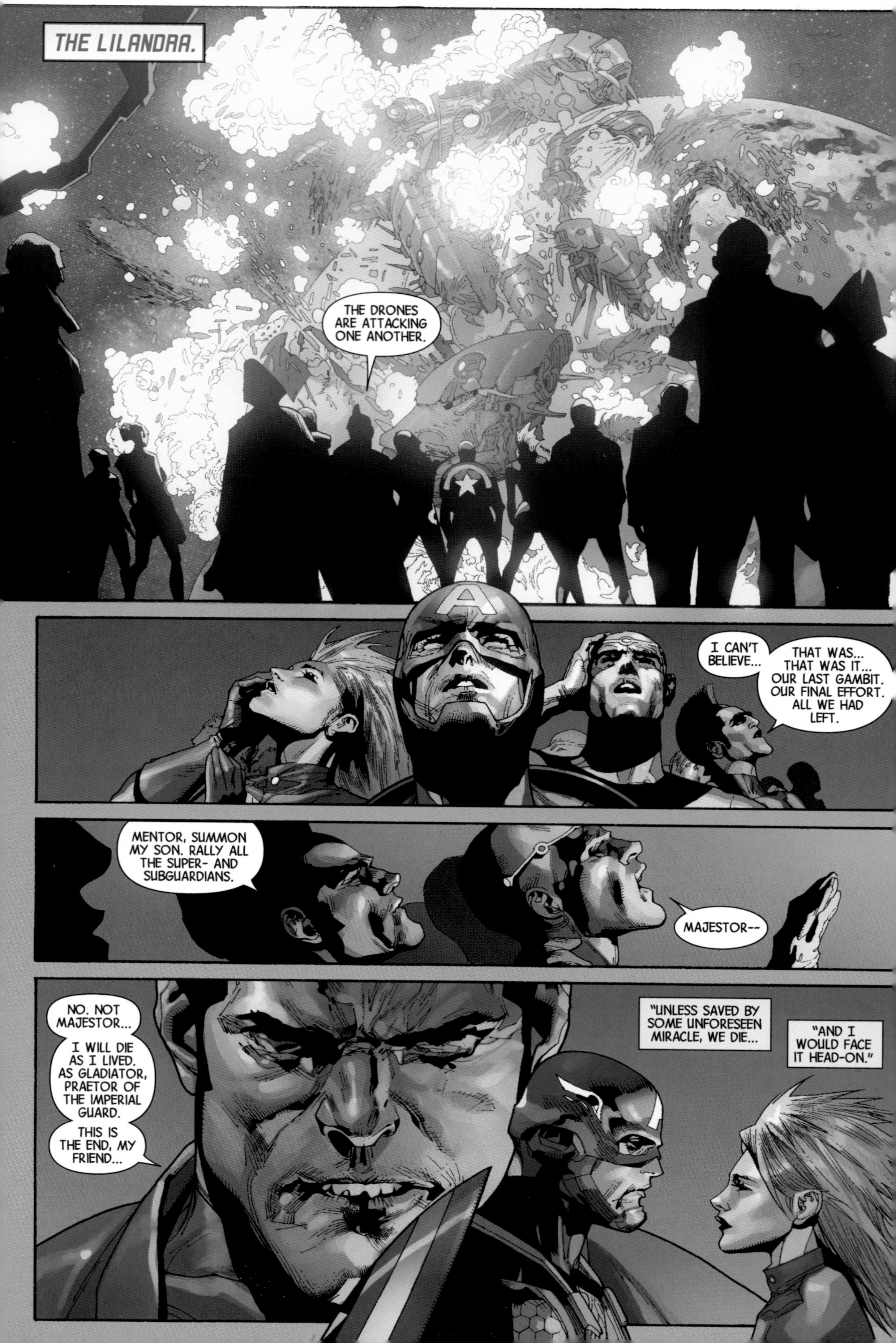
THE LILANDRA.
THE DRONES ARE ATTACKING ONE ANOTHER.
I CAN'T BELIEVE...
THAT WAS... THAT WAS IT... OUR LAST GAMBIT. OUR FINAL EFFORT. ALL WE HAD LEFT.
MENTOR, SUMMON MY SON. RALLY ALL THE SUPER- AND SUBGUARDIANS.
MAJESTOR--
NO. NOT MAJESTOR...
I WILL DIE AS I LIVED. AS GLADIATOR, PRAETOR OF THE IMPERIAL GUARD.
THIS IS THE END, MY FRIEND...
"UNLESS SAVED BY SOME UNFORESEEN MIRACLE, WE DIE...
"AND I WOULD FACE IT HEAD-ON."

THE PROMISE
FULFILLED

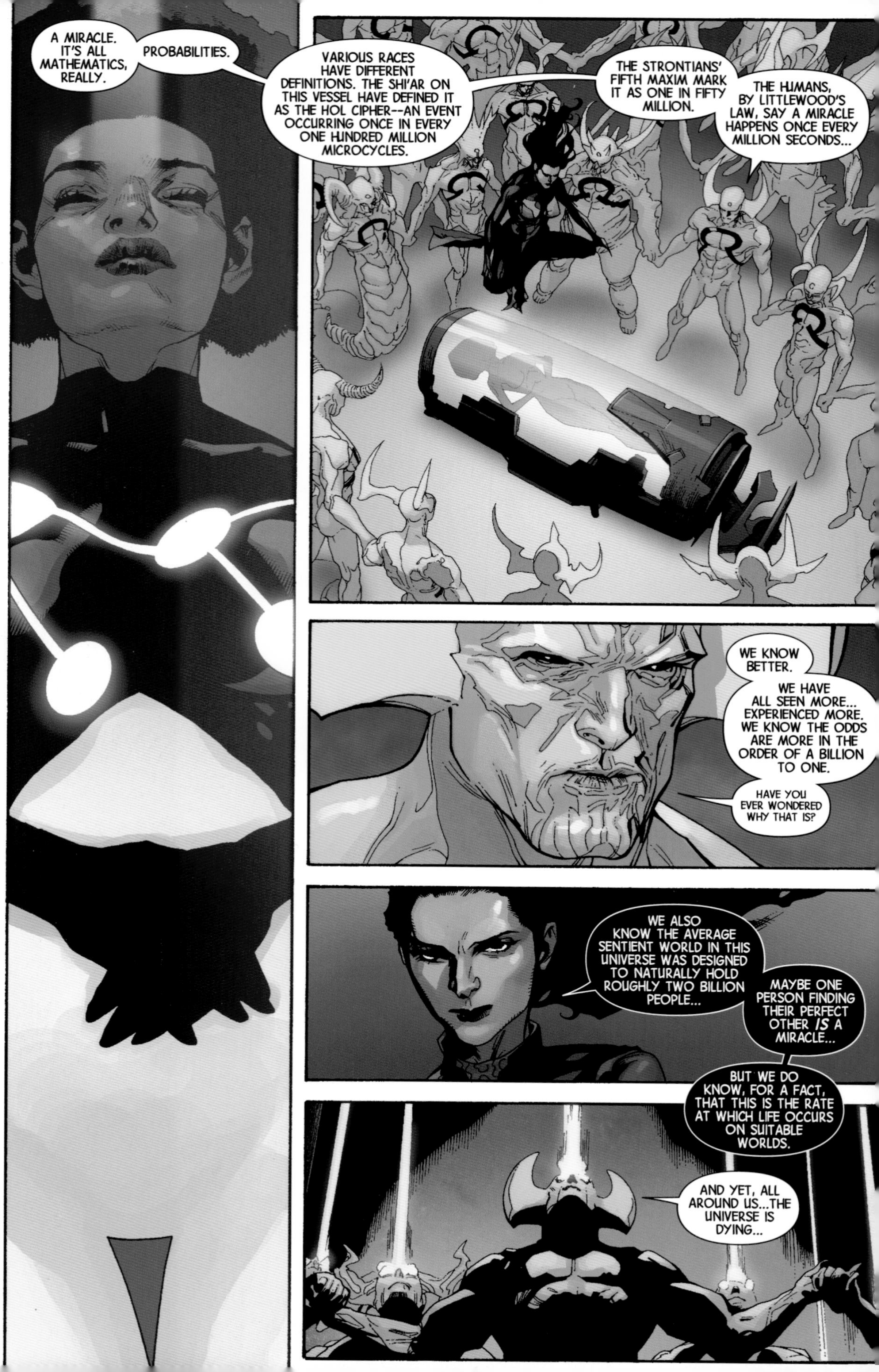
A MIRACLE. IT'S ALL MATHEMATICS, REALLY.
PROBABILITIES.
VARIOUS RACES HAVE DIFFERENT DEFINITIONS. THE SHI'AR ON THIS VESSEL HAVE DEFINED IT AS THE HOL CIPHER--AN EVENT OCCURRING ONCE IN EVERY ONE HUNDRED MILLION MICROCYCLES.
THE STRONTIANS' FIFTH MAXIM MARK IT AS ONE IN FIFTY MILLION.
THE HUMANS, BY LITTLEWOOD'S LAW, SAY A MIRACLE HAPPENS ONCE EVERY MILLION SECONDS...
WE KNOW BETTER.
WE HAVE ALL SEEN MORE... EXPERIENCED MORE. WE KNOW THE ODDS ARE MORE IN THE ORDER OF A BILLION TO ONE.
HAVE YOU EVER WONDERED WHY THAT IS?
WE ALSO KNOW THE AVERAGE SENTIENT WORLD IN THIS UNIVERSE WAS DESIGNED TO NATURALLY HOLD ROUGHLY TWO BILLION PEOPLE...
MAYBE ONE PERSON FINDING THEIR PERFECT OTHER *IS* A MIRACLE...
BUT WE DO KNOW, FOR A FACT, THAT THIS IS THE RATE AT WHICH LIFE OCCURS ON SUITABLE WORLDS.
AND YET, ALL AROUND US...THE UNIVERSE IS DYING...

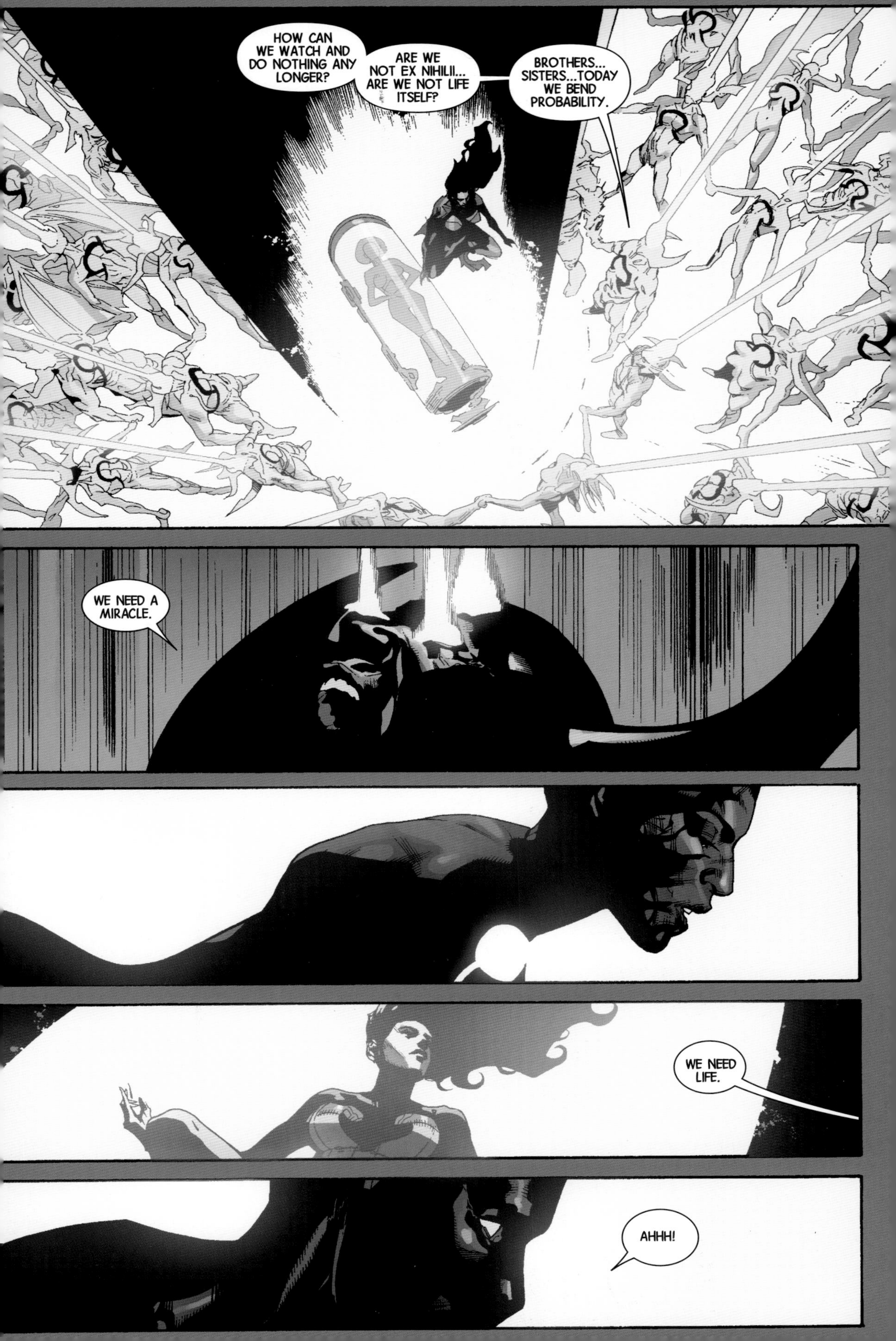
HOW CAN WE WATCH AND DO NOTHING ANY LONGER?
ARE WE NOT EX NIHILII... ARE WE NOT LIFE ITSELF?
BROTHERS... SISTERS...TODAY WE BEND PROBABILITY.
WE NEED A MIRACLE.
WE NEED LIFE.
AHHH!

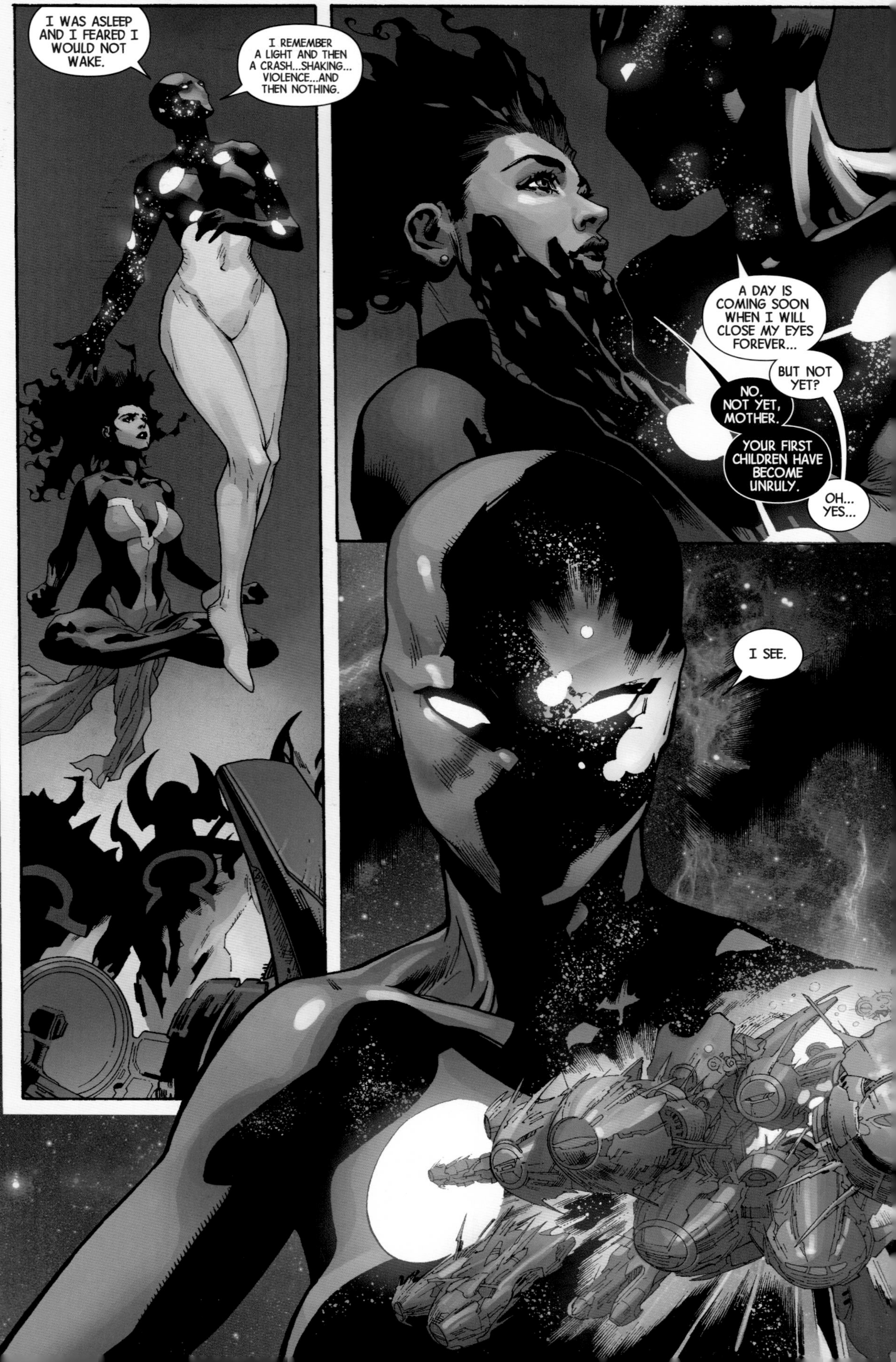

I WAS ASLEEP AND I FEARED I WOULD NOT WAKE.
I REMEMBER A LIGHT AND THEN A CRASH...SHAKING... VIOLENCE...AND THEN NOTHING.
A DAY IS COMING SOON WHEN I WILL CLOSE MY EYES FOREVER...
BUT NOT YET?
NO. NOT YET, MOTHER.
YOUR FIRST CHILDREN HAVE BECOME UNRULY.
OH... YES...
I SEE.

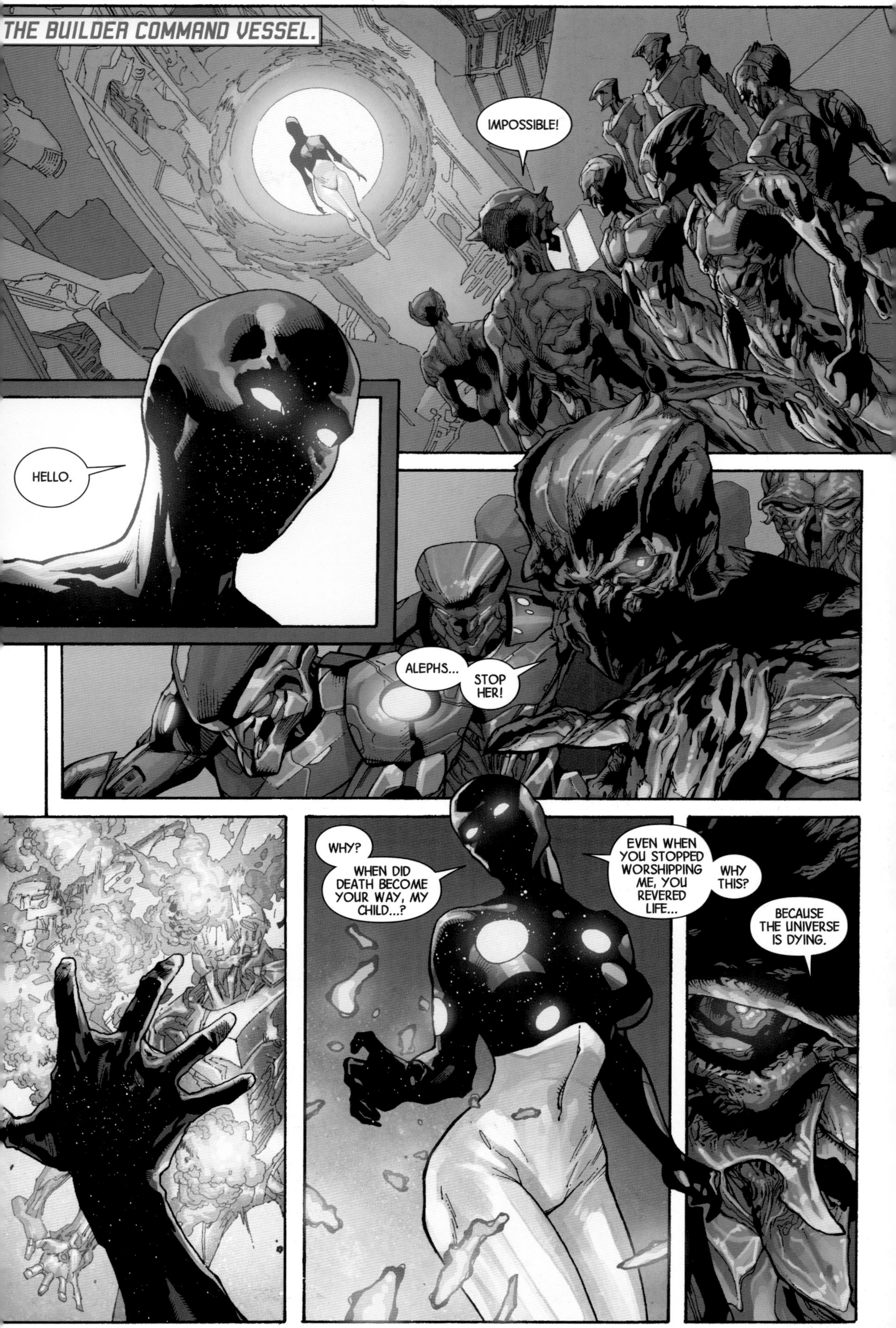
THE BUILDER COMMAND VESSEL.
IMPOSSIBLE!
HELLO.
ALEPHS...
STOP HER!
WHY?
WHEN DID DEATH BECOME YOUR WAY, MY CHILD...?
EVEN WHEN YOU STOPPED WORSHIPPING ME, YOU REVERED LIFE...
WHY THIS?
BECAUSE THE UNIVERSE IS DYING.

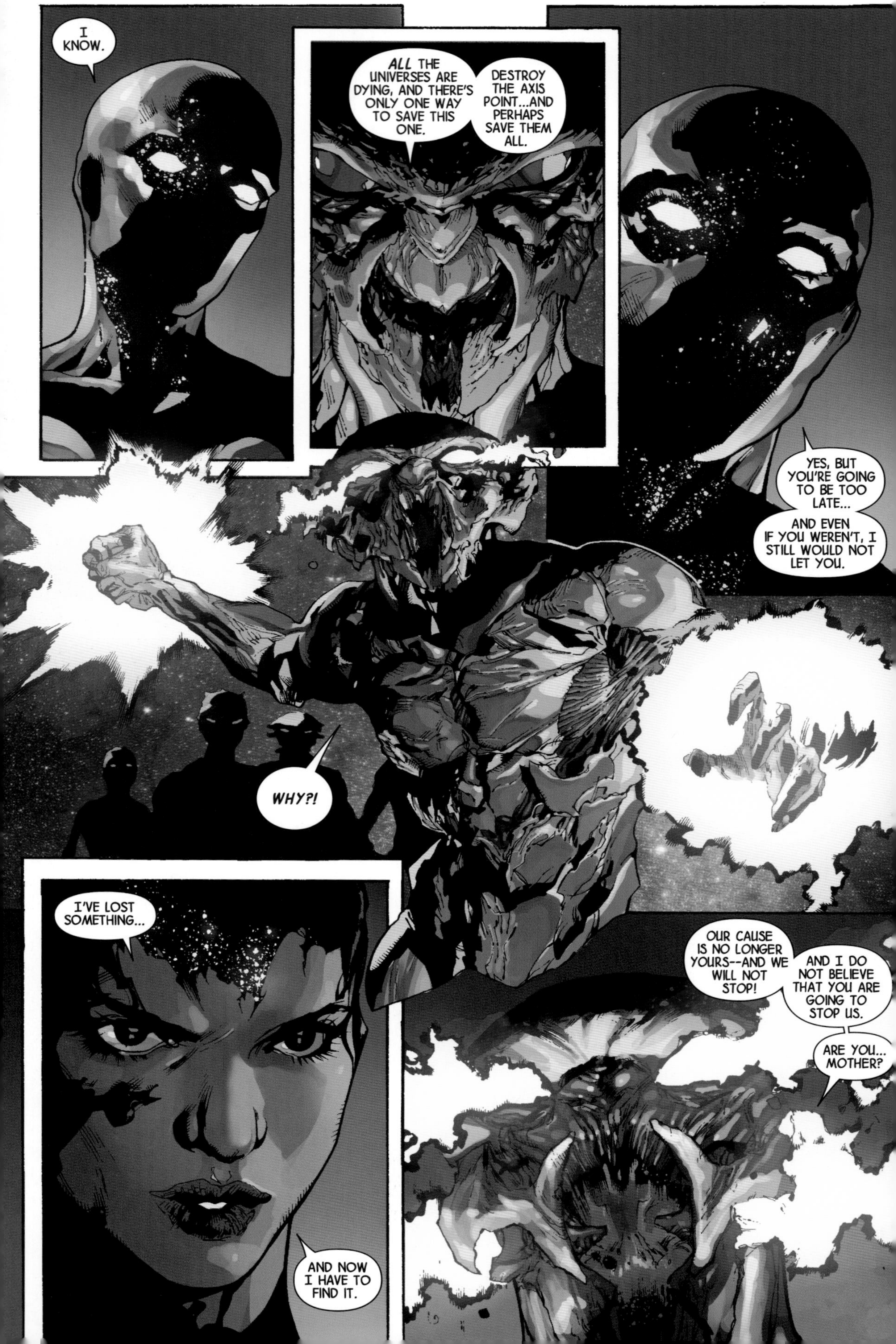
I KNOW.
ALL THE UNIVERSES ARE DYING, AND THERE'S ONLY ONE WAY TO SAVE THIS ONE.
DESTROY THE AXIS POINT...AND PERHAPS SAVE THEM ALL.
YES, BUT YOU'RE GOING TO BE TOO LATE...
AND EVEN IF YOU WEREN'T, I STILL WOULD NOT LET YOU.
WHY?!
I'VE LOST SOMETHING...
AND NOW I HAVE TO FIND IT.
OUR CAUSE IS NO LONGER YOURS--AND WE WILL NOT STOP!
AND I DO NOT BELIEVE THAT YOU ARE GOING TO STOP US.
ARE YOU... MOTHER?

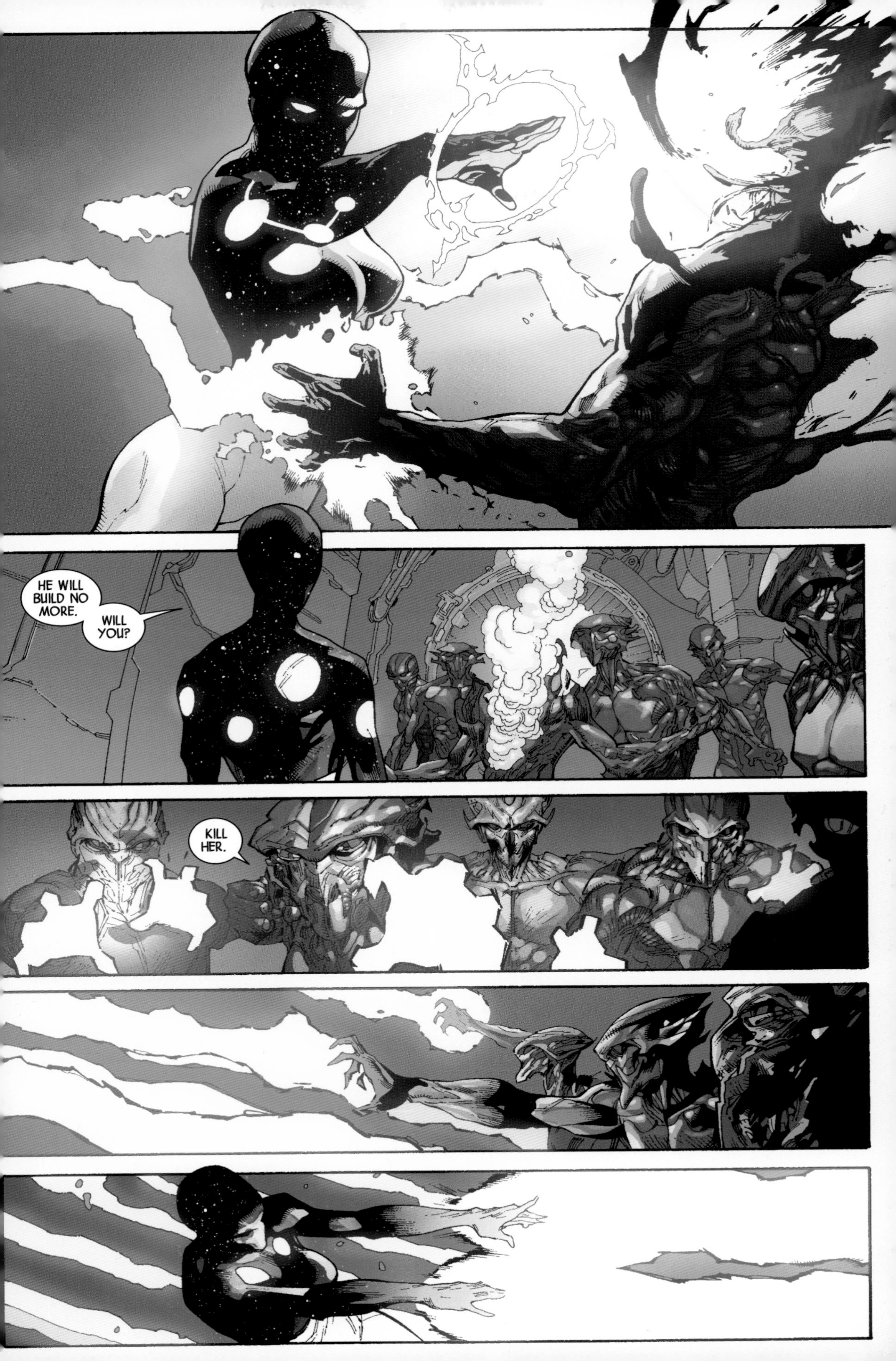
HE WILL BUILD NO MORE.
WILL YOU?
KILL HER.

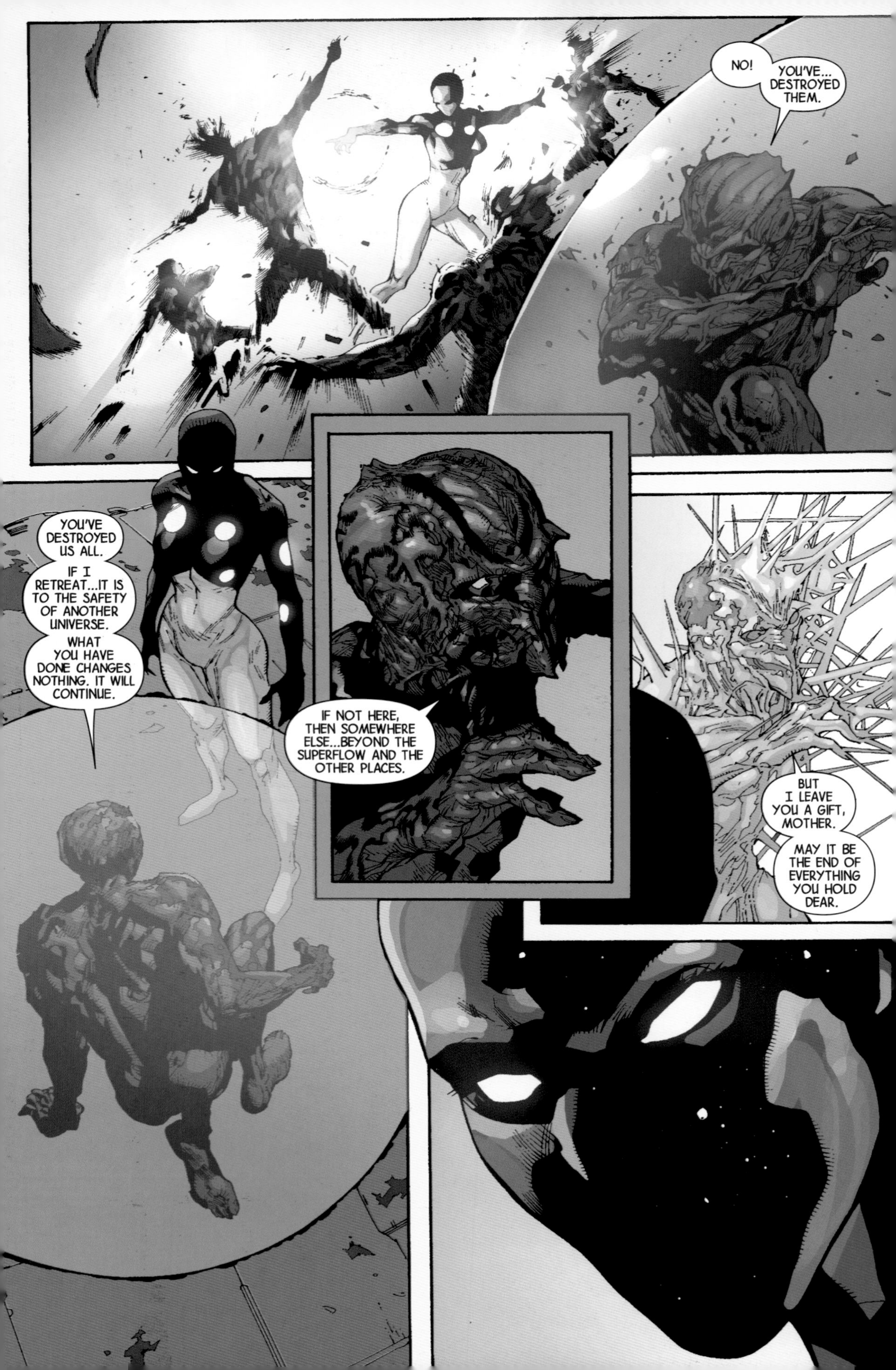
NO!
YOU'VE... DESTROYED THEM.
YOU'VE DESTROYED US ALL.
IF I RETREAT...IT IS TO THE SAFETY OF ANOTHER UNIVERSE.
WHAT YOU HAVE DONE CHANGES NOTHING. IT WILL CONTINUE.
IF NOT HERE, THEN SOMEWHERE ELSE...BEYOND THE SUPERFLOW AND THE OTHER PLACES.
BUT I LEAVE YOU A GIFT, MOTHER.
MAY IT BE THE END OF EVERYTHING YOU HOLD DEAR.

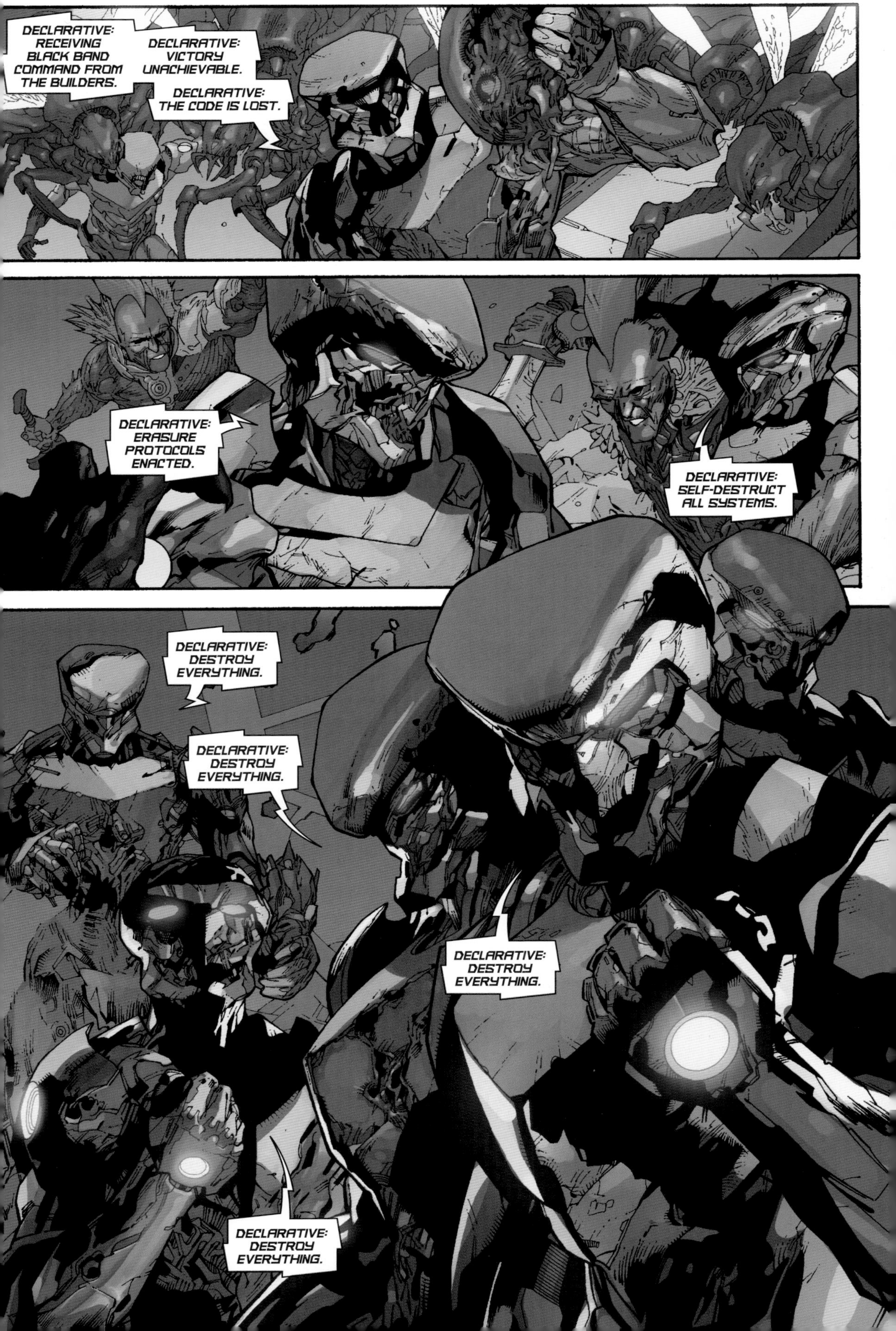
DECLARATIVE: RECEIVING BLACK BAND COMMAND FROM THE BUILDERS.
DECLARATIVE: VICTORY UNACHIEVABLE.
DECLARATIVE: THE CODE IS LOST.
DECLARATIVE: ERASURE PROTOCOLS ENACTED.
DECLARATIVE: SELF-DESTRUCT ALL SYSTEMS.
DECLARATIVE: DESTROY EVERYTHING.
DECLARATIVE: DESTROY EVERYTHING.
DECLARATIVE: DESTROY EVERYTHING.
DECLARATIVE: DESTROY EVERYTHING.

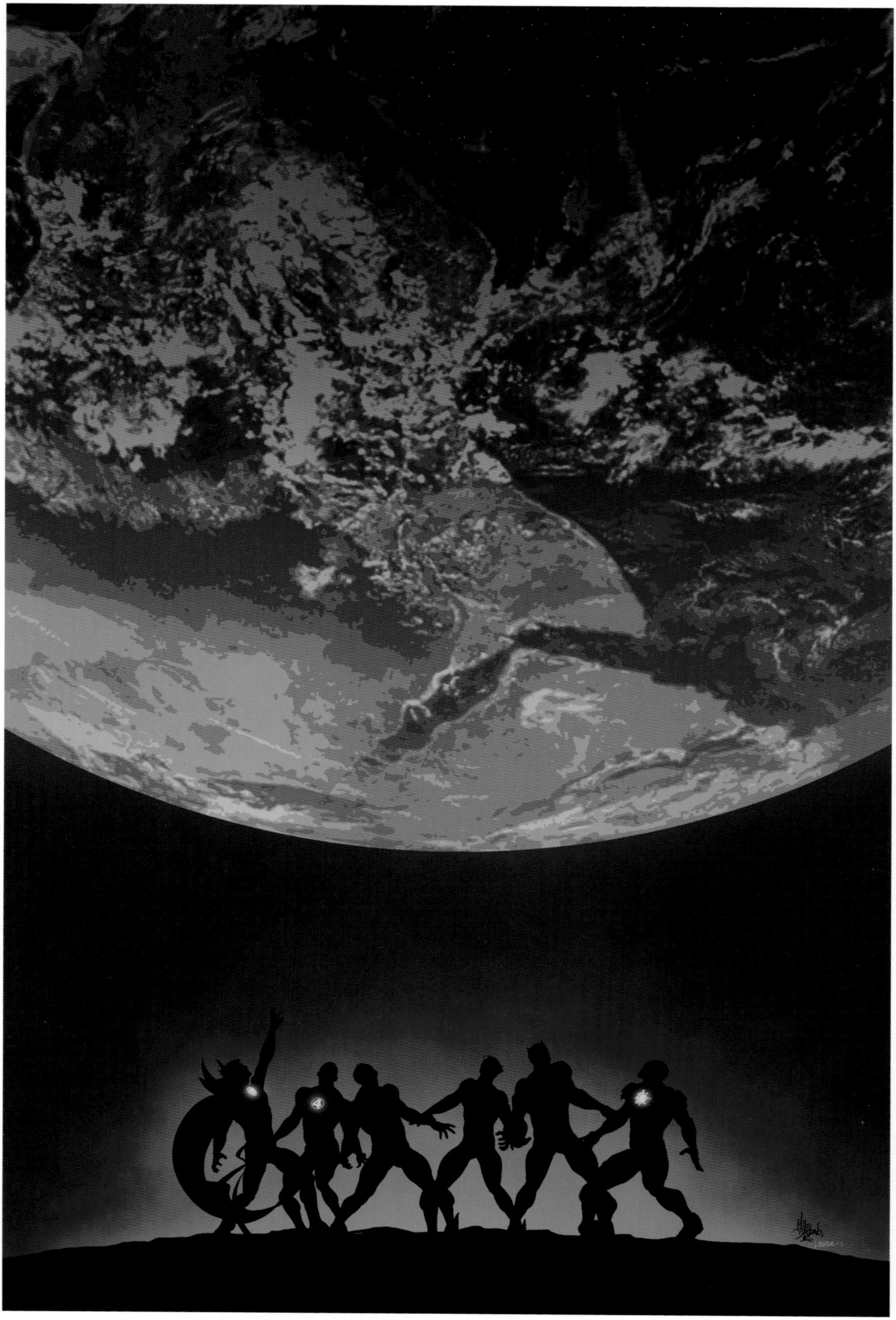

ALL THESE WORLDS

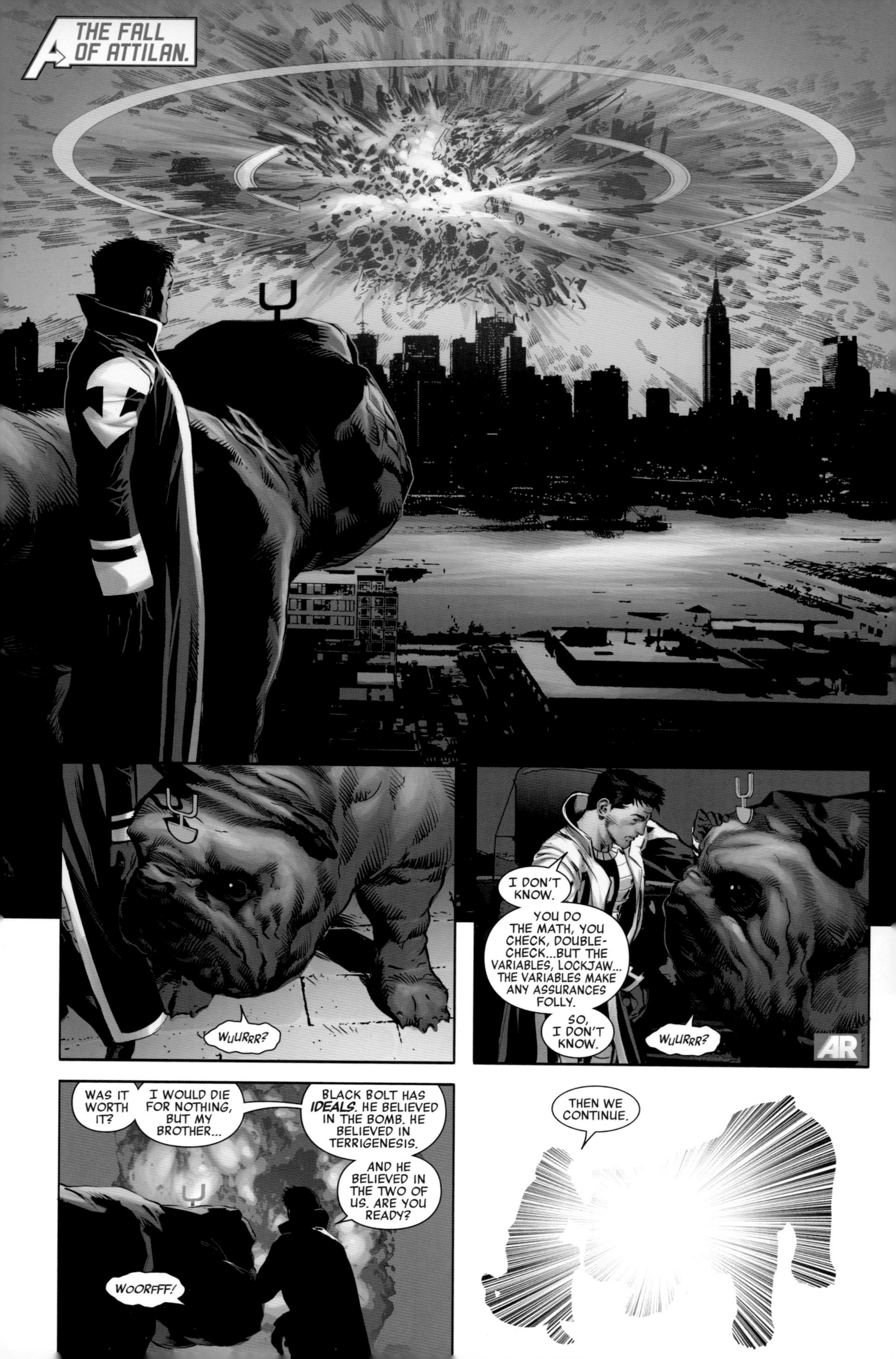
THE FALL OF ATTILAN.
WUURRR?
I DON'T KNOW.
YOU DO THE MATH, YOU CHECK, DOUBLE-CHECK...BUT THE VARIABLES, LOCKJAW... THE VARIABLES MAKE ANY ASSURANCES FOLLY.
SO, I DON'T KNOW.
WUURRR?
AR
WAS IT WORTH IT?
I WOULD DIE FOR NOTHING, BUT MY BROTHER...
BLACK BOLT HAS IDEALS. HE BELIEVED IN THE BOMB. HE BELIEVED IN TERRIGENESIS.
AND HE BELIEVED IN THE TWO OF US. ARE YOU READY?
WOORFFF!
THEN WE CONTINUE.

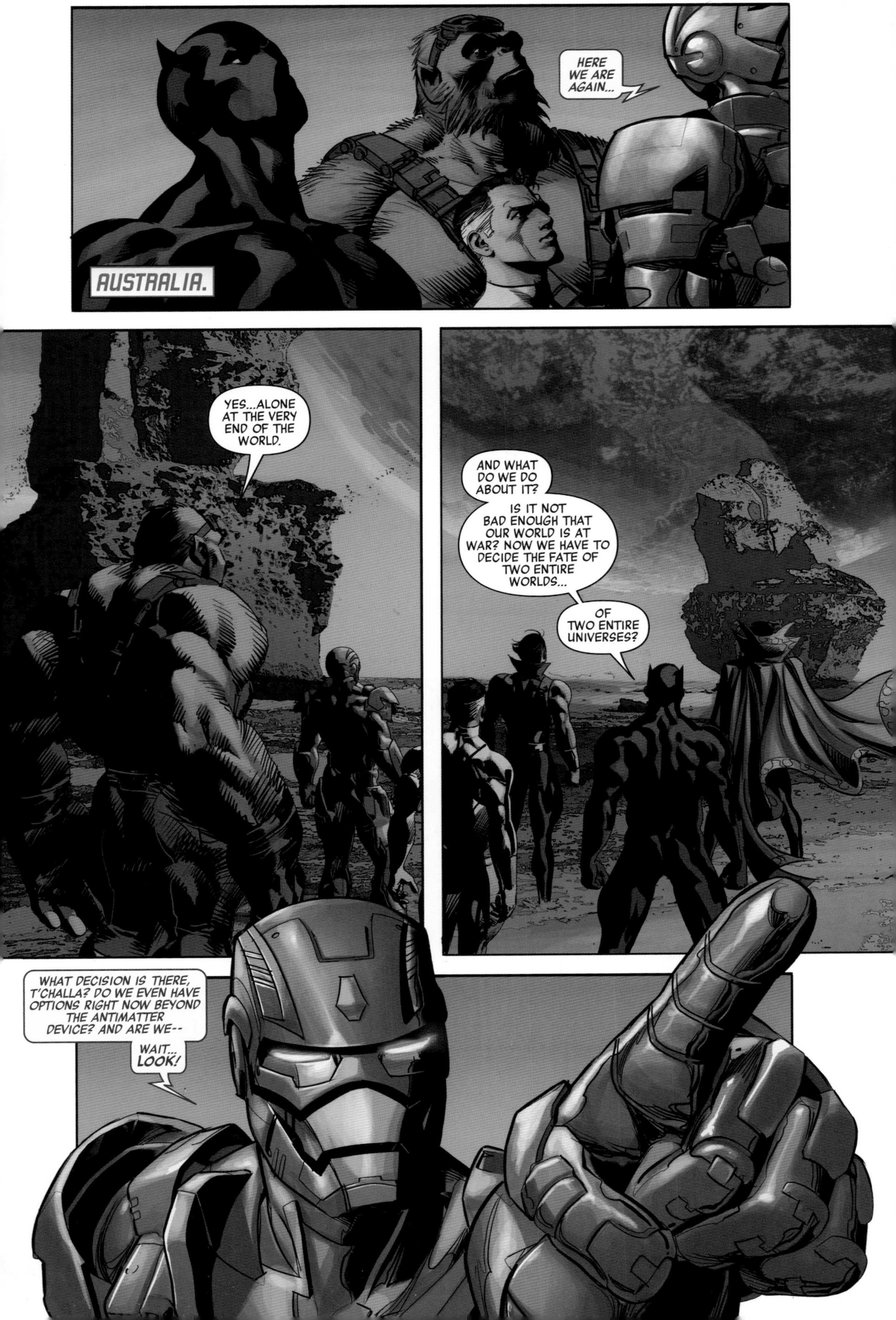
HERE WE ARE AGAIN...
AUSTRALIA.
YES...ALONE AT THE VERY END OF THE WORLD.
AND WHAT DO WE DO ABOUT IT?
IS IT NOT BAD ENOUGH THAT OUR WORLD IS AT WAR? NOW WE HAVE TO DECIDE THE FATE OF TWO ENTIRE WORLDS...
OF TWO ENTIRE UNIVERSES?
WHAT DECISION IS THERE, T'CHALLA? DO WE EVEN HAVE OPTIONS RIGHT NOW BEYOND THE ANTIMATTER DEVICE? AND ARE WE--
WAIT... LOOK!

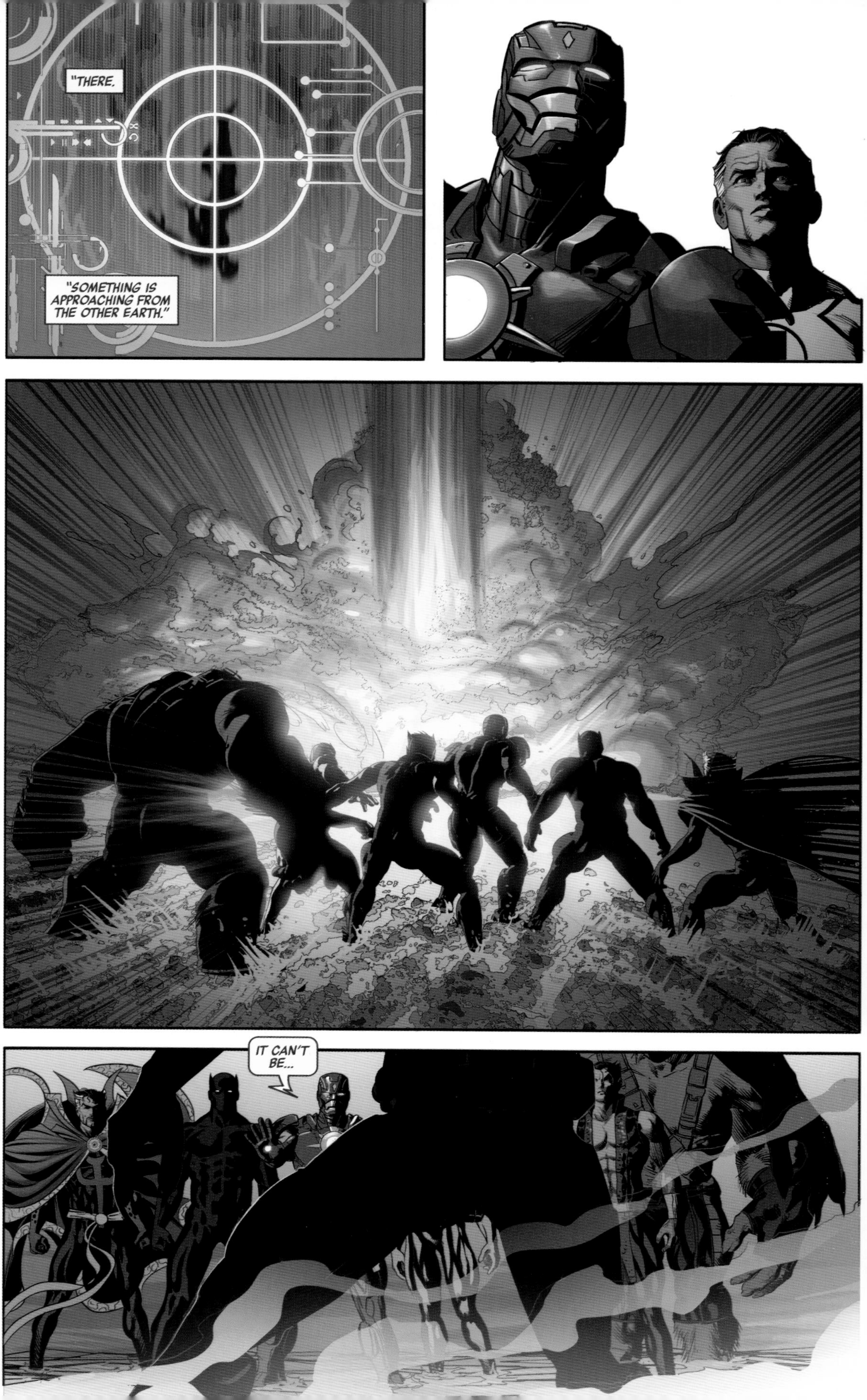
"THERE.
"SOMETHING IS APPROACHING FROM THE OTHER EARTH."
IT CAN'T BE...

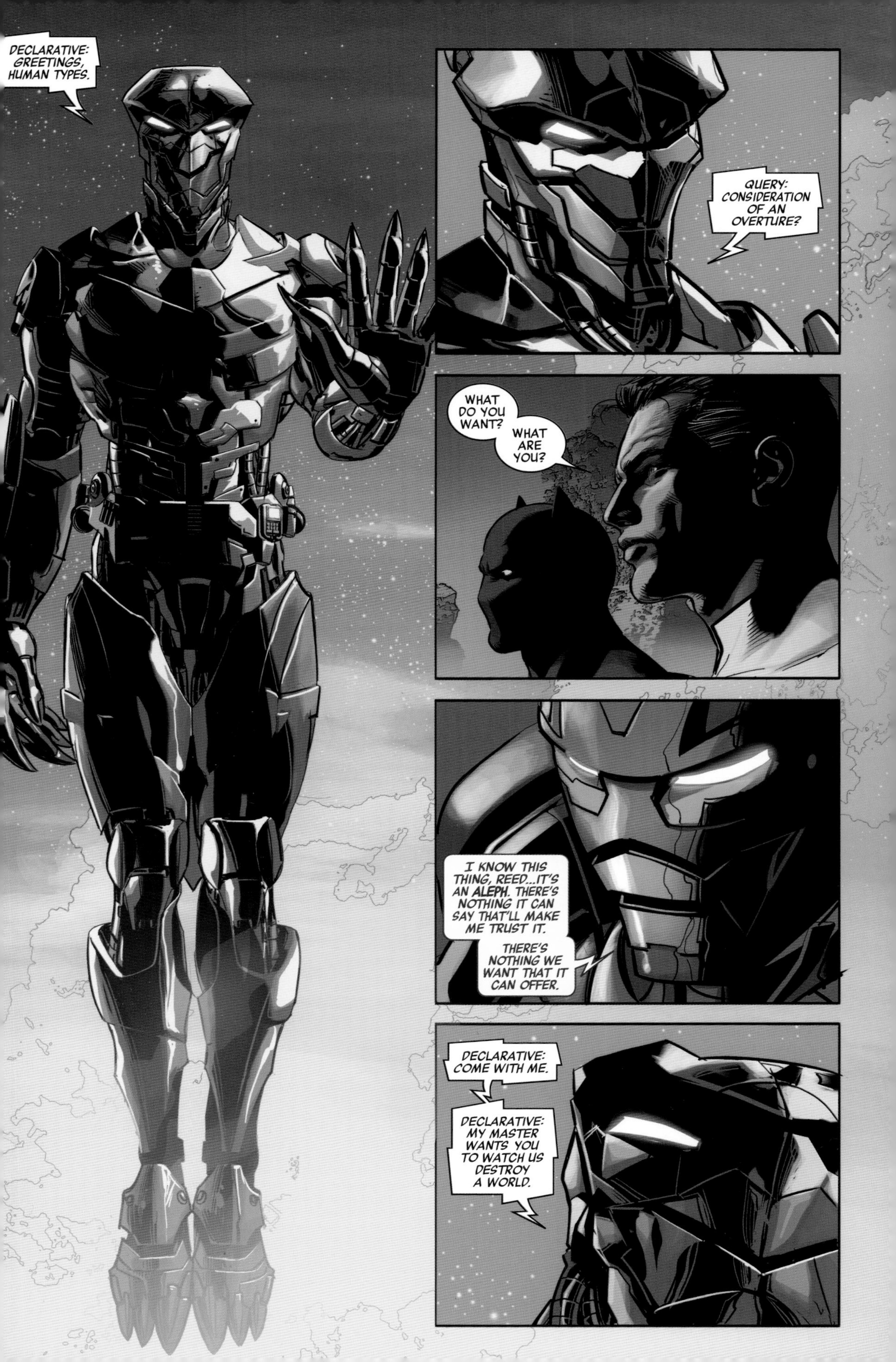
DECLARATIVE: GREETINGS, HUMAN TYPES.
QUERY: CONSIDERATION OF AN OVERTURE?
WHAT DO YOU WANT?
WHAT ARE YOU?
I KNOW THIS THING, REED...IT'S AN ALEPH. THERE'S NOTHING IT CAN SAY THAT'LL MAKE ME TRUST IT.
THERE'S NOTHING WE WANT THAT IT CAN OFFER.
DECLARATIVE: COME WITH ME.
DECLARATIVE: MY MASTER WANTS YOU TO WATCH US DESTROY A WORLD.

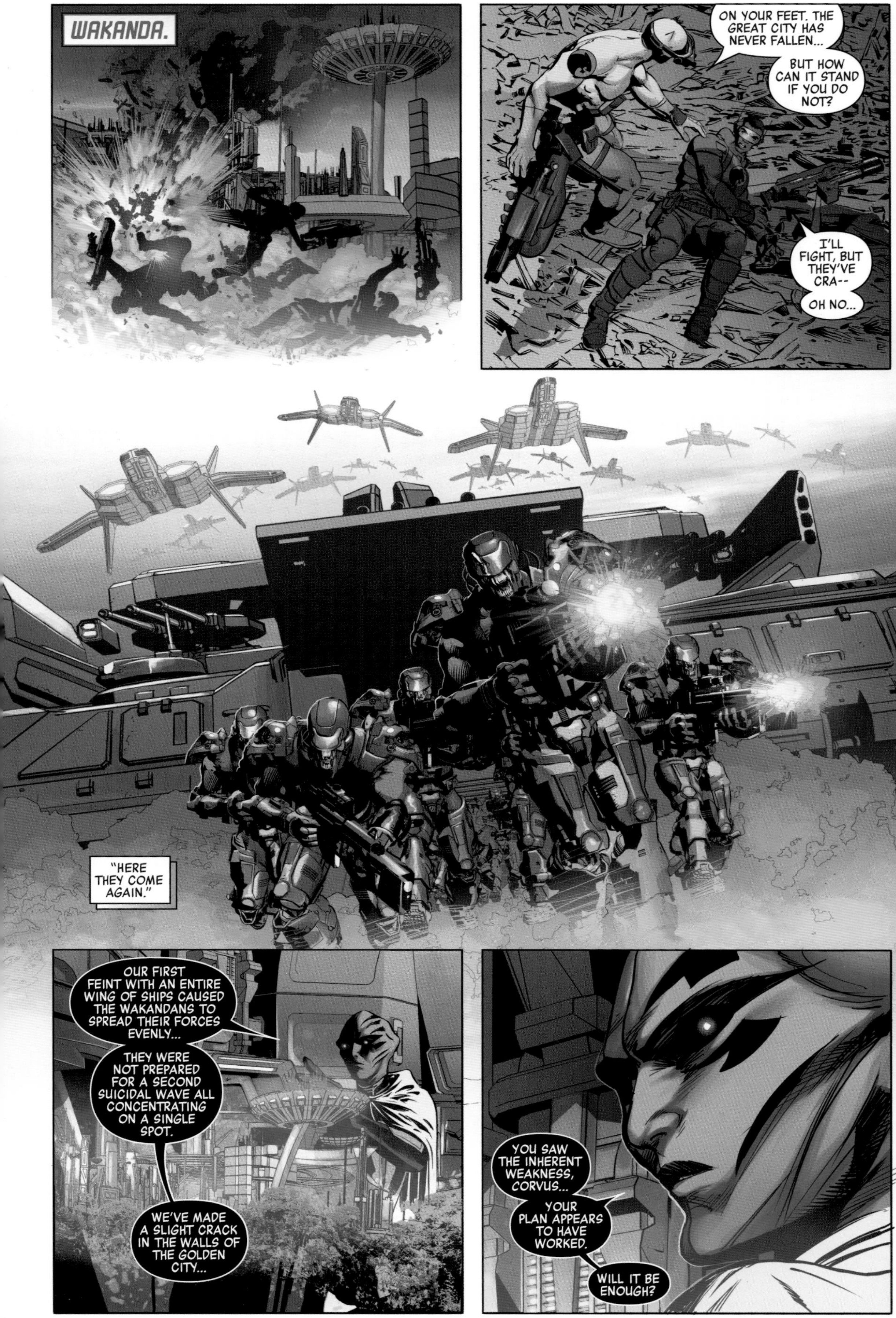
WAKANDA.
ON YOUR FEET. THE GREAT CITY HAS NEVER FALLEN...
BUT HOW CAN IT STAND IF YOU DO NOT?
I'LL FIGHT, BUT THEY'VE CRA--
OH NO...
"HERE THEY COME AGAIN."
OUR FIRST FEINT WITH AN ENTIRE WING OF SHIPS CAUSED THE WAKANDANS TO SPREAD THEIR FORCES EVENLY...
THEY WERE NOT PREPARED FOR A SECOND SUICIDAL WAVE ALL CONCENTRATING ON A SINGLE SPOT.
WE'VE MADE A SLIGHT CRACK IN THE WALLS OF THE GOLDEN CITY...
YOU SAW THE INHERENT WEAKNESS, CORVUS...
YOUR PLAN APPEARS TO HAVE WORKED.
WILL IT BE ENOUGH?

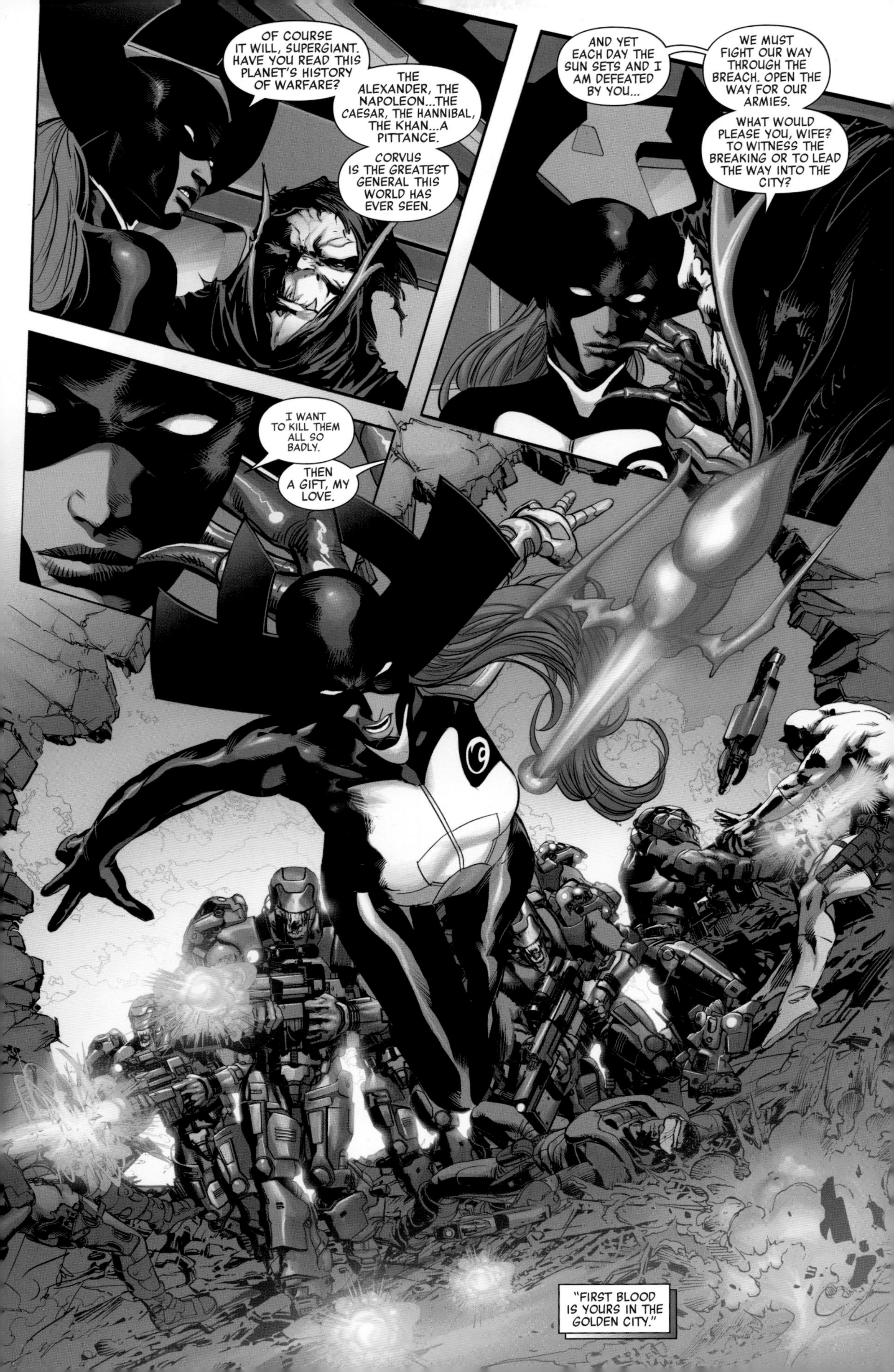
OF COURSE IT WILL, SUPERGIANT. HAVE YOU READ THIS PLANET'S HISTORY OF WARFARE?
THE ALEXANDER, THE NAPOLEON...THE CAESAR, THE HANNIBAL, THE KHAN...A PITTANCE.
CORVUS IS THE GREATEST GENERAL THIS WORLD HAS EVER SEEN.
AND YET EACH DAY THE SUN SETS AND I AM DEFEATED BY YOU...
WE MUST FIGHT OUR WAY THROUGH THE BREACH. OPEN THE WAY FOR OUR ARMIES.
WHAT WOULD PLEASE YOU, WIFE? TO WITNESS THE BREAKING OR TO LEAD THE WAY INTO THE CITY?
I WANT TO KILL THEM ALL SO BADLY.
THEN A GIFT, MY LOVE.
"FIRST BLOOD IS YOURS IN THE GOLDEN CITY."

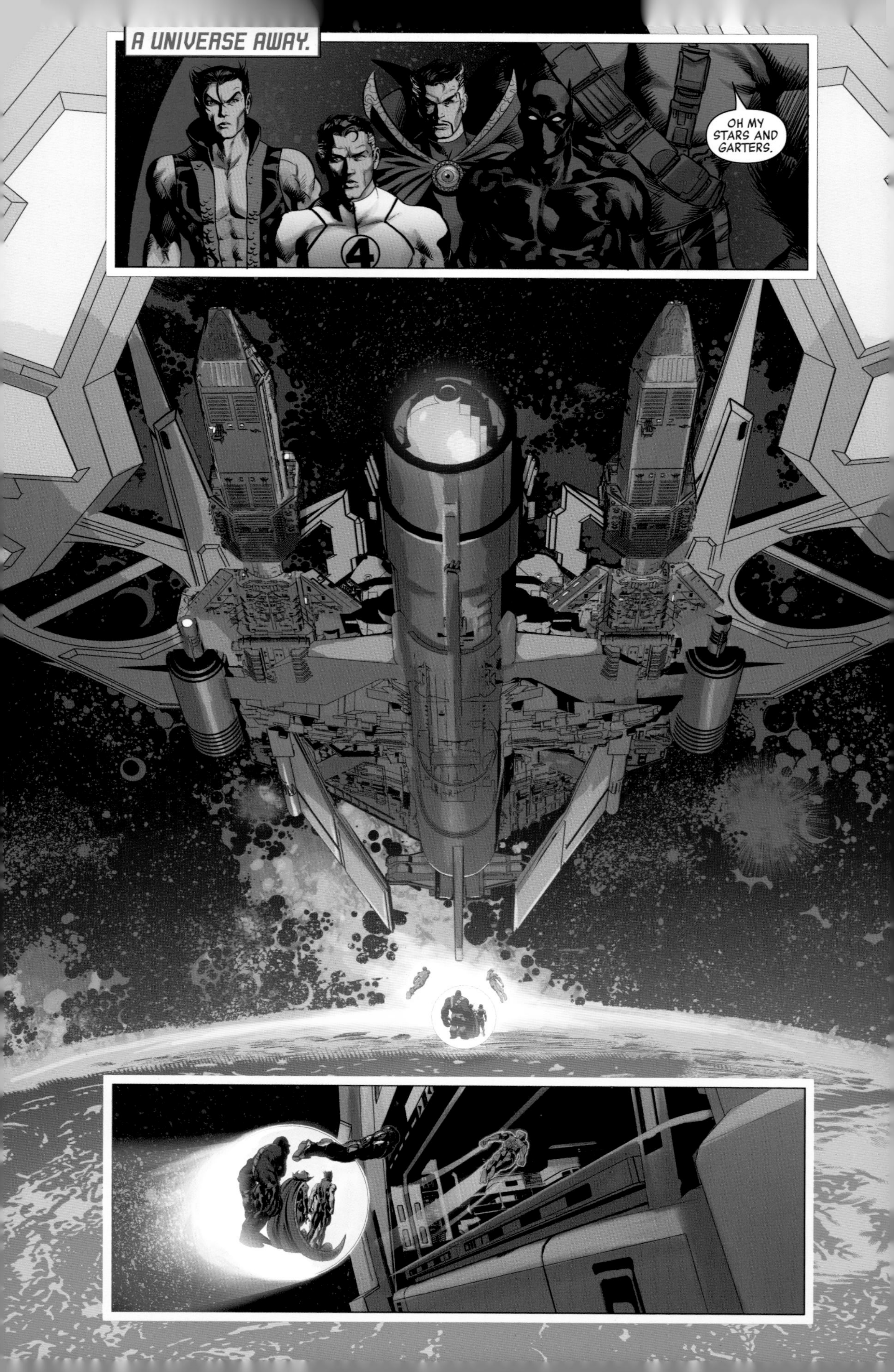
A UNIVERSE AWAY.
OH MY STARS AND GARTERS.

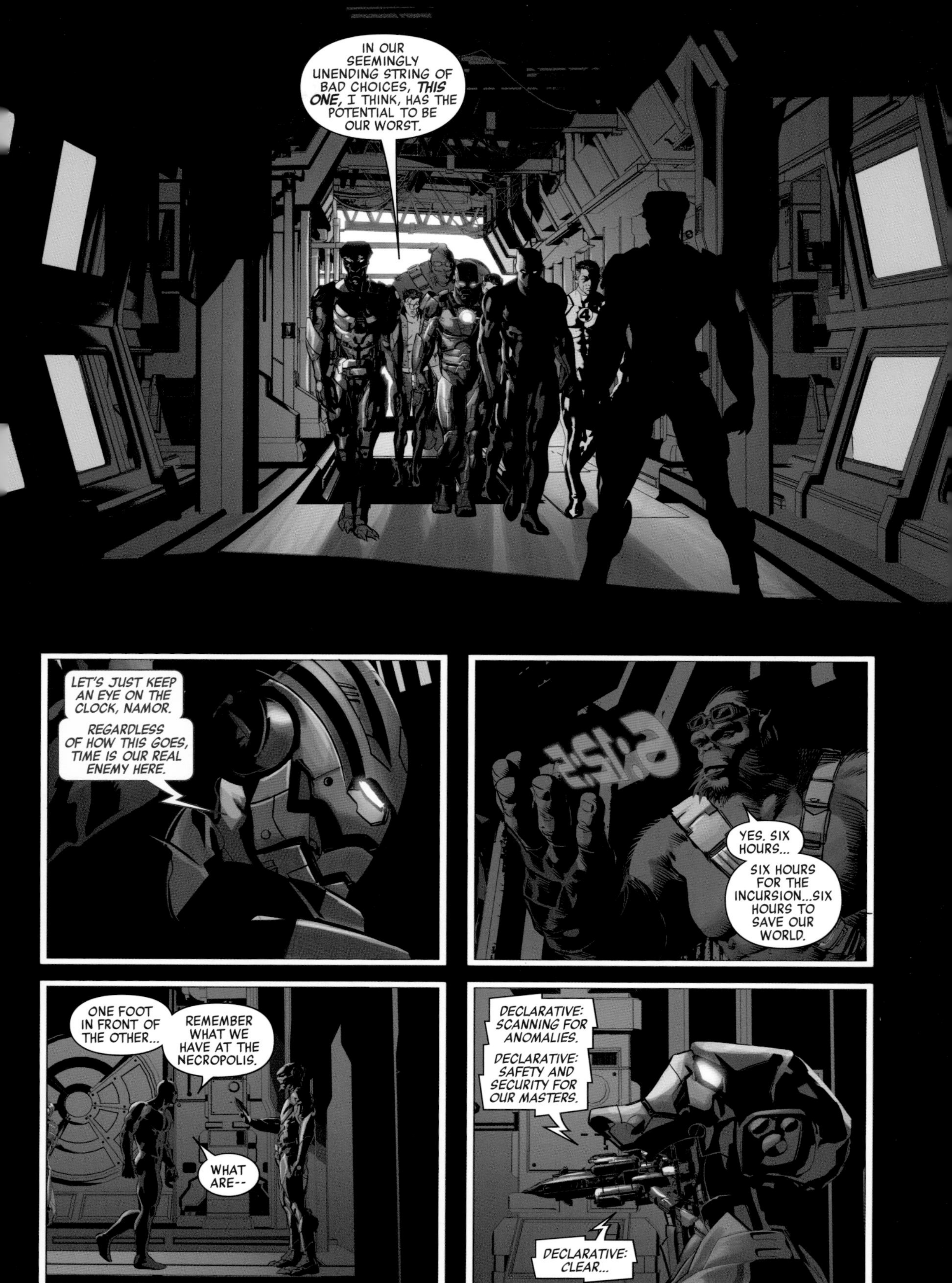
IN OUR SEEMINGLY UNENDING STRING OF BAD CHOICES, **THIS ONE,** I THINK, HAS THE POTENTIAL TO BE OUR WORST.
LET'S JUST KEEP AN EYE ON THE CLOCK, NAMOR.
REGARDLESS OF HOW THIS GOES, TIME IS OUR REAL ENEMY HERE.
YES. SIX HOURS...
SIX HOURS FOR THE INCURSION...SIX HOURS TO SAVE OUR WORLD.
ONE FOOT IN FRONT OF THE OTHER...
REMEMBER WHAT WE HAVE AT THE NECROPOLIS.
WHAT ARE--
DECLARATIVE: SCANNING FOR ANOMALIES.
DECLARATIVE: SAFETY AND SECURITY FOR OUR MASTERS.
DECLARATIVE: CLEAR...

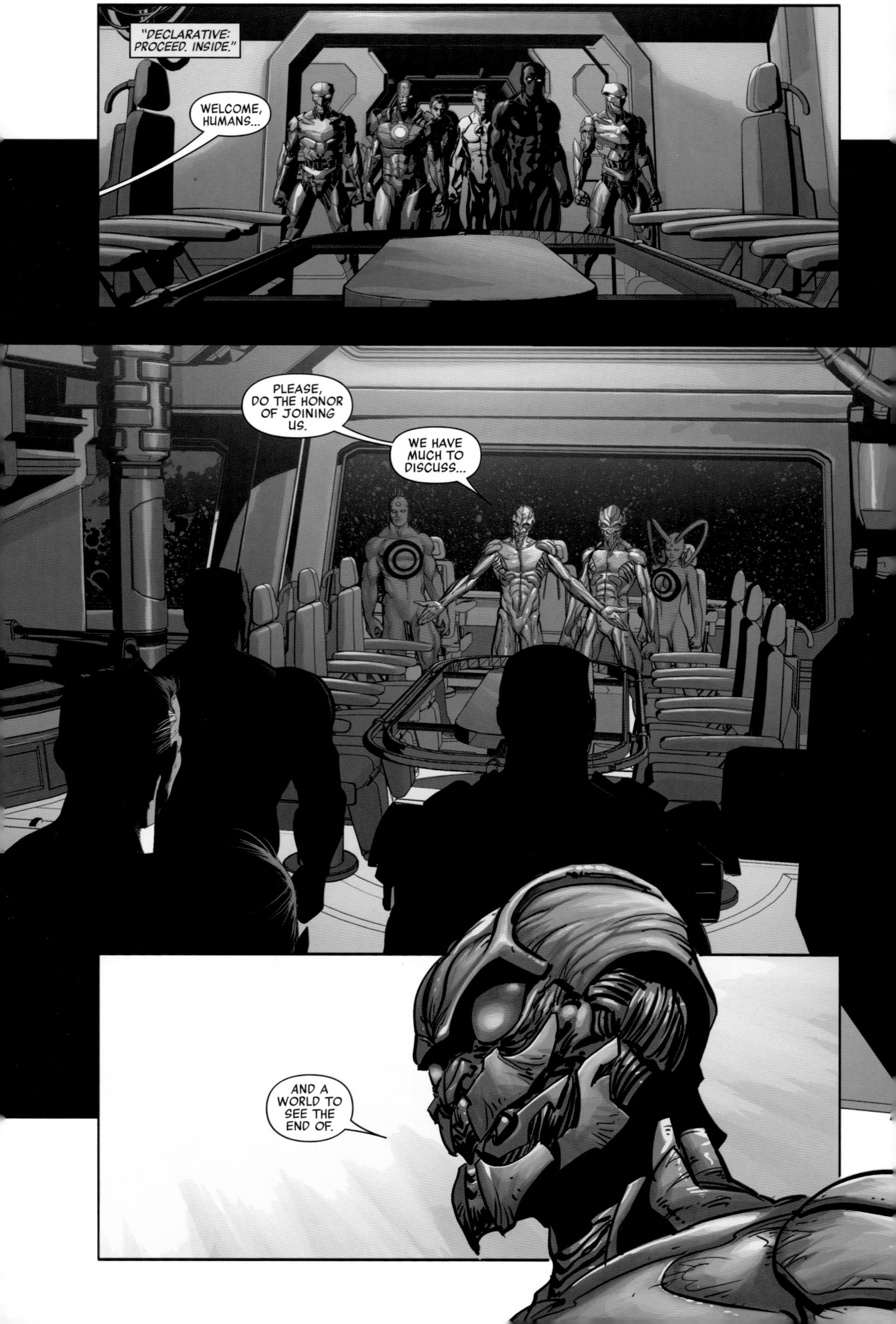
"DECLARATIVE: PROCEED. INSIDE."
WELCOME, HUMANS...
PLEASE, DO THE HONOR OF JOINING US.
WE HAVE MUCH TO DISCUSS...
AND A WORLD TO SEE THE END OF.

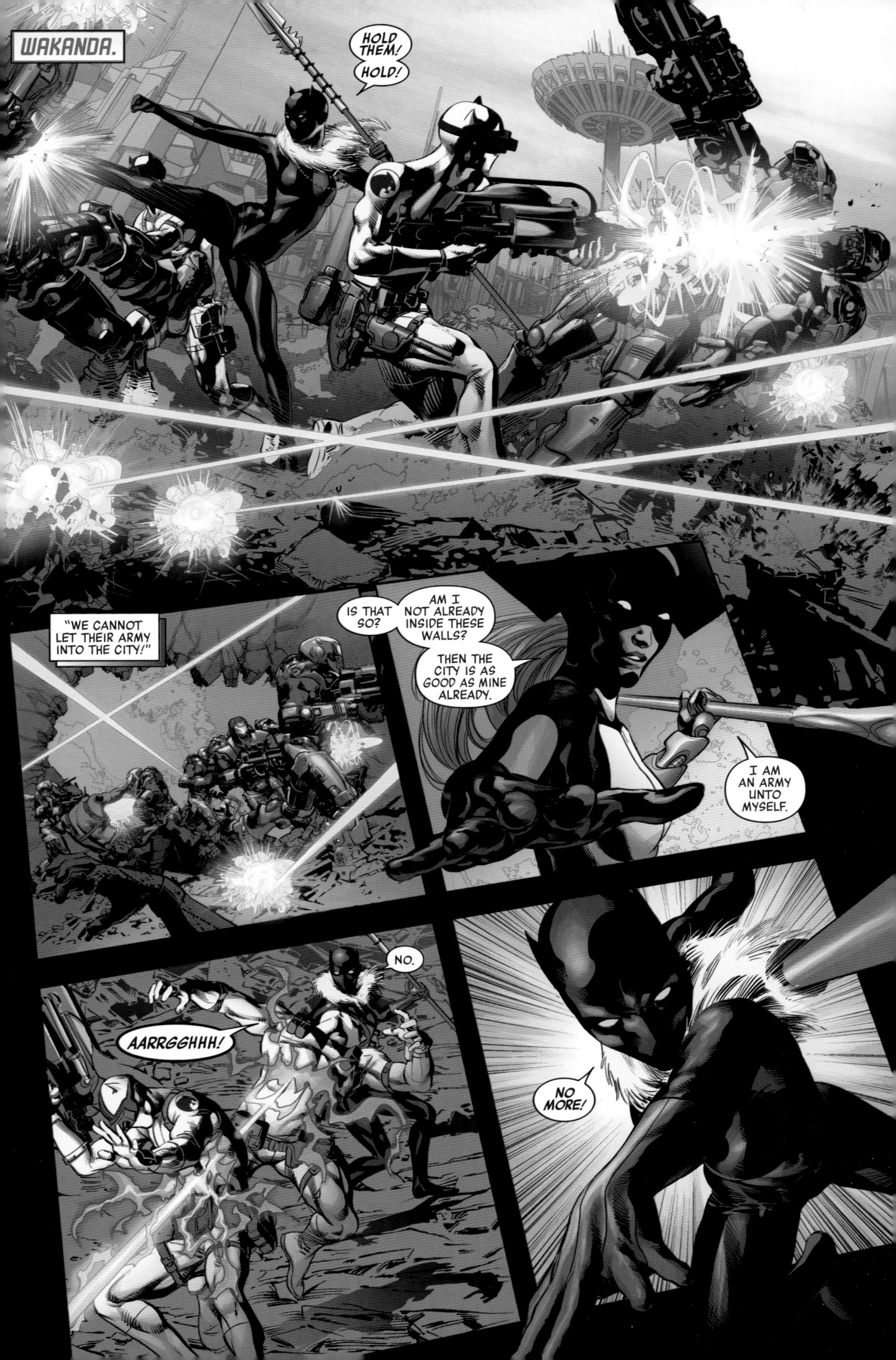
WAKANDA.
HOLD THEM!
HOLD!
"WE CANNOT LET THEIR ARMY INTO THE CITY!"
IS THAT SO?
AM I NOT ALREADY INSIDE THESE WALLS?
THEN THE CITY IS AS GOOD AS MINE ALREADY.
I AM AN ARMY UNTO MYSELF.
NO.
AARRGGHHH!
NO MORE!

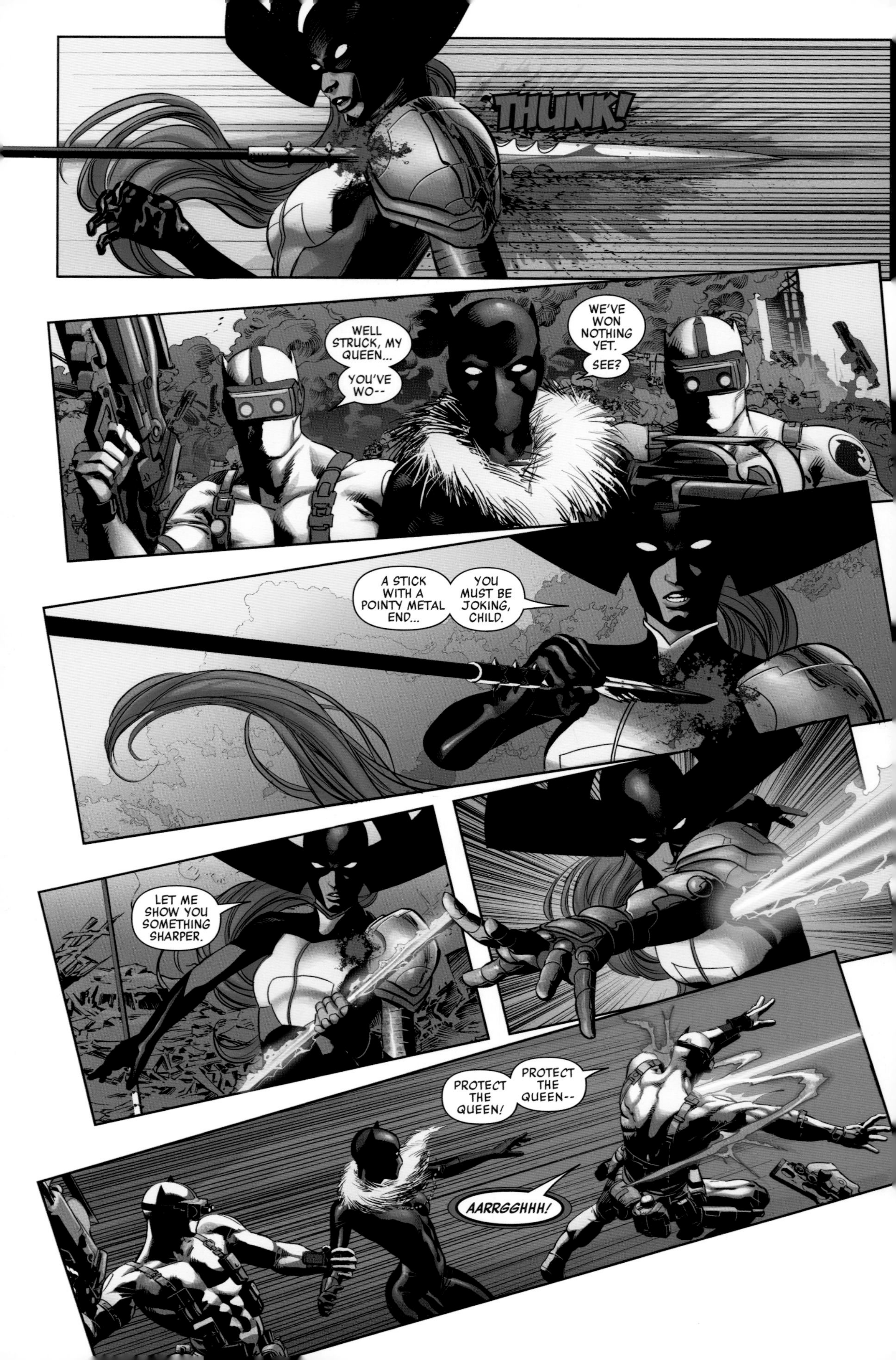
THUNK!
WELL STRUCK, MY QUEEN...
YOU'VE WO--
WE'VE WON NOTHING YET.
SEE?
A STICK WITH A POINTY METAL END...
YOU MUST BE JOKING, CHILD.
LET ME SHOW YOU SOMETHING SHARPER.
PROTECT THE QUEEN!
PROTECT THE QUEEN--
AARRGGHHH!

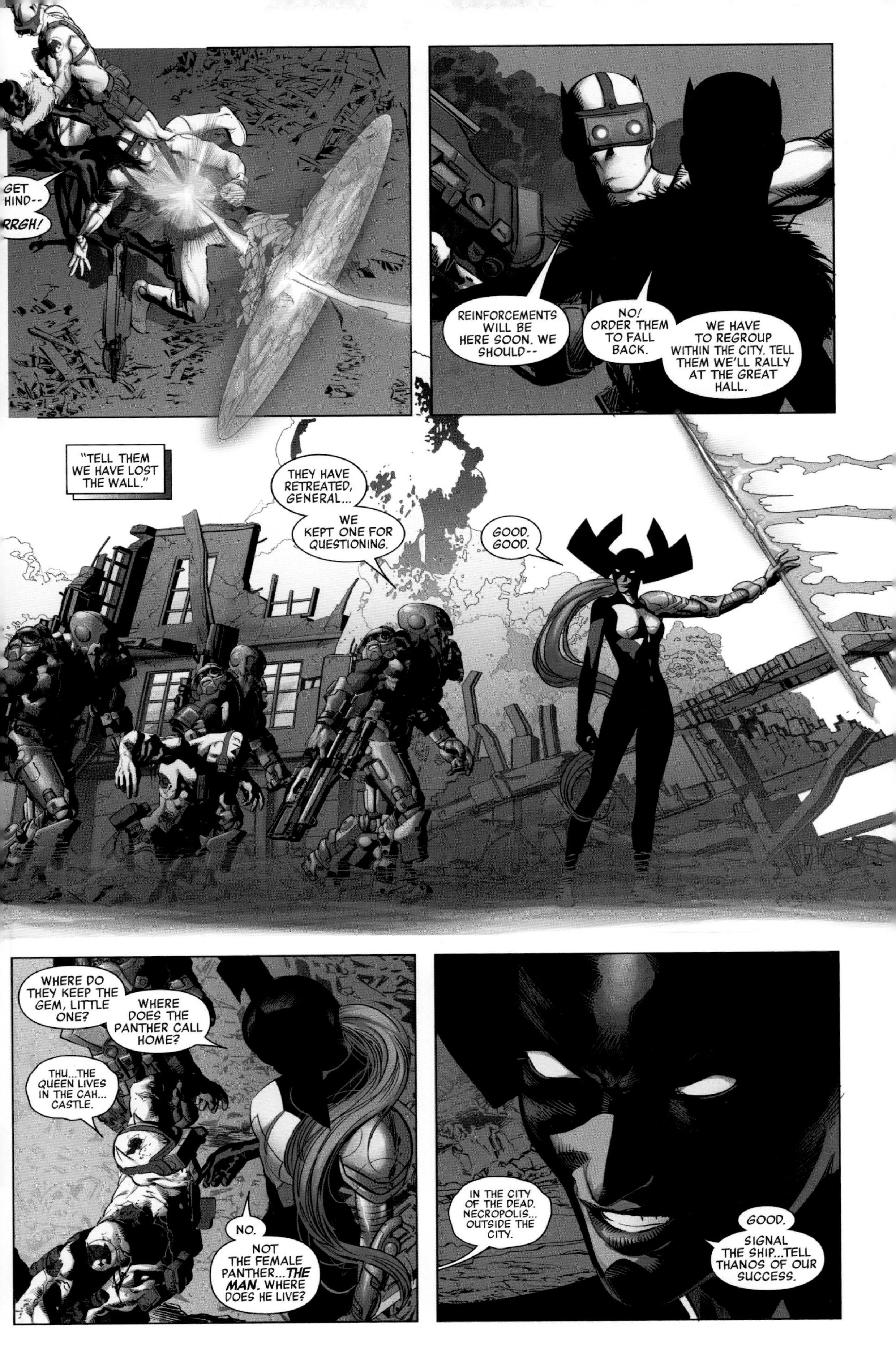
GET
HIND--
RRGH!
REINFORCEMENTS WILL BE HERE SOON. WE SHOULD--
NO! ORDER THEM TO FALL BACK.
WE HAVE TO REGROUP WITHIN THE CITY. TELL THEM WE'LL RALLY AT THE GREAT HALL.
"TELL THEM WE HAVE LOST THE WALL."
THEY HAVE RETREATED, GENERAL...
WE KEPT ONE FOR QUESTIONING.
GOOD. GOOD.
WHERE DO THEY KEEP THE GEM, LITTLE ONE?
WHERE DOES THE PANTHER CALL HOME?
THU...THE QUEEN LIVES IN THE CAH... CASTLE.
NO.
NOT THE FEMALE PANTHER...*THE MAN.* WHERE DOES HE LIVE?
IN THE CITY OF THE DEAD. NECROPOLIS... OUTSIDE THE CITY.
GOOD.
SIGNAL THE SHIP...TELL THANOS OF OUR SUCCESS.

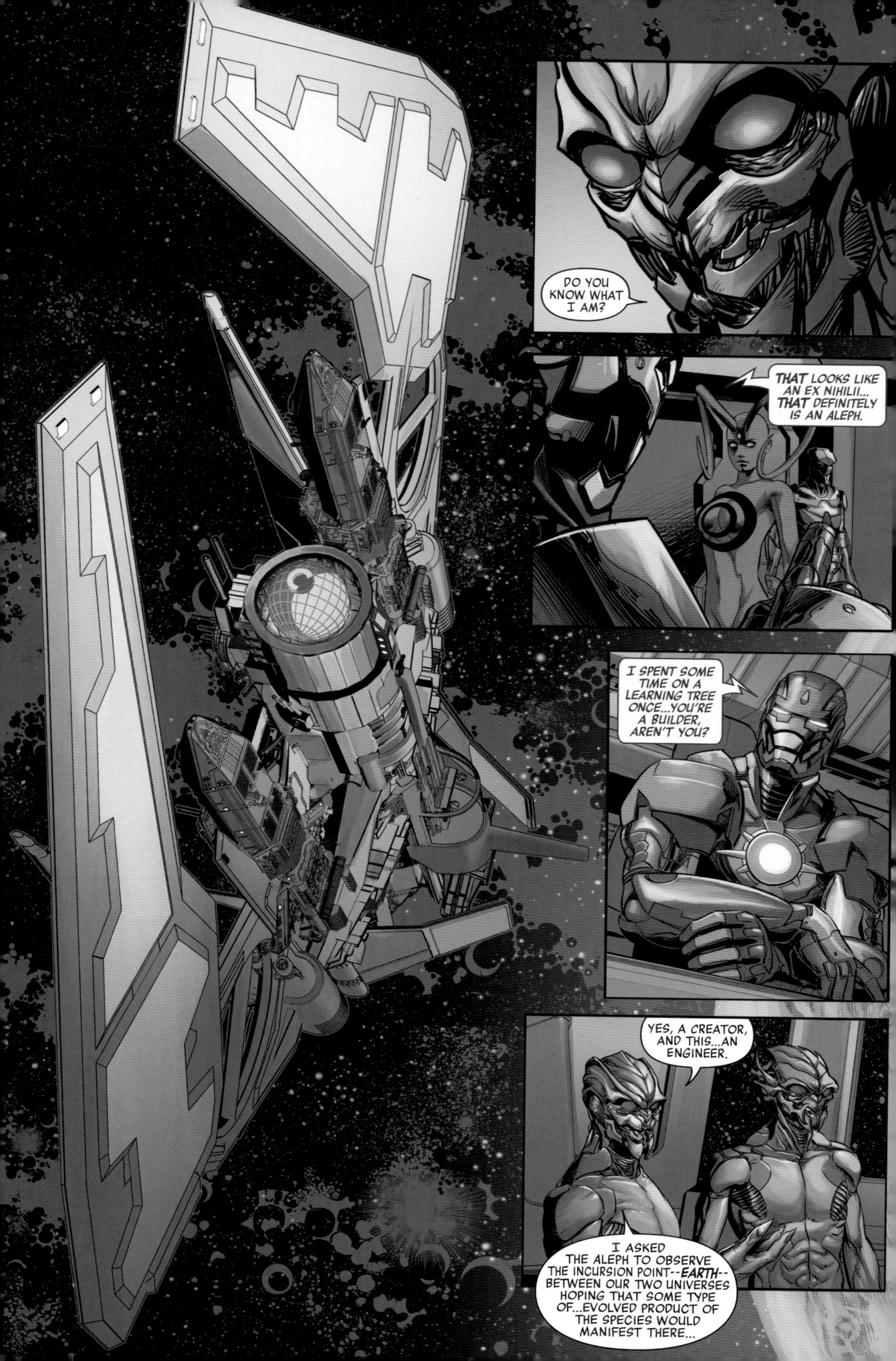
DO YOU KNOW WHAT I AM?
THAT LOOKS LIKE AN EX NIHILII... THAT DEFINITELY IS AN ALEPH.
I SPENT SOME TIME ON A LEARNING TREE ONCE...YOU'RE A BUILDER, AREN'T YOU?
YES, A CREATOR, AND THIS...AN ENGINEER.
I ASKED THE ALEPH TO OBSERVE THE INCURSION POINT--EARTH--BETWEEN OUR TWO UNIVERSES HOPING THAT SOME TYPE OF...EVOLVED PRODUCT OF THE SPECIES WOULD MANIFEST THERE...

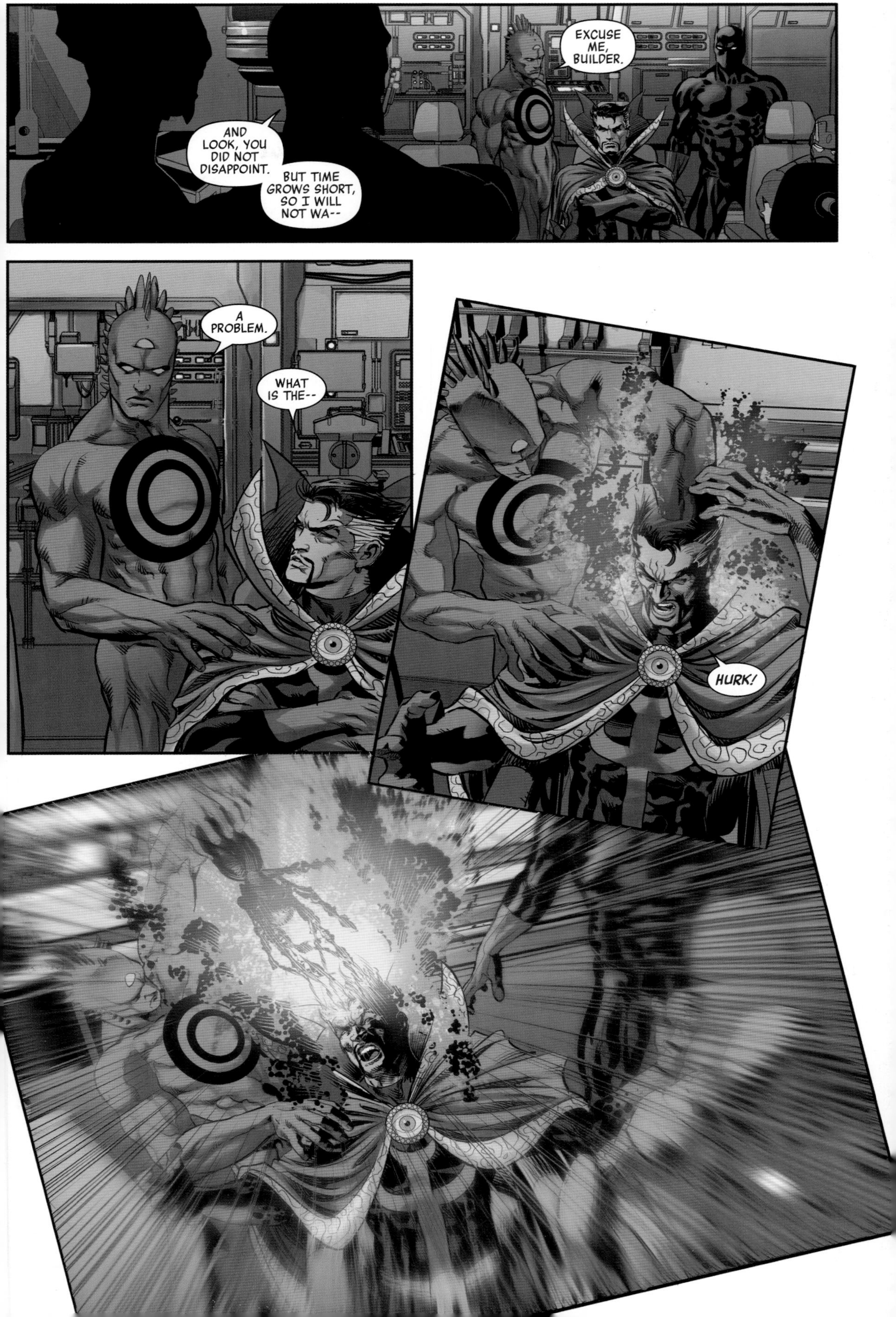
EXCUSE ME, BUILDER.
AND LOOK, YOU DID NOT DISAPPOINT.
BUT TIME GROWS SHORT, SO I WILL NOT WA--
A PROBLEM.
WHAT IS THE--
HURK!

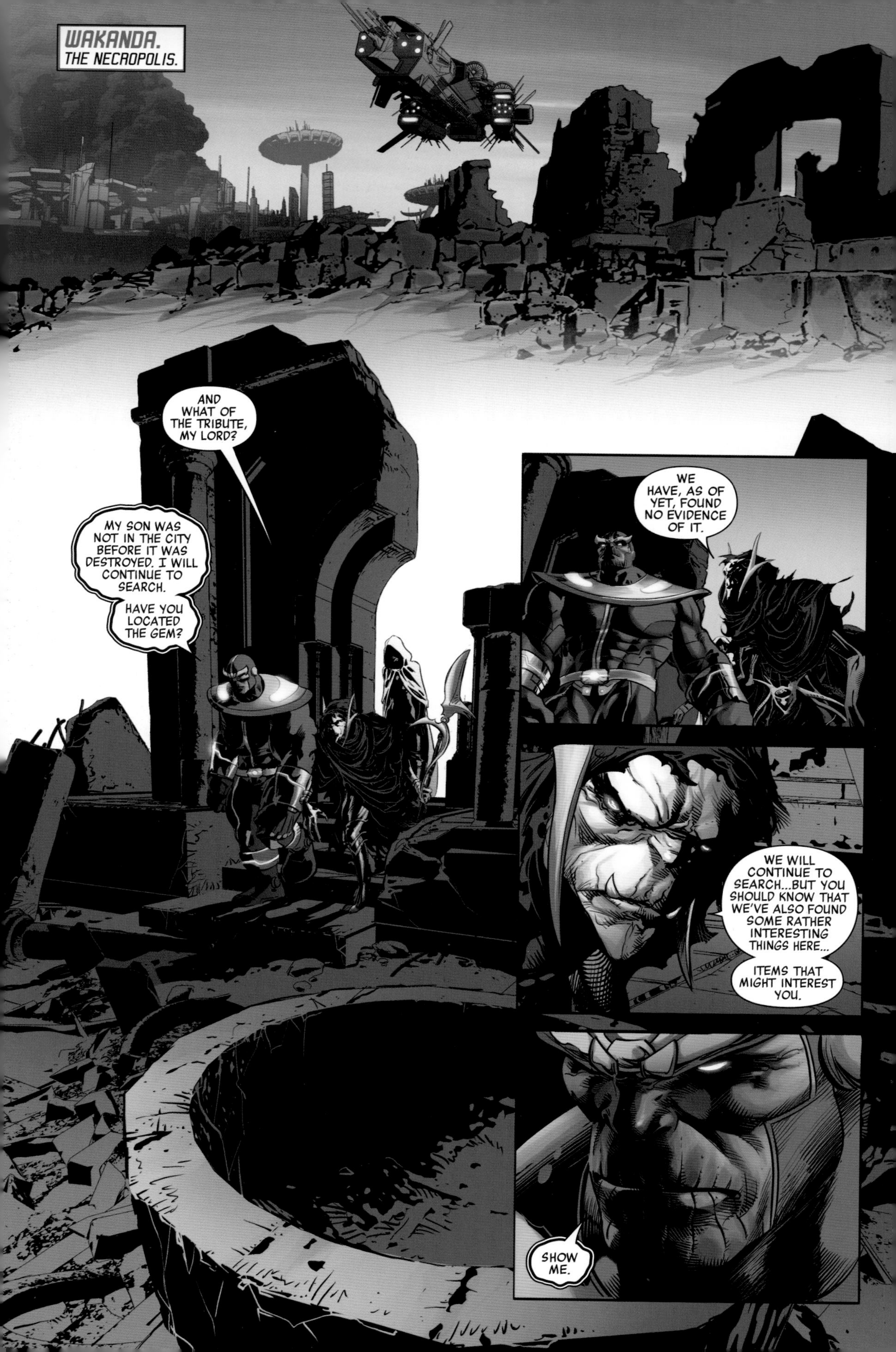
WAKANDA. THE NECROPOLIS.
AND WHAT OF THE TRIBUTE, MY LORD?
MY SON WAS NOT IN THE CITY BEFORE IT WAS DESTROYED. I WILL CONTINUE TO SEARCH.
HAVE YOU LOCATED THE GEM?
WE HAVE, AS OF YET, FOUND NO EVIDENCE OF IT.
WE WILL CONTINUE TO SEARCH...BUT YOU SHOULD KNOW THAT WE'VE ALSO FOUND SOME RATHER INTERESTING THINGS HERE...
ITEMS THAT MIGHT INTEREST YOU.
SHOW ME.

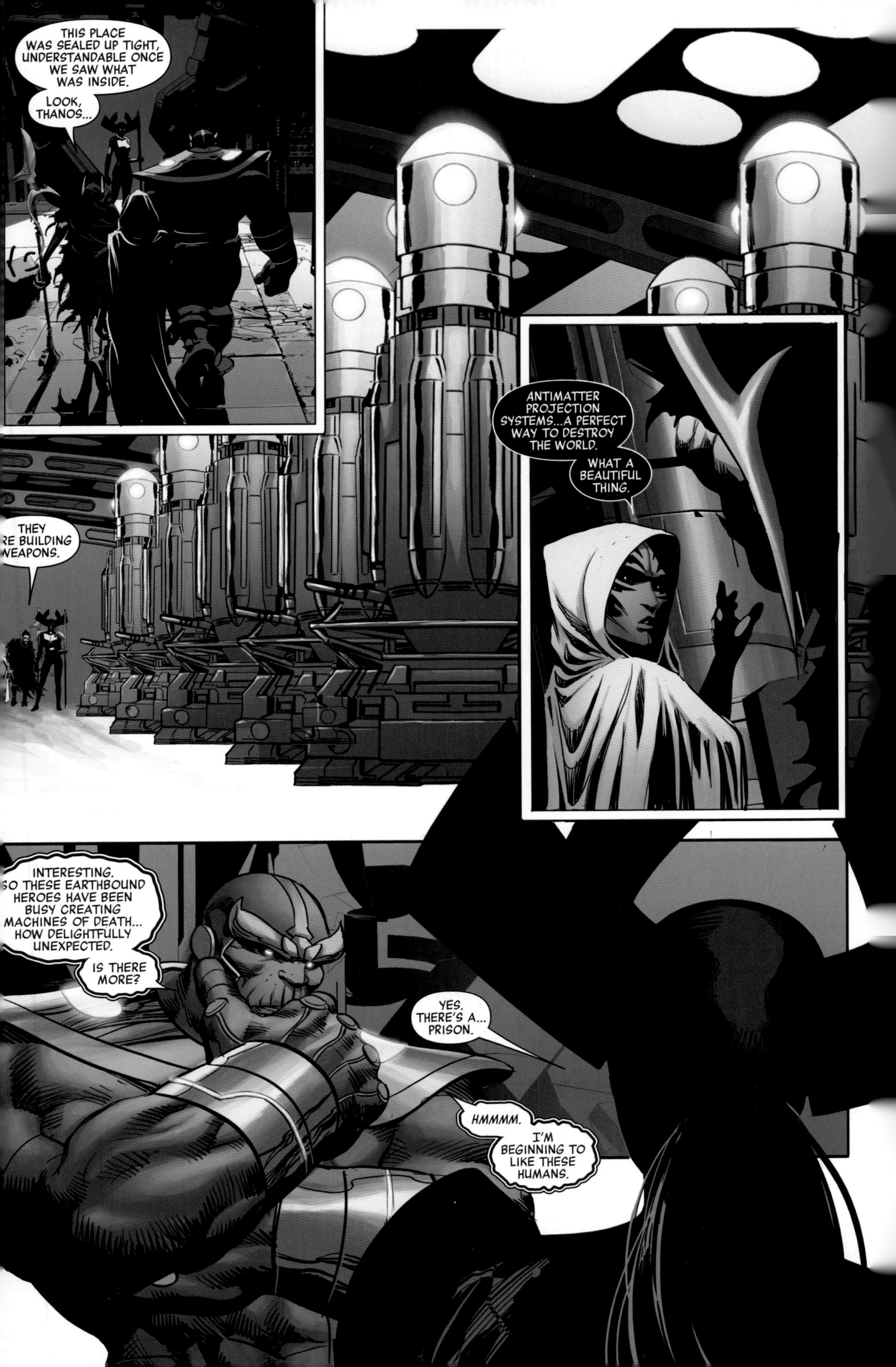
THIS PLACE WAS SEALED UP TIGHT, UNDERSTANDABLE ONCE WE SAW WHAT WAS INSIDE.
LOOK, THANOS...
ANTIMATTER PROJECTION SYSTEMS...A PERFECT WAY TO DESTROY THE WORLD.
WHAT A BEAUTIFUL THING.
THEY RE BUILDING WEAPONS.
INTERESTING. SO THESE EARTHBOUND HEROES HAVE BEEN BUSY CREATING MACHINES OF DEATH... HOW DELIGHTFULLY UNEXPECTED.
IS THERE MORE?
YES. THERE'S A... PRISON.
HMMMM.
I'M BEGINNING TO LIKE THESE HUMANS.

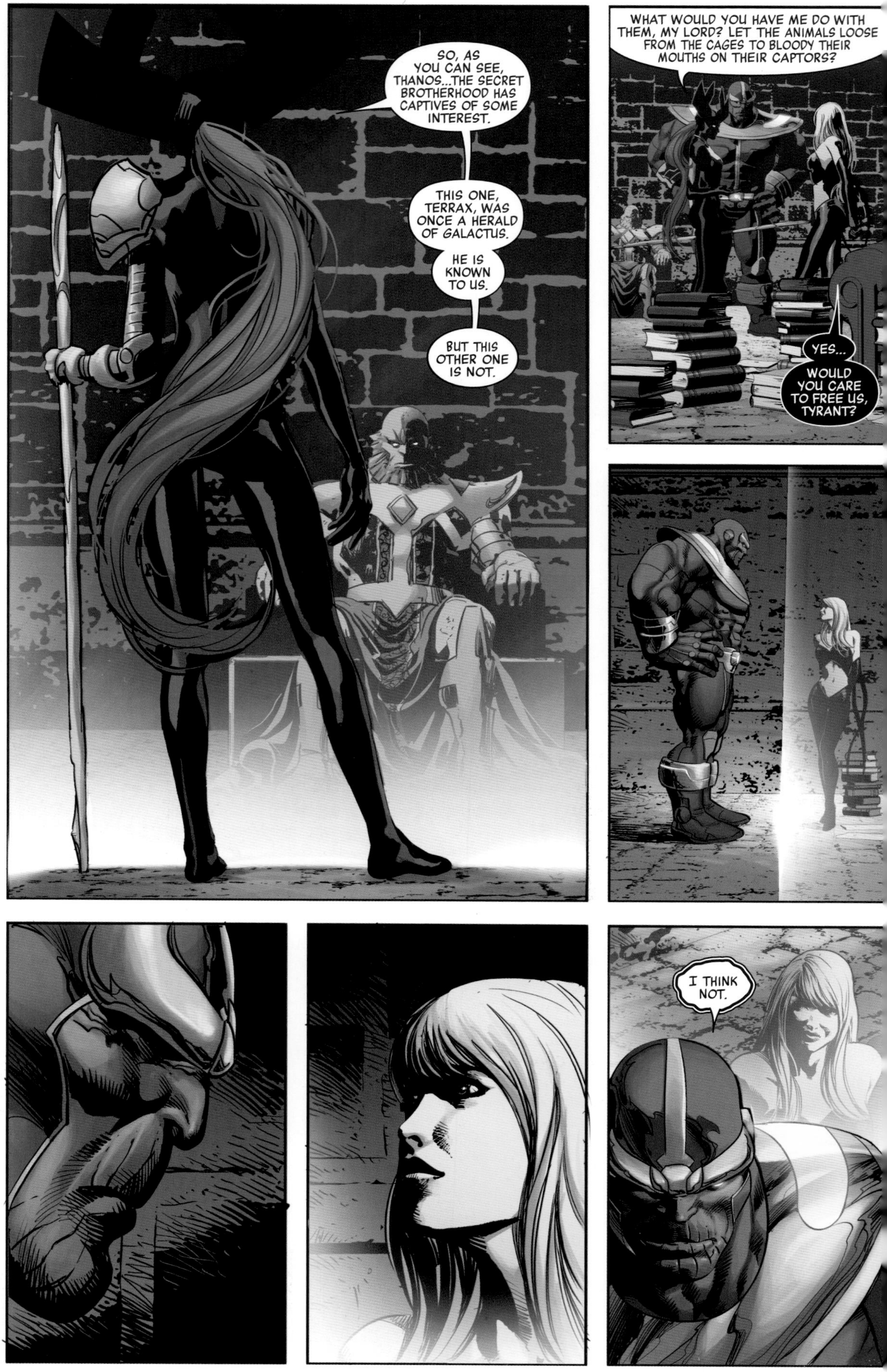
SO, AS YOU CAN SEE, THANOS...THE SECRET BROTHERHOOD HAS CAPTIVES OF SOME INTEREST.
THIS ONE, TERRAX, WAS ONCE A HERALD OF GALACTUS.
HE IS KNOWN TO US.
BUT THIS OTHER ONE IS NOT.
WHAT WOULD YOU HAVE ME DO WITH THEM, MY LORD? LET THE ANIMALS LOOSE FROM THE CAGES TO BLOODY THEIR MOUTHS ON THEIR CAPTORS?
YES...
WOULD YOU CARE TO FREE US, TYRANT?
I THINK NOT.

A HIDDEN INHUMAN TRIBE. THE GEM IS LOST. LOCATED IN THE GREAT SOUTHERN CREVICE OF GREENLAND. ALL THESE MEN ARE LIARS AND KINGS. THE SON IS THERE. THE SON OF THANOS IS IN LOR.

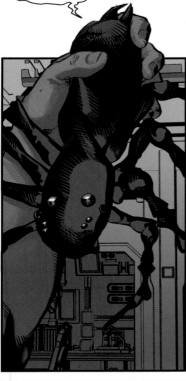

AH, A MIND WEB, THE INFECTIOUS NETWORKED REMNANTS OF A WHISPERER--*ARTIFACTING* LEFTOVER FROM A *POSSESSION.*

I CAN TELL YOU THE EFFECTS WILL PASS. THERE ARE NO WHISPERERS IN THIS UNIVERSE, BUT IN THE PAST, WE HAVE STUDIED THEM IN YOURS.

EXCUSE ME... I HAVE TO ASK, WHERE ARE YOU FROM? YOU KNOW ABOUT THIS THING, SO DID YOUR SPECIES BEGIN IN OUR UNIVERSE?

WHERE ANYONE BEGINS IS INCONSEQUENTIAL, HUMAN...IT'S WHERE YOU END UP THAT MATTERS.

FOR US, IT WAS THE ENTIRE MULTIVERSE.

WAS?

"YES. A VERY SHORT TIME AGO, WE MOVED FREELY FROM UNIVERSE TO UNIVERSE, ACCESSING EACH FROM THE OTHERSPACE THAT EXISTED BETWEEN THEM--THE SUPERFLOW."

"BUT ALL THAT HAS COLLAPSED. DESTROYED. THE SUPERFLOW... FRACTURED AND NO LONGER ABLE TO BE SAFELY NAVIGATED."

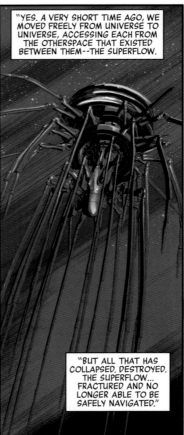

THE HARBINGER OF THE END OF EVERYTHING.

WHICH MY PEOPLE HAVE PLEDGED TO PREVENT. *WHICH IS WHY WE ARE SPEAKING...*

...AS RIGHT NOW, A GROUP OF...ENTITIES, SUCH AS YOURSELF, HAVE JUST DEFEATED THE BUILDERS EXISTING IN YOUR UNIVERSE.

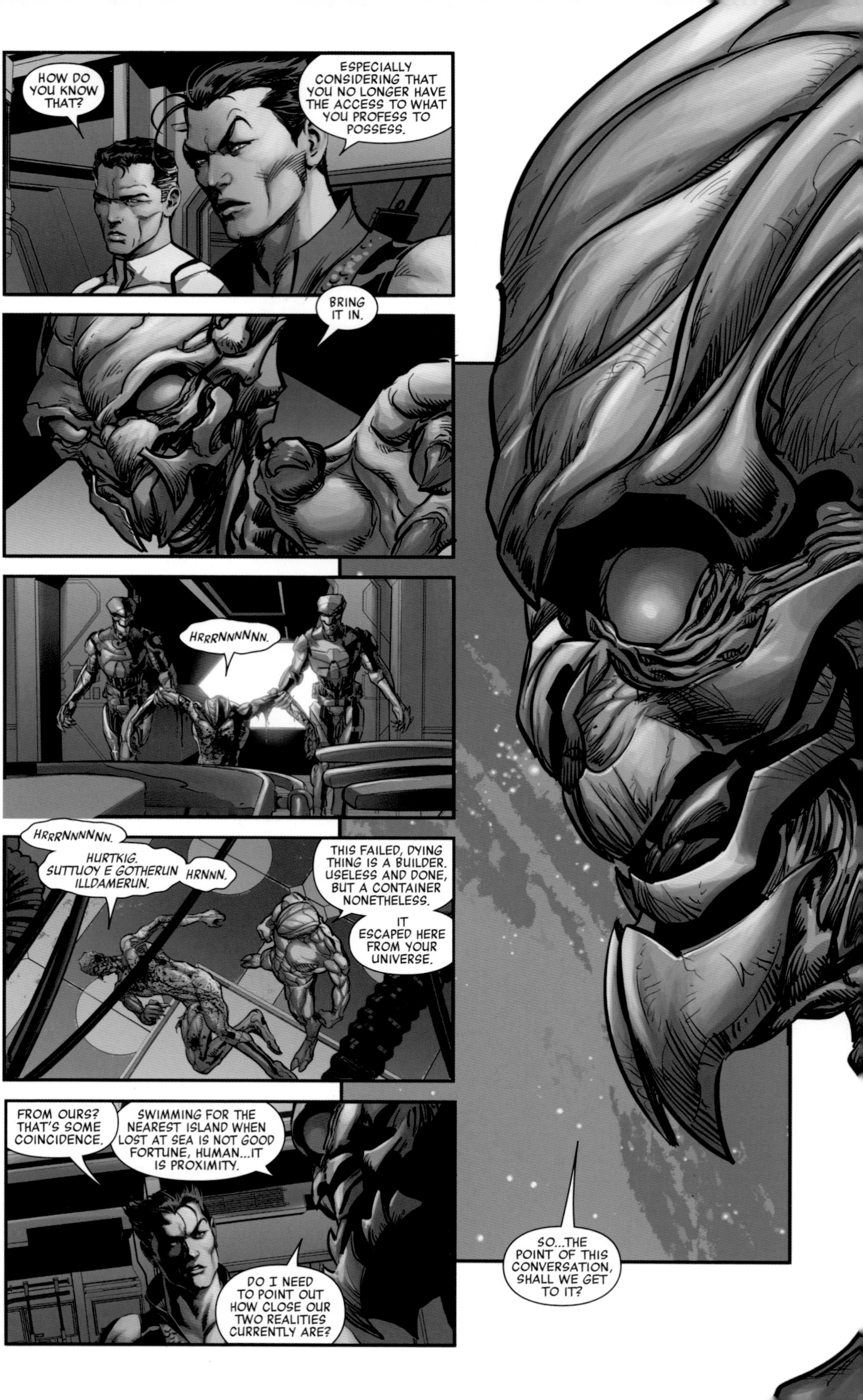
HOW DO YOU KNOW THAT?
ESPECIALLY CONSIDERING THAT YOU NO LONGER HAVE THE ACCESS TO WHAT YOU PROFESS TO POSSESS.
BRING IT IN.
HRRRNNNNNN.
HRRRNNNNNN.
HURTKIG. SUTTUOY E GOTHERUN ILLDAMERUN.
HRNNN.
THIS FAILED, DYING THING IS A BUILDER. USELESS AND DONE, BUT A CONTAINER NONETHELESS.
IT ESCAPED HERE FROM YOUR UNIVERSE.
FROM OURS? THAT'S SOME COINCIDENCE.
SWIMMING FOR THE NEAREST ISLAND WHEN LOST AT SEA IS NOT GOOD FORTUNE, HUMAN...IT IS PROXIMITY.
DO I NEED TO POINT OUT HOW CLOSE OUR TWO REALITIES CURRENTLY ARE?
SO...THE POINT OF THIS CONVERSATION, SHALL WE GET TO IT?

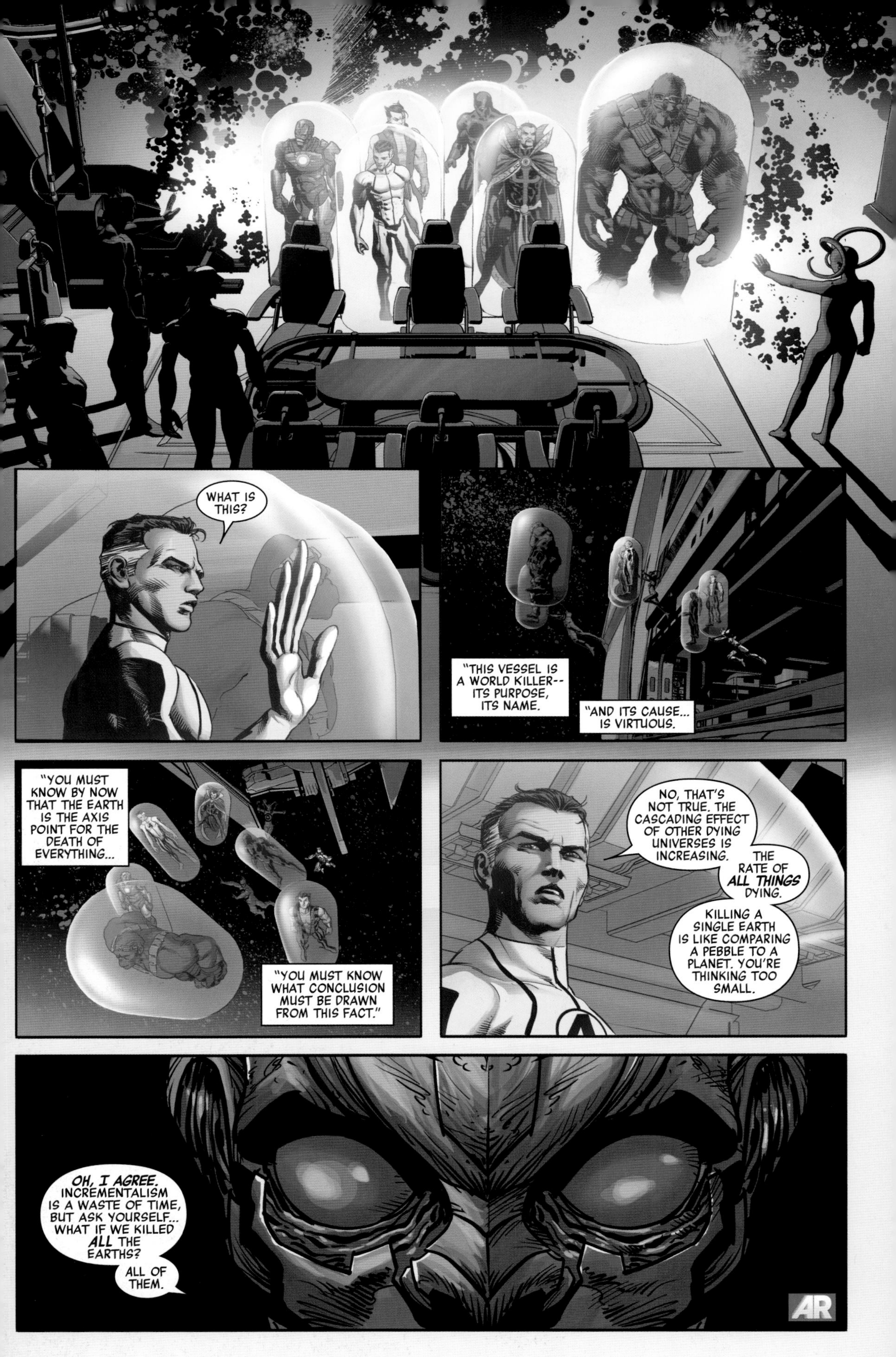
WHAT IS THIS?
"THIS VESSEL IS A WORLD KILLER-- ITS PURPOSE, ITS NAME.
"AND ITS CAUSE... IS VIRTUOUS.
"YOU MUST KNOW BY NOW THAT THE EARTH IS THE AXIS POINT FOR THE DEATH OF EVERYTHING...
"YOU MUST KNOW WHAT CONCLUSION MUST BE DRAWN FROM THIS FACT."
NO, THAT'S NOT TRUE. THE CASCADING EFFECT OF OTHER DYING UNIVERSES IS INCREASING.
THE RATE OF *ALL THINGS* DYING.
KILLING A SINGLE EARTH IS LIKE COMPARING A PEBBLE TO A PLANET. YOU'RE THINKING TOO SMALL.
OH, I AGREE. INCREMENTALISM IS A WASTE OF TIME, BUT ASK YOURSELF... WHAT IF WE KILLED *ALL* THE EARTHS?
ALL OF THEM.
AR

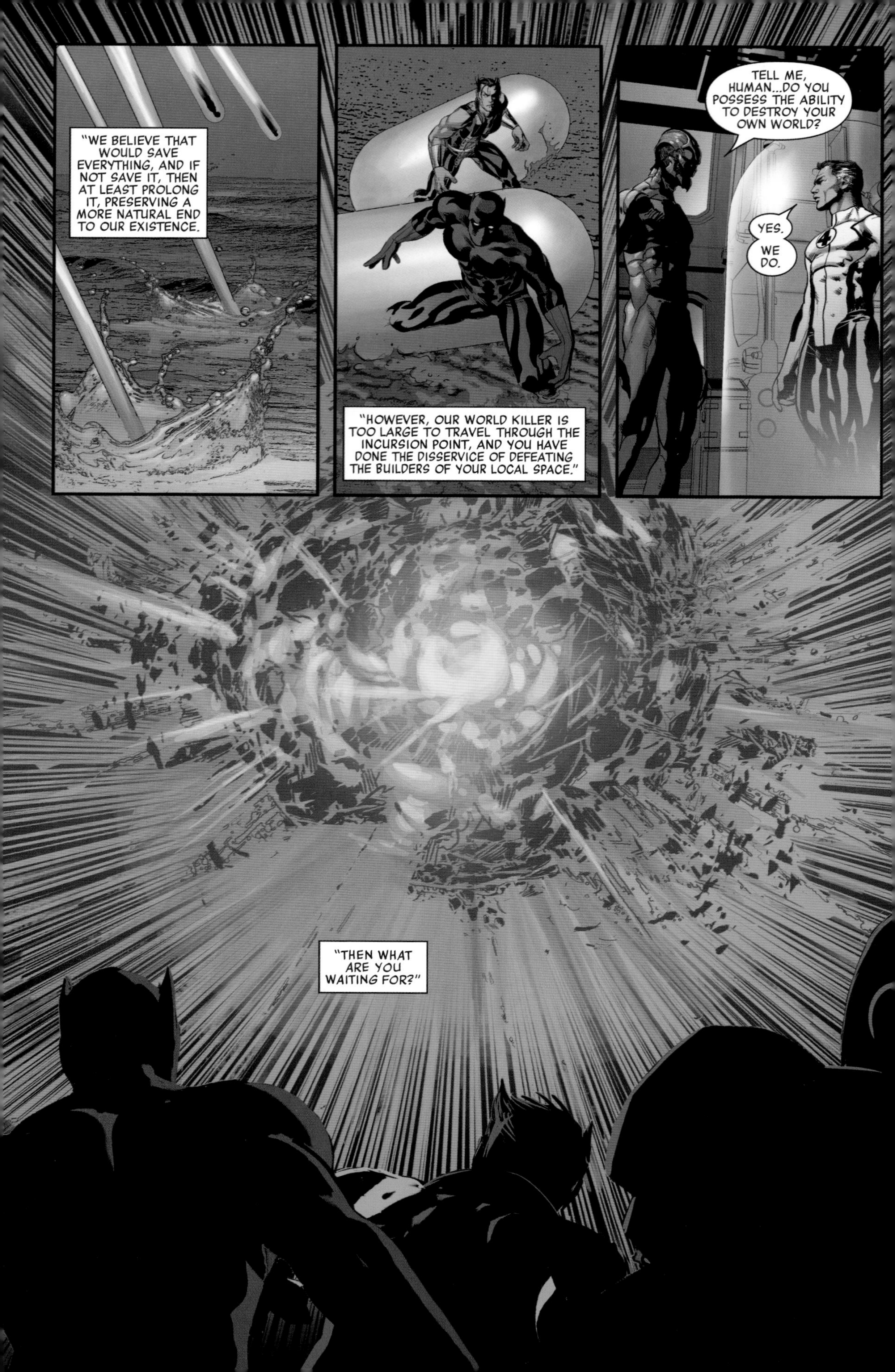
"WE BELIEVE THAT WOULD SAVE EVERYTHING, AND IF NOT SAVE IT, THEN AT LEAST PROLONG IT, PRESERVING A MORE NATURAL END TO OUR EXISTENCE.
"HOWEVER, OUR WORLD KILLER IS TOO LARGE TO TRAVEL THROUGH THE INCURSION POINT, AND YOU HAVE DONE THE DISSERVICE OF DEFEATING THE BUILDERS OF YOUR LOCAL SPACE."
TELL ME, HUMAN...DO YOU POSSESS THE ABILITY TO DESTROY YOUR OWN WORLD?
YES.
WE DO.
"THEN WHAT ARE YOU WAITING FOR?"

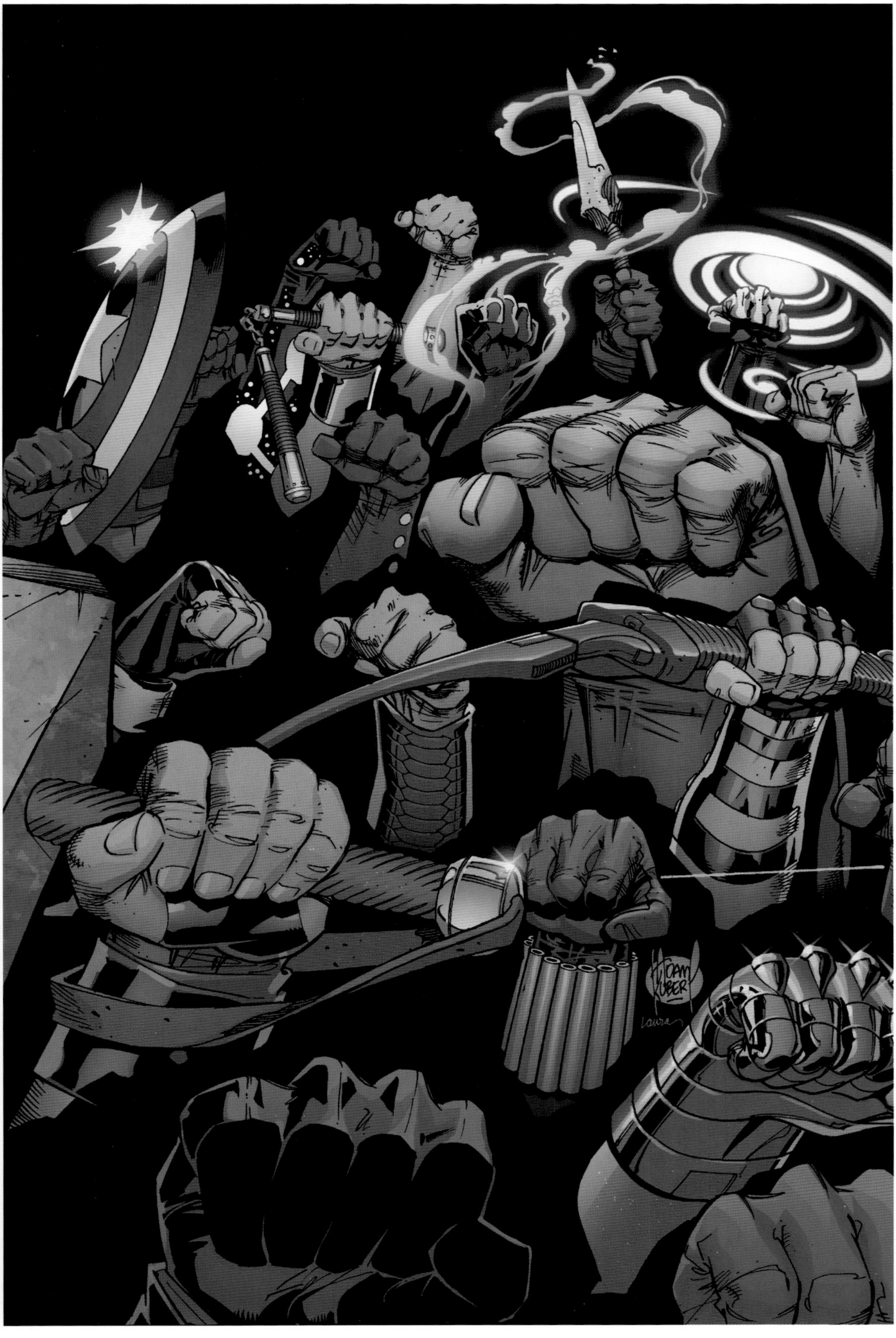

OF SUNS AND STORMS

◆

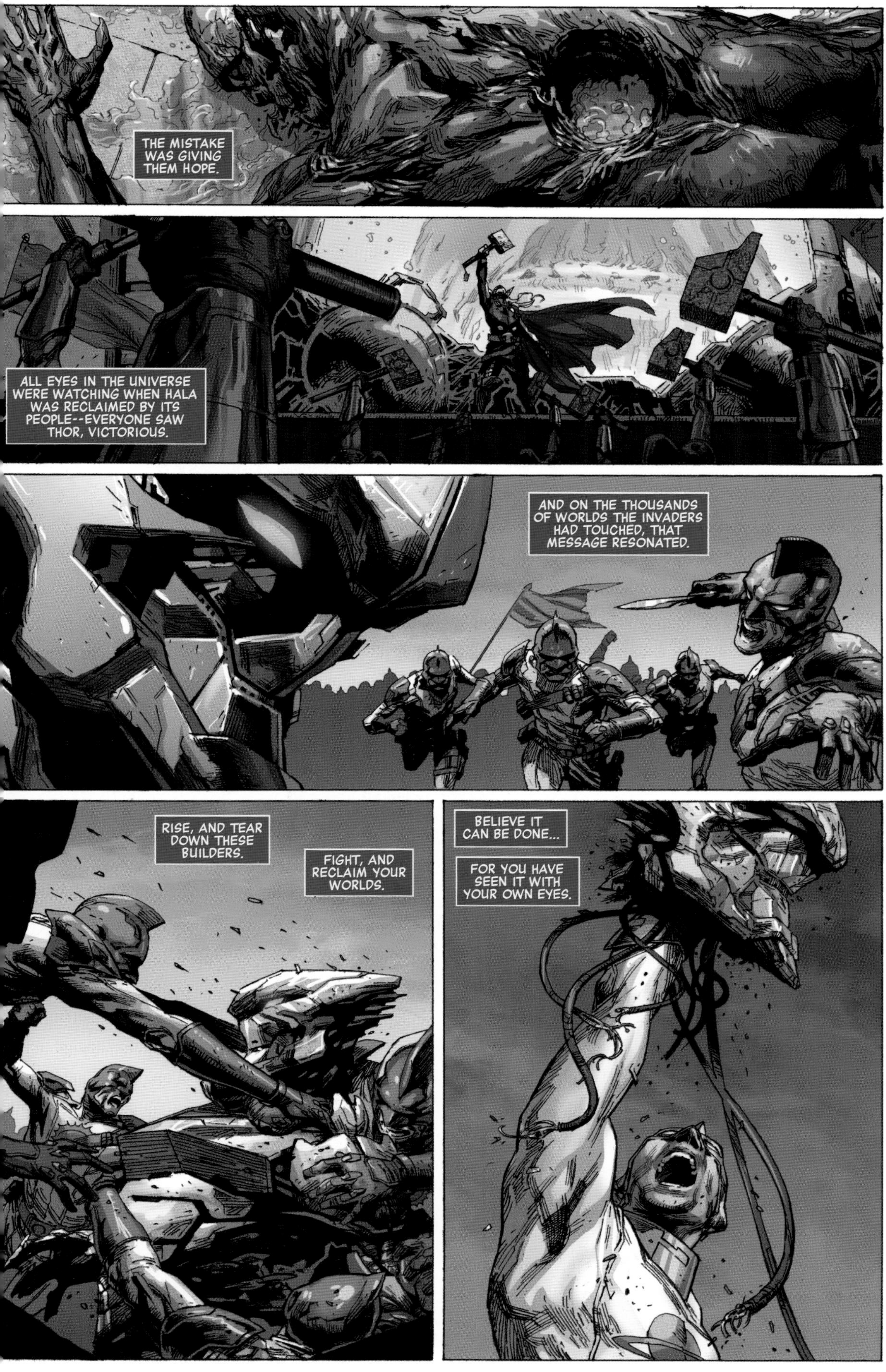
THE MISTAKE WAS GIVING THEM HOPE.
ALL EYES IN THE UNIVERSE WERE WATCHING WHEN HALA WAS RECLAIMED BY ITS PEOPLE--EVERYONE SAW THOR, VICTORIOUS.
AND ON THE THOUSANDS OF WORLDS THE INVADERS HAD TOUCHED, THAT MESSAGE RESONATED.
RISE, AND TEAR DOWN THESE BUILDERS.
FIGHT, AND RECLAIM YOUR WORLDS.
BELIEVE IT CAN BE DONE...
FOR YOU HAVE SEEN IT WITH YOUR OWN EYES.

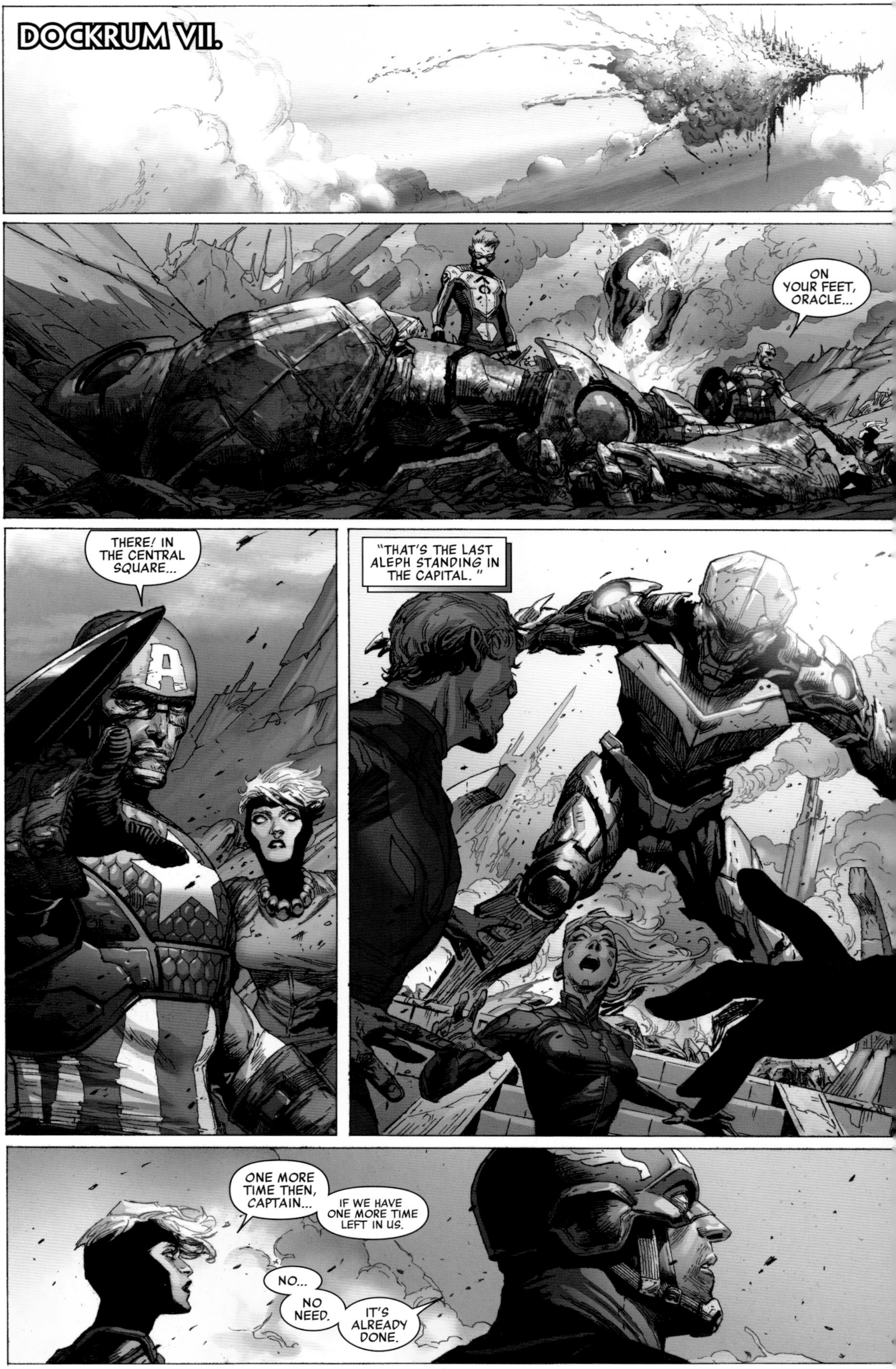
DOCKRUM VII.
ON YOUR FEET, ORACLE...
THERE! IN THE CENTRAL SQUARE...
"THAT'S THE LAST ALEPH STANDING IN THE CAPITAL."
ONE MORE TIME THEN, CAPTAIN...
IF WE HAVE ONE MORE TIME LEFT IN US.
NO...
NO NEED.
IT'S ALREADY DONE.

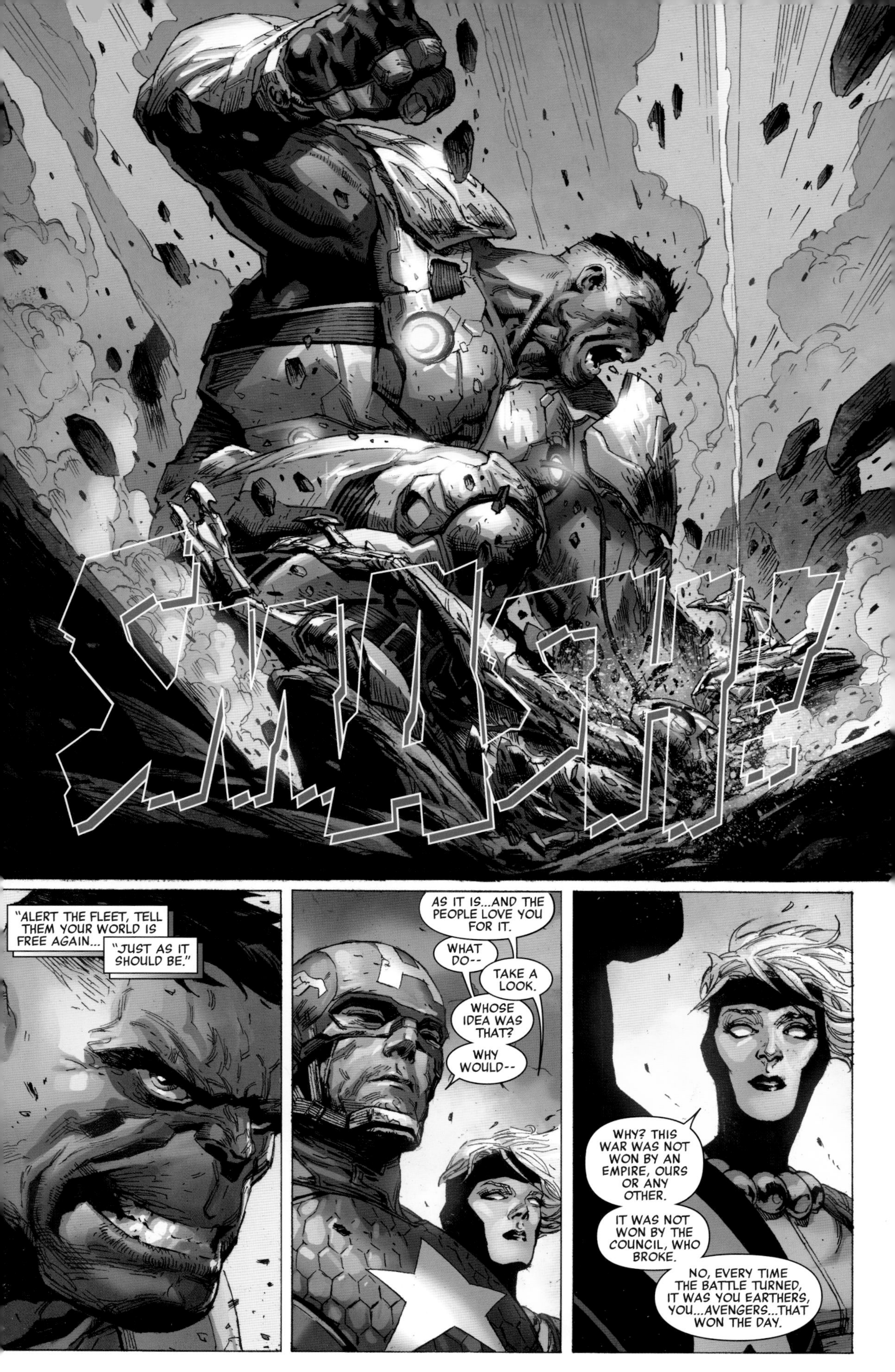
SMASH!!
"ALERT THE FLEET, TELL THEM YOUR WORLD IS FREE AGAIN...
"JUST AS IT SHOULD BE."
AS IT IS...AND THE PEOPLE LOVE YOU FOR IT.
WHAT DO--
TAKE A LOOK.
WHOSE IDEA WAS THAT?
WHY WOULD--
WHY? THIS WAR WAS NOT WON BY AN EMPIRE, OURS OR ANY OTHER.
IT WAS NOT WON BY THE COUNCIL, WHO BROKE.
NO, EVERY TIME THE BATTLE TURNED, IT WAS YOU EARTHERS, YOU...AVENGERS...THAT WON THE DAY.

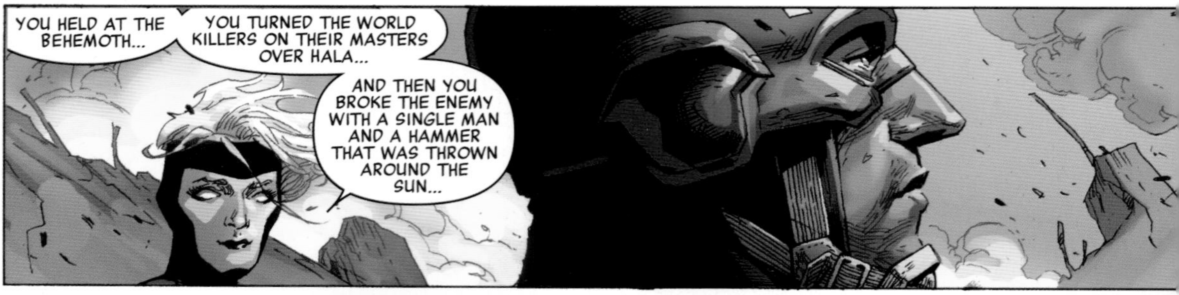
YOU HELD AT THE BEHEMOTH...
YOU TURNED THE WORLD KILLERS ON THEIR MASTERS OVER HALA...
AND THEN YOU BROKE THE ENEMY WITH A SINGLE MAN AND A HAMMER THAT WAS THROWN AROUND THE SUN...

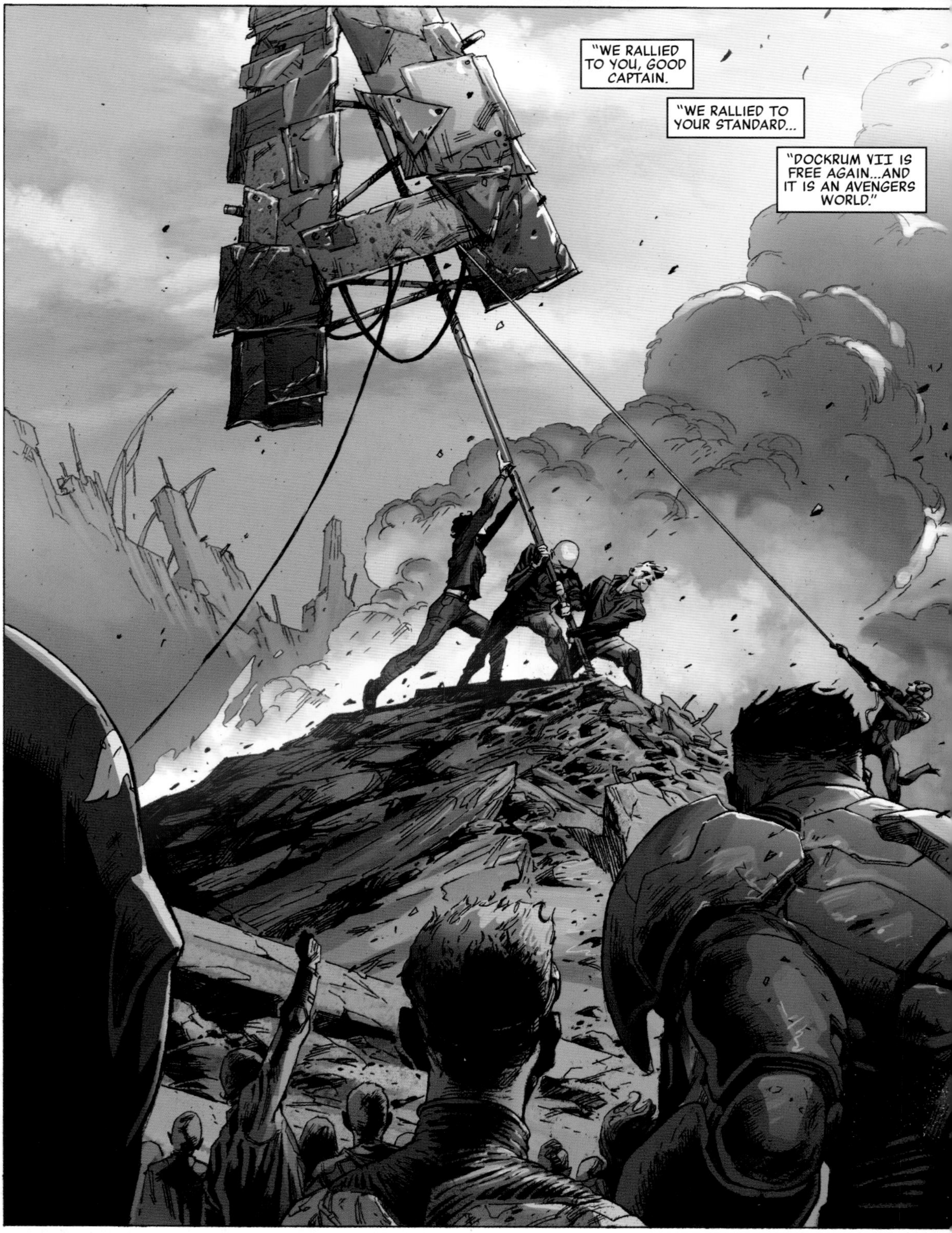
"WE RALLIED TO YOU, GOOD CAPTAIN.
"WE RALLIED TO YOUR STANDARD...
"DOCKRUM VII IS FREE AGAIN...AND IT IS AN AVENGERS WORLD."

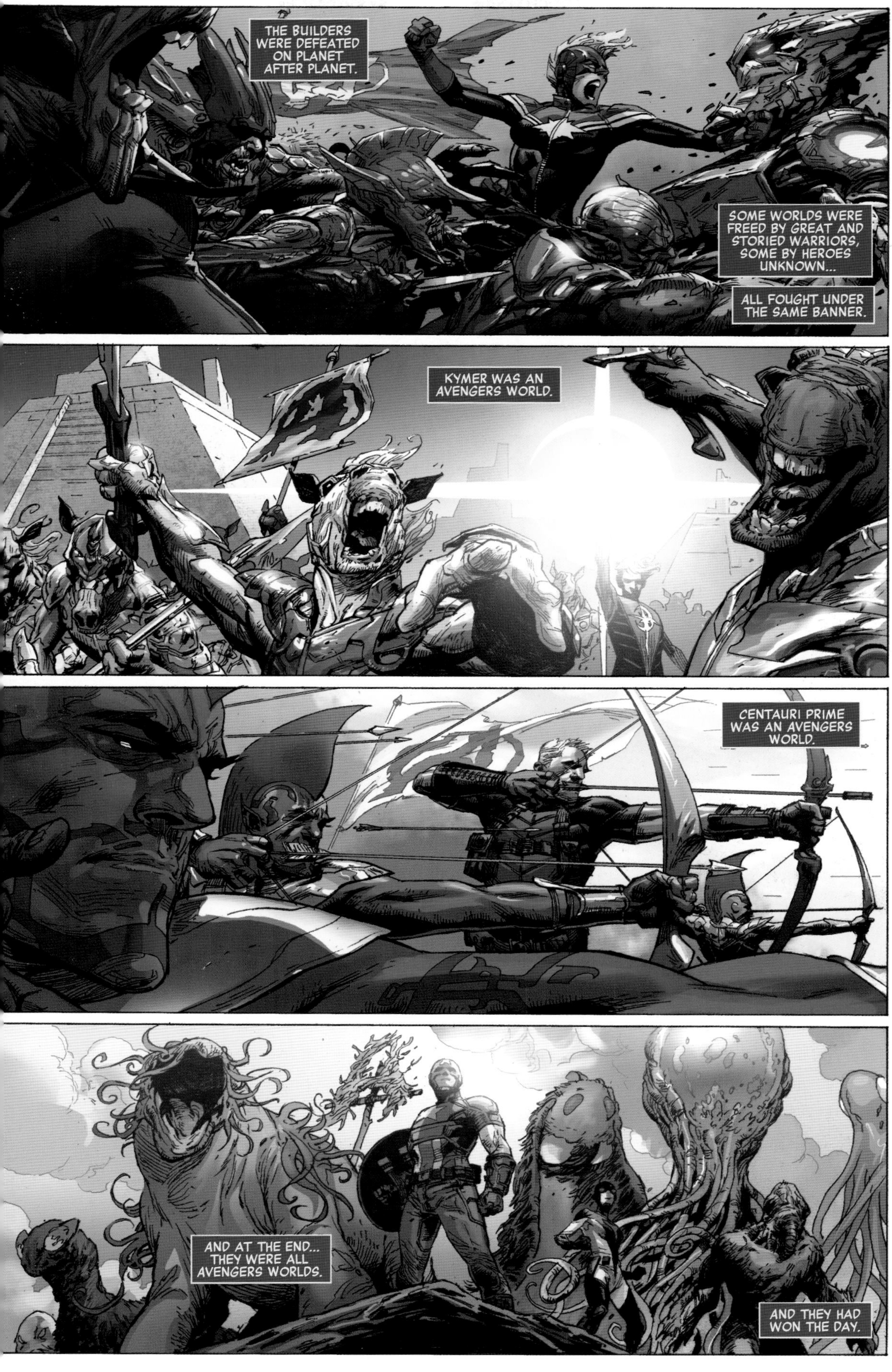
THE BUILDERS WERE DEFEATED ON PLANET AFTER PLANET.
SOME WORLDS WERE FREED BY GREAT AND STORIED WARRIORS, SOME BY HEROES UNKNOWN...
ALL FOUGHT UNDER THE SAME BANNER.
KYMER WAS AN AVENGERS WORLD.
CENTAURI PRIME WAS AN AVENGERS WORLD.
AND AT THE END... THEY WERE ALL AVENGERS WORLDS.
AND THEY HAD WON THE DAY.

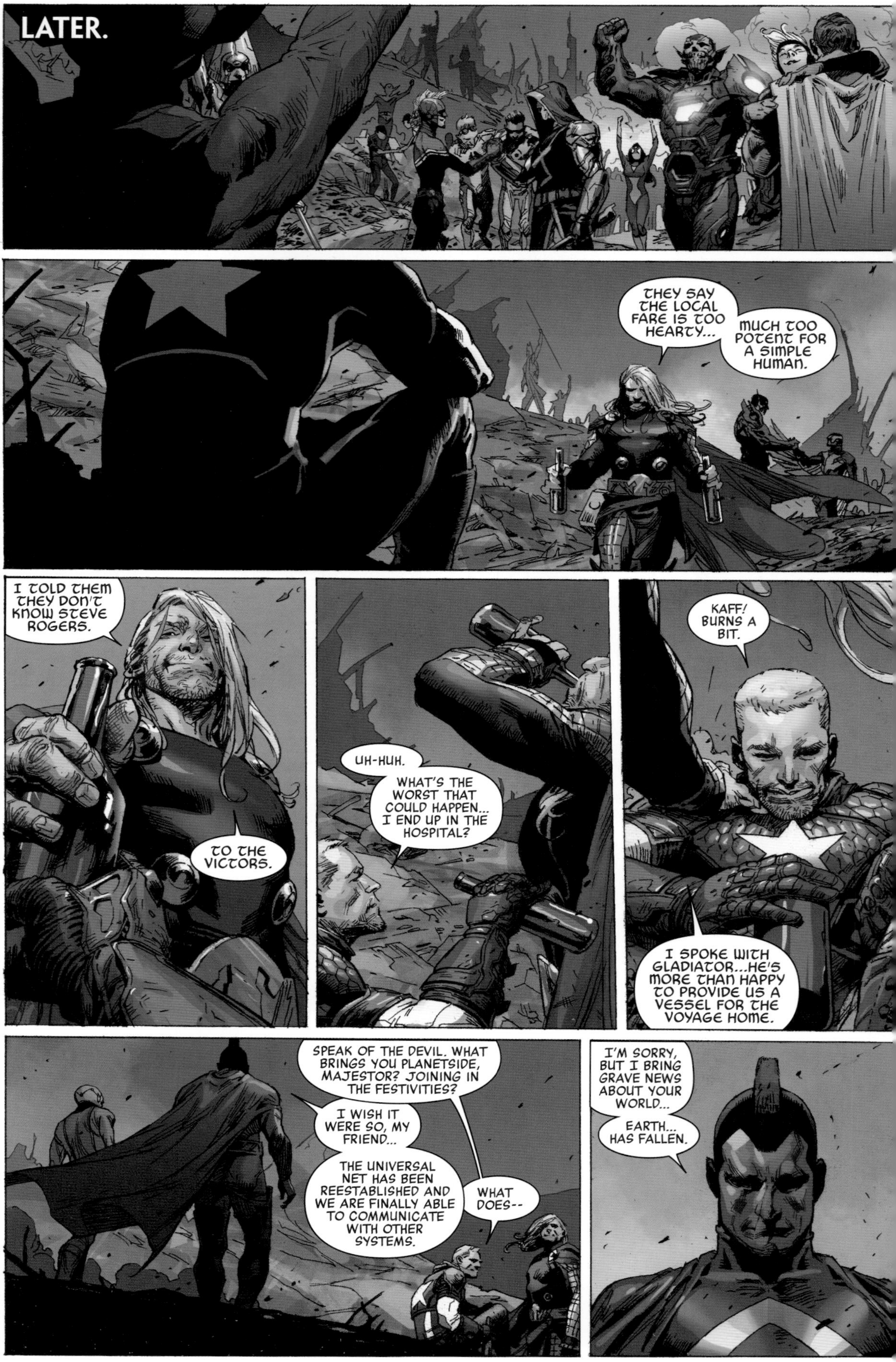

LATER.
THEY SAY THE LOCAL FARE IS TOO HEARTY...
MUCH TOO POTENT FOR A SIMPLE HUMAN.
I TOLD THEM THEY DON'T KNOW STEVE ROGERS.
TO THE VICTORS.
UH-HUH.
WHAT'S THE WORST THAT COULD HAPPEN... I END UP IN THE HOSPITAL?
KAFF! BURNS A BIT.
I SPOKE WITH GLADIATOR...HE'S MORE THAN HAPPY TO PROVIDE US A VESSEL FOR THE VOYAGE HOME.
SPEAK OF THE DEVIL. WHAT BRINGS YOU PLANETSIDE, MAJESTOR? JOINING IN THE FESTIVITIES?
I WISH IT WERE SO, MY FRIEND...
THE UNIVERSAL NET HAS BEEN REESTABLISHED AND WE ARE FINALLY ABLE TO COMMUNICATE WITH OTHER SYSTEMS.
WHAT DOES--
I'M SORRY, BUT I BRING GRAVE NEWS ABOUT YOUR WORLD...
EARTH... HAS FALLEN.

THIS EBONY NOW

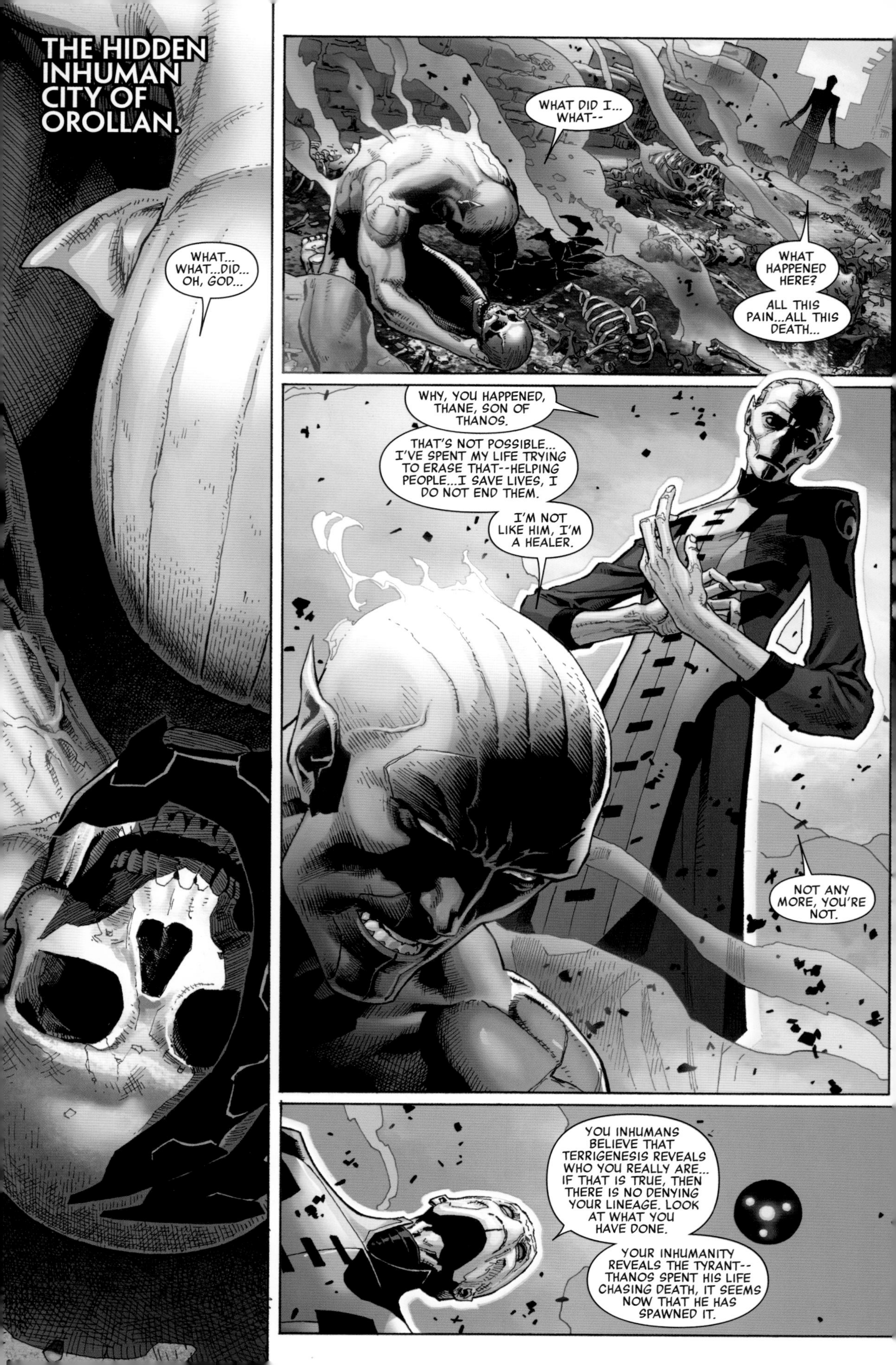
THE HIDDEN INHUMAN CITY OF OROLLAN.
WHAT... WHAT...DID... OH, GOD...
WHAT DID I... WHAT--
WHAT HAPPENED HERE?
ALL THIS PAIN...ALL THIS DEATH...
WHY, YOU HAPPENED, THANE, SON OF THANOS.
THAT'S NOT POSSIBLE... I'VE SPENT MY LIFE TRYING TO ERASE THAT--HELPING PEOPLE...I SAVE LIVES, I DO NOT END THEM.
I'M NOT LIKE HIM, I'M A HEALER.
NOT ANY MORE, YOU'RE NOT.
YOU INHUMANS BELIEVE THAT TERRIGENESIS REVEALS WHO YOU REALLY ARE... IF THAT IS TRUE, THEN THERE IS NO DENYING YOUR LINEAGE. LOOK AT WHAT YOU HAVE DONE.
YOUR INHUMANITY REVEALS THE TYRANT--THANOS SPENT HIS LIFE CHASING DEATH, IT SEEMS NOW THAT HE HAS SPAWNED IT.

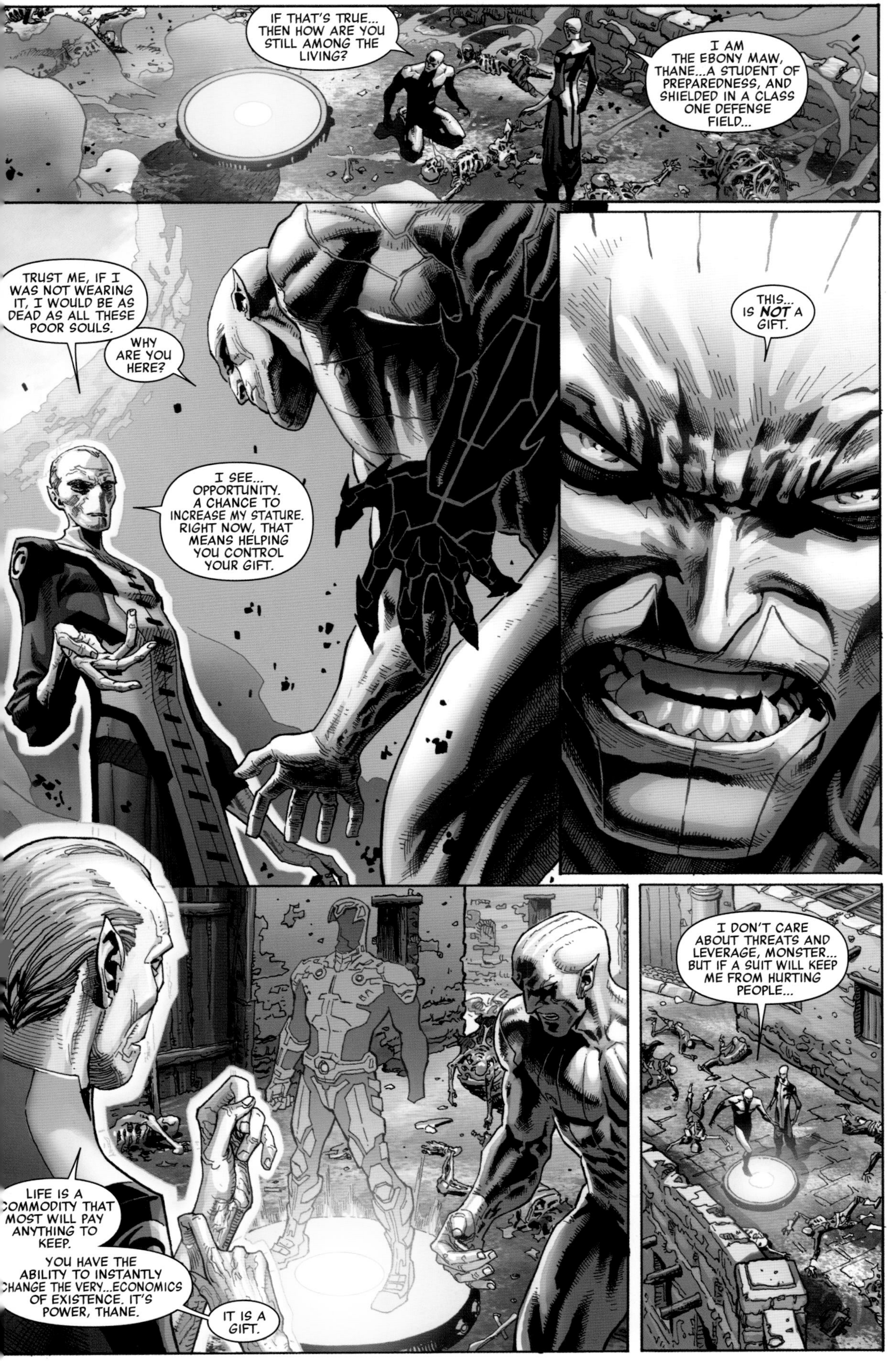
IF THAT'S TRUE... THEN HOW ARE YOU STILL AMONG THE LIVING?
I AM THE EBONY MAW, THANE...A STUDENT OF PREPAREDNESS, AND SHIELDED IN A CLASS ONE DEFENSE FIELD...
TRUST ME, IF I WAS NOT WEARING IT, I WOULD BE AS DEAD AS ALL THESE POOR SOULS.
WHY ARE YOU HERE?
I SEE... OPPORTUNITY. A CHANCE TO INCREASE MY STATURE. RIGHT NOW, THAT MEANS HELPING YOU CONTROL YOUR GIFT.
THIS... IS NOT A GIFT.
LIFE IS A COMMODITY THAT MOST WILL PAY ANYTHING TO KEEP.
YOU HAVE THE ABILITY TO INSTANTLY CHANGE THE VERY...ECONOMICS OF EXISTENCE. IT'S POWER, THANE.
IT IS A GIFT.
I DON'T CARE ABOUT THREATS AND LEVERAGE, MONSTER... BUT IF A SUIT WILL KEEP ME FROM HURTING PEOPLE...

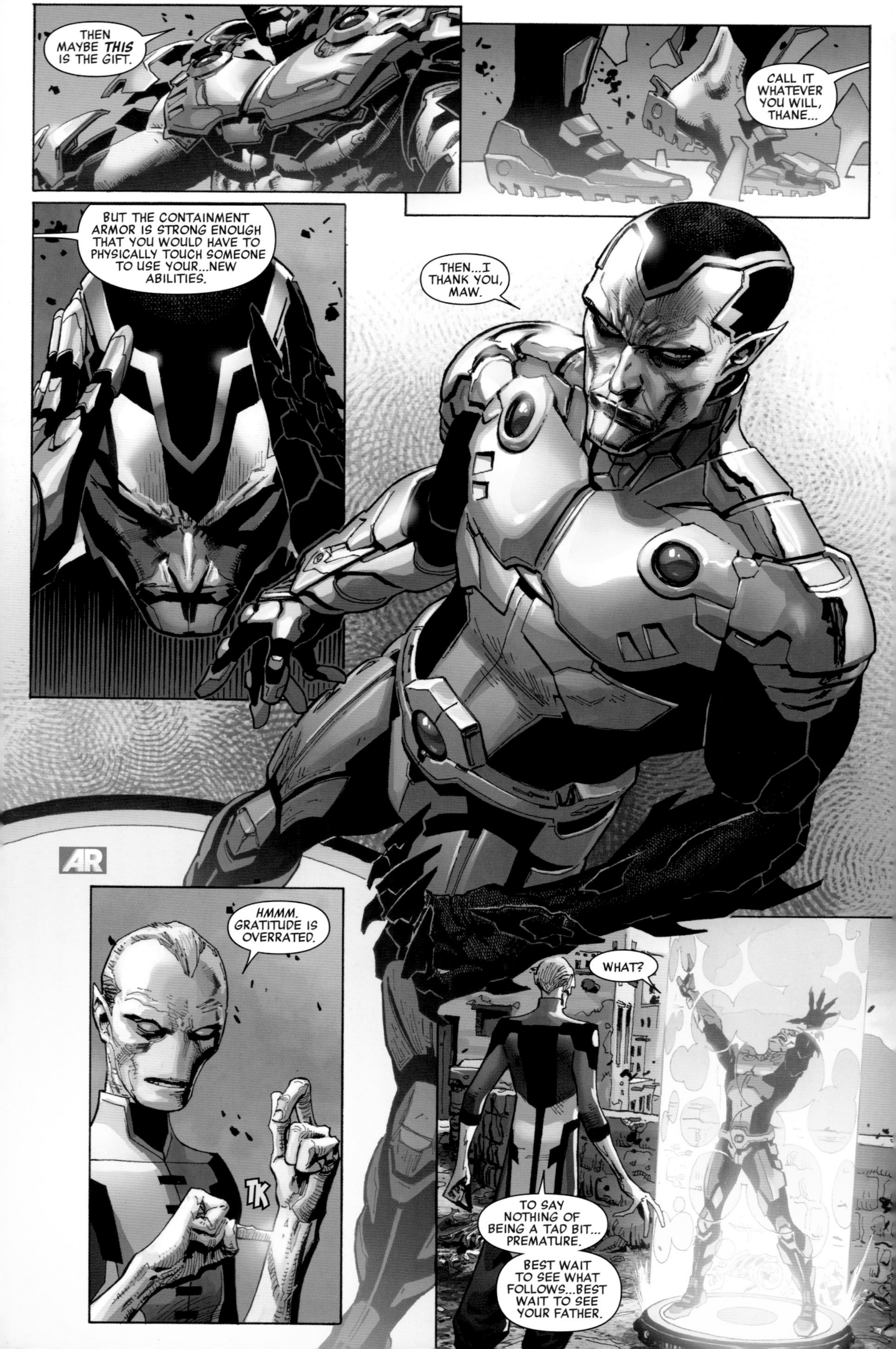
THEN MAYBE THIS IS THE GIFT.
CALL IT WHATEVER YOU WILL, THANE...
BUT THE CONTAINMENT ARMOR IS STRONG ENOUGH THAT YOU WOULD HAVE TO PHYSICALLY TOUCH SOMEONE TO USE YOUR...NEW ABILITIES.
THEN...I THANK YOU, MAW.
AR
HMMM. GRATITUDE IS OVERRATED.
TK
WHAT?
TO SAY NOTHING OF BEING A TAD BIT... PREMATURE.
BEST WAIT TO SEE WHAT FOLLOWS...BEST WAIT TO SEE YOUR FATHER.

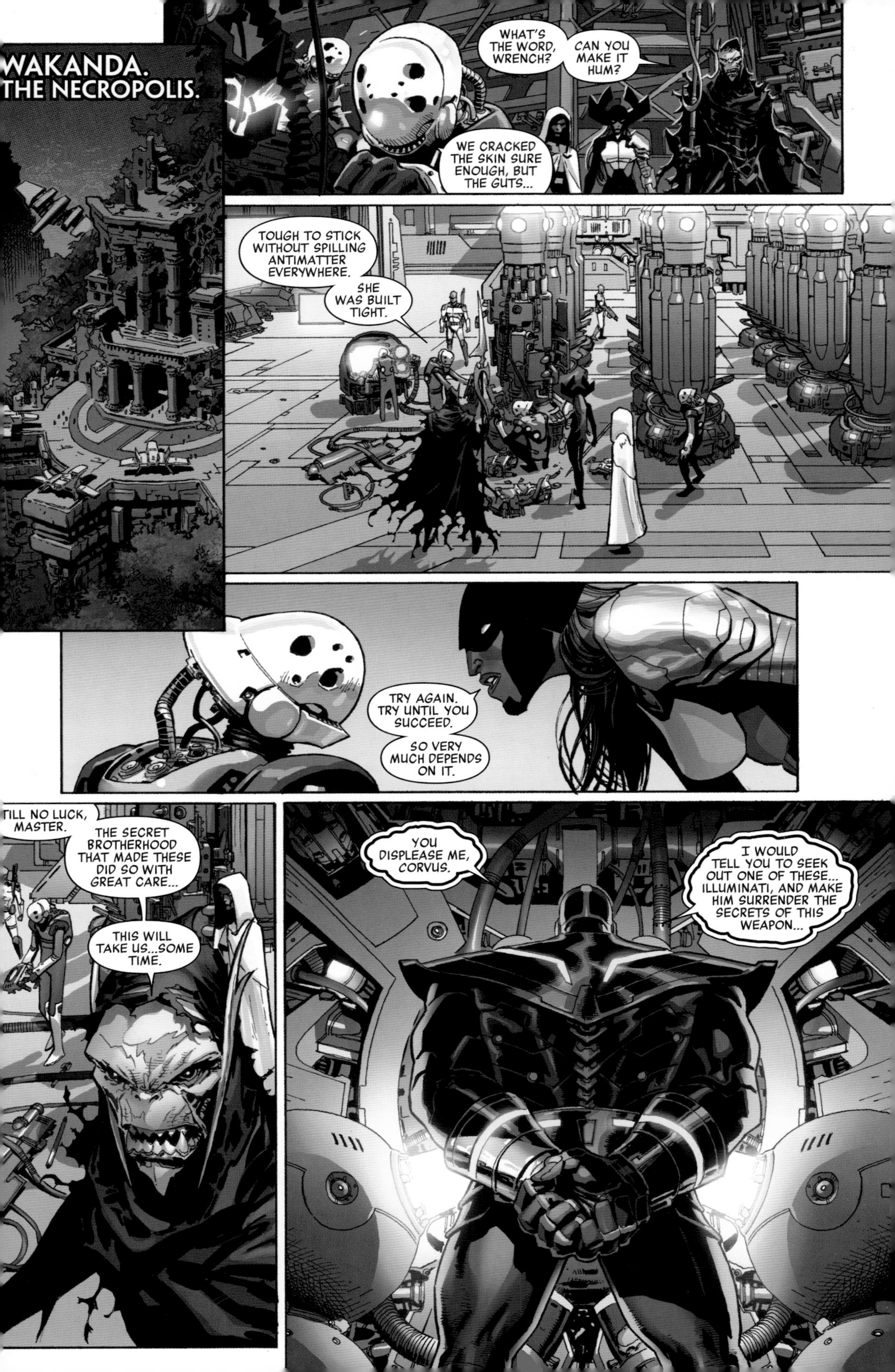
WAKANDA. THE NECROPOLIS.
WHAT'S THE WORD, WRENCH?
CAN YOU MAKE IT HUM?
WE CRACKED THE SKIN SURE ENOUGH, BUT THE GUTS...
TOUGH TO STICK WITHOUT SPILLING ANTIMATTER EVERYWHERE.
SHE WAS BUILT TIGHT.
TRY AGAIN. TRY UNTIL YOU SUCCEED.
SO VERY MUCH DEPENDS ON IT.
TILL NO LUCK, MASTER.
THE SECRET BROTHERHOOD THAT MADE THESE DID SO WITH GREAT CARE...
THIS WILL TAKE US...SOME TIME.
YOU DISPLEASE ME, CORVUS.
I WOULD TELL YOU TO SEEK OUT ONE OF THESE... ILLUMINATI, AND MAKE HIM SURRENDER THE SECRETS OF THIS WEAPON...

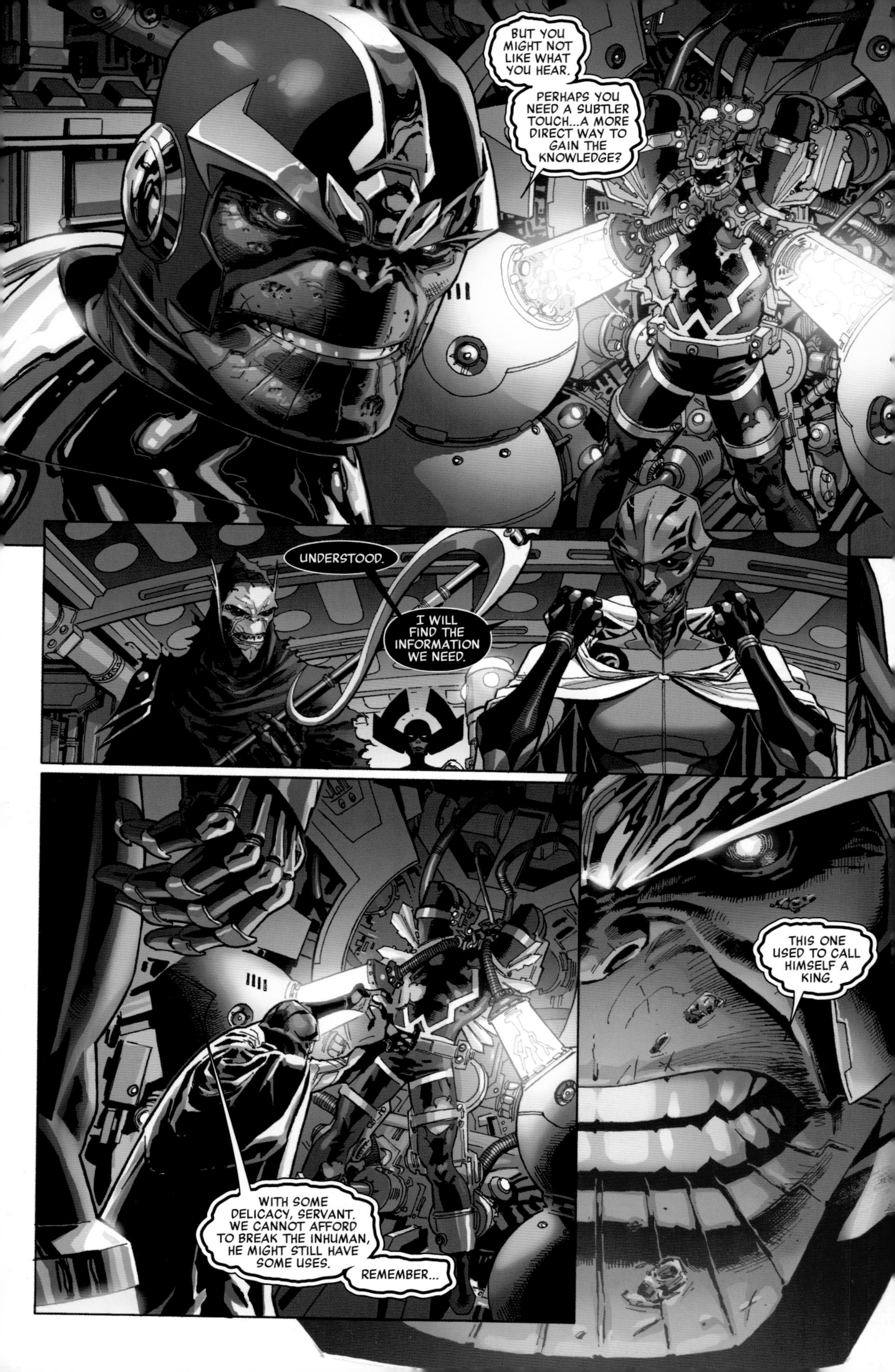
BUT YOU MIGHT NOT LIKE WHAT YOU HEAR.
PERHAPS YOU NEED A SUBTLER TOUCH...A MORE DIRECT WAY TO GAIN THE KNOWLEDGE?
UNDERSTOOD.
I WILL FIND THE INFORMATION WE NEED.
WITH SOME DELICACY, SERVANT. WE CANNOT AFFORD TO BREAK THE INHUMAN, HE MIGHT STILL HAVE SOME USES.
REMEMBER...
THIS ONE USED TO CALL HIMSELF A KING.

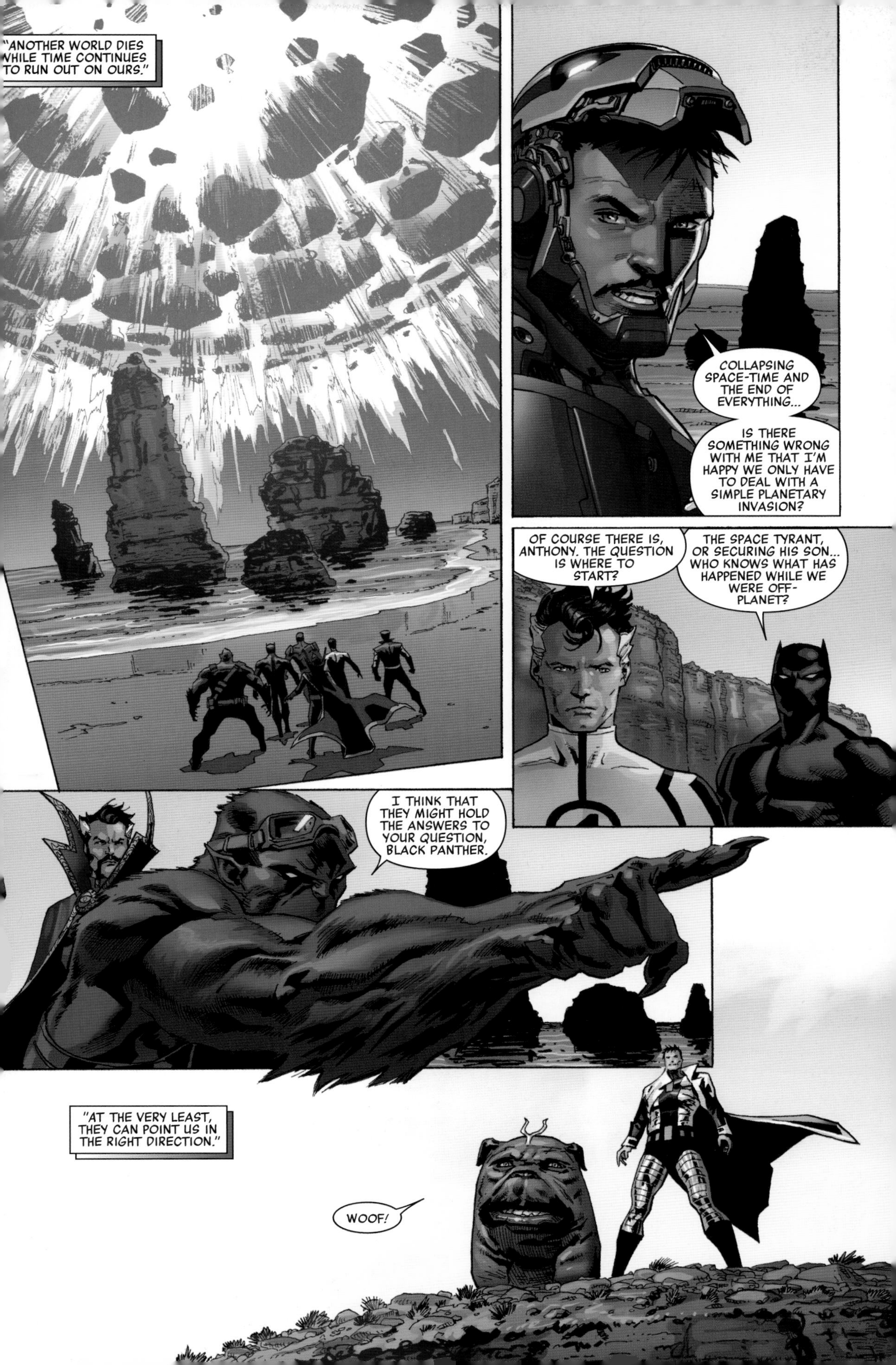
"ANOTHER WORLD DIES WHILE TIME CONTINUES TO RUN OUT ON OURS."
COLLAPSING SPACE-TIME AND THE END OF EVERYTHING...
IS THERE SOMETHING WRONG WITH ME THAT I'M HAPPY WE ONLY HAVE TO DEAL WITH A SIMPLE PLANETARY INVASION?
OF COURSE THERE IS, ANTHONY. THE QUESTION IS WHERE TO START?
THE SPACE TYRANT, OR SECURING HIS SON... WHO KNOWS WHAT HAS HAPPENED WHILE WE WERE OFF-PLANET?
I THINK THAT THEY MIGHT HOLD THE ANSWERS TO YOUR QUESTION, BLACK PANTHER.
"AT THE VERY LEAST, THEY CAN POINT US IN THE RIGHT DIRECTION."
WOOF!

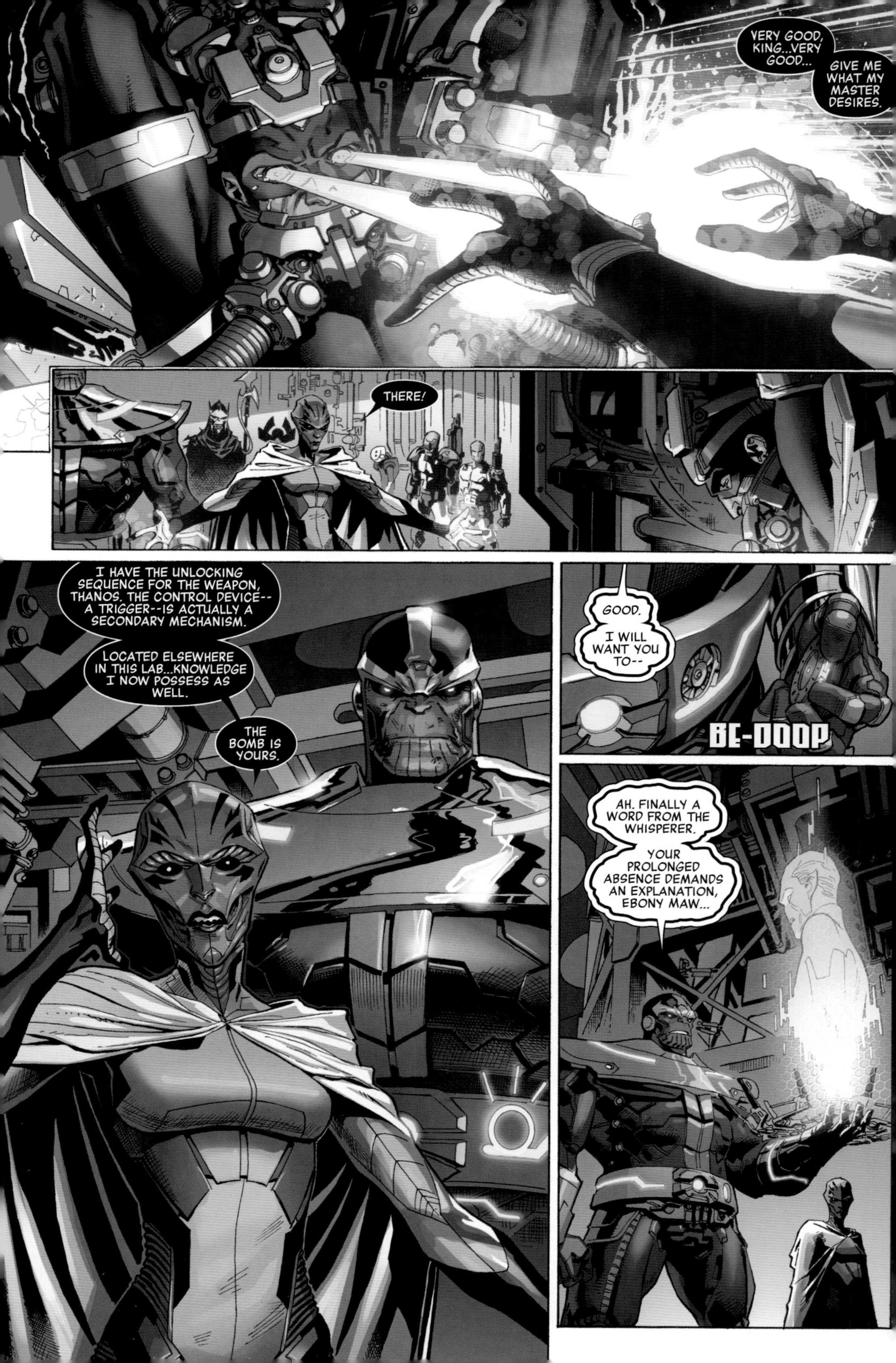
VERY GOOD, KING...VERY GOOD...
GIVE ME WHAT MY MASTER DESIRES.
THERE!
I HAVE THE UNLOCKING SEQUENCE FOR THE WEAPON, THANOS. THE CONTROL DEVICE--A TRIGGER--IS ACTUALLY A SECONDARY MECHANISM.
LOCATED ELSEWHERE IN THIS LAB...KNOWLEDGE I NOW POSSESS AS WELL.
THE BOMB IS YOURS.
GOOD.
I WILL WANT YOU TO--
BE-DOOP
AH. FINALLY A WORD FROM THE WHISPERER.
YOUR PROLONGED ABSENCE DEMANDS AN EXPLANATION, EBONY MAW...

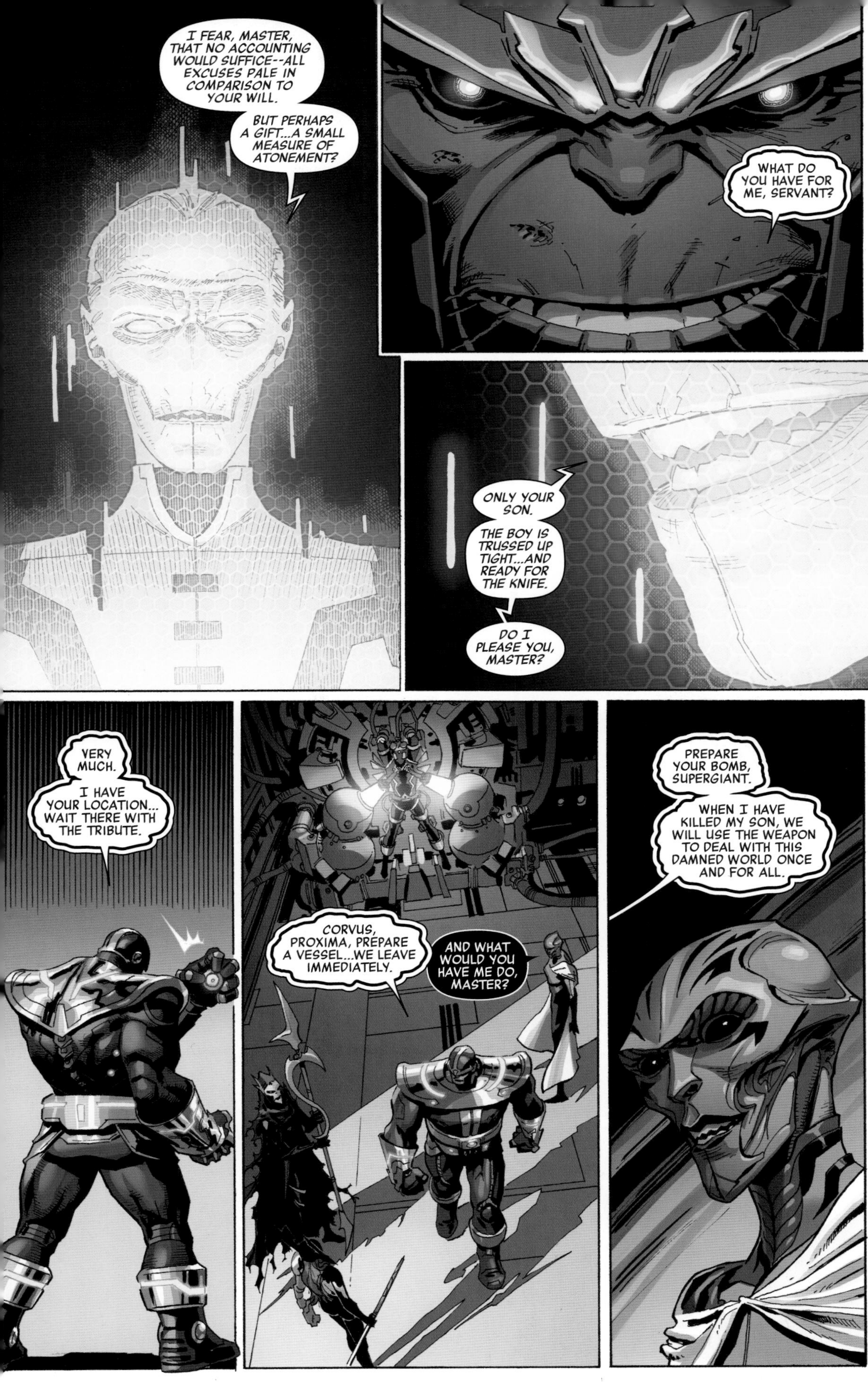
I FEAR, MASTER, THAT NO ACCOUNTING WOULD SUFFICE--ALL EXCUSES PALE IN COMPARISON TO YOUR WILL.
BUT PERHAPS A GIFT...A SMALL MEASURE OF ATONEMENT?
WHAT DO YOU HAVE FOR ME, SERVANT?
ONLY YOUR SON.
THE BOY IS TRUSSED UP TIGHT...AND READY FOR THE KNIFE.
DO I PLEASE YOU, MASTER?
VERY MUCH.
I HAVE YOUR LOCATION... WAIT THERE WITH THE TRIBUTE.
CORVUS, PROXIMA, PREPARE A VESSEL...WE LEAVE IMMEDIATELY.
AND WHAT WOULD YOU HAVE ME DO, MASTER?
PREPARE YOUR BOMB, SUPERGIANT.
WHEN I HAVE KILLED MY SON, WE WILL USE THE WEAPON TO DEAL WITH THIS DAMNED WORLD ONCE AND FOR ALL.

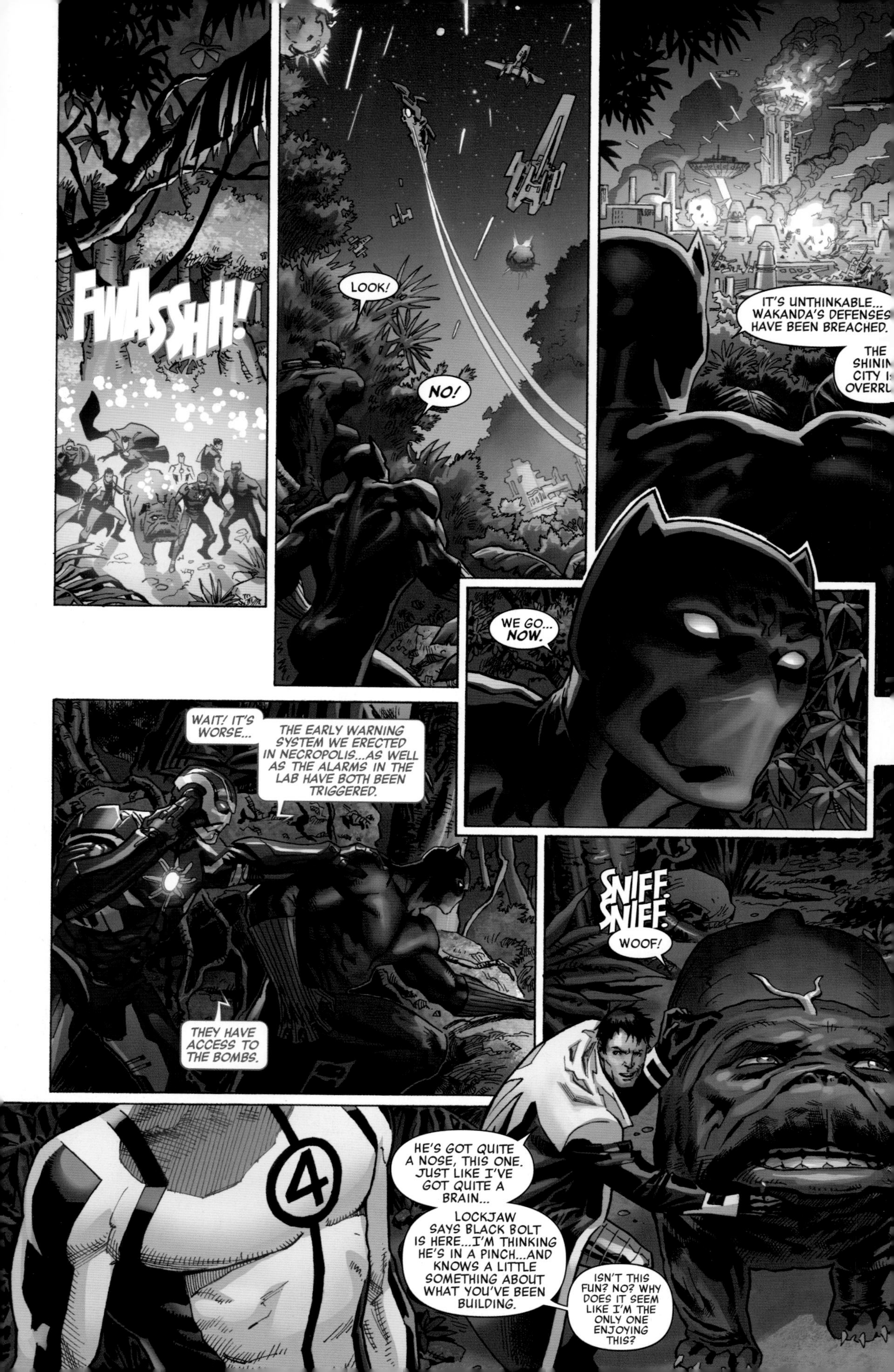
FWASSHH!
LOOK!
NO!
IT'S UNTHINKABLE... WAKANDA'S DEFENSES HAVE BEEN BREACHED.
THE SHININ CITY IS OVERRU
WE GO... NOW.
WAIT! IT'S WORSE...
THE EARLY WARNING SYSTEM WE ERECTED IN NECROPOLIS...AS WELL AS THE ALARMS IN THE LAB HAVE BOTH BEEN TRIGGERED.
THEY HAVE ACCESS TO THE BOMBS.
SNIFF. SNIFF.
WOOF!
HE'S GOT QUITE A NOSE, THIS ONE. JUST LIKE I'VE GOT QUITE A BRAIN...
LOCKJAW SAYS BLACK BOLT IS HERE...I'M THINKING HE'S IN A PINCH...AND KNOWS A LITTLE SOMETHING ABOUT WHAT YOU'VE BEEN BUILDING.
ISN'T THIS FUN? NO? WHY DOES IT SEEM LIKE I'M THE ONLY ONE ENJOYING THIS?

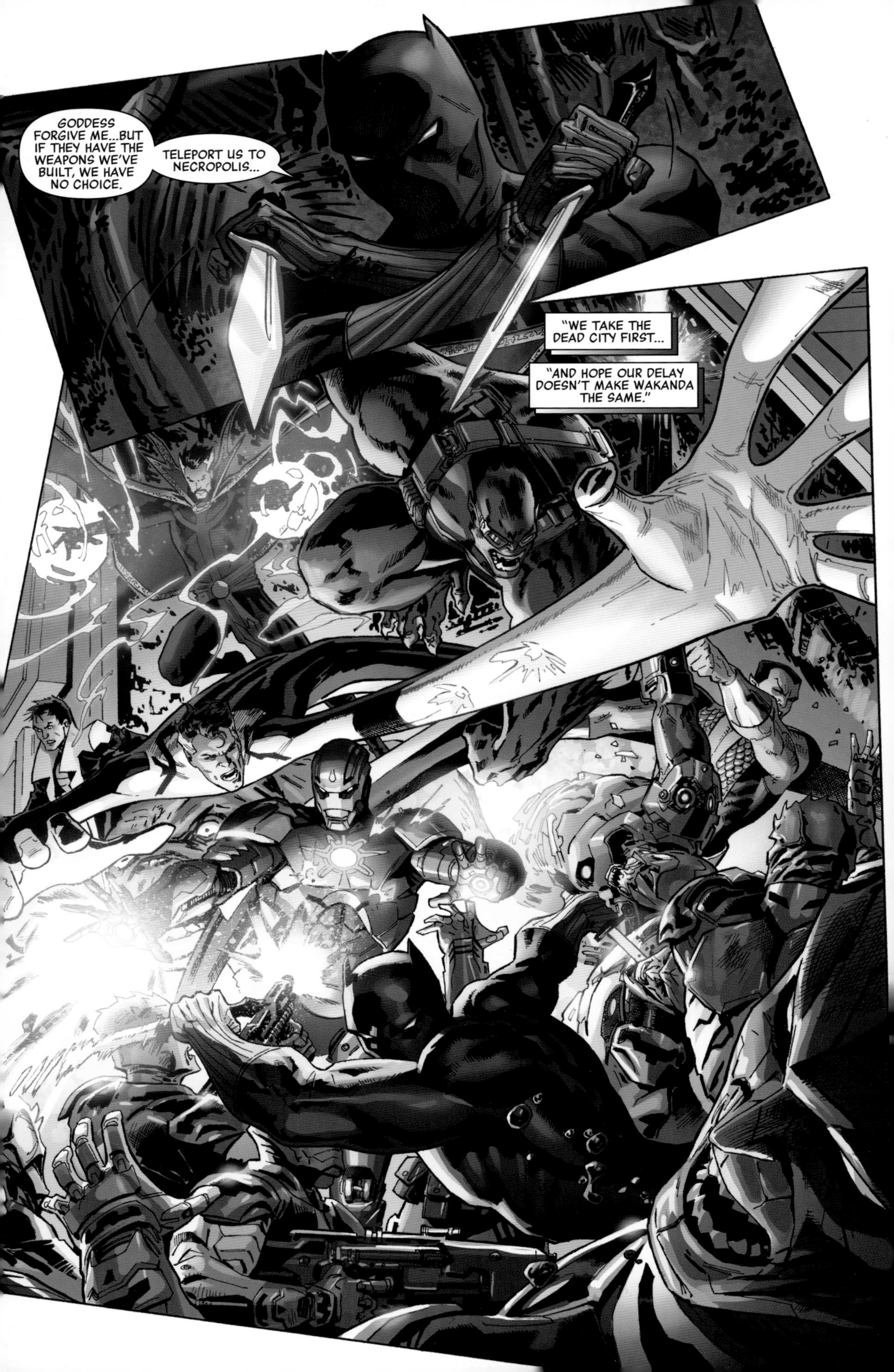
GODDESS FORGIVE ME...BUT IF THEY HAVE THE WEAPONS WE'VE BUILT, WE HAVE NO CHOICE.
TELEPORT US TO NECROPOLIS...
"WE TAKE THE DEAD CITY FIRST...
"AND HOPE OUR DELAY DOESN'T MAKE WAKANDA THE SAME."

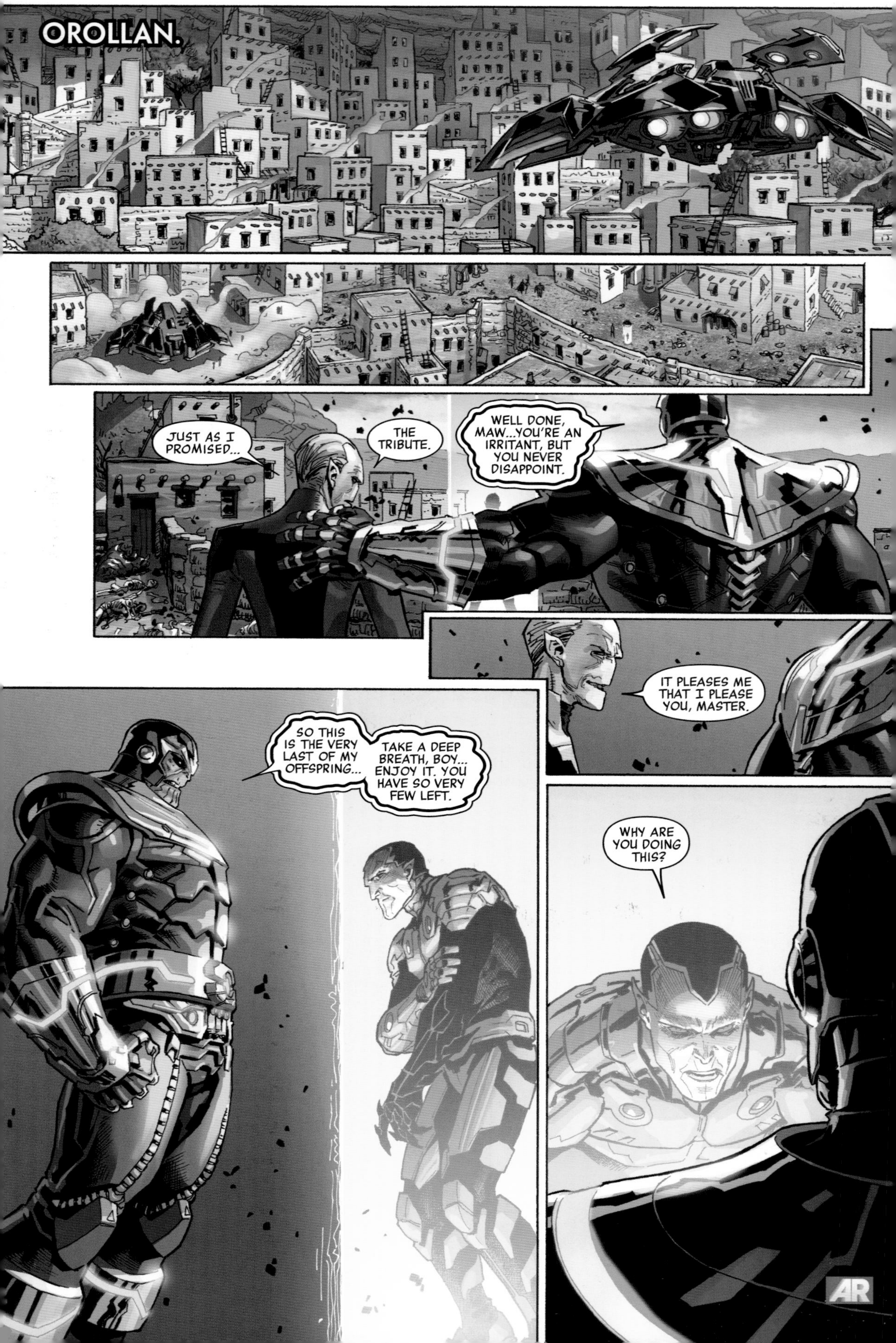
OROLLAN.
JUST AS I PROMISED...
THE TRIBUTE.
WELL DONE, MAW...YOU'RE AN IRRITANT, BUT YOU NEVER DISAPPOINT.
IT PLEASES ME THAT I PLEASE YOU, MASTER.
SO THIS IS THE VERY LAST OF MY OFFSPRING...
TAKE A DEEP BREATH, BOY... ENJOY IT. YOU HAVE SO VERY FEW LEFT.
WHY ARE YOU DOING THIS?

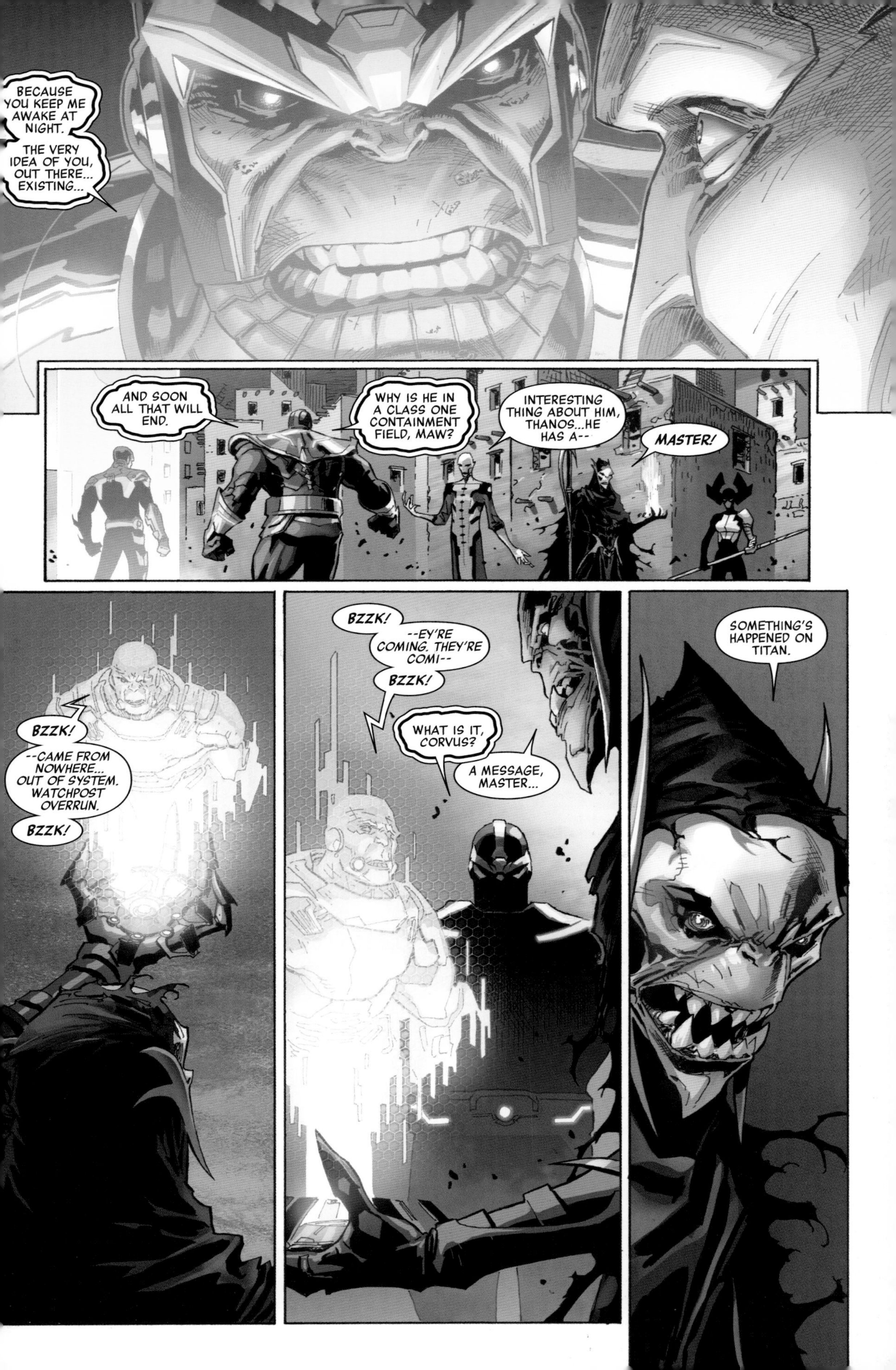
BECAUSE YOU KEEP ME AWAKE AT NIGHT.
THE VERY IDEA OF YOU, OUT THERE... EXISTING...
AND SOON ALL THAT WILL END.
WHY IS HE IN A CLASS ONE CONTAINMENT FIELD, MAW?
INTERESTING THING ABOUT HIM, THANOS...HE HAS A--
MASTER!
BZZK!
--CAME FROM NOWHERE... OUT OF SYSTEM. WATCHPOST OVERRUN.
BZZK!
BZZK!
--EY'RE COMING. THEY'RE COMI--
BZZK!
WHAT IS IT, CORVUS?
A MESSAGE, MASTER...
SOMETHING'S HAPPENED ON TITAN.

IN THE SHADOW OF
THE GIANTS

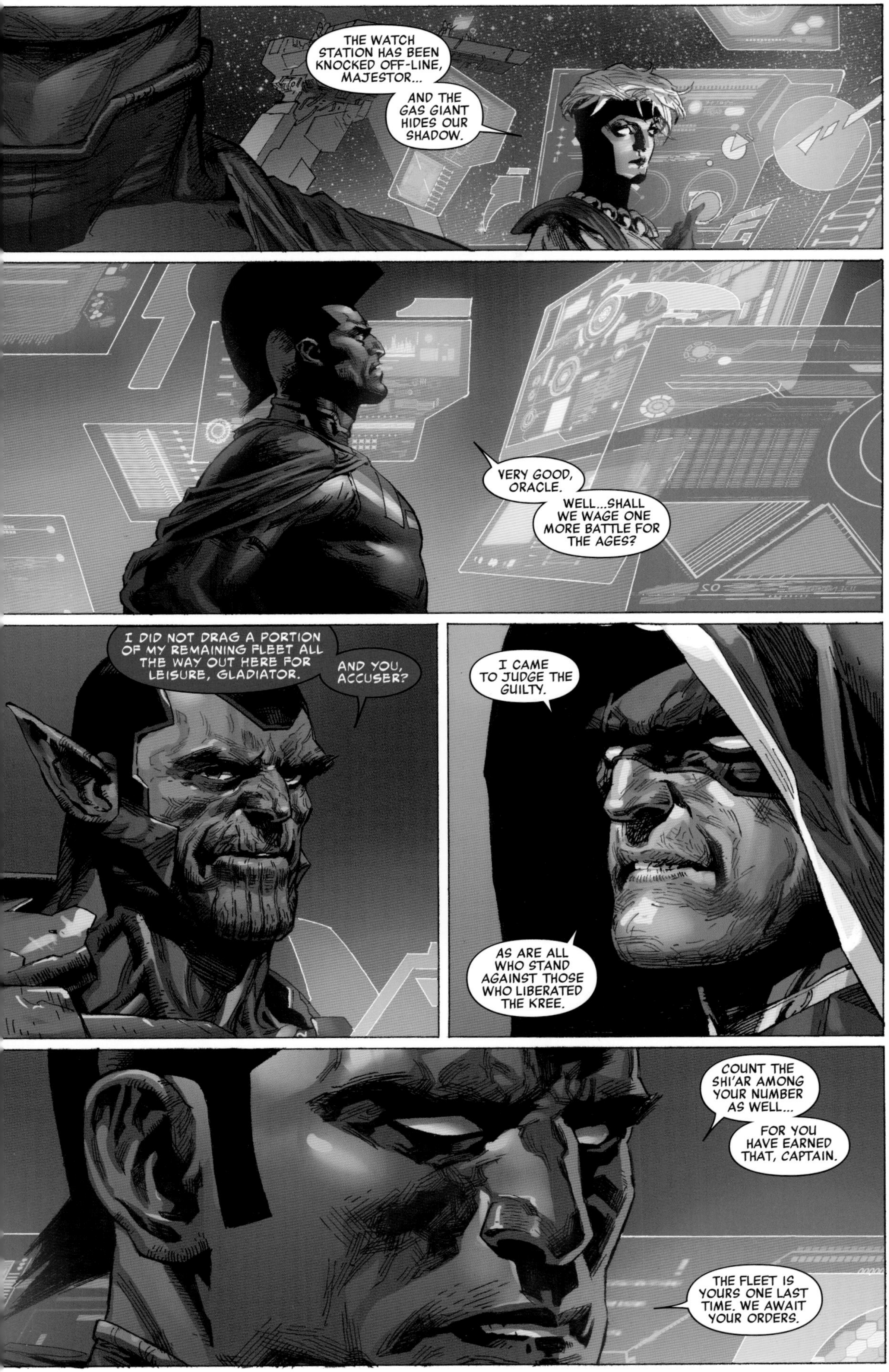
THE WATCH STATION HAS BEEN KNOCKED OFF-LINE, MAJESTOR...
AND THE GAS GIANT HIDES OUR SHADOW.
VERY GOOD, ORACLE.
WELL...SHALL WE WAGE ONE MORE BATTLE FOR THE AGES?
I DID NOT DRAG A PORTION OF MY REMAINING FLEET ALL THE WAY OUT HERE FOR LEISURE, GLADIATOR.
AND YOU, ACCUSER?
I CAME TO JUDGE THE GUILTY.
AS ARE ALL WHO STAND AGAINST THOSE WHO LIBERATED THE KREE.
COUNT THE SHI'AR AMONG YOUR NUMBER AS WELL...
FOR YOU HAVE EARNED THAT, CAPTAIN.
THE FLEET IS YOURS ONE LAST TIME. WE AWAIT YOUR ORDERS.

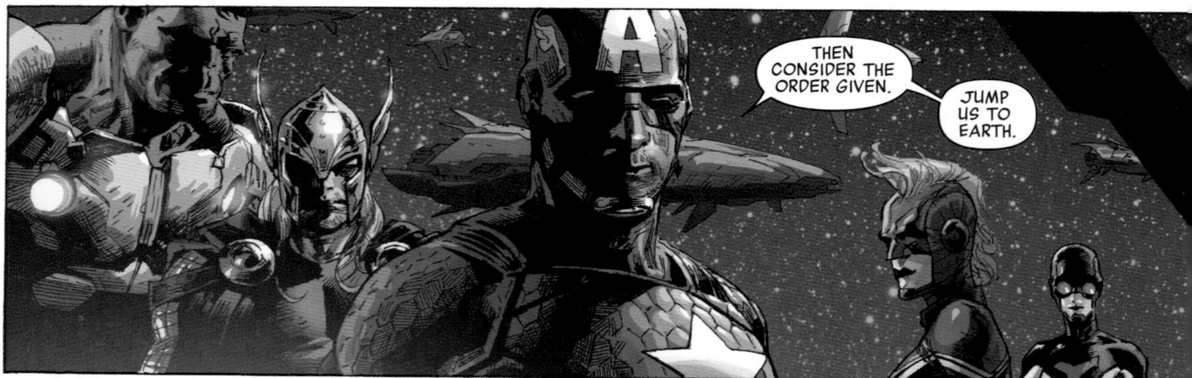
THEN CONSIDER THE ORDER GIVEN.
JUMP US TO EARTH.

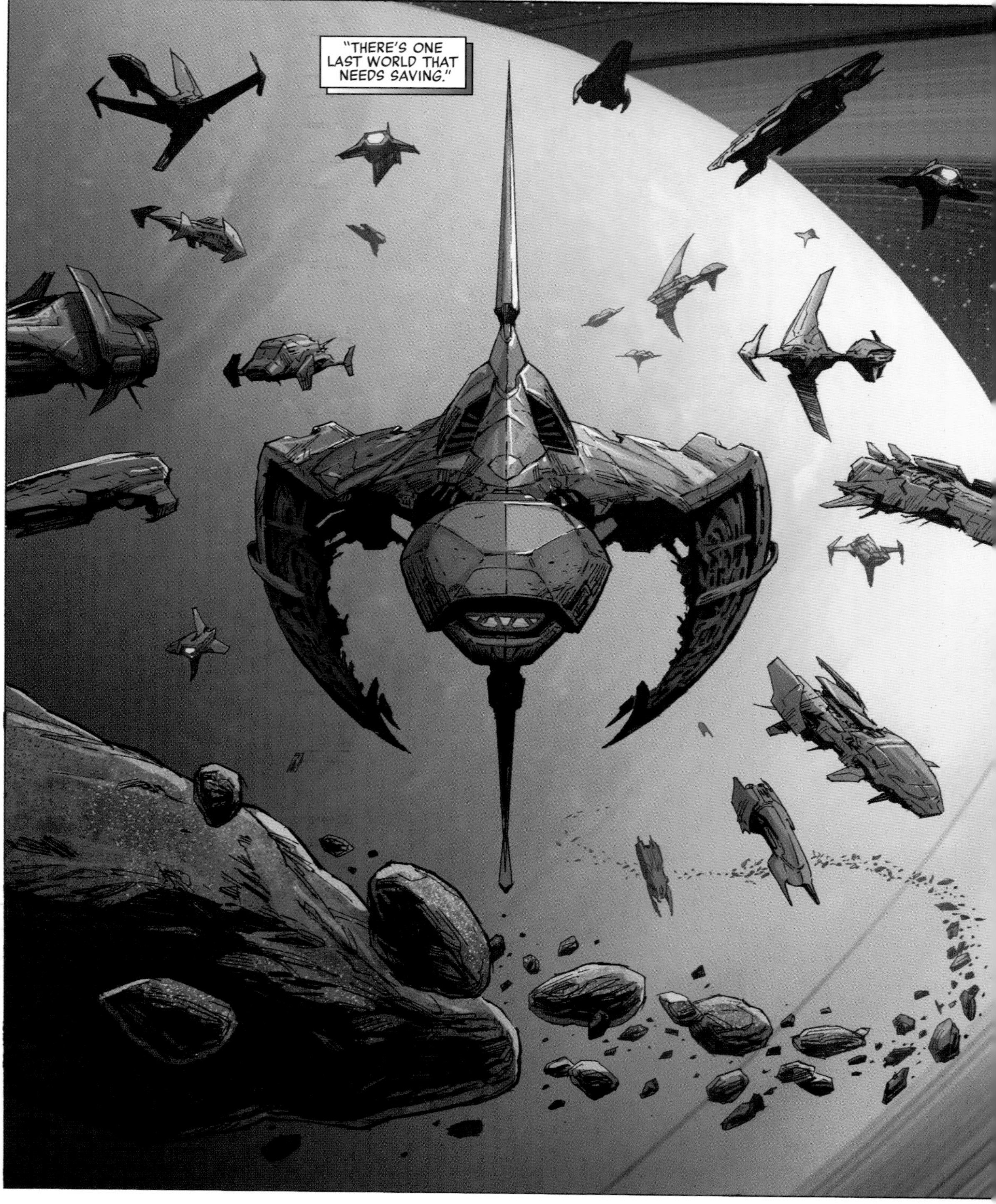
"THERE'S ONE LAST WORLD THAT NEEDS SAVING."

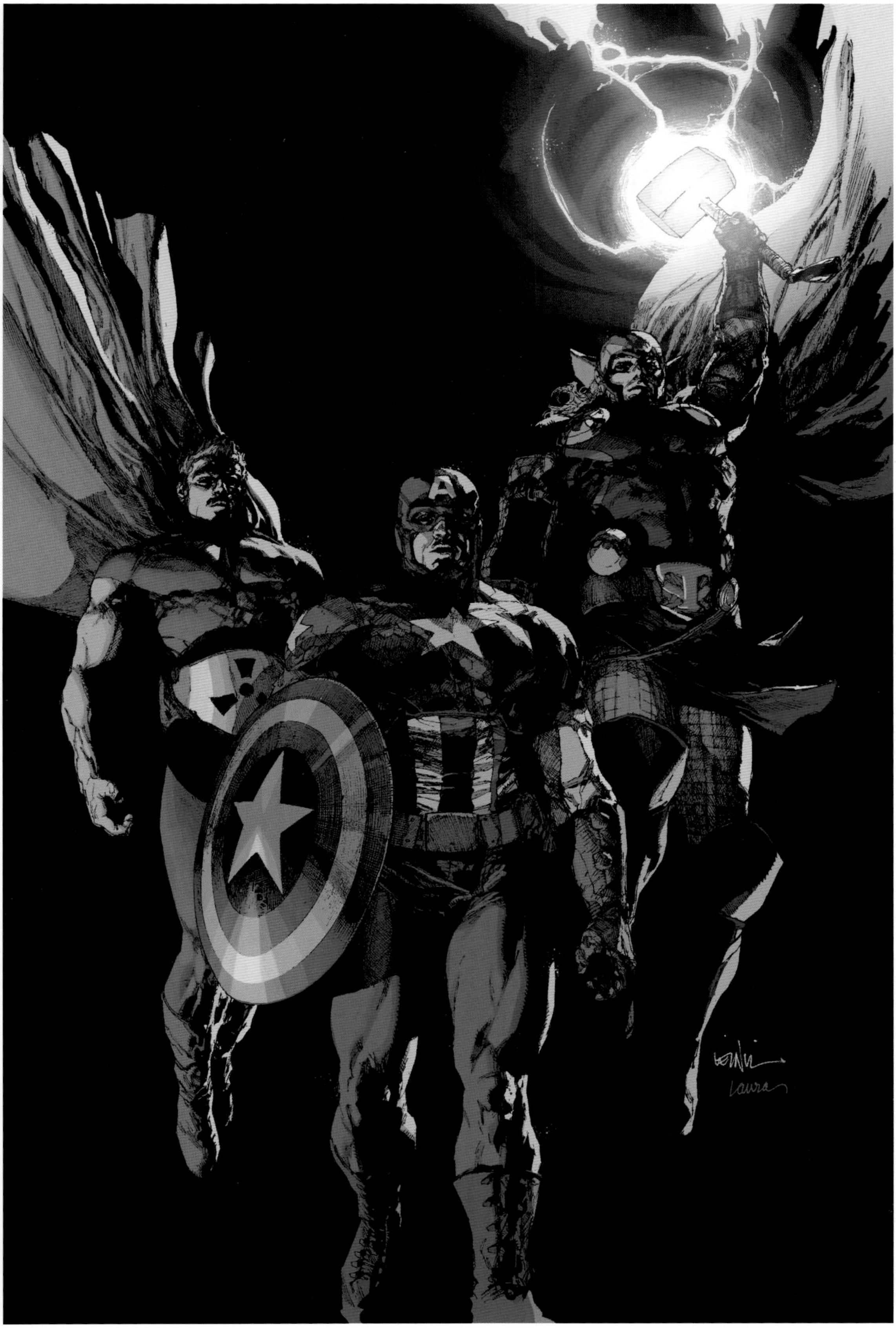

HOMECOMING

◆

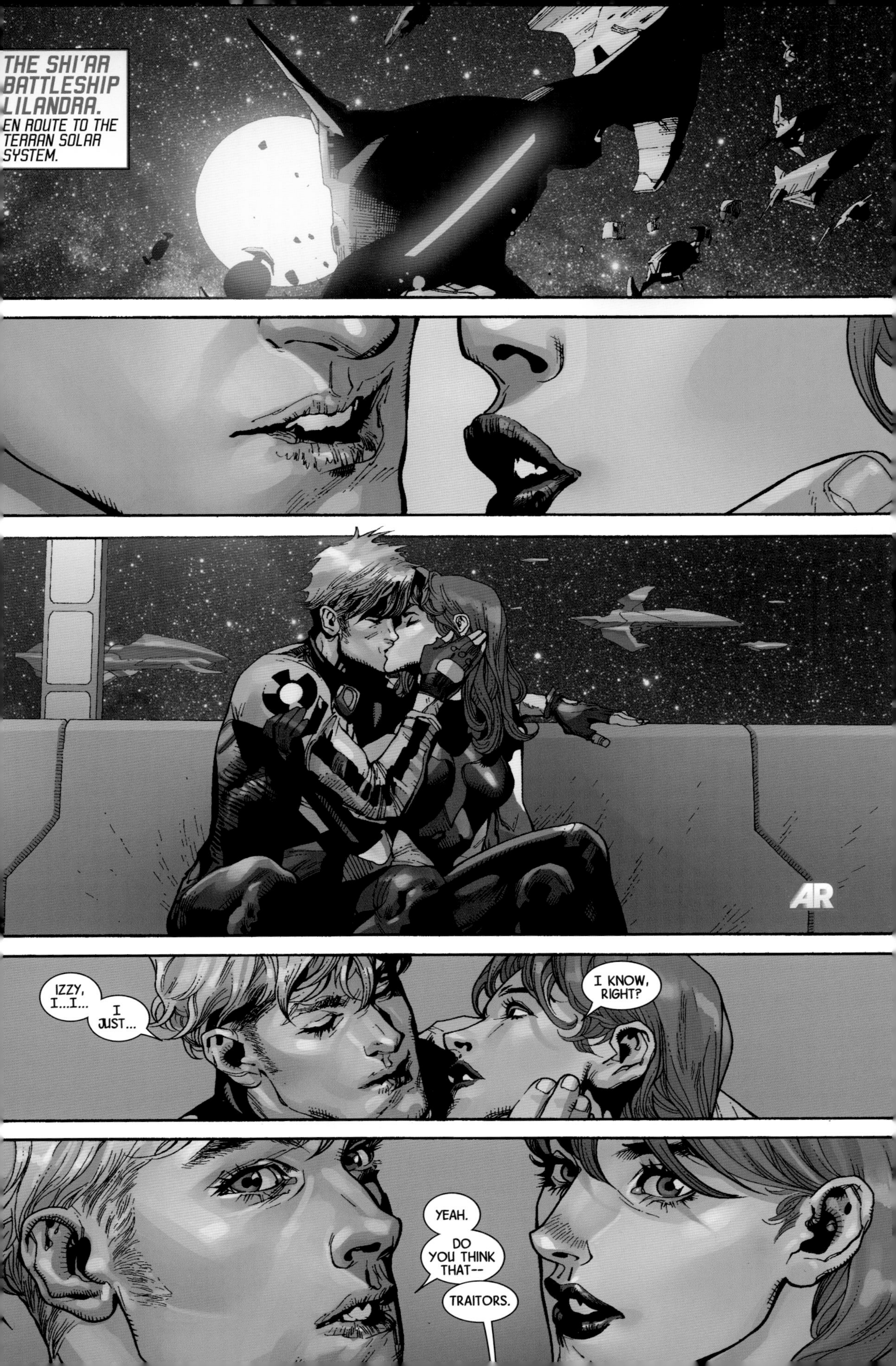

THE SHI'AR BATTLESHIP LILANDRA.
EN ROUTE TO THE TERRAN SOLAR SYSTEM.
AR
IZZY, I...I...
I JUST...
I KNOW, RIGHT?
YEAH.
DO YOU THINK THAT--
TRAITORS.

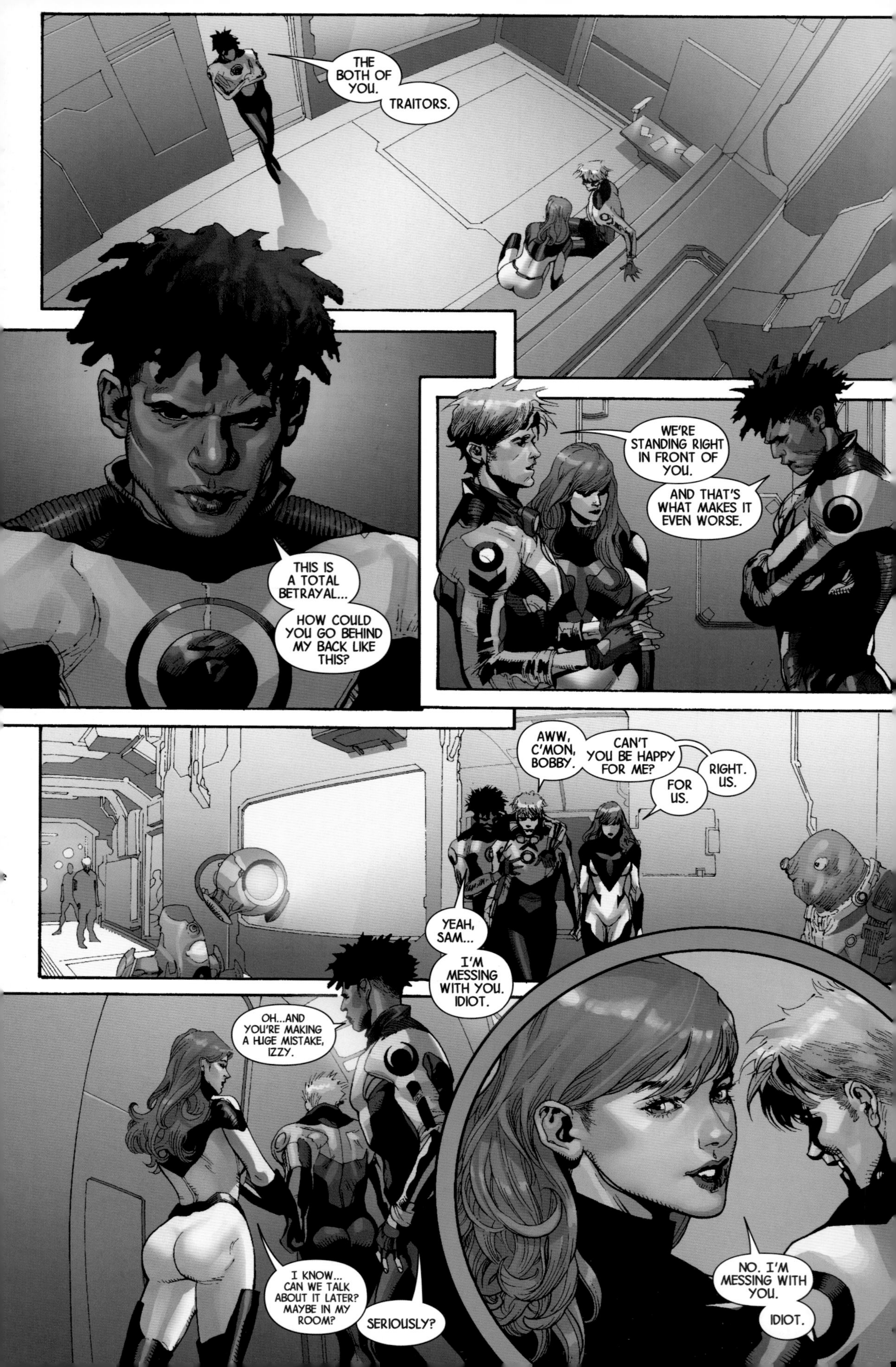
THE BOTH OF YOU.
TRAITORS.
THIS IS A TOTAL BETRAYAL...
HOW COULD YOU GO BEHIND MY BACK LIKE THIS?
WE'RE STANDING RIGHT IN FRONT OF YOU.
AND THAT'S WHAT MAKES IT EVEN WORSE.
AWW, C'MON, BOBBY.
CAN'T YOU BE HAPPY FOR ME?
FOR US.
RIGHT. US.
YEAH, SAM...
I'M MESSING WITH YOU. IDIOT.
OH...AND YOU'RE MAKING A HUGE MISTAKE, IZZY.
I KNOW... CAN WE TALK ABOUT IT LATER? MAYBE IN MY ROOM?
SERIOUSLY?
NO. I'M MESSING WITH YOU.
IDIOT.

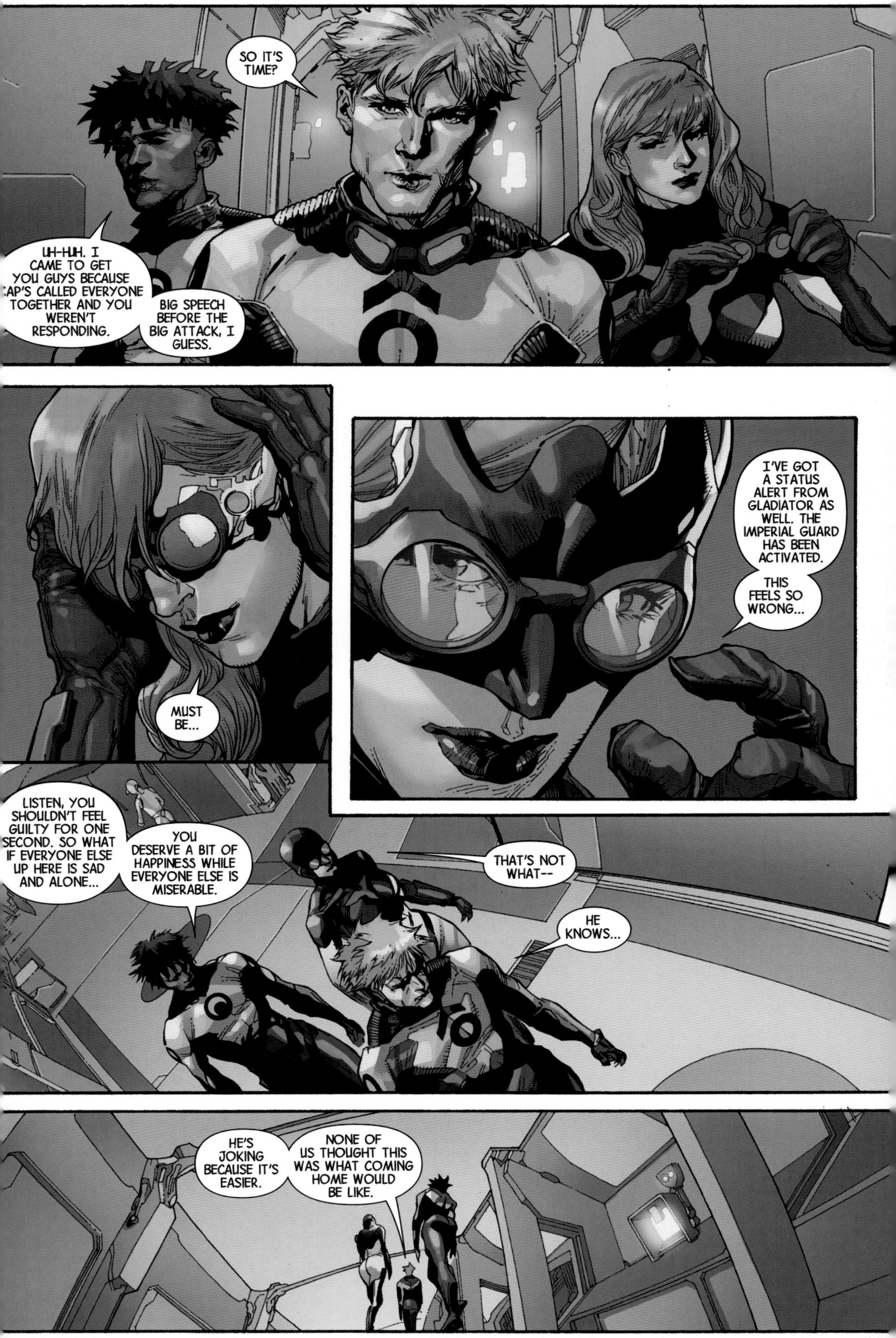
SO IT'S TIME?
UH-HUH. I CAME TO GET YOU GUYS BECAUSE CAP'S CALLED EVERYONE TOGETHER AND YOU WEREN'T RESPONDING.
BIG SPEECH BEFORE THE BIG ATTACK, I GUESS.
MUST BE...
I'VE GOT A STATUS ALERT FROM GLADIATOR AS WELL. THE IMPERIAL GUARD HAS BEEN ACTIVATED.
THIS FEELS SO WRONG...
LISTEN, YOU SHOULDN'T FEEL GUILTY FOR ONE SECOND. SO WHAT IF EVERYONE ELSE UP HERE IS SAD AND ALONE...
YOU DESERVE A BIT OF HAPPINESS WHILE EVERYONE ELSE IS MISERABLE.
THAT'S NOT WHAT--
HE KNOWS...
HE'S JOKING BECAUSE IT'S EASIER.
NONE OF US THOUGHT THIS WAS WHAT COMING HOME WOULD BE LIKE.

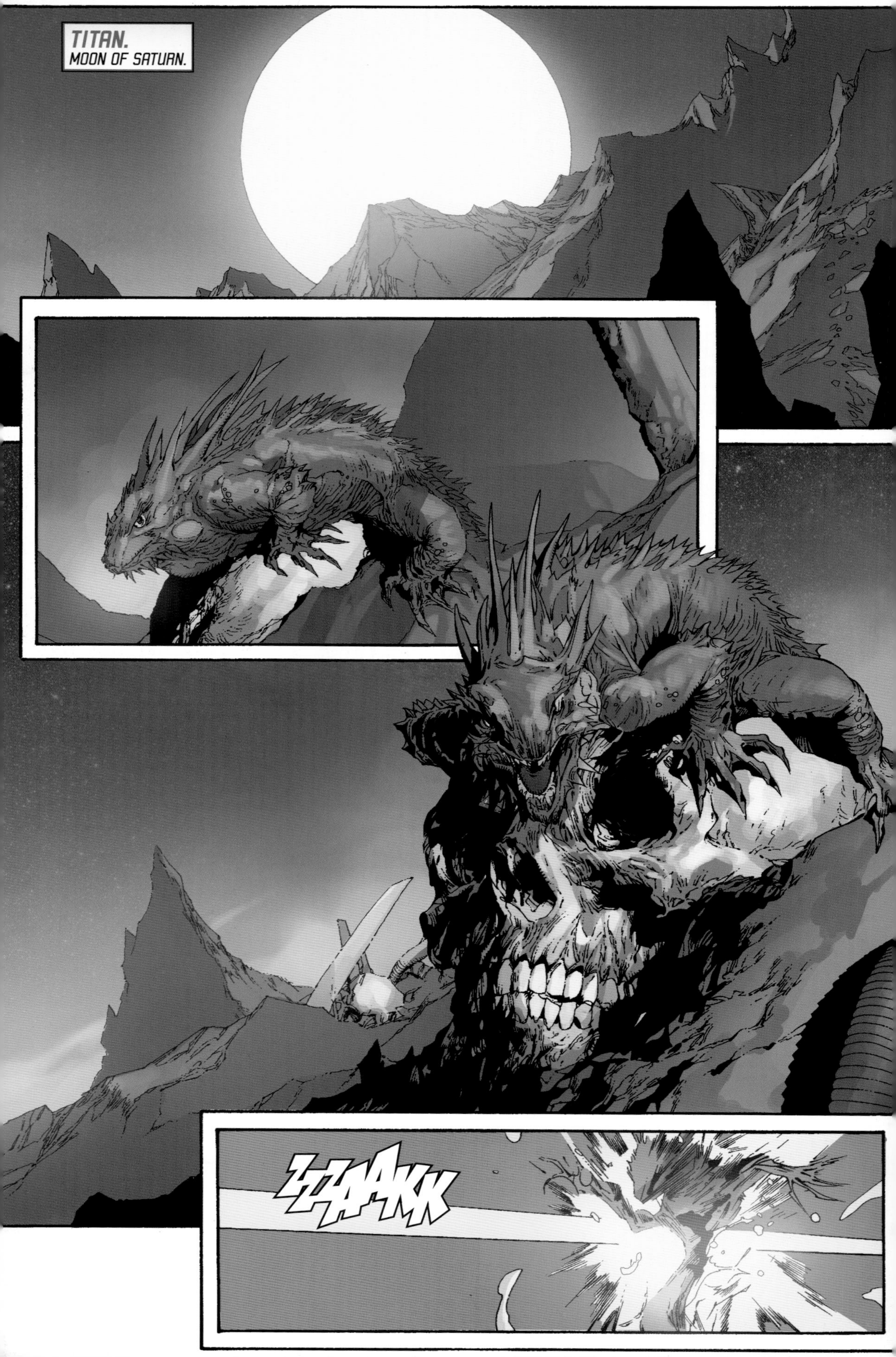
TITAN.
MOON OF SATURN.
ZZZAAKK

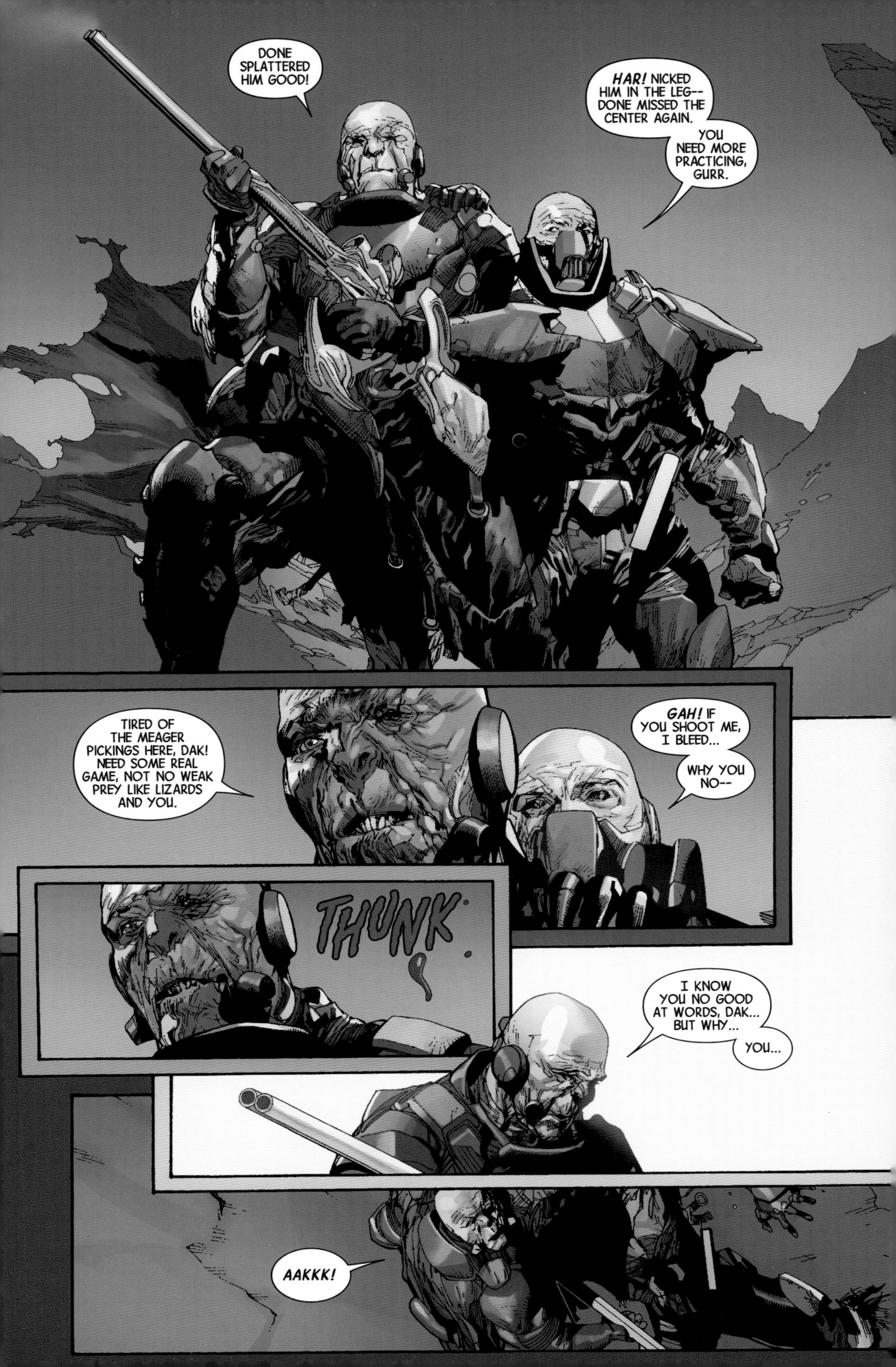
DONE SPLATTERED HIM GOOD!
HAR! NICKED HIM IN THE LEG-- DONE MISSED THE CENTER AGAIN.
YOU NEED MORE PRACTICING, GURR.
TIRED OF THE MEAGER PICKINGS HERE, DAK! NEED SOME REAL GAME, NOT NO WEAK PREY LIKE LIZARDS AND YOU.
GAH! IF YOU SHOOT ME, I BLEED...
WHY YOU NO--
THUNK
I KNOW YOU NO GOOD AT WORDS, DAK... BUT WHY...
YOU...
AAKKK!

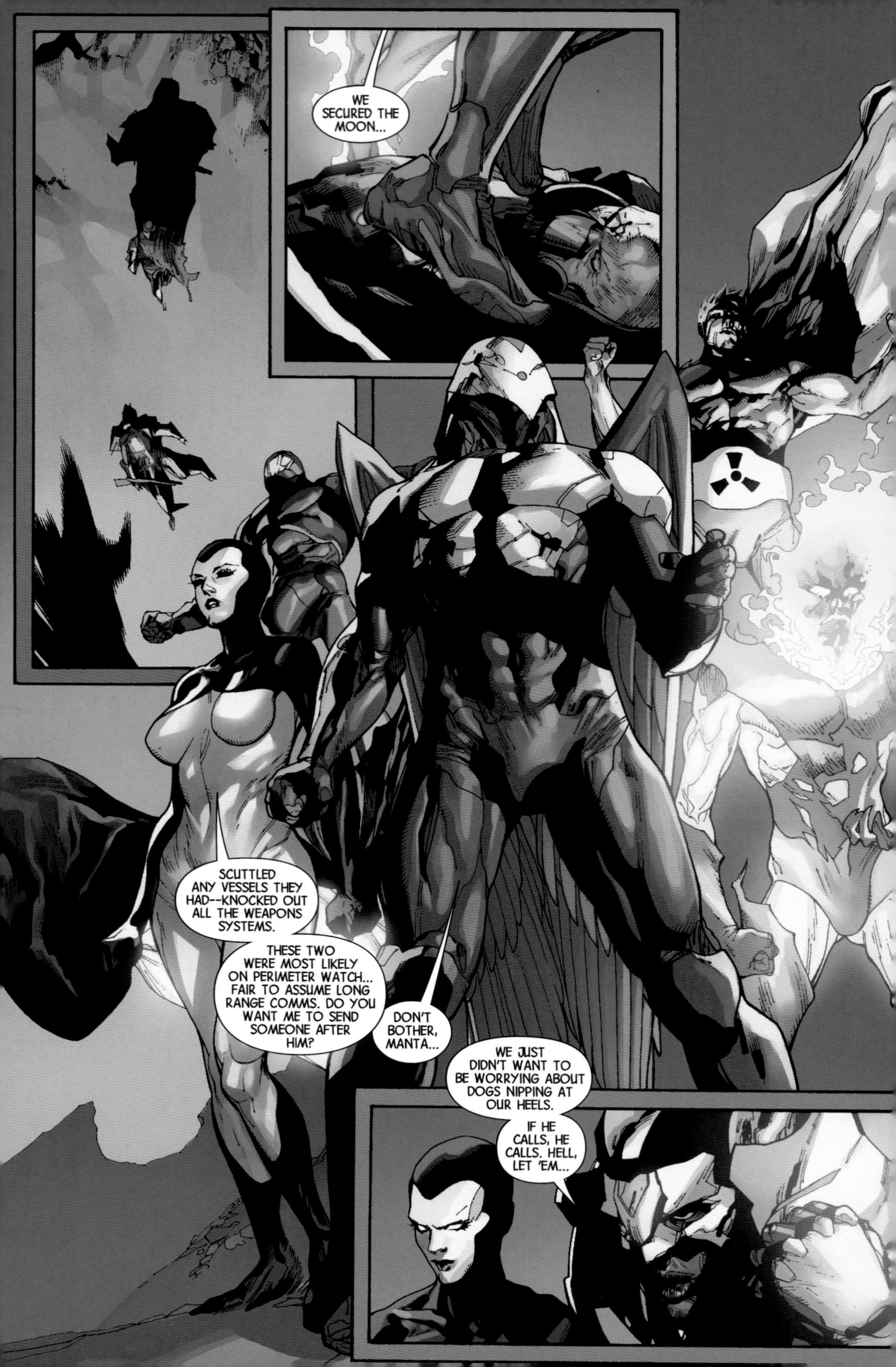
WE SECURED THE MOON...
SCUTTLED ANY VESSELS THEY HAD--KNOCKED OUT ALL THE WEAPONS SYSTEMS.
THESE TWO WERE MOST LIKELY ON PERIMETER WATCH... FAIR TO ASSUME LONG RANGE COMMS. DO YOU WANT ME TO SEND SOMEONE AFTER HIM?
DON'T BOTHER, MANTA...
WE JUST DIDN'T WANT TO BE WORRYING ABOUT DOGS NIPPING AT OUR HEELS.
IF HE CALLS, HE CALLS. HELL, LET 'EM...

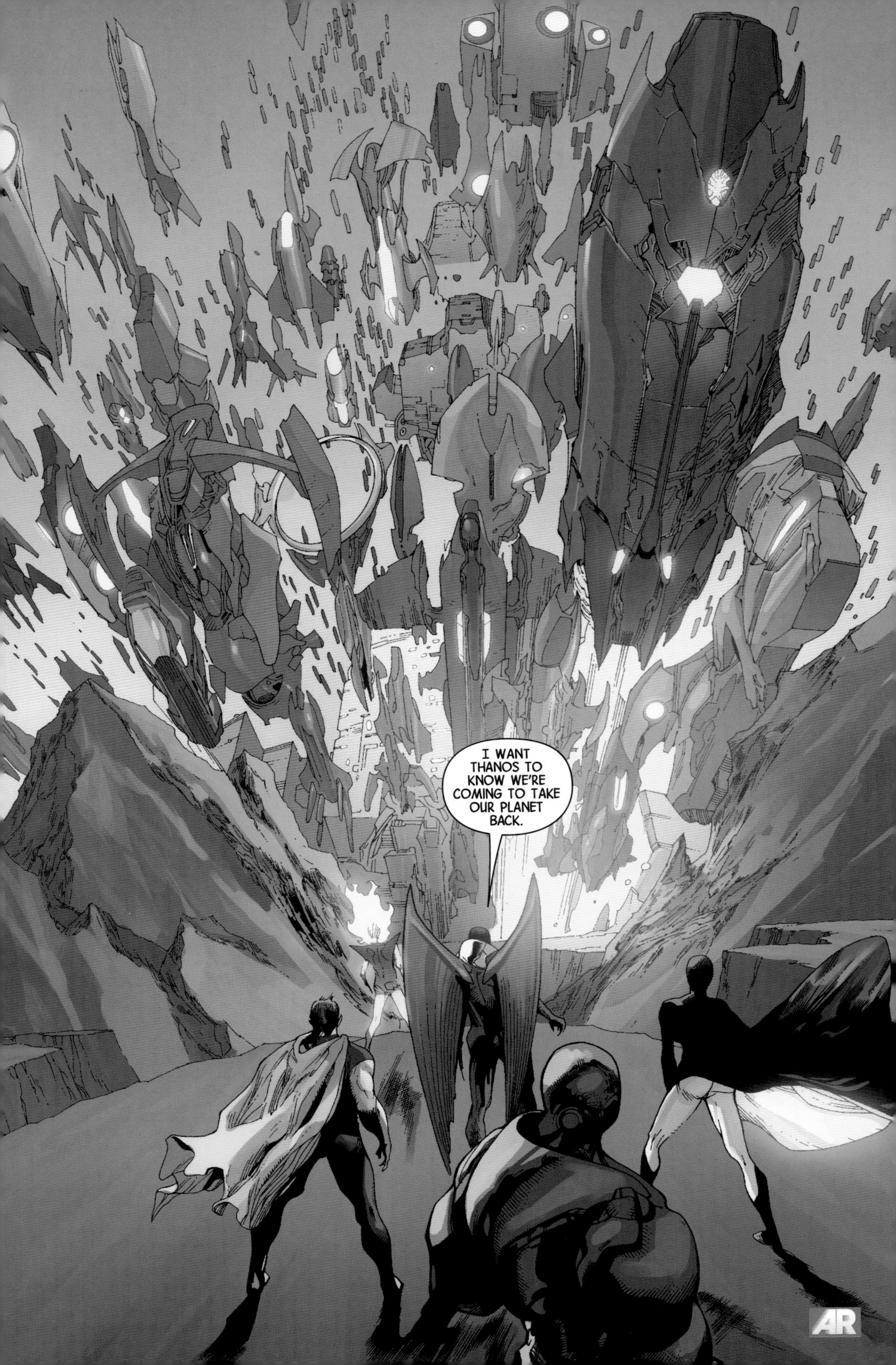
I WANT THANOS TO KNOW WE'RE COMING TO TAKE OUR PLANET BACK.

PLANS AND INTENTIONS

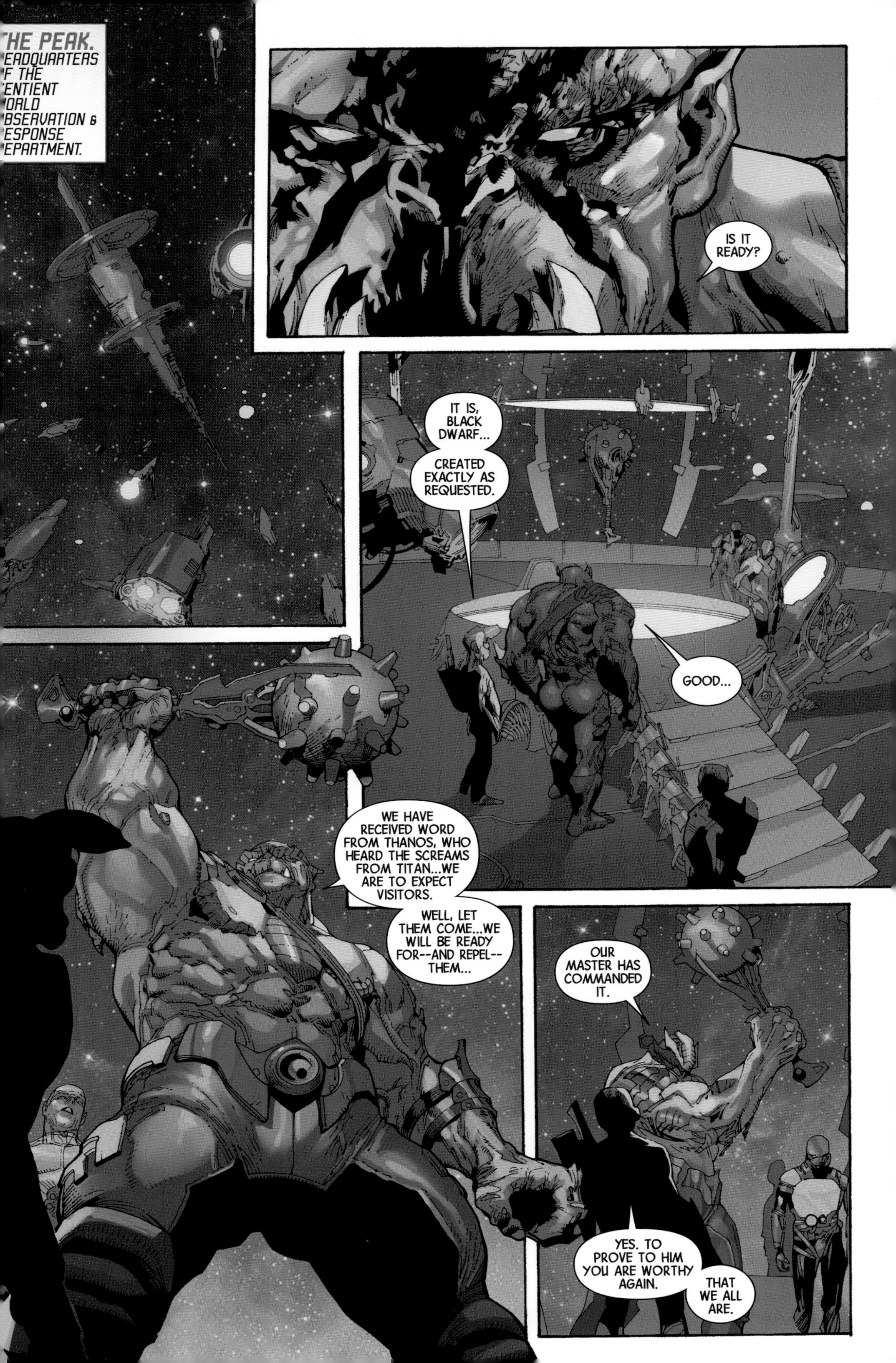
THE PEAK. HEADQUARTERS OF THE SENTIENT WORLD OBSERVATION & RESPONSE DEPARTMENT.
IS IT READY?
IT IS, BLACK DWARF...
CREATED EXACTLY AS REQUESTED.
GOOD...
WE HAVE RECEIVED WORD FROM THANOS, WHO HEARD THE SCREAMS FROM TITAN...WE ARE TO EXPECT VISITORS.
WELL, LET THEM COME...WE WILL BE READY FOR--AND REPEL--THEM...
OUR MASTER HAS COMMANDED IT.
YES. TO PROVE TO HIM YOU ARE WORTHY AGAIN.
THAT WE ALL ARE.

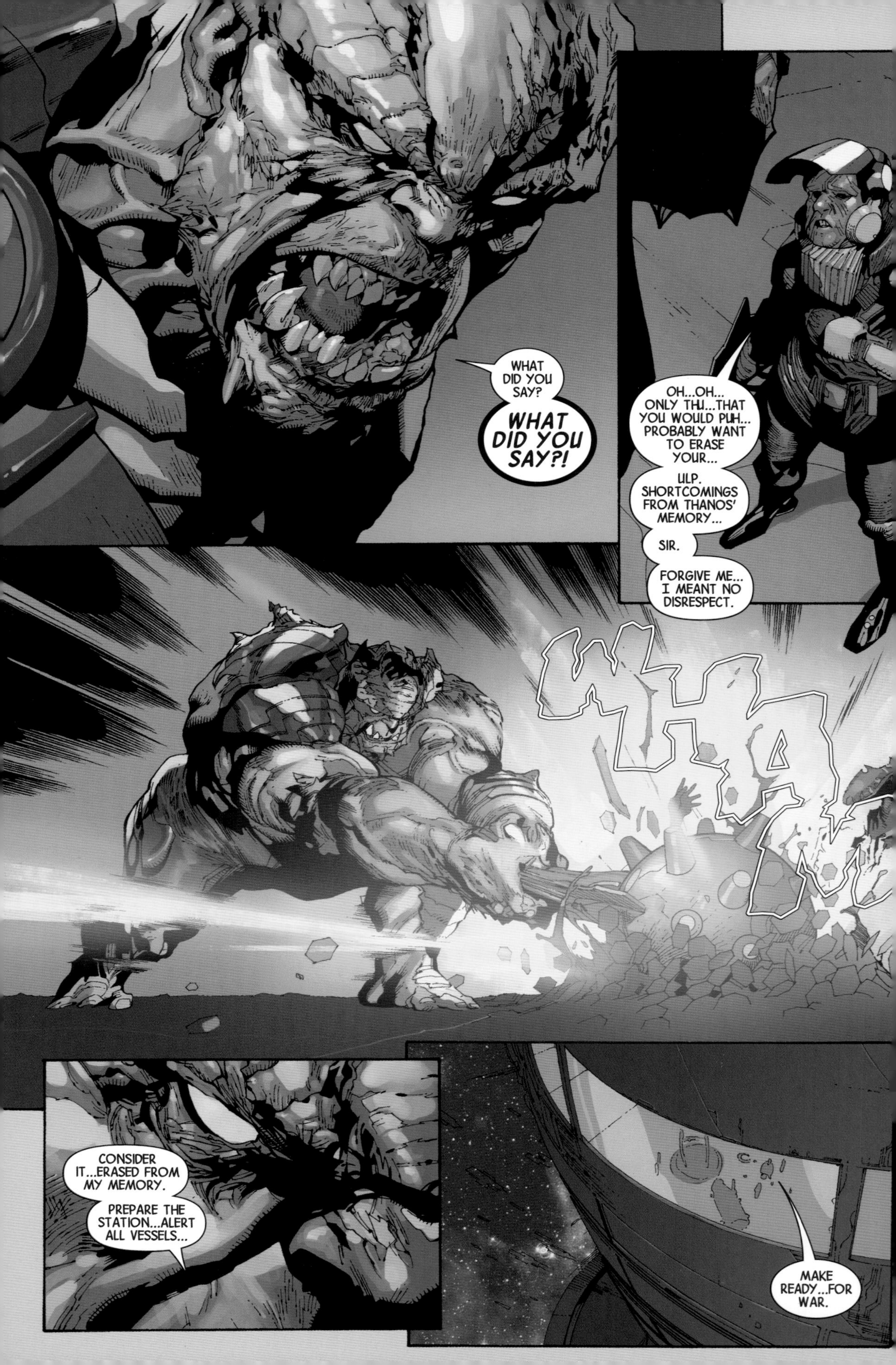
WHAT DID YOU SAY?
WHAT DID YOU SAY?!
OH...OH... ONLY THU...THAT YOU WOULD PUH... PROBABLY WANT TO ERASE YOUR...
ULP. SHORTCOMINGS FROM THANOS' MEMORY...
SIR.
FORGIVE ME... I MEANT NO DISRESPECT.
CONSIDER IT...ERASED FROM MY MEMORY.
PREPARE THE STATION...ALERT ALL VESSELS...
MAKE READY...FOR WAR.

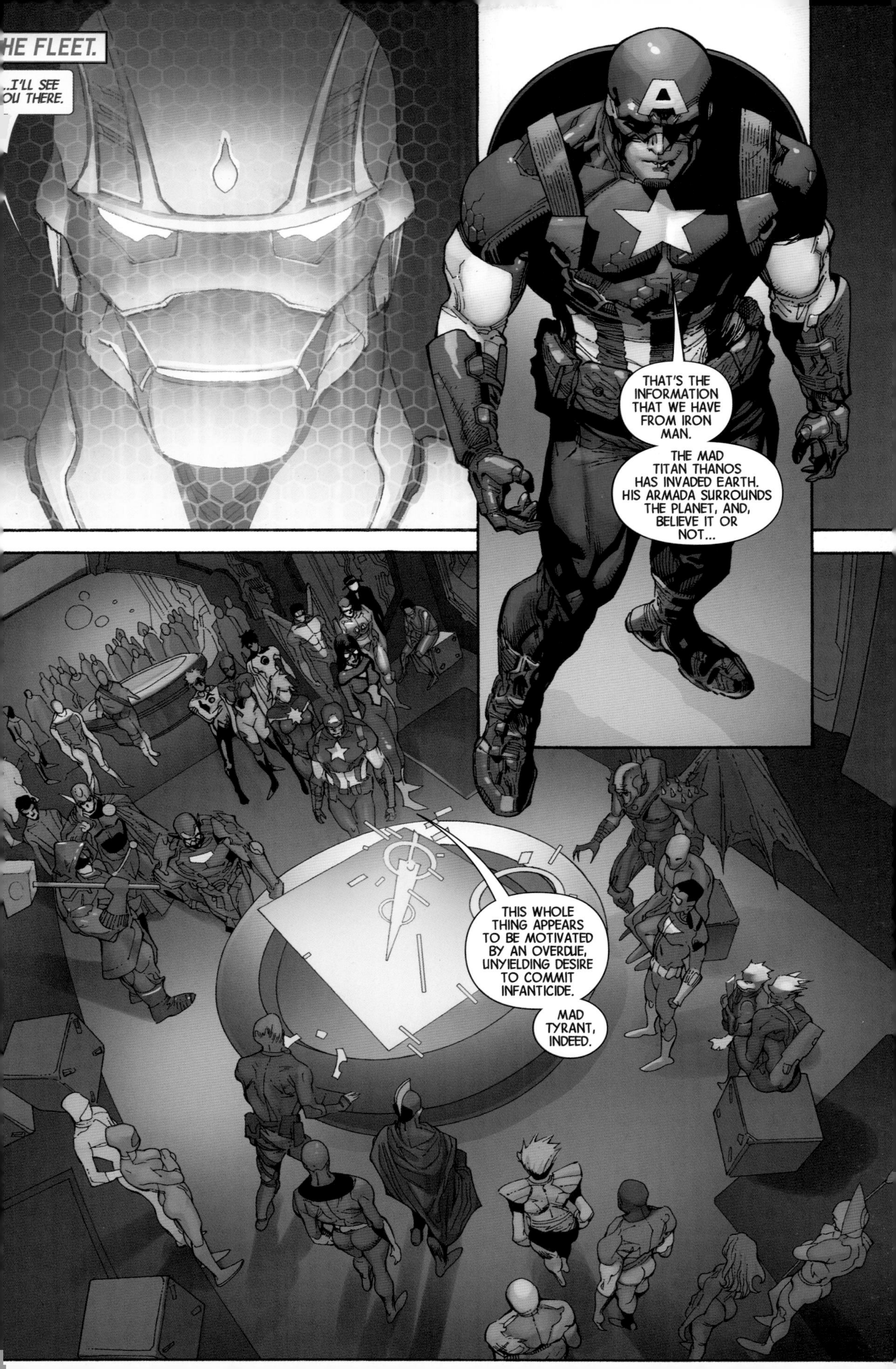
HE FLEET.
...I'LL SEE
OU THERE.
THAT'S THE INFORMATION THAT WE HAVE FROM IRON MAN.
THE MAD TITAN THANOS HAS INVADED EARTH. HIS ARMADA SURROUNDS THE PLANET, AND, BELIEVE IT OR NOT...
THIS WHOLE THING APPEARS TO BE MOTIVATED BY AN OVERDUE, UNYIELDING DESIRE TO COMMIT INFANTICIDE.
MAD TYRANT, INDEED.

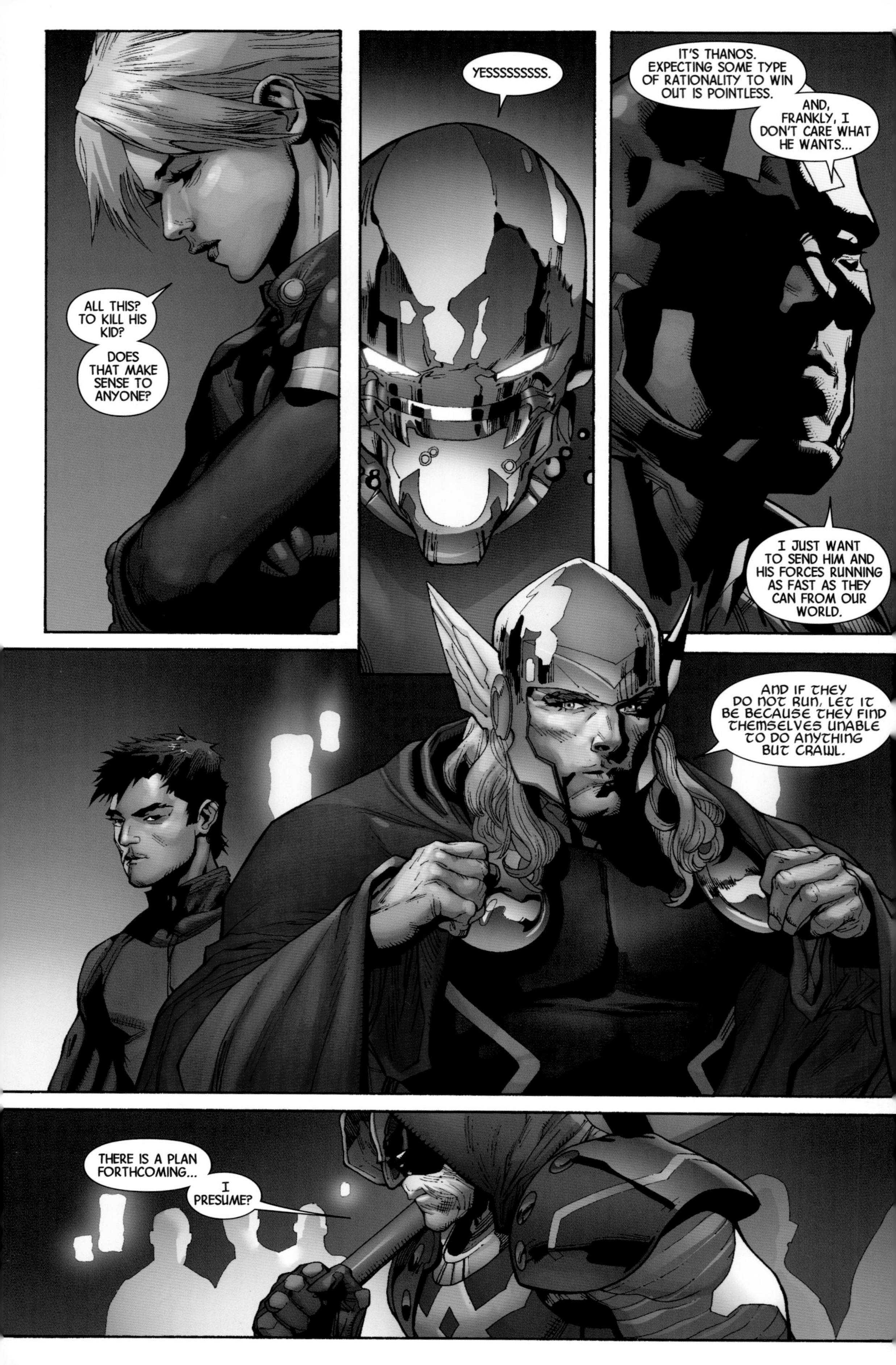
ALL THIS? TO KILL HIS KID?
DOES THAT MAKE SENSE TO ANYONE?
YESSSSSSSSS.
IT'S THANOS. EXPECTING SOME TYPE OF RATIONALITY TO WIN OUT IS POINTLESS.
AND, FRANKLY, I DON'T CARE WHAT HE WANTS...
I JUST WANT TO SEND HIM AND HIS FORCES RUNNING AS FAST AS THEY CAN FROM OUR WORLD.
AND IF THEY DO NOT RUN, LET IT BE BECAUSE THEY FIND THEMSELVES UNABLE TO DO ANYTHING BUT CRAWL.
THERE IS A PLAN FORTHCOMING...
I PRESUME?

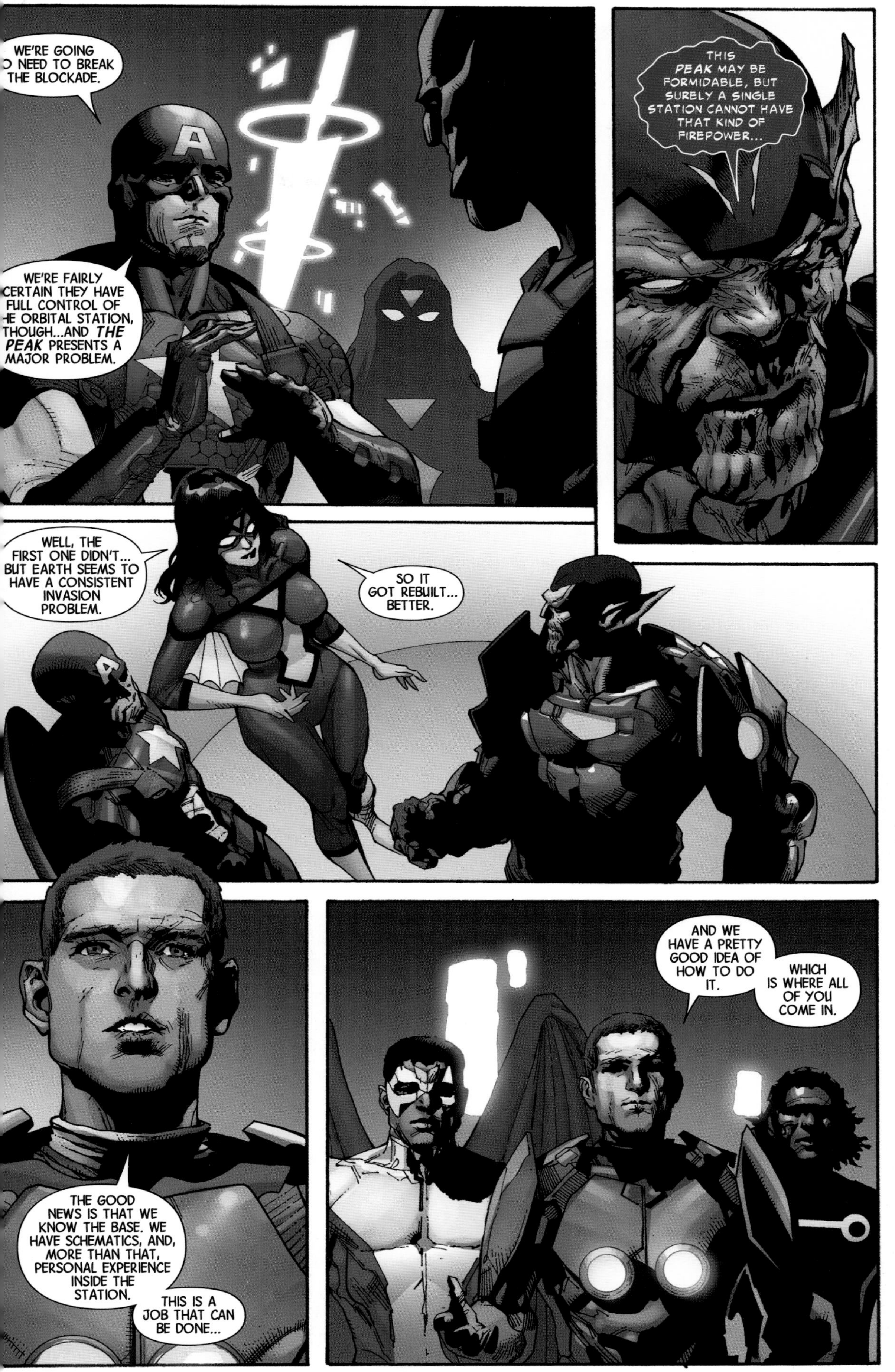

WE'RE GOING TO NEED TO BREAK THE BLOCKADE.
WE'RE FAIRLY CERTAIN THEY HAVE FULL CONTROL OF THE ORBITAL STATION, THOUGH...AND THE PEAK PRESENTS A MAJOR PROBLEM.
THIS PEAK MAY BE FORMIDABLE, BUT SURELY A SINGLE STATION CANNOT HAVE THAT KIND OF FIREPOWER...
WELL, THE FIRST ONE DIDN'T... BUT EARTH SEEMS TO HAVE A CONSISTENT INVASION PROBLEM.
SO IT GOT REBUILT... BETTER.
THE GOOD NEWS IS THAT WE KNOW THE BASE. WE HAVE SCHEMATICS, AND, MORE THAN THAT, PERSONAL EXPERIENCE INSIDE THE STATION.
THIS IS A JOB THAT CAN BE DONE...
AND WE HAVE A PRETTY GOOD IDEA OF HOW TO DO IT.
WHICH IS WHERE ALL OF YOU COME IN.

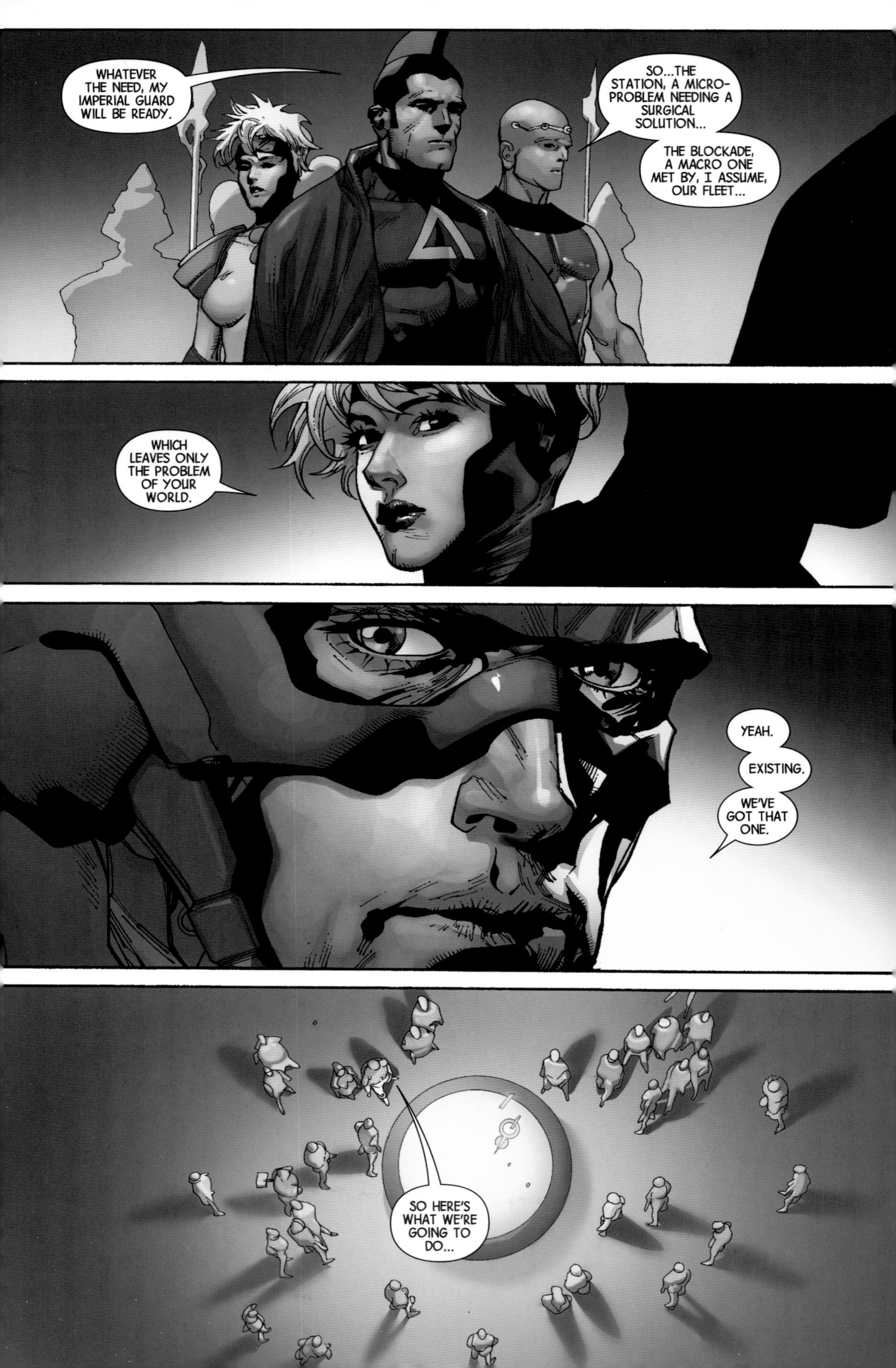
WHATEVER THE NEED, MY IMPERIAL GUARD WILL BE READY.
SO...THE STATION, A MICRO-PROBLEM NEEDING A SURGICAL SOLUTION...
THE BLOCKADE, A MACRO ONE MET BY, I ASSUME, OUR FLEET...
WHICH LEAVES ONLY THE PROBLEM OF YOUR WORLD.
YEAH.
EXISTING.
WE'VE GOT THAT ONE.
SO HERE'S WHAT WE'RE GOING TO DO...

A GREATER PURPOSE

◆

JUMP'S COMPLETED. ON OUR FINAL APPROACH NOW. A FORERUNNER HAS CONFIRMED WHAT THE SHI'AR LONG RANGE SCANS PICKED UP.

WE'RE BASICALLY GOING TO BE CRASHING A BLOCKADE.

AS EXPECTED. NUMBERS?

THE COUNCIL WORLDS SPARED WHAT THEY COULD IN THE HOPES THAT WE WOULD OVERWHELM THE PIRATES...SEND THEM RUNNING WHEN THEY SAW WHAT WAS COMING.

BUT THEY'VE GOT ABOUT WHAT WE HAVE...

AND IN ADDITION TO THAT--

THEY'RE FRESH, RESTED...NOT BROKEN AND BEATEN.

LIKE BEASTS WAITING ON WOUNDED PREY.

SOMETHING YOU WANT TO SAY, EDEN?

I'M TIRED. I CAN'T BELIEVE WHAT I JUST LIVED THROUGH AND NOW I HAVE TO DO IT AGAIN...

AND THIS TIME WITH THE LIVES OF MY FAMILY AND PEOPLE AT STAKE.

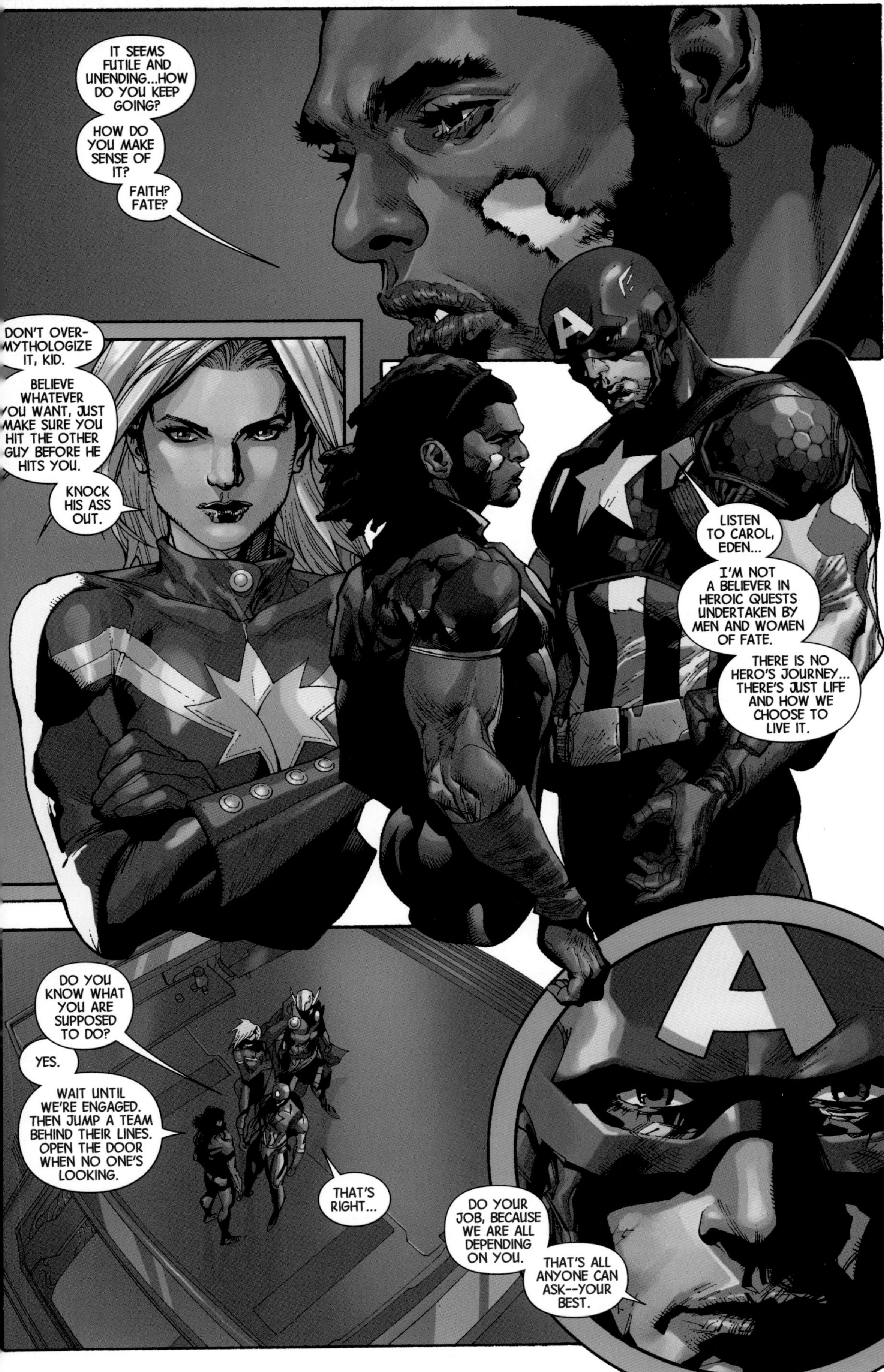

IT SEEMS FUTILE AND UNENDING...HOW DO YOU KEEP GOING?
HOW DO YOU MAKE SENSE OF IT?
FAITH? FATE?
DON'T OVER-MYTHOLOGIZE IT, KID.
BELIEVE WHATEVER YOU WANT, JUST MAKE SURE YOU HIT THE OTHER GUY BEFORE HE HITS YOU.
KNOCK HIS ASS OUT.
LISTEN TO CAROL, EDEN...
I'M NOT A BELIEVER IN HEROIC QUESTS UNDERTAKEN BY MEN AND WOMEN OF FATE.
THERE IS NO HERO'S JOURNEY... THERE'S JUST LIFE AND HOW WE CHOOSE TO LIVE IT.
DO YOU KNOW WHAT YOU ARE SUPPOSED TO DO?
YES.
WAIT UNTIL WE'RE ENGAGED. THEN JUMP A TEAM BEHIND THEIR LINES. OPEN THE DOOR WHEN NO ONE'S LOOKING.
THAT'S RIGHT...
DO YOUR JOB, BECAUSE WE ARE ALL DEPENDING ON YOU.
THAT'S ALL ANYONE CAN ASK--YOUR BEST.

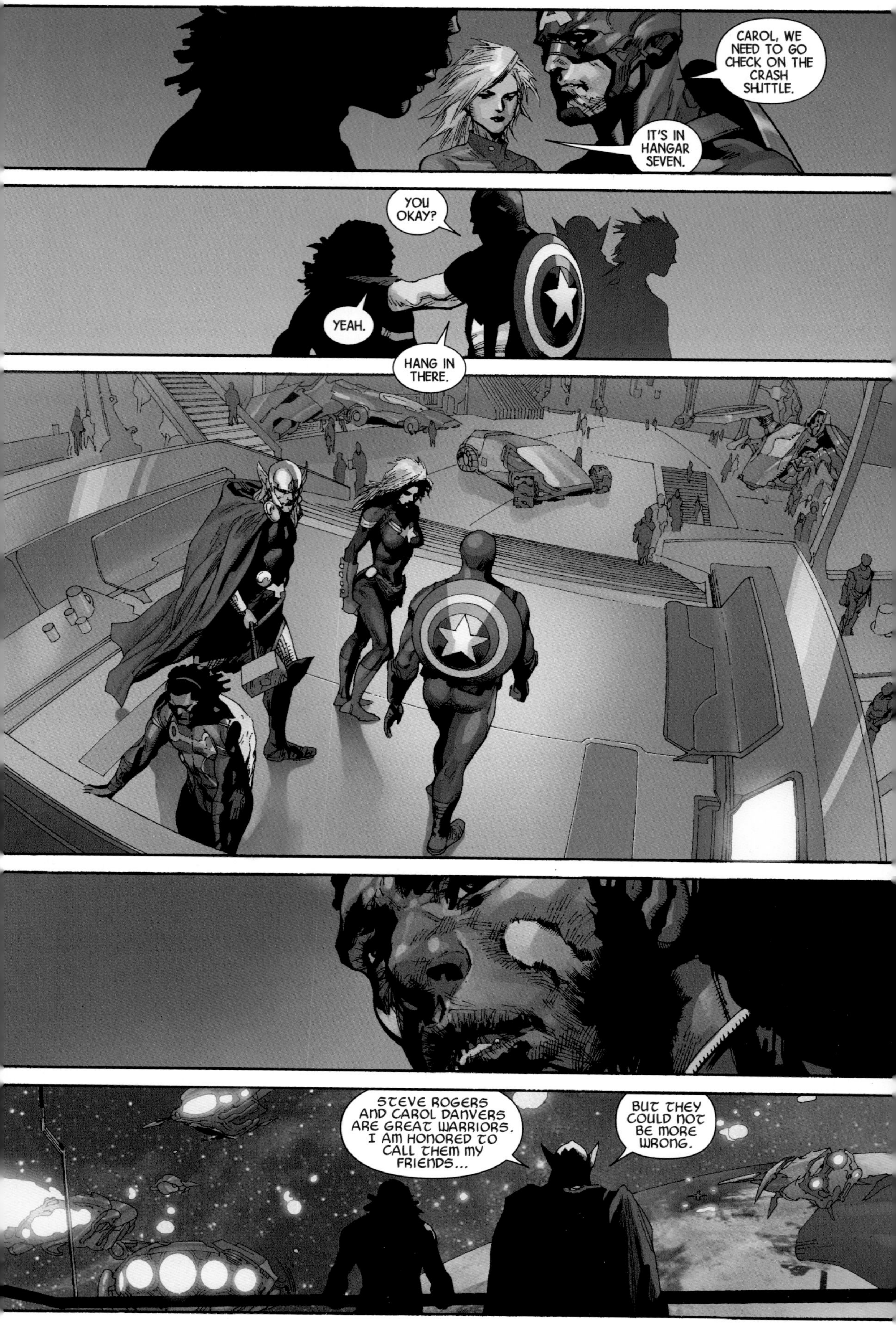
CAROL, WE NEED TO GO CHECK ON THE CRASH SHUTTLE.
IT'S IN HANGAR SEVEN.
YOU OKAY?
YEAH.
HANG IN THERE.
STEVE ROGERS AND CAROL DANVERS ARE GREAT WARRIORS. I AM HONORED TO CALL THEM MY FRIENDS...
BUT THEY COULD NOT BE MORE WRONG.

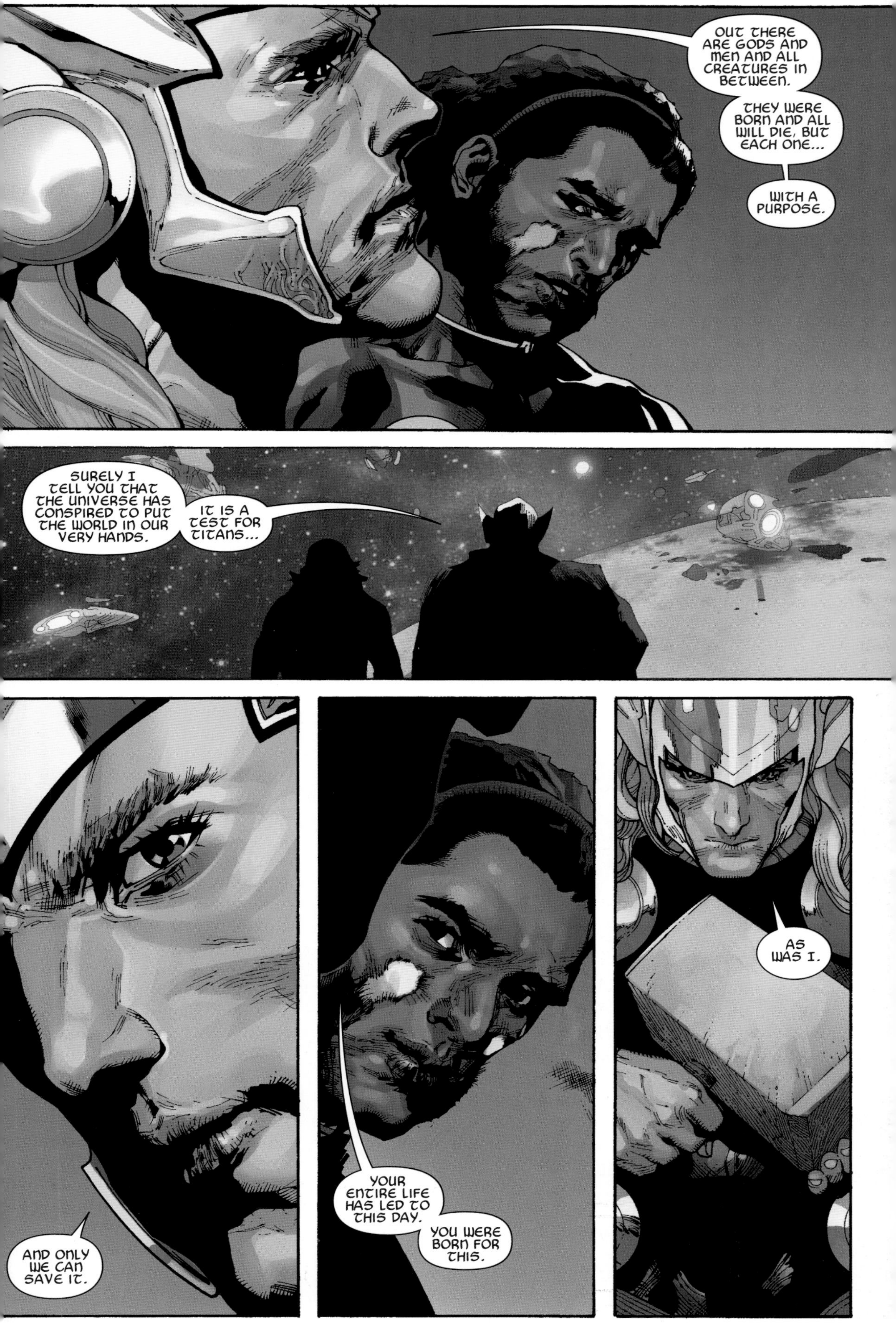
OUT THERE ARE GODS AND MEN AND ALL CREATURES IN BETWEEN.
THEY WERE BORN AND ALL WILL DIE, BUT EACH ONE...
WITH A PURPOSE.
SURELY I TELL YOU THAT THE UNIVERSE HAS CONSPIRED TO PUT THE WORLD IN OUR VERY HANDS.
IT IS A TEST FOR TITANS...
AND ONLY WE CAN SAVE IT.
YOUR ENTIRE LIFE HAS LED TO THIS DAY.
YOU WERE BORN FOR THIS.
AS WAS I.

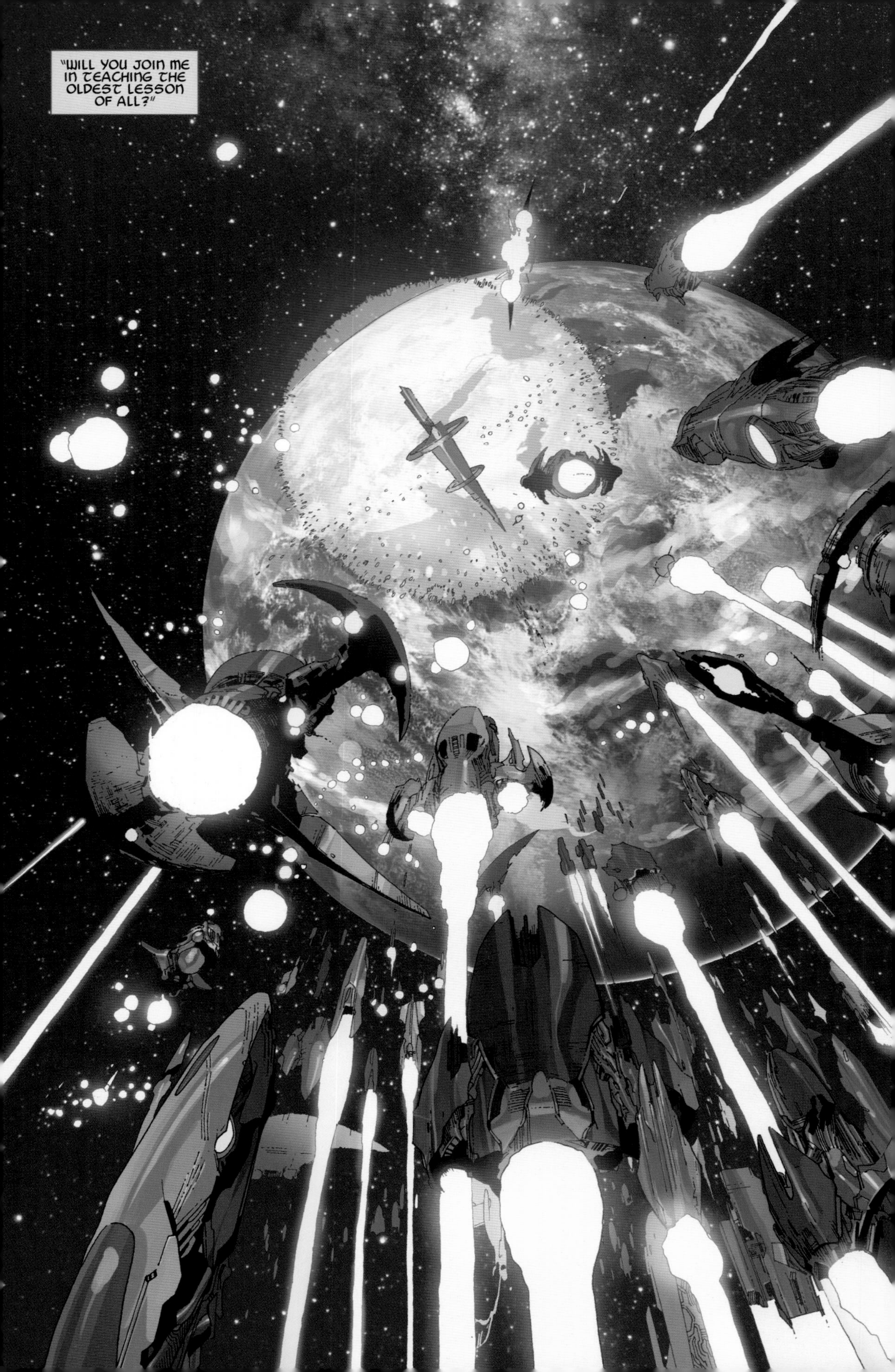
"WILL YOU JOIN ME IN TEACHING THE OLDEST LESSON OF ALL?"

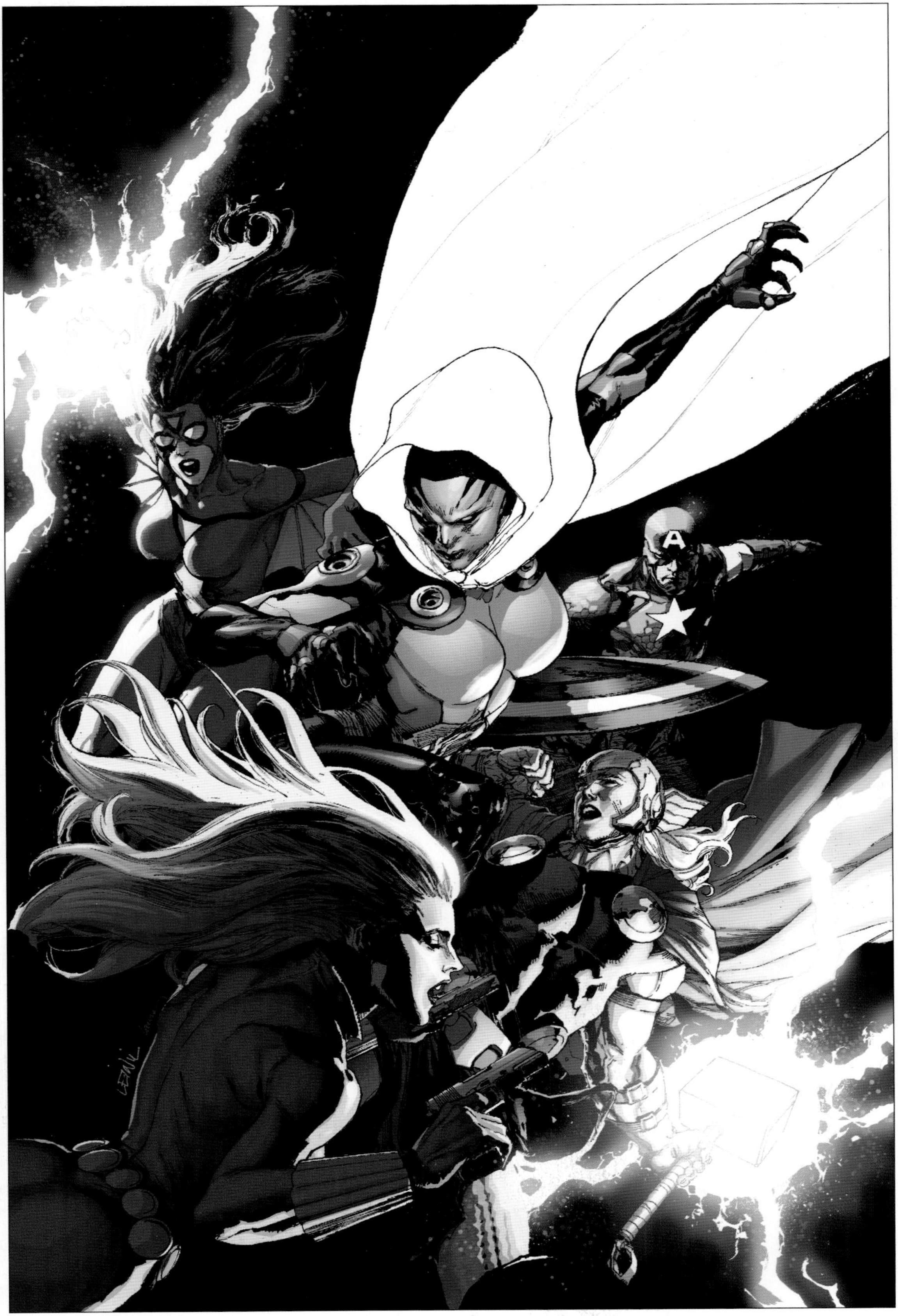

A WORD FROM THE HEAVENS

◆

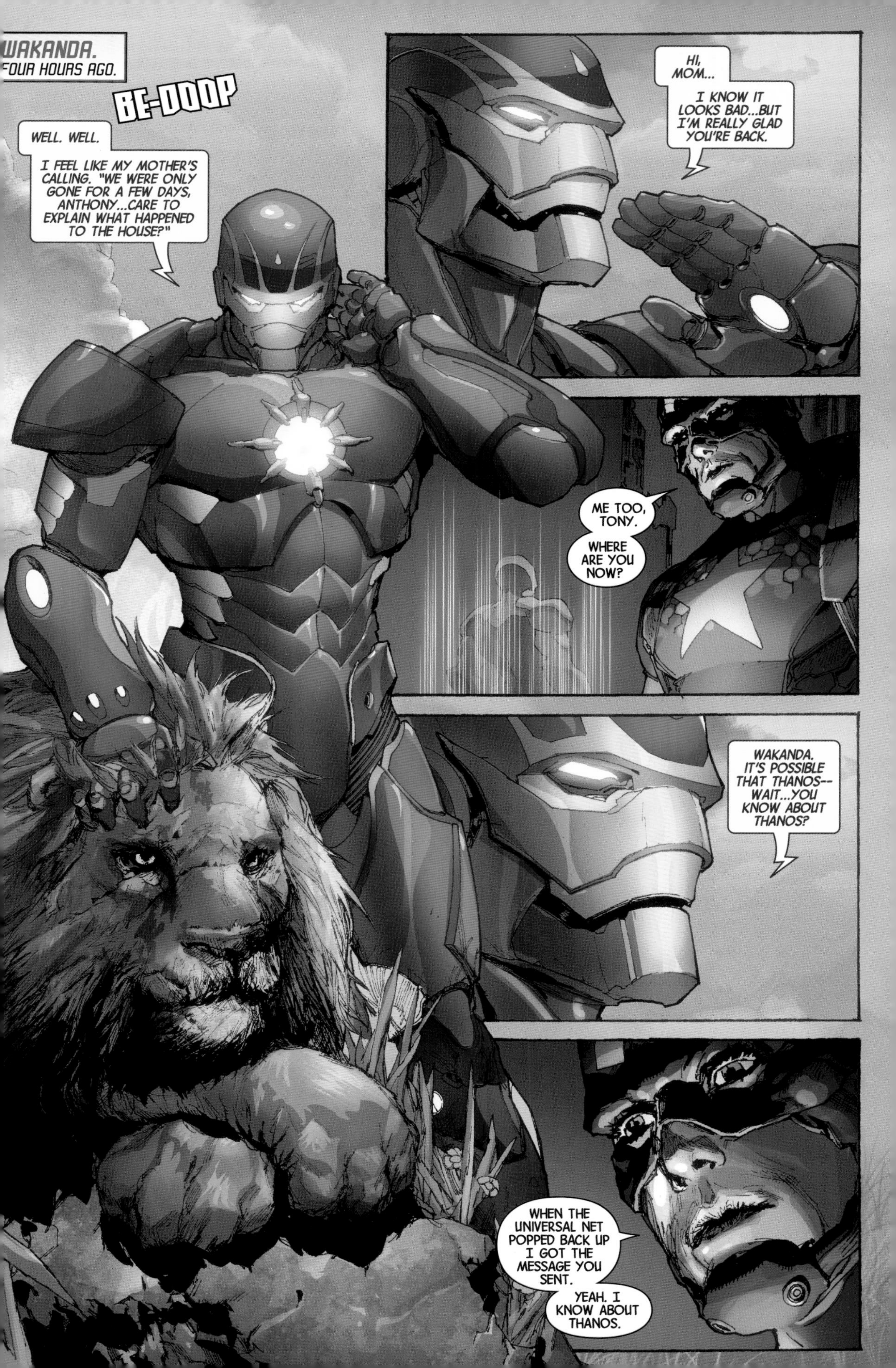
WAKANDA. FOUR HOURS AGO.
BE-DOOP
WELL. WELL.
I FEEL LIKE MY MOTHER'S CALLING. "WE WERE ONLY GONE FOR A FEW DAYS, ANTHONY...CARE TO EXPLAIN WHAT HAPPENED TO THE HOUSE?"
HI, MOM...
I KNOW IT LOOKS BAD...BUT I'M REALLY GLAD YOU'RE BACK.
ME TOO, TONY.
WHERE ARE YOU NOW?
WAKANDA. IT'S POSSIBLE THAT THANOS--WAIT...YOU KNOW ABOUT THANOS?
WHEN THE UNIVERSAL NET POPPED BACK UP I GOT THE MESSAGE YOU SENT.
YEAH. I KNOW ABOUT THANOS.

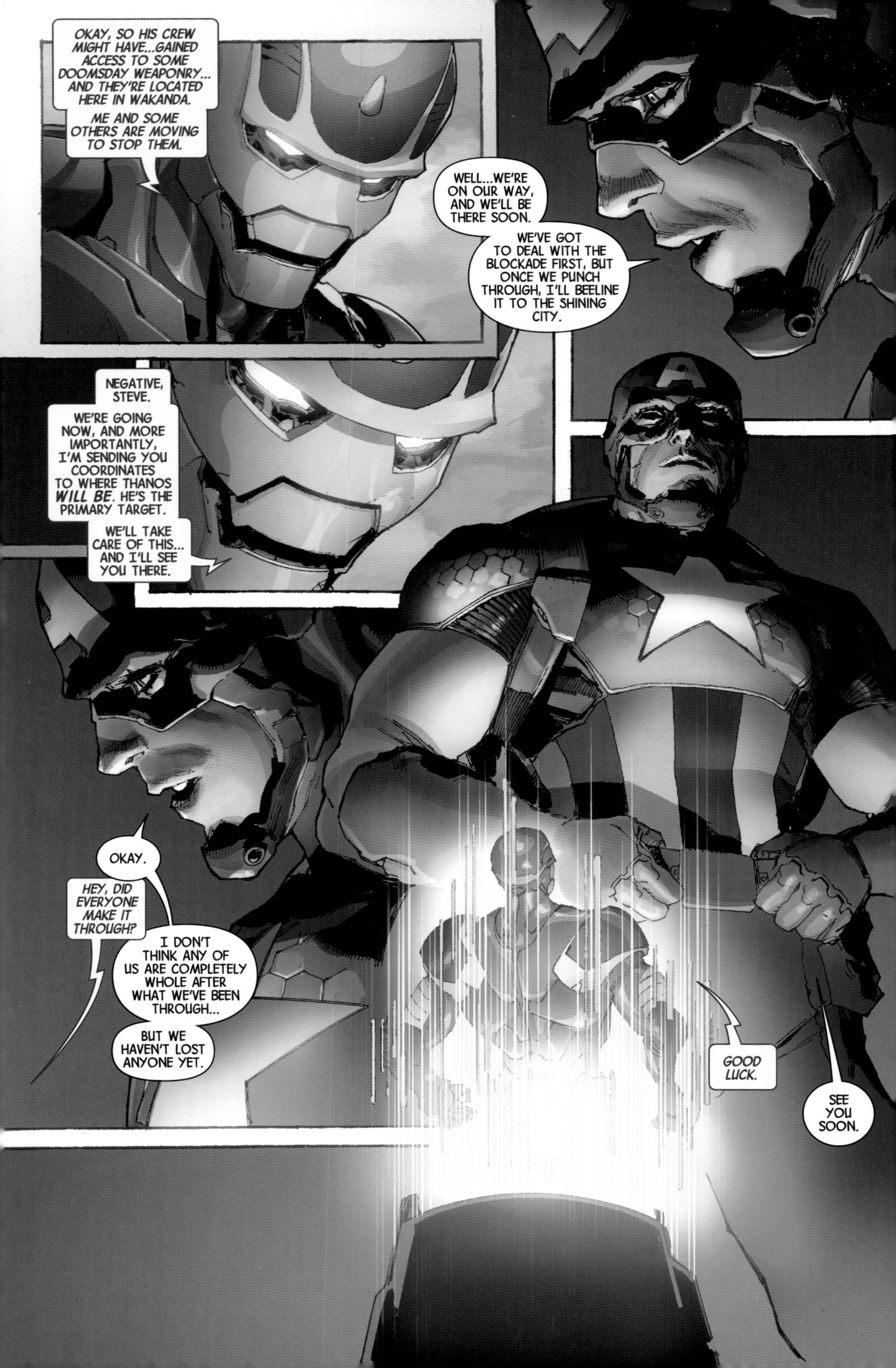
OKAY, SO HIS CREW MIGHT HAVE...GAINED ACCESS TO SOME DOOMSDAY WEAPONRY... AND THEY'RE LOCATED HERE IN WAKANDA.
ME AND SOME OTHERS ARE MOVING TO STOP THEM.
WELL...WE'RE ON OUR WAY, AND WE'LL BE THERE SOON.
WE'VE GOT TO DEAL WITH THE BLOCKADE FIRST, BUT ONCE WE PUNCH THROUGH, I'LL BEELINE IT TO THE SHINING CITY.
NEGATIVE, STEVE.
WE'RE GOING NOW, AND MORE IMPORTANTLY, I'M SENDING YOU COORDINATES TO WHERE THANOS WILL BE. HE'S THE PRIMARY TARGET.
WE'LL TAKE CARE OF THIS... AND I'LL SEE YOU THERE.
OKAY.
HEY, DID EVERYONE MAKE IT THROUGH?
I DON'T THINK ANY OF US ARE COMPLETELY WHOLE AFTER WHAT WE'VE BEEN THROUGH...
BUT WE HAVEN'T LOST ANYONE YET.
GOOD LUCK.
SEE YOU SOON.

HOMECOMING

◆

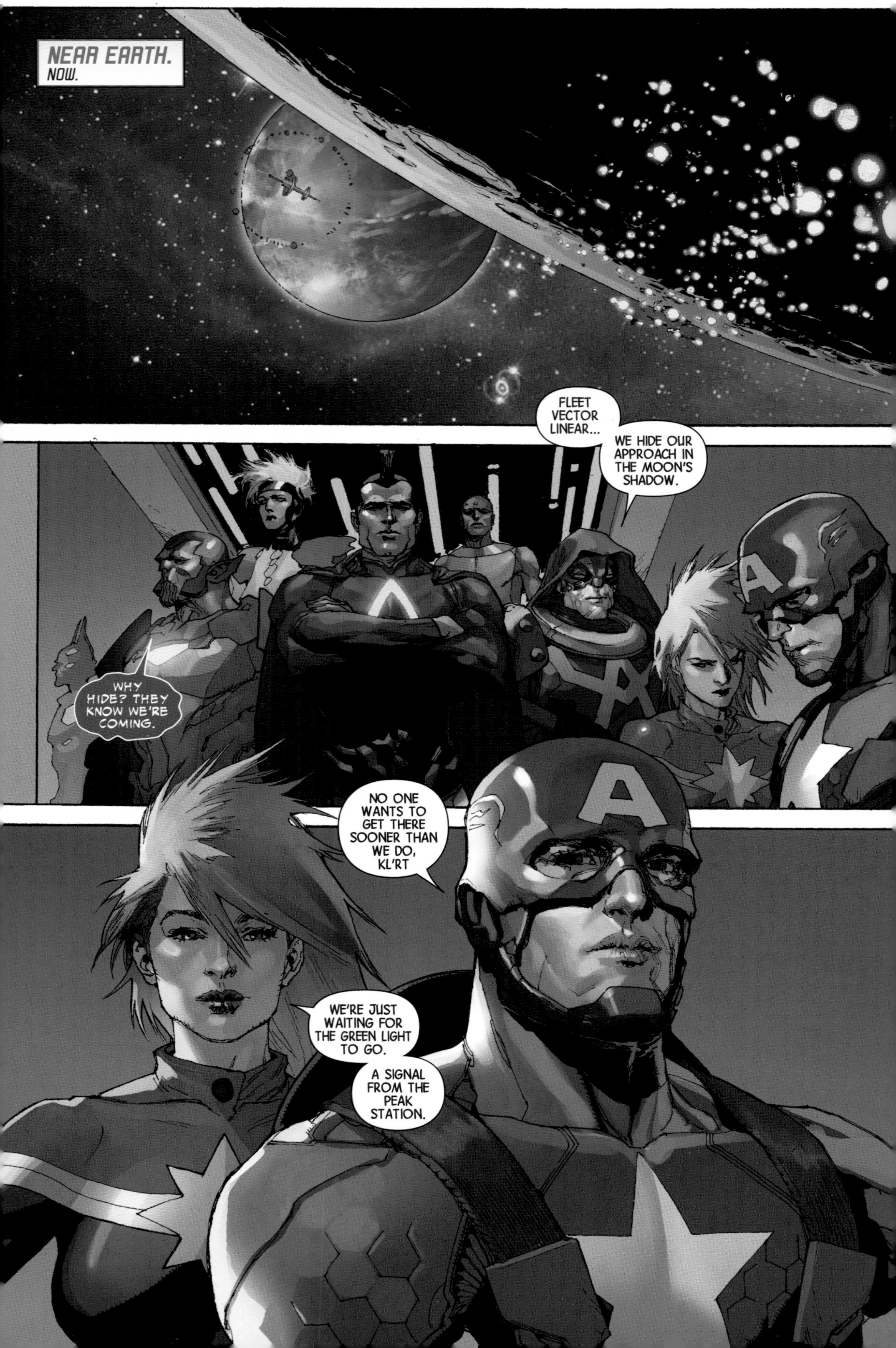
NEAR EARTH. NOW.
FLEET VECTOR LINEAR...
WE HIDE OUR APPROACH IN THE MOON'S SHADOW.
WHY HIDE? THEY KNOW WE'RE COMING.
NO ONE WANTS TO GET THERE SOONER THAN WE DO, KL'RT
WE'RE JUST WAITING FOR THE GREEN LIGHT TO GO.
A SIGNAL FROM THE PEAK STATION.

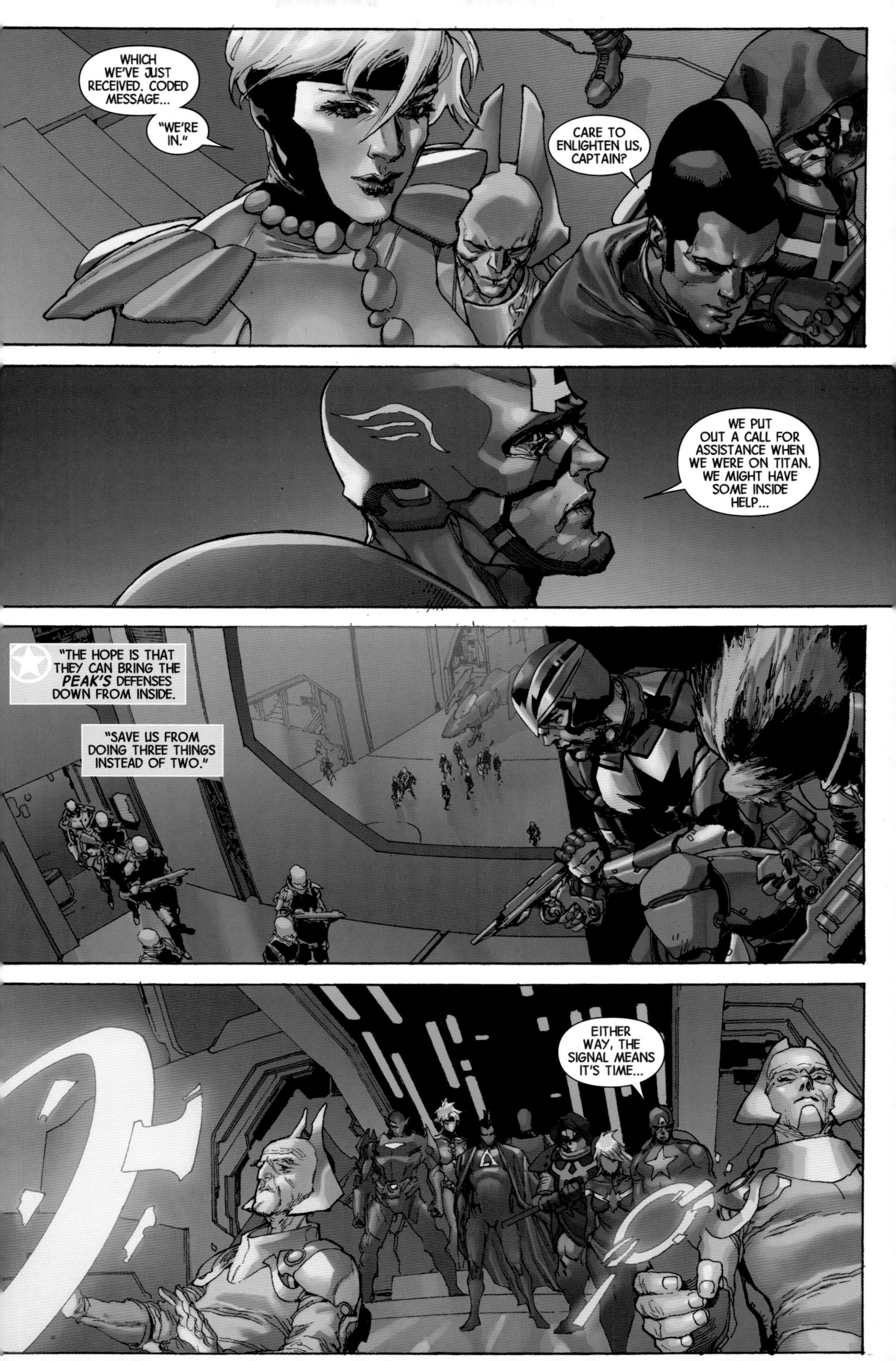
WHICH WE'VE JUST RECEIVED. CODED MESSAGE...
"WE'RE IN."
CARE TO ENLIGHTEN US, CAPTAIN?
WE PUT OUT A CALL FOR ASSISTANCE WHEN WE WERE ON TITAN. WE MIGHT HAVE SOME INSIDE HELP...
"THE HOPE IS THAT THEY CAN BRING THE PEAK'S DEFENSES DOWN FROM INSIDE.
"SAVE US FROM DOING THREE THINGS INSTEAD OF TWO."
EITHER WAY, THE SIGNAL MEANS IT'S TIME...

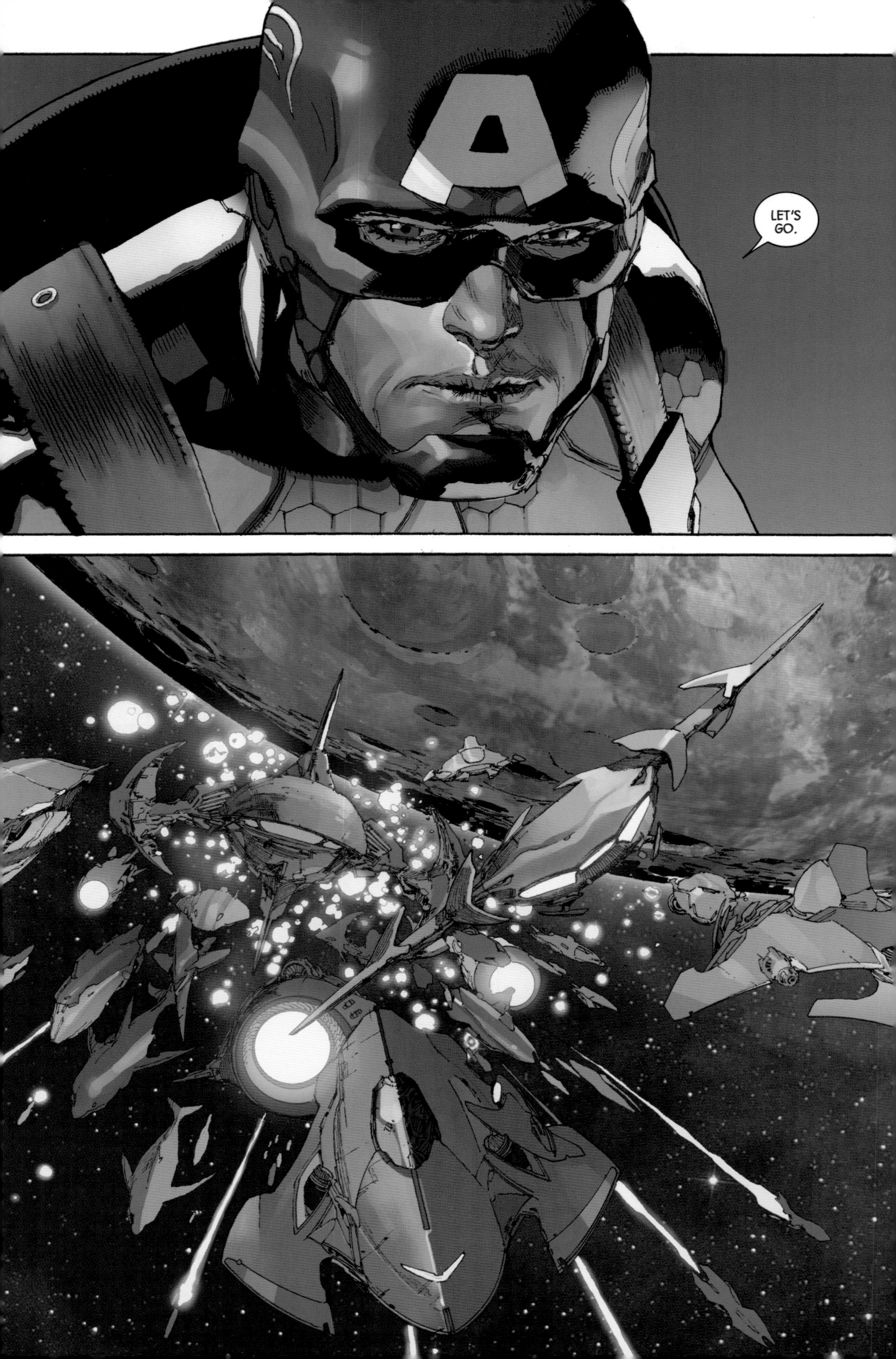
LET'S GO.

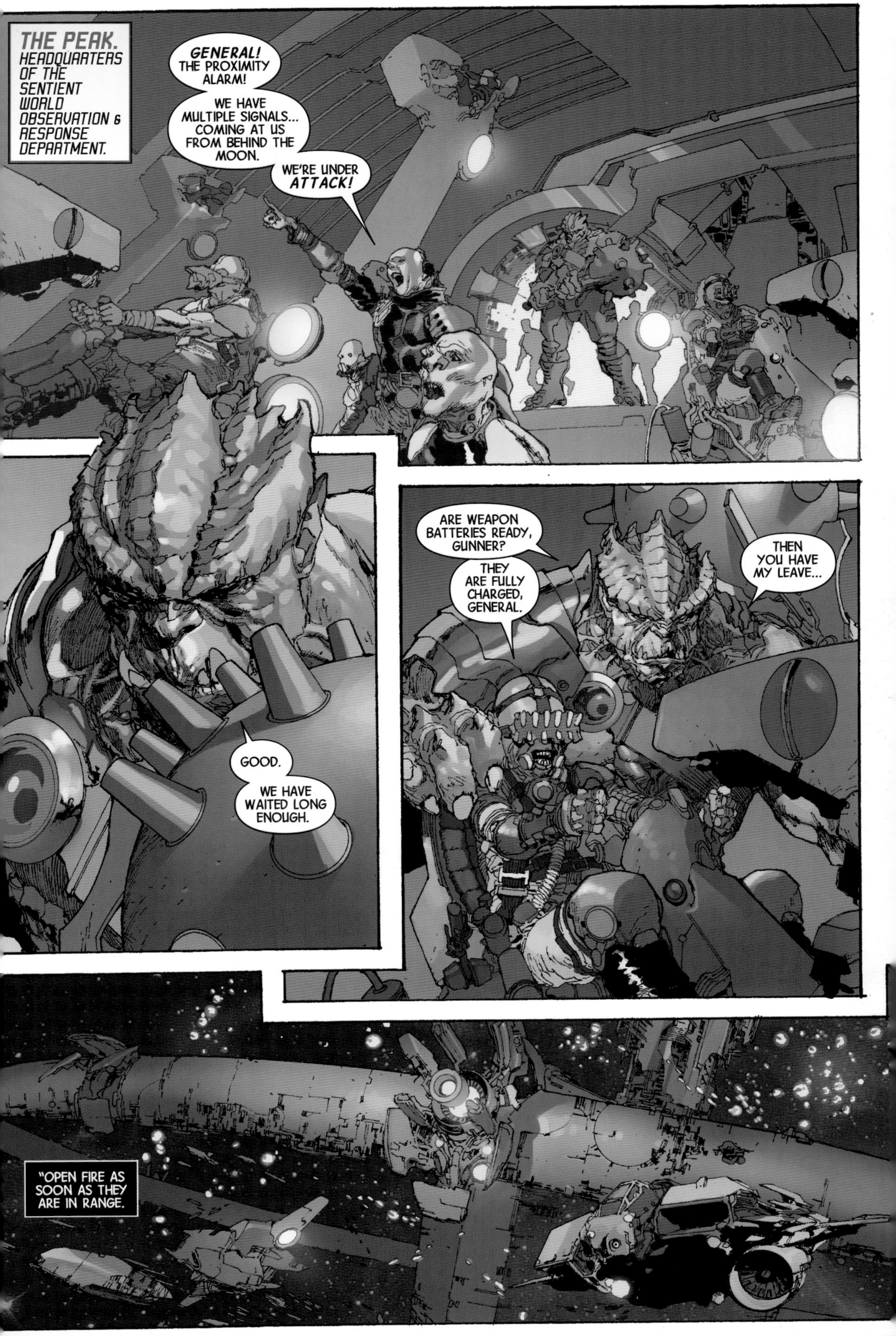
THE PEAK.
HEADQUARTERS OF THE SENTIENT WORLD OBSERVATION & RESPONSE DEPARTMENT.
GENERAL! THE PROXIMITY ALARM!
WE HAVE MULTIPLE SIGNALS... COMING AT US FROM BEHIND THE MOON.
WE'RE UNDER ATTACK!
GOOD.
WE HAVE WAITED LONG ENOUGH.
ARE WEAPON BATTERIES READY, GUNNER?
THEY ARE FULLY CHARGED, GENERAL.
THEN YOU HAVE MY LEAVE...
"OPEN FIRE AS SOON AS THEY ARE IN RANGE.

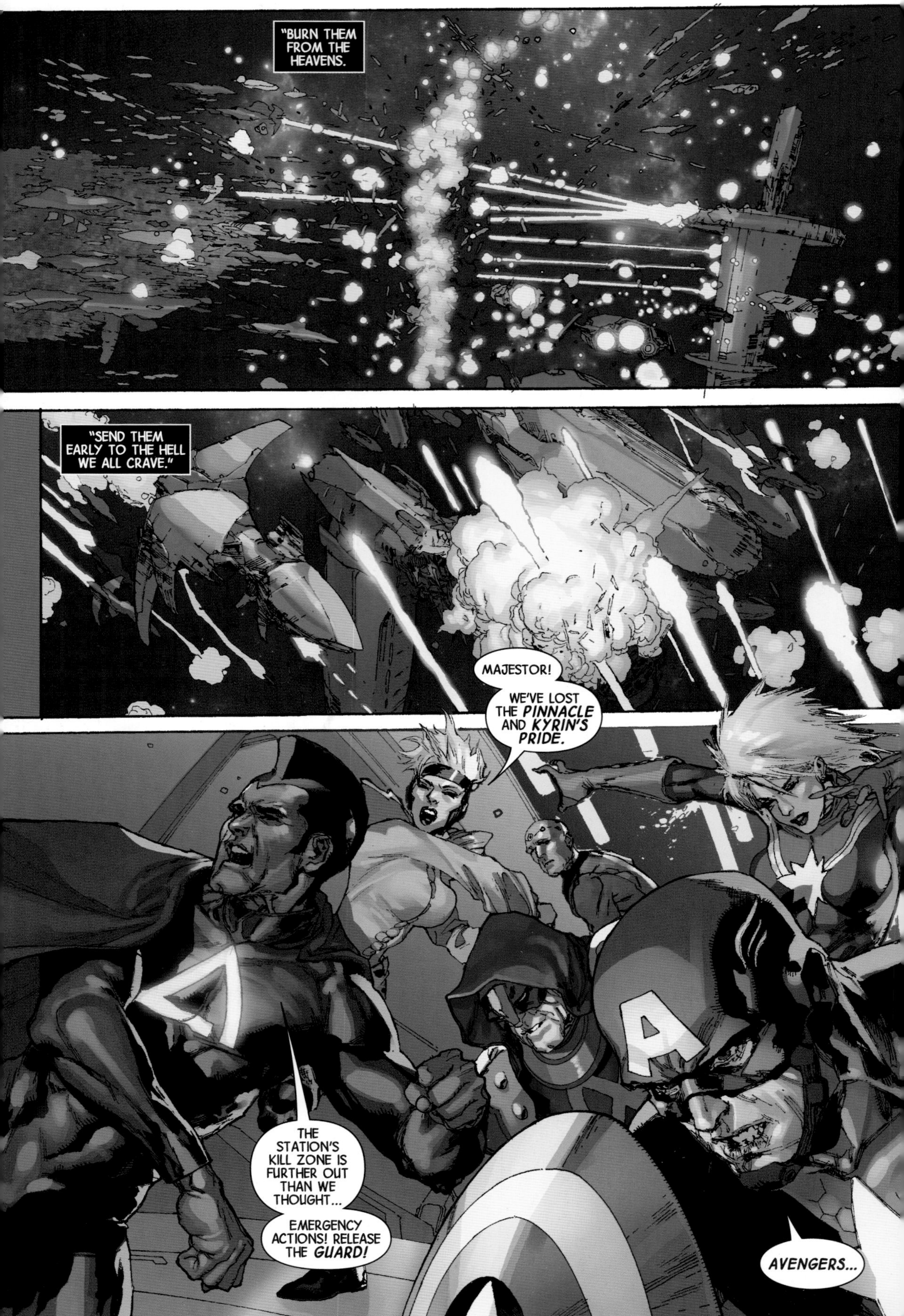
"BURN THEM FROM THE HEAVENS.
"SEND THEM EARLY TO THE HELL WE ALL CRAVE."
MAJESTOR!
WE'VE LOST THE *PINNACLE* AND *KYRIN'S PRIDE.*
THE STATION'S KILL ZONE IS FURTHER OUT THAN WE THOUGHT...
EMERGENCY ACTIONS! RELEASE THE *GUARD!*
AVENGERS...

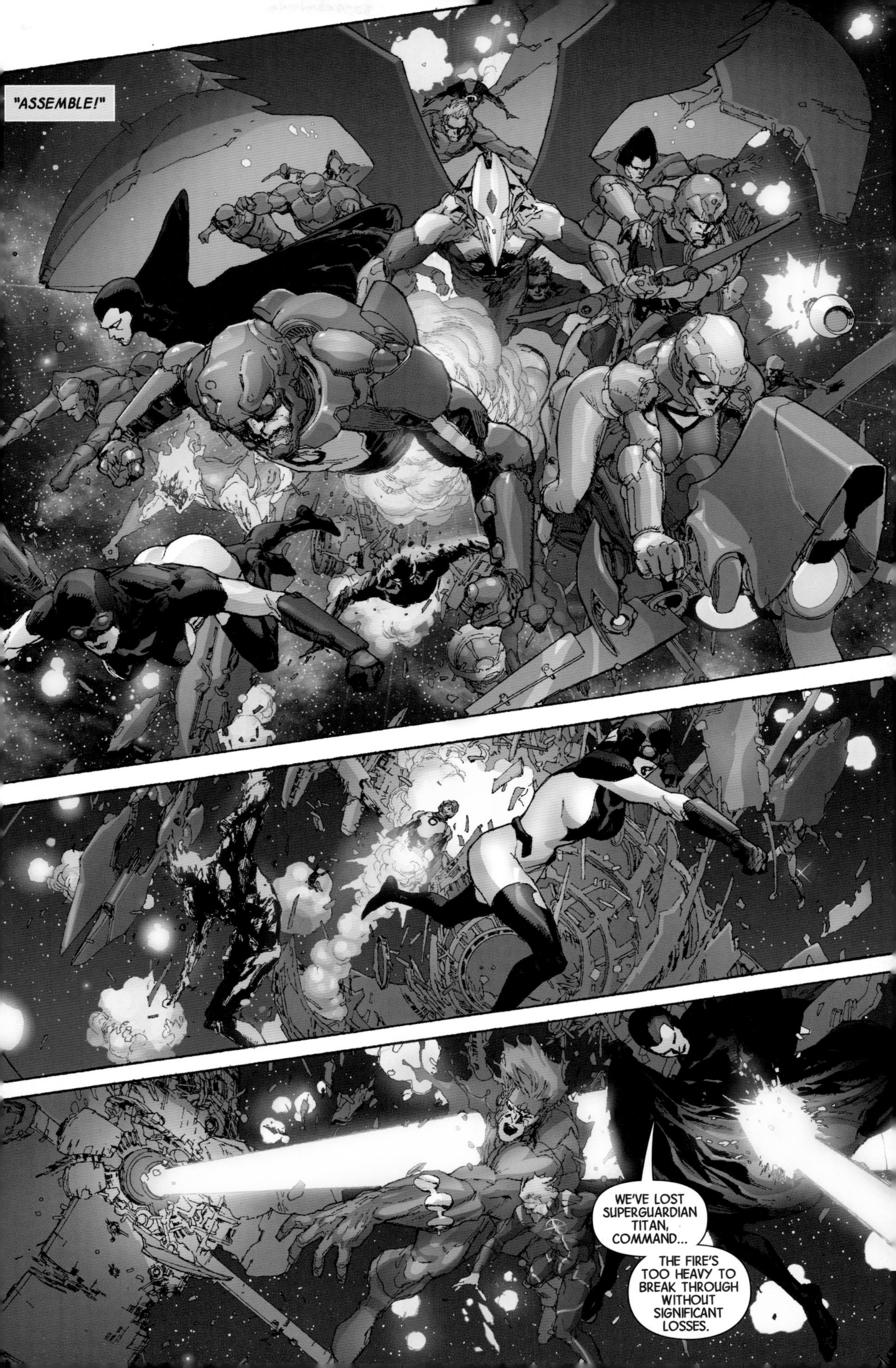
"ASSEMBLE!"
WE'VE LOST SUPERGUARDIAN TITAN, COMMAND...
THE FIRE'S TOO HEAVY TO BREAK THROUGH WITHOUT SIGNIFICANT LOSSES.

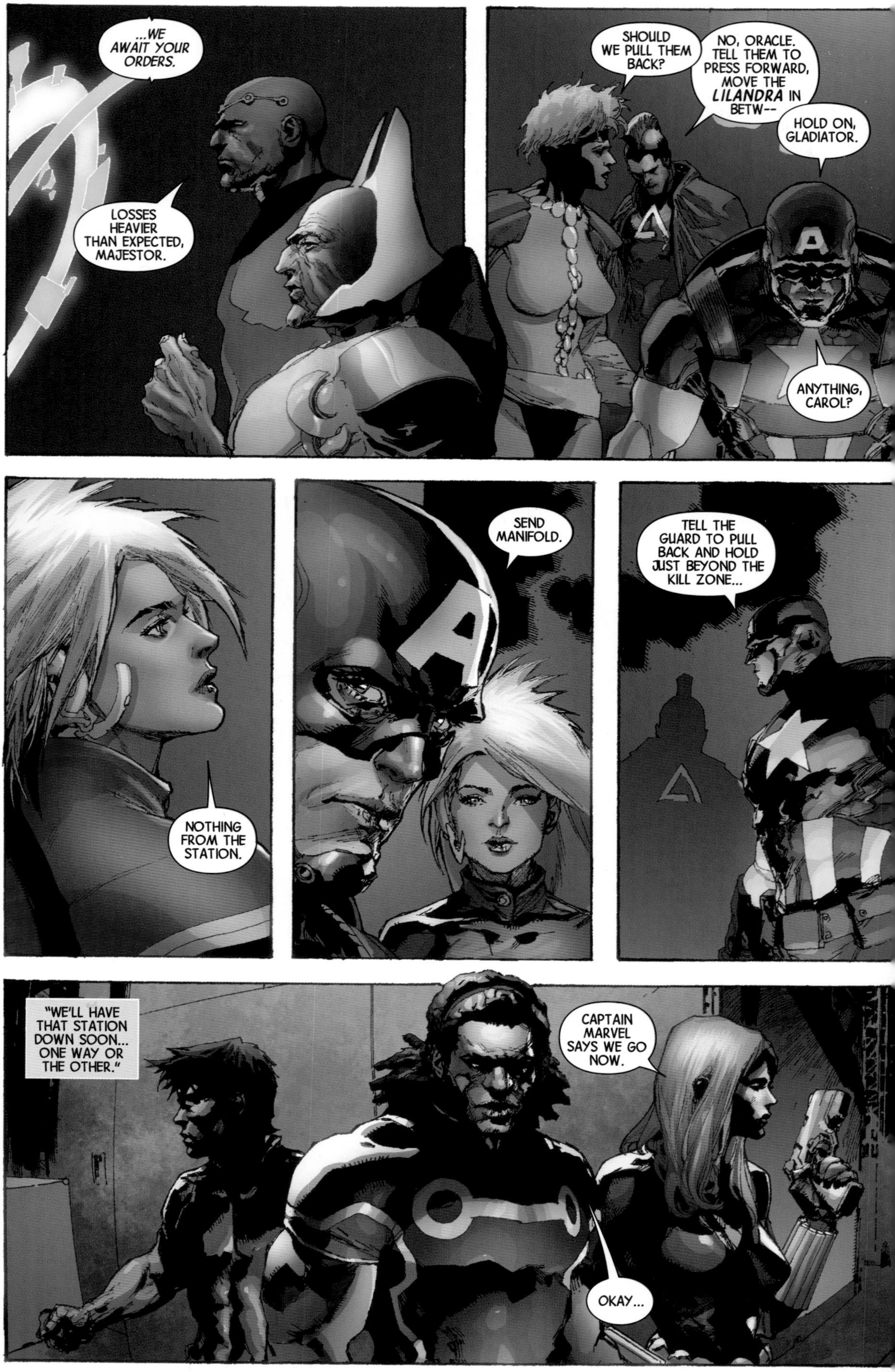
...WE AWAIT YOUR ORDERS.
LOSSES HEAVIER THAN EXPECTED, MAJESTOR.
SHOULD WE PULL THEM BACK?
NO, ORACLE. TELL THEM TO PRESS FORWARD, MOVE THE LILANDRA IN BETW--
HOLD ON, GLADIATOR.
ANYTHING, CAROL?
NOTHING FROM THE STATION.
SEND MANIFOLD.
TELL THE GUARD TO PULL BACK AND HOLD JUST BEYOND THE KILL ZONE...
"WE'LL HAVE THAT STATION DOWN SOON... ONE WAY OR THE OTHER."
CAPTAIN MARVEL SAYS WE GO NOW.
OKAY...

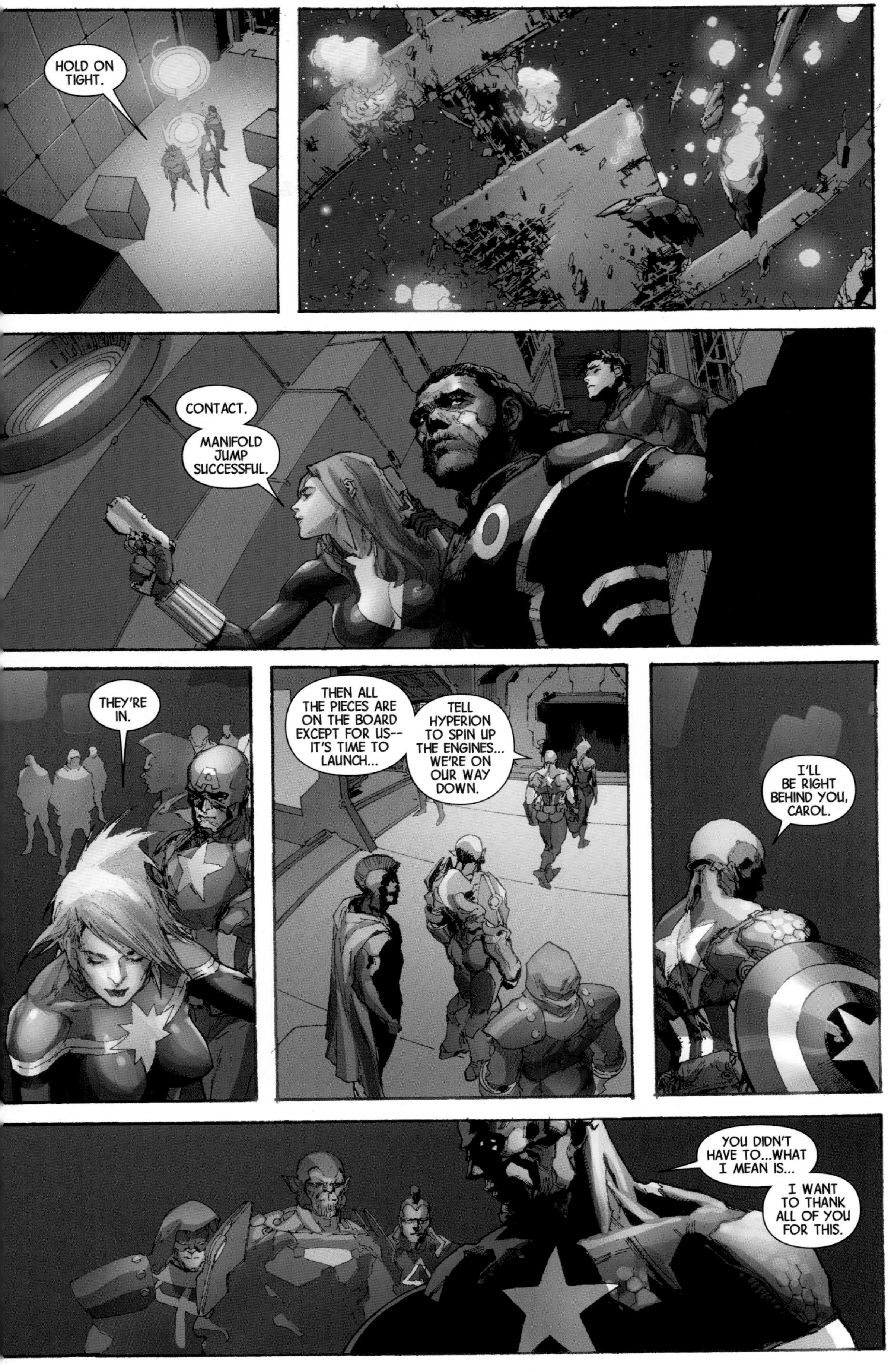
HOLD ON TIGHT.
CONTACT.
MANIFOLD JUMP SUCCESSFUL.
THEY'RE IN.
THEN ALL THE PIECES ARE ON THE BOARD EXCEPT FOR US-- IT'S TIME TO LAUNCH...
TELL HYPERION TO SPIN UP THE ENGINES... WE'RE ON OUR WAY DOWN.
I'LL BE RIGHT BEHIND YOU, CAROL.
YOU DIDN'T HAVE TO...WHAT I MEAN IS...
I WANT TO THANK ALL OF YOU FOR THIS.

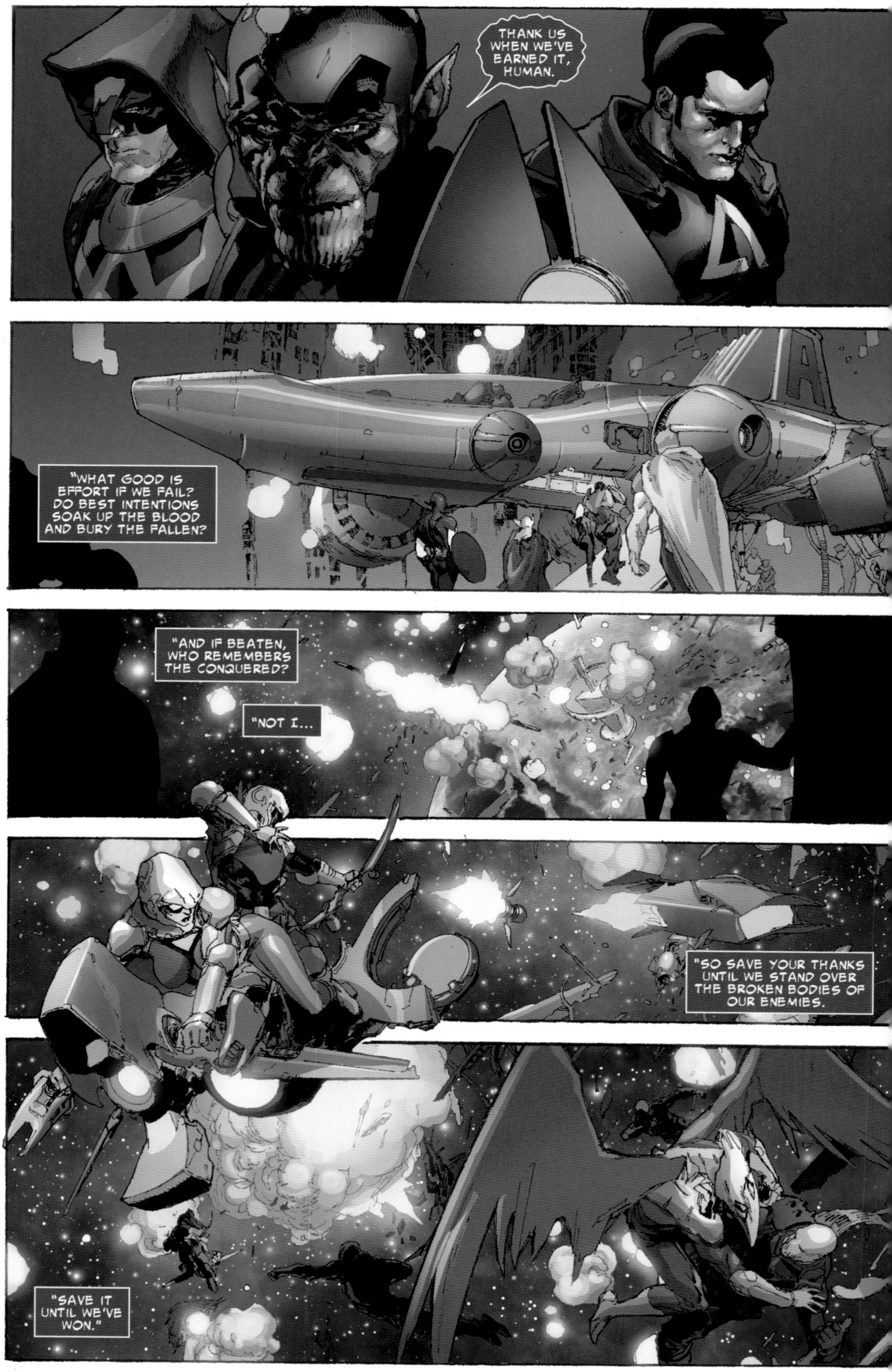
THANK US WHEN WE'VE EARNED IT, HUMAN.
"WHAT GOOD IS EFFORT IF WE FAIL? DO BEST INTENTIONS SOAK UP THE BLOOD AND BURY THE FALLEN?
"AND IF BEATEN, WHO REMEMBERS THE CONQUERED?
"NOT I...
"SO SAVE YOUR THANKS UNTIL WE STAND OVER THE BROKEN BODIES OF OUR ENEMIES.
"SAVE IT UNTIL WE'VE WON."

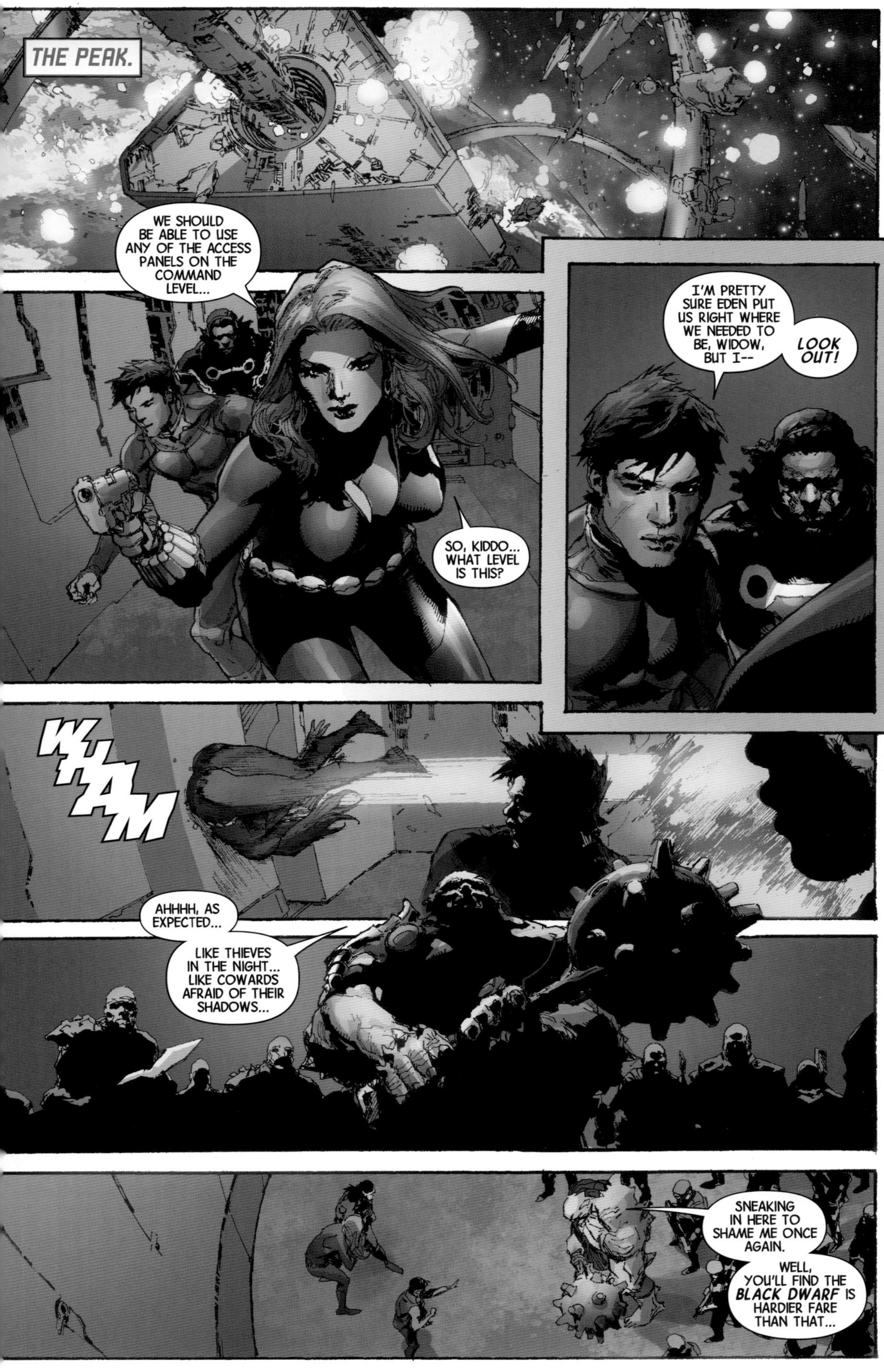
THE PEAK.
WE SHOULD BE ABLE TO USE ANY OF THE ACCESS PANELS ON THE COMMAND LEVEL...
SO, KIDDO... WHAT LEVEL IS THIS?
I'M PRETTY SURE EDEN PUT US RIGHT WHERE WE NEEDED TO BE, WIDOW, BUT I--
LOOK OUT!
WHAM
AHHHH, AS EXPECTED...
LIKE THIEVES IN THE NIGHT... LIKE COWARDS AFRAID OF THEIR SHADOWS...
SNEAKING IN HERE TO SHAME ME ONCE AGAIN.
WELL, YOU'LL FIND THE BLACK DWARF IS HARDIER FARE THAN THAT...

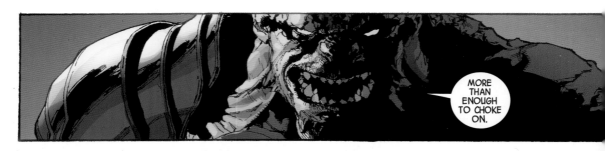

MORE THAN ENOUGH TO CHOKE ON.

MANIFOLD! GET BACK TO THE SHIP...

TELL THEM WE'RE NOT GOING TO GET THE FIELD DOWN IN TIME!

BRING BACKUP!

ZZZNNNN

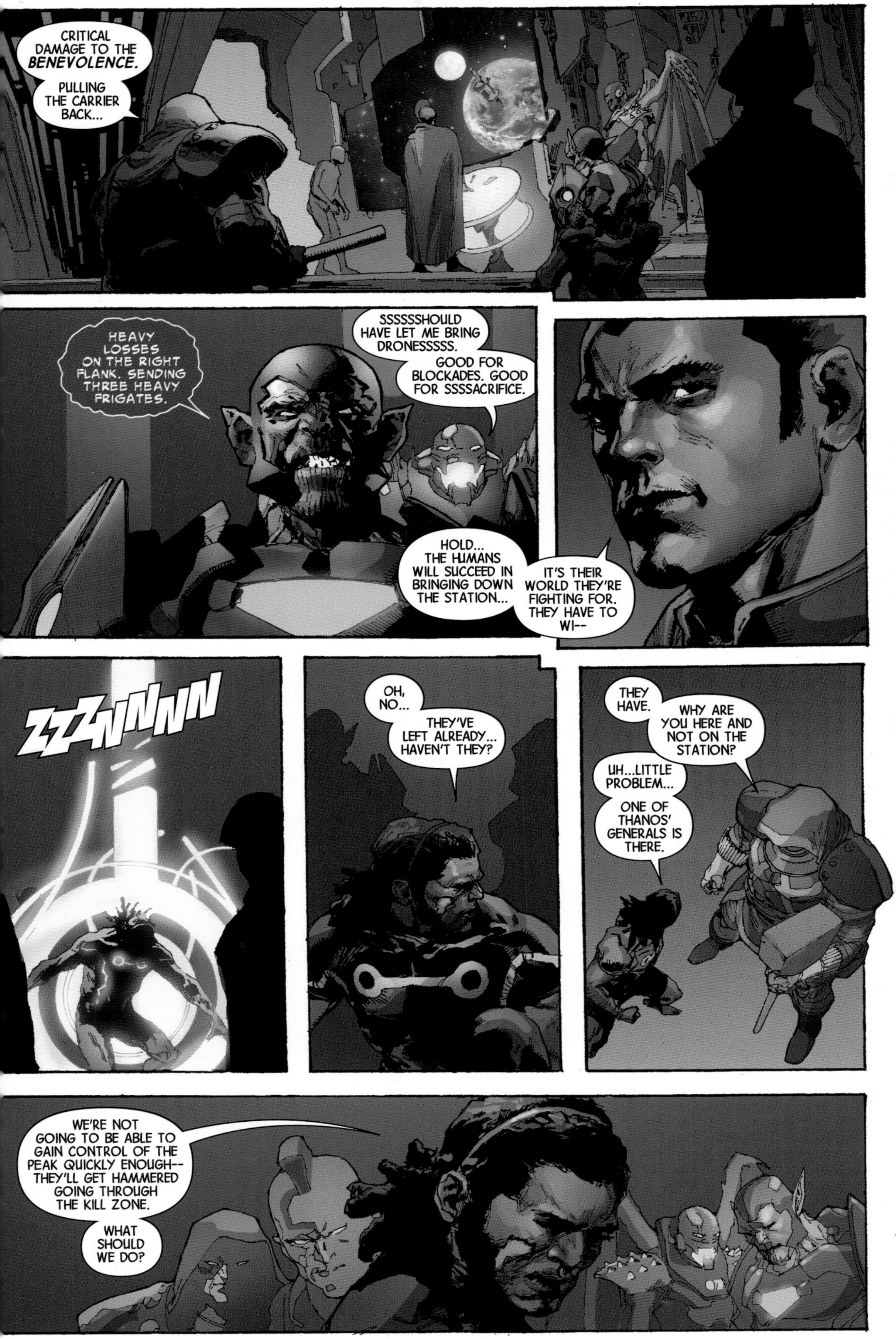
CRITICAL DAMAGE TO THE *BENEVOLENCE.*
PULLING THE CARRIER BACK...
HEAVY LOSSES ON THE RIGHT FLANK. SENDING THREE HEAVY FRIGATES.
SSSSSSHOULD HAVE LET ME BRING DRONESSSSS.
GOOD FOR BLOCKADES. GOOD FOR SSSSACRIFICE.
HOLD... THE HUMANS WILL SUCCEED IN BRINGING DOWN THE STATION...
IT'S THEIR WORLD THEY'RE FIGHTING FOR. THEY HAVE TO WI--
ZZZNNNNN
OH, NO...
THEY'VE LEFT ALREADY... HAVEN'T THEY?
THEY HAVE.
WHY ARE YOU HERE AND NOT ON THE STATION?
UH...LITTLE PROBLEM...
ONE OF THANOS' GENERALS IS THERE.
WE'RE NOT GOING TO BE ABLE TO GAIN CONTROL OF THE PEAK QUICKLY ENOUGH-- THEY'LL GET HAMMERED GOING THROUGH THE KILL ZONE.
WHAT SHOULD WE DO?

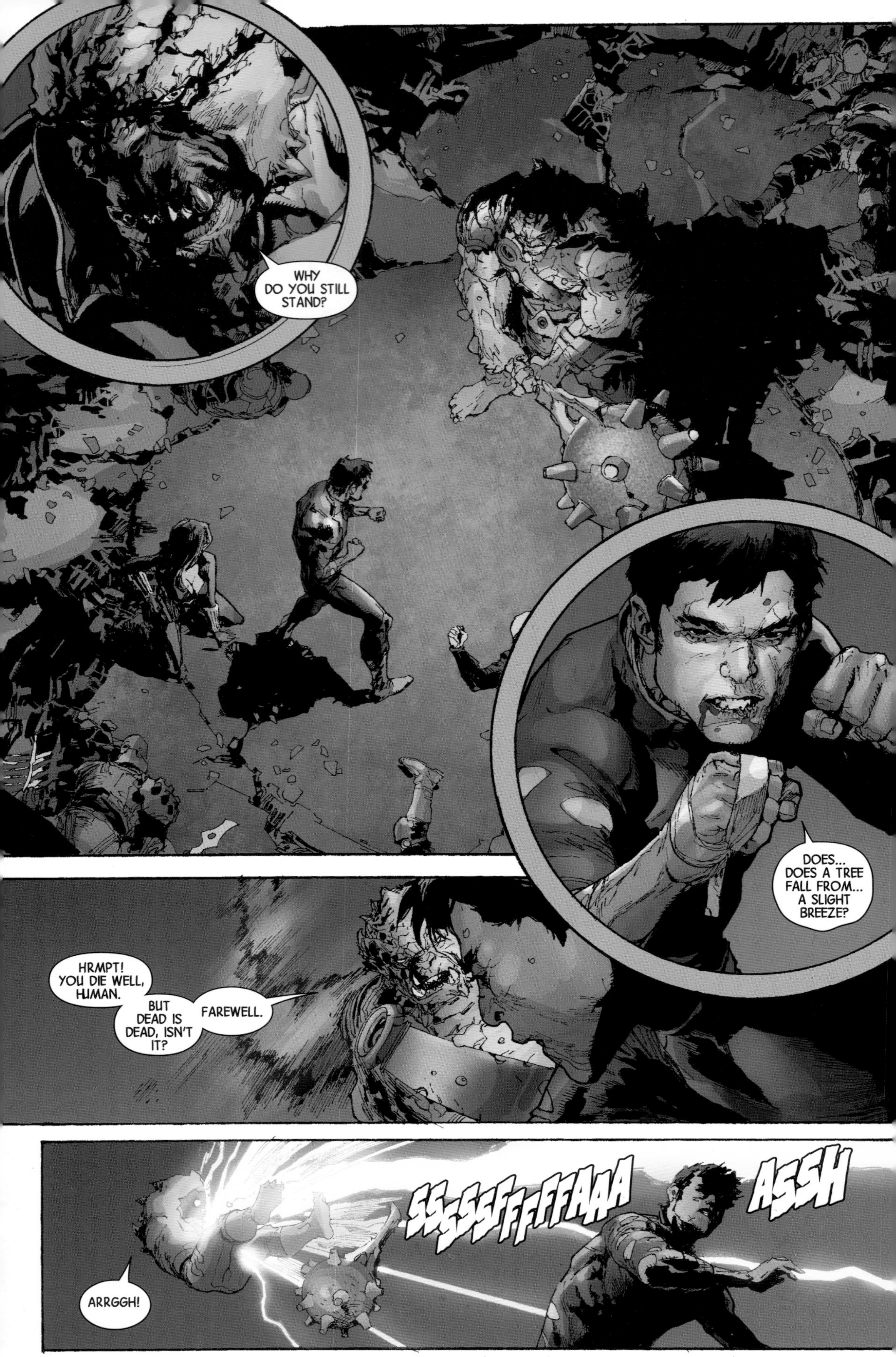
WHY DO YOU STILL STAND?
DOES... DOES A TREE FALL FROM... A SLIGHT BREEZE?
HRMPT! YOU DIE WELL, HUMAN.
BUT DEAD IS DEAD, ISN'T IT?
FAREWELL.
SSSSSFFFFFAAA
ASSH
ARRGGH!

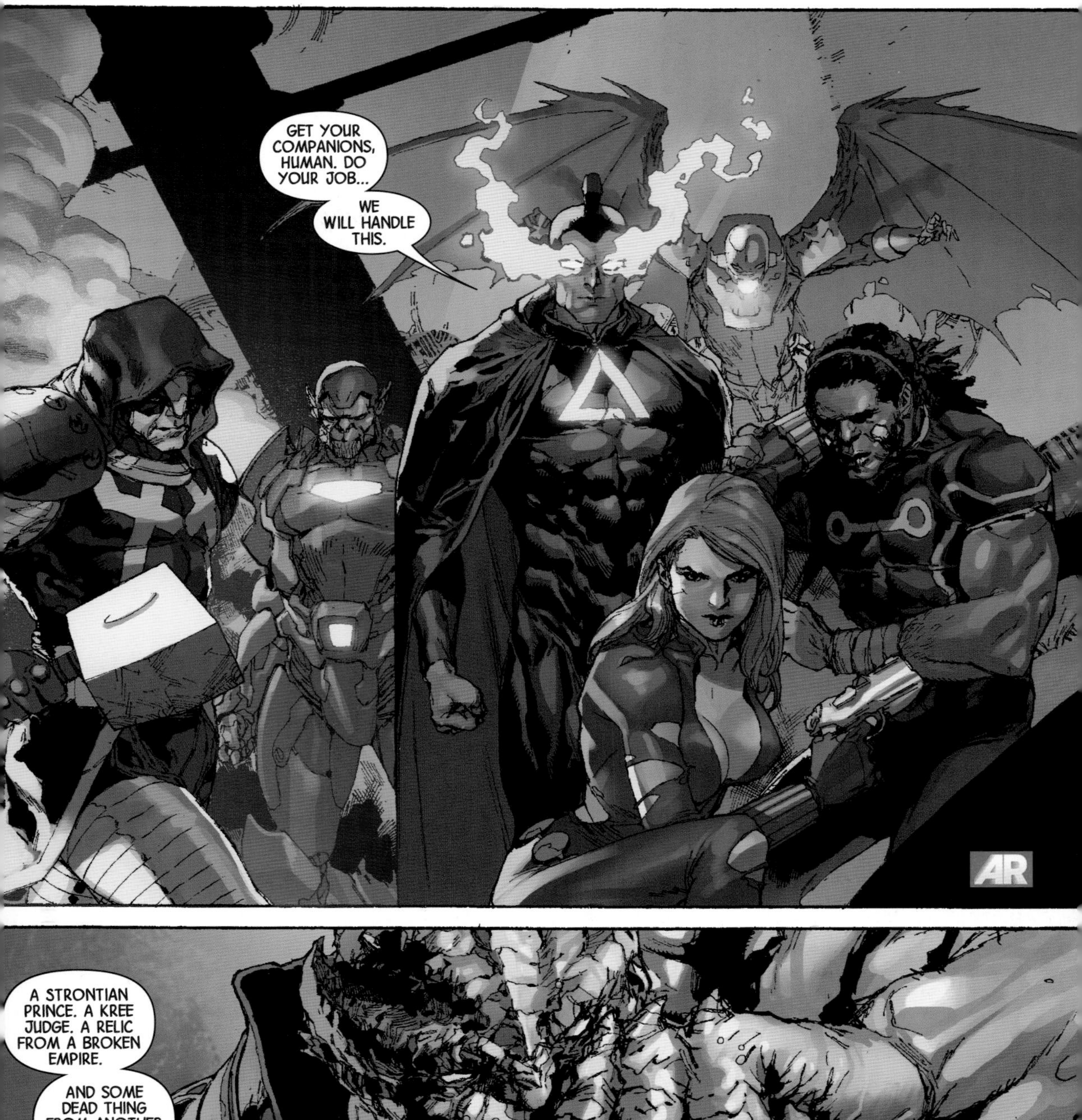
GET YOUR COMPANIONS, HUMAN. DO YOUR JOB...
WE WILL HANDLE THIS.
AR

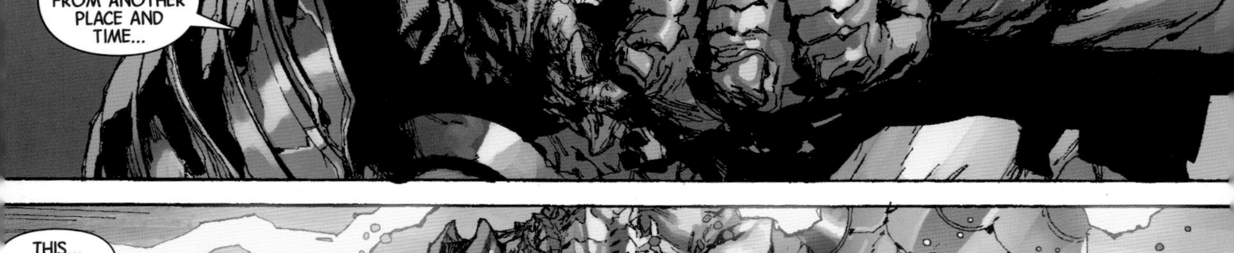
A STRONTIAN PRINCE. A KREE JUDGE. A RELIC FROM A BROKEN EMPIRE.
AND SOME DEAD THING FROM ANOTHER PLACE AND TIME...

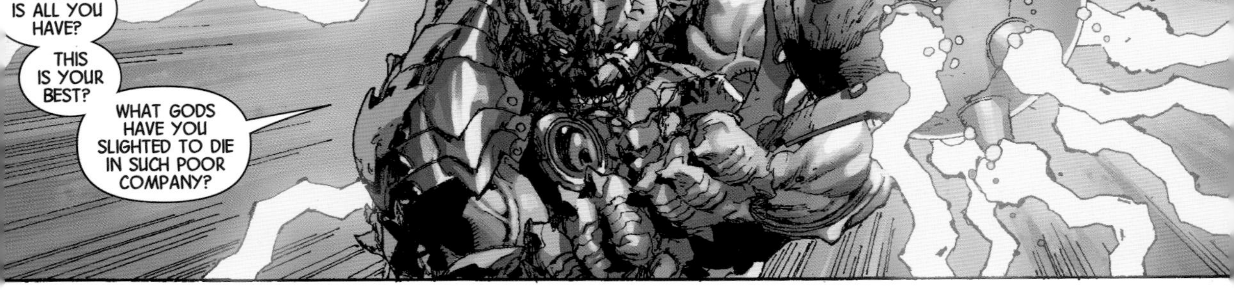
THIS... IS ALL YOU HAVE?
THIS IS YOUR BEST?
WHAT GODS HAVE YOU SLIGHTED TO DIE IN SUCH POOR COMPANY?

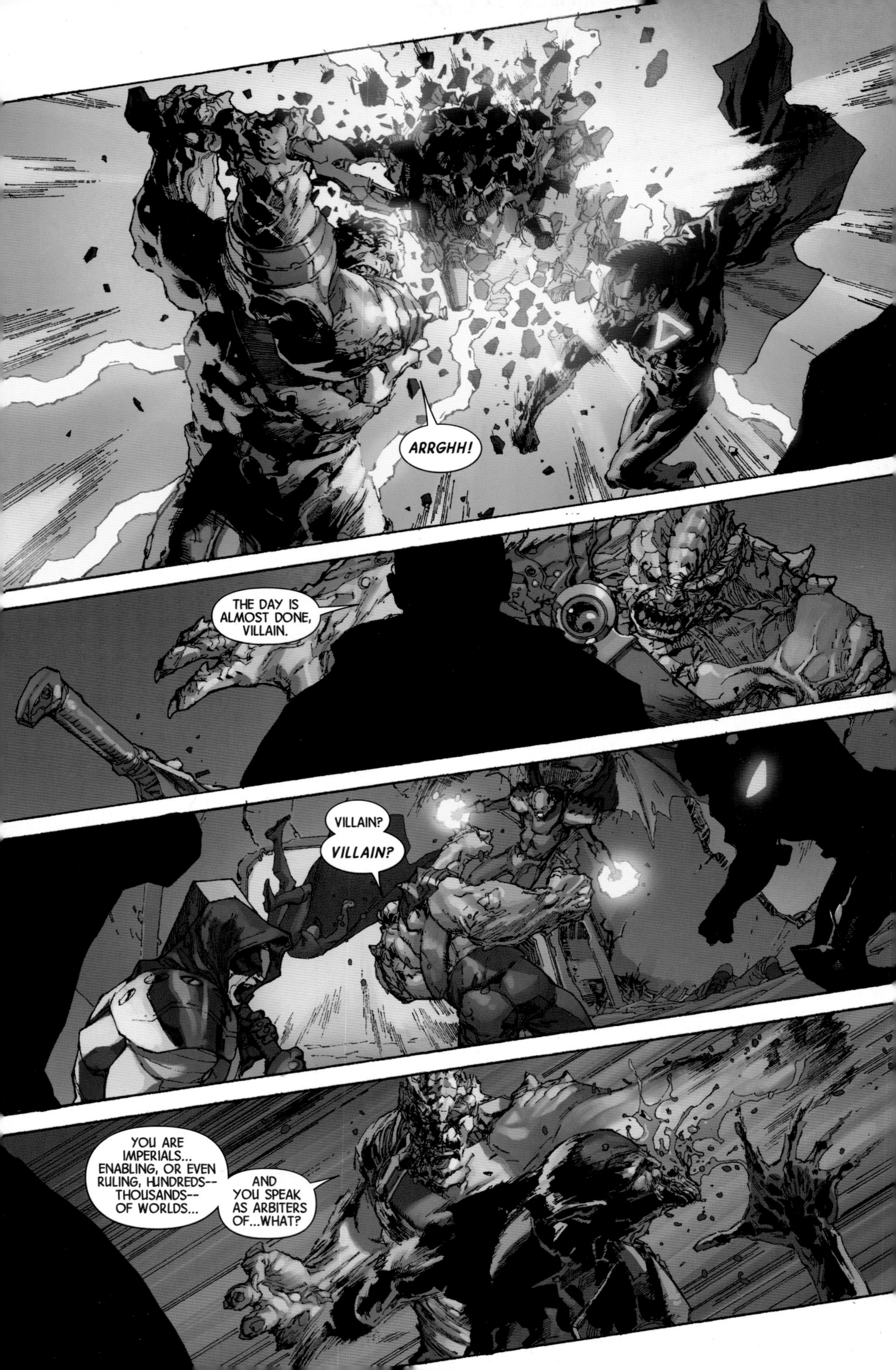
ARRGHH!
THE DAY IS ALMOST DONE, VILLAIN.
VILLAIN?
VILLAIN?
YOU ARE IMPERIALS... ENABLING, OR EVEN RULING, HUNDREDS-- THOUSANDS-- OF WORLDS...
AND YOU SPEAK AS ARBITERS OF...WHAT?

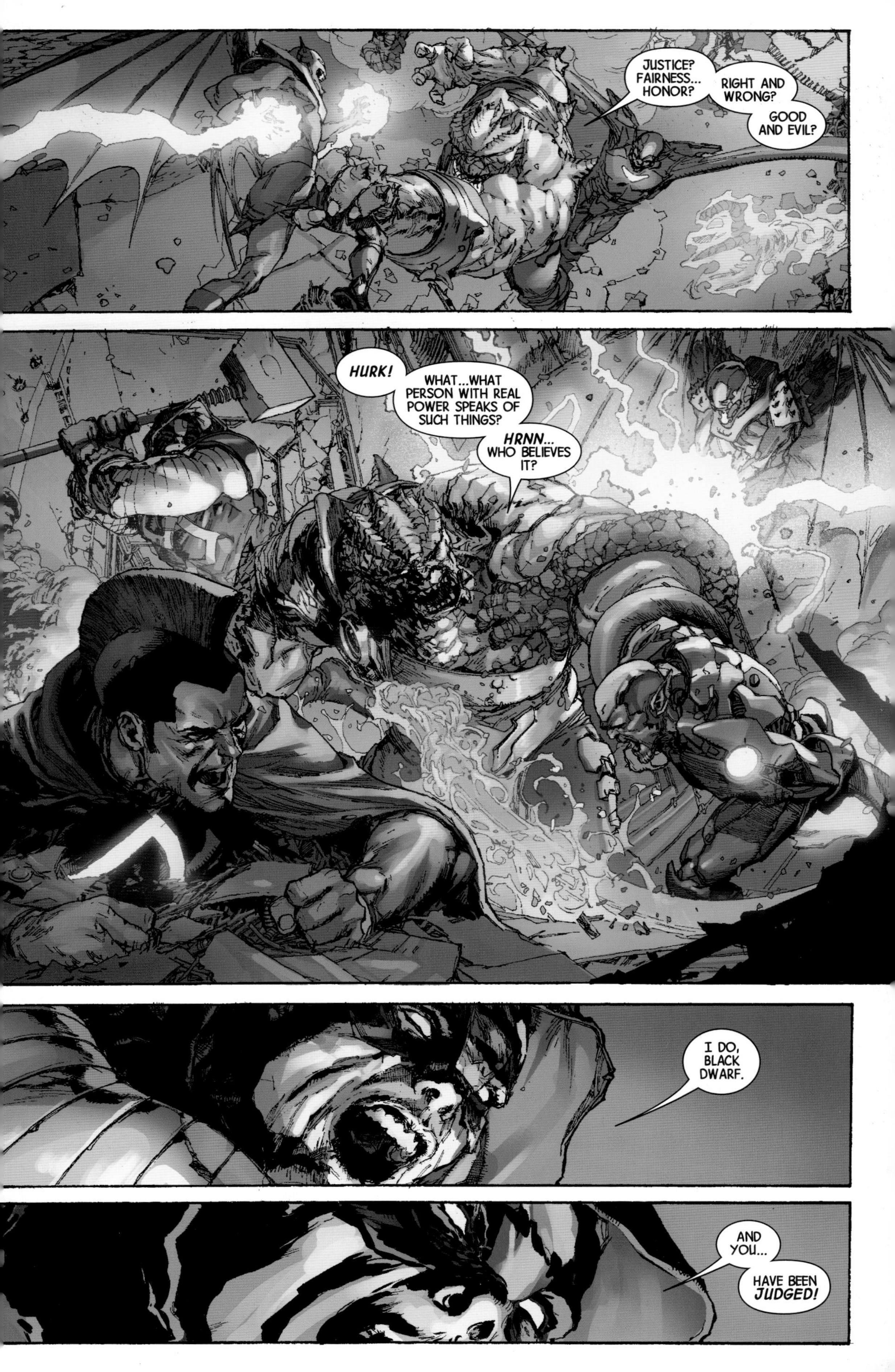
JUSTICE? FAIRNESS... HONOR?
RIGHT AND WRONG?
GOOD AND EVIL?
HURK!
WHAT...WHAT PERSON WITH REAL POWER SPEAKS OF SUCH THINGS?
HRNN... WHO BELIEVES IT?
I DO, BLACK DWARF.
AND YOU...
HAVE BEEN JUDGED!

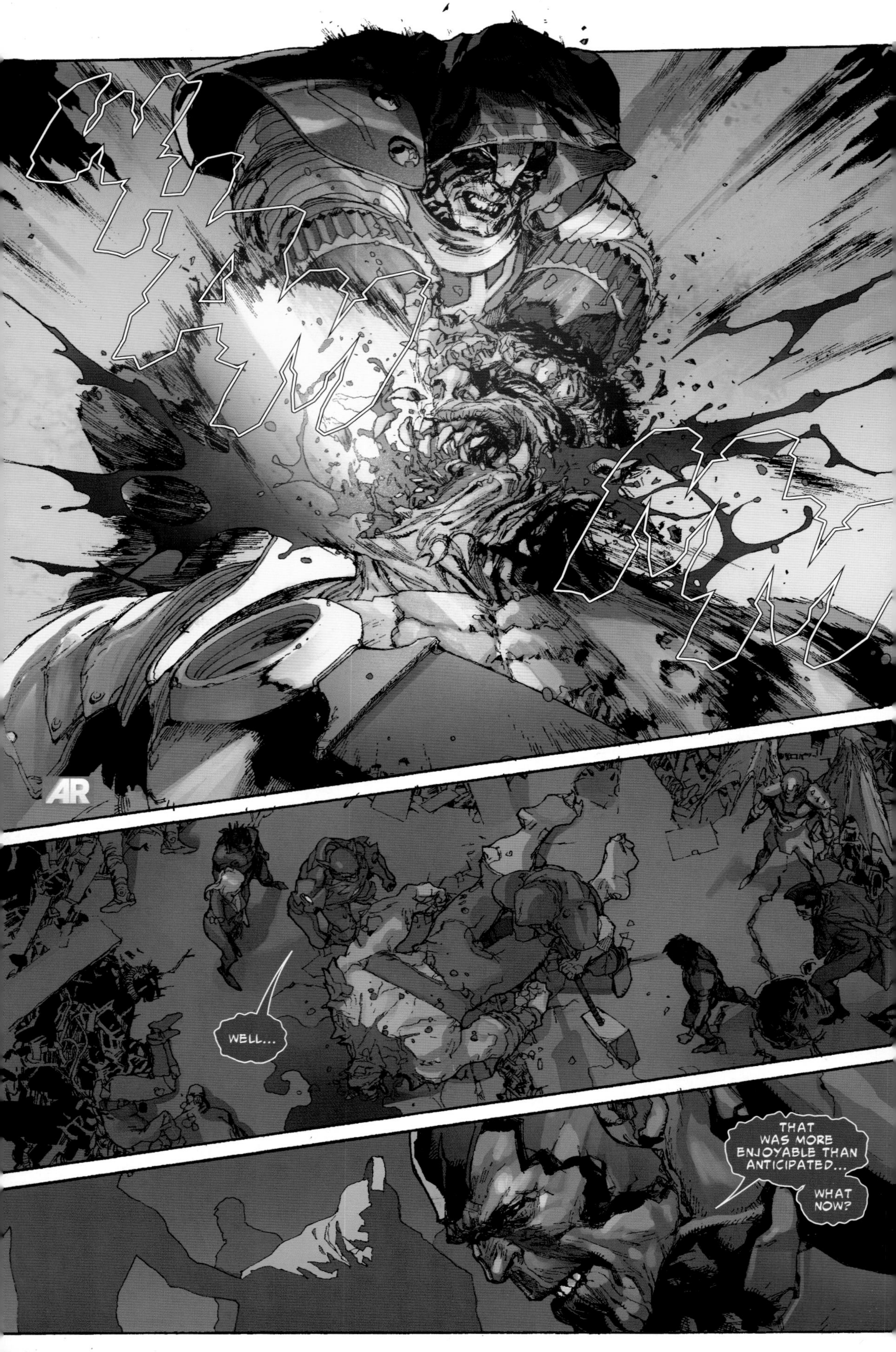
WELL...
THAT WAS MORE ENJOYABLE THAN ANTICIPATED...
WHAT NOW?

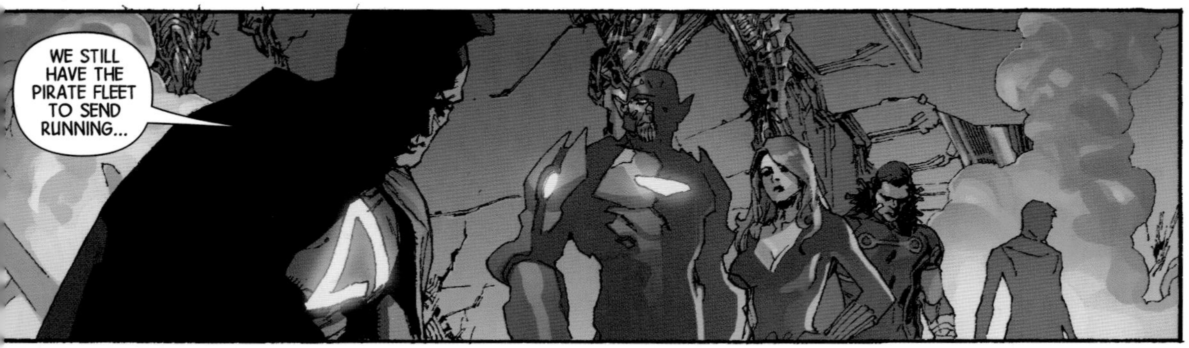
WE STILL HAVE THE PIRATE FLEET TO SEND RUNNING...

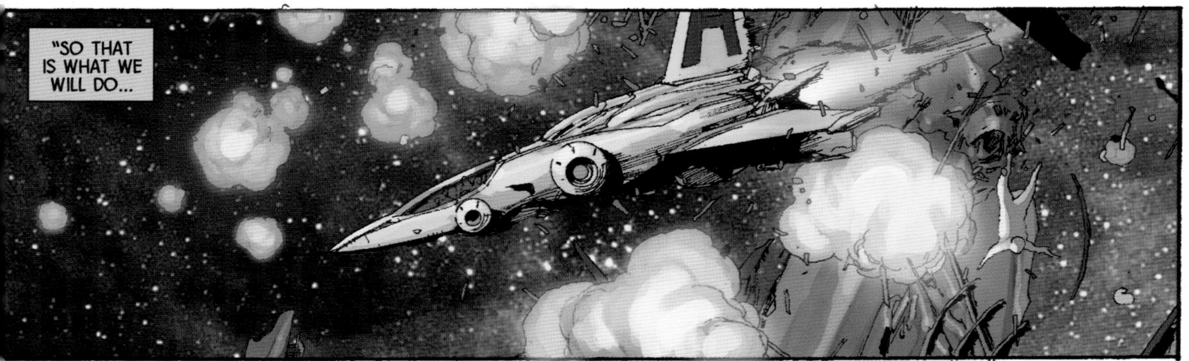
"SO THAT IS WHAT WE WILL DO...

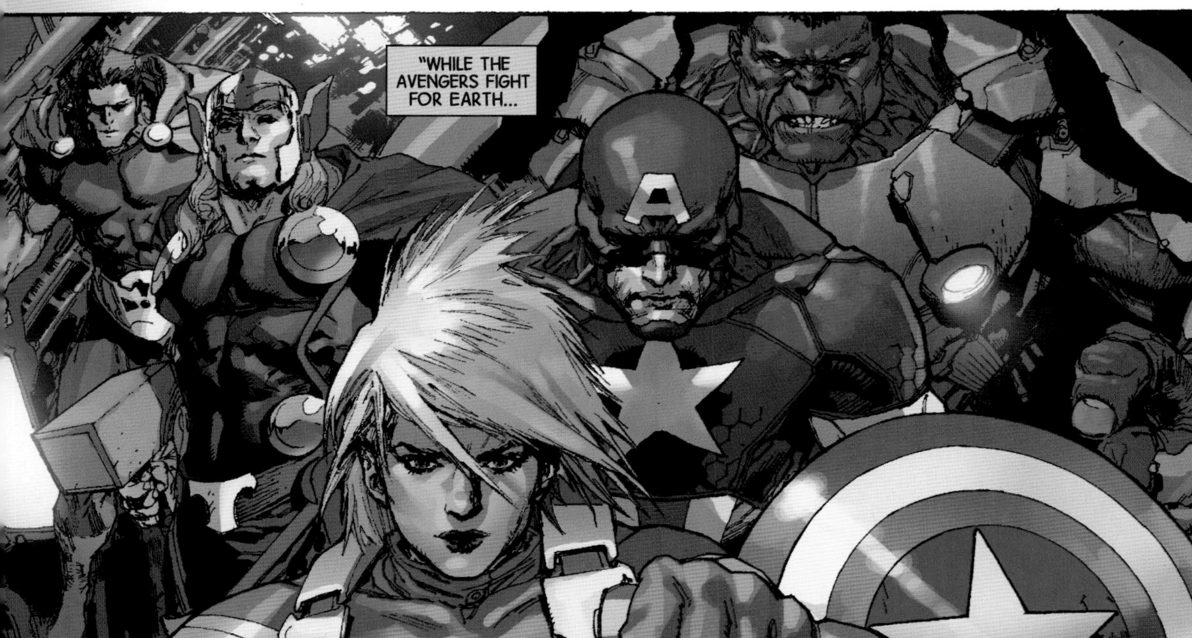
"WHILE THE AVENGERS FIGHT FOR EARTH...

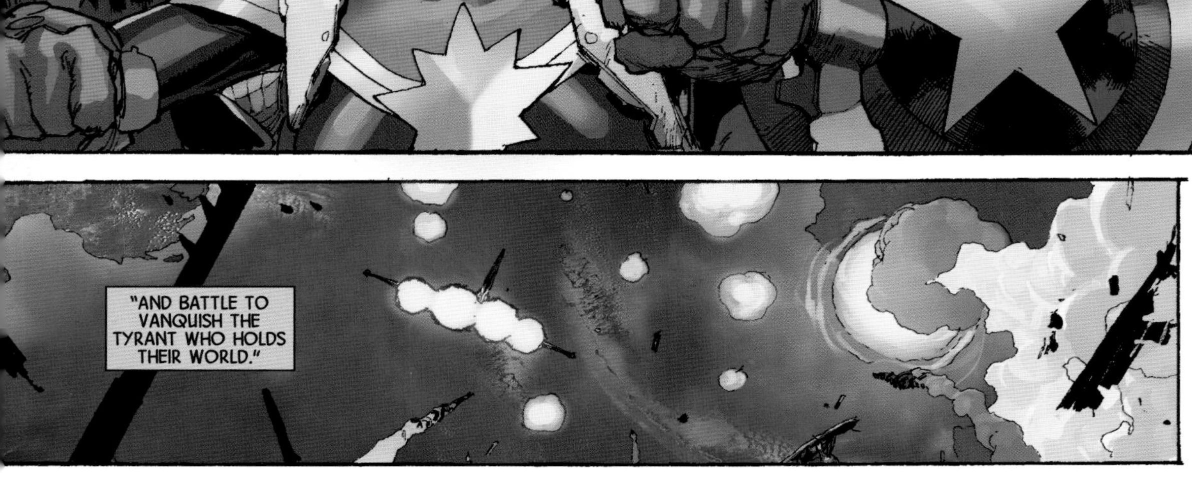
"AND BATTLE TO VANQUISH THE TYRANT WHO HOLDS THEIR WORLD."

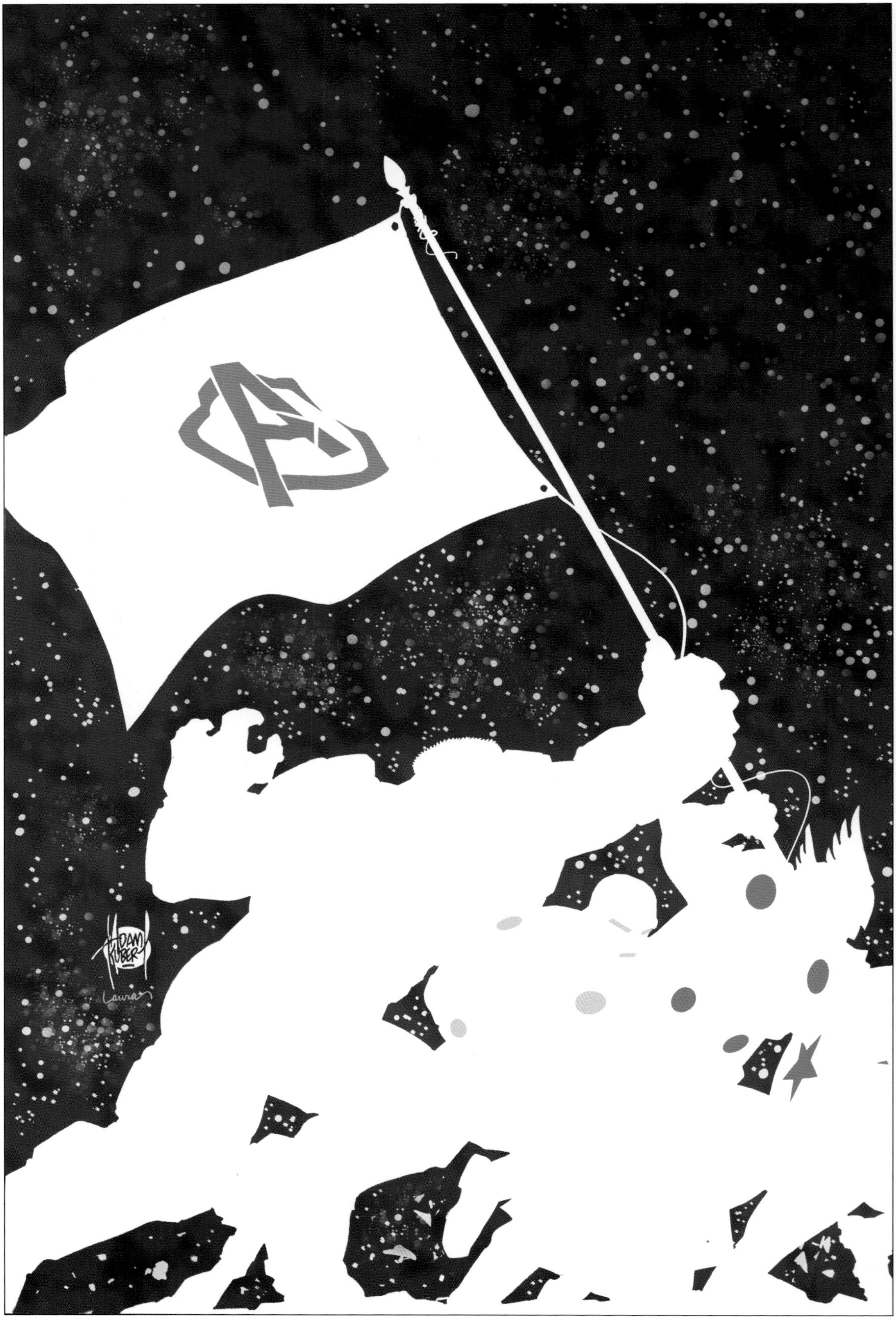

TYRANT

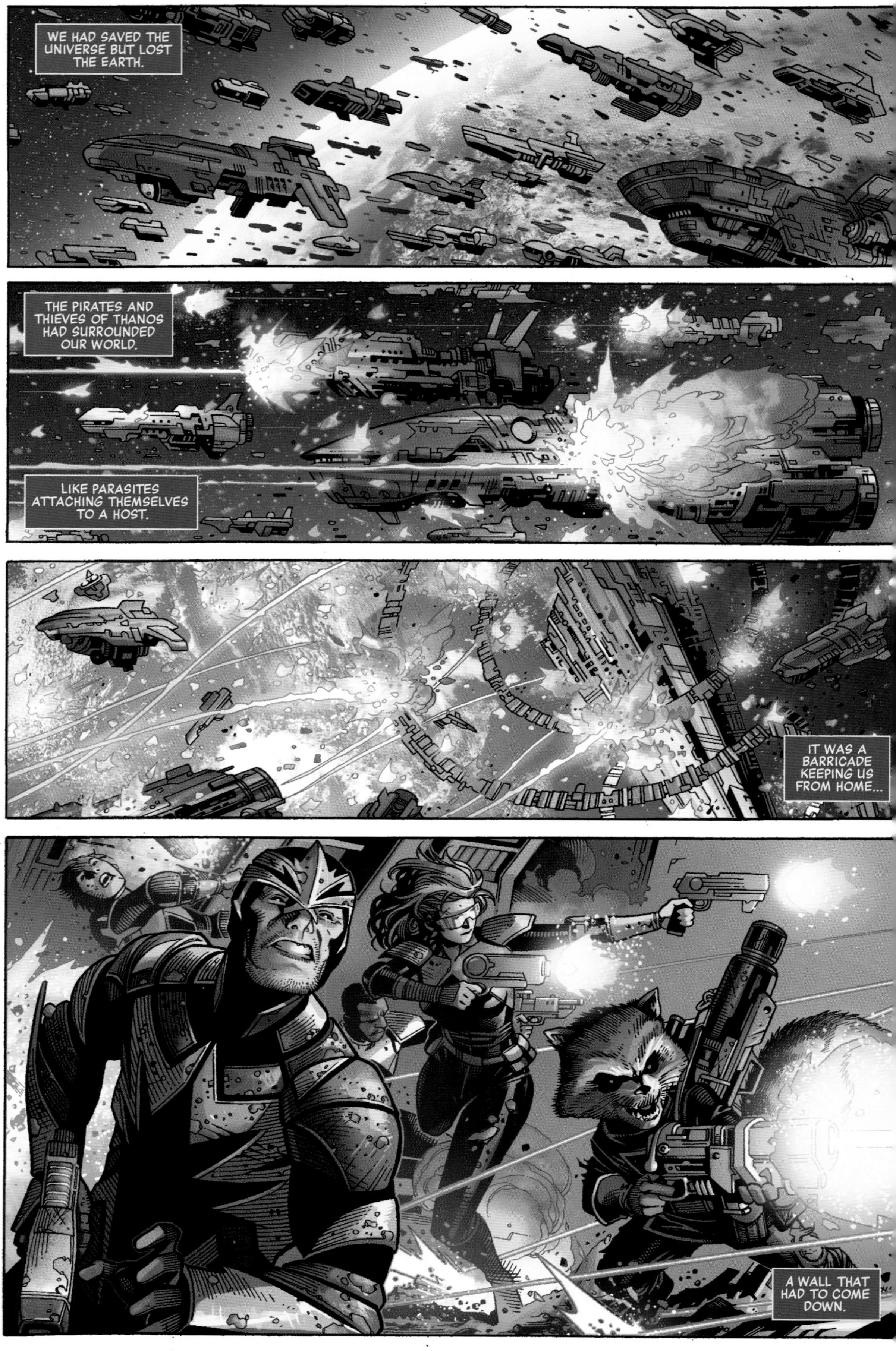
WE HAD SAVED THE UNIVERSE BUT LOST THE EARTH.
THE PIRATES AND THIEVES OF THANOS HAD SURROUNDED OUR WORLD.
LIKE PARASITES ATTACHING THEMSELVES TO A HOST.
IT WAS A BARRICADE KEEPING US FROM HOME...
A WALL THAT HAD TO COME DOWN.

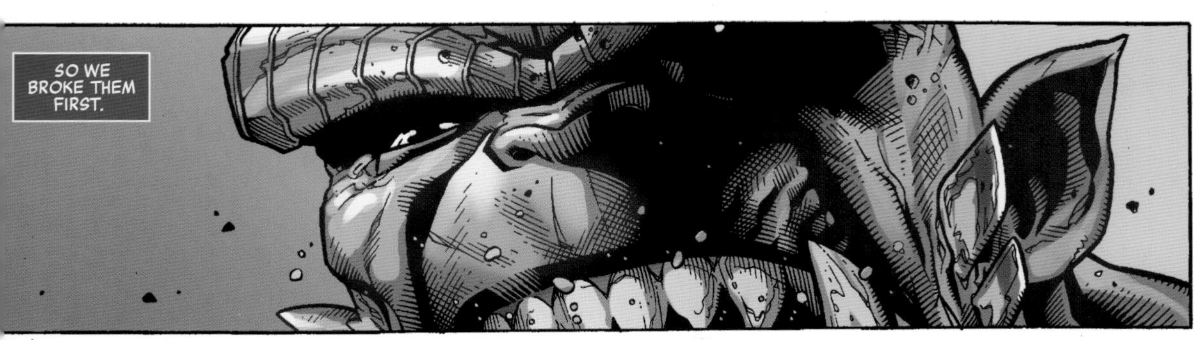
SO WE BROKE THEM FIRST.

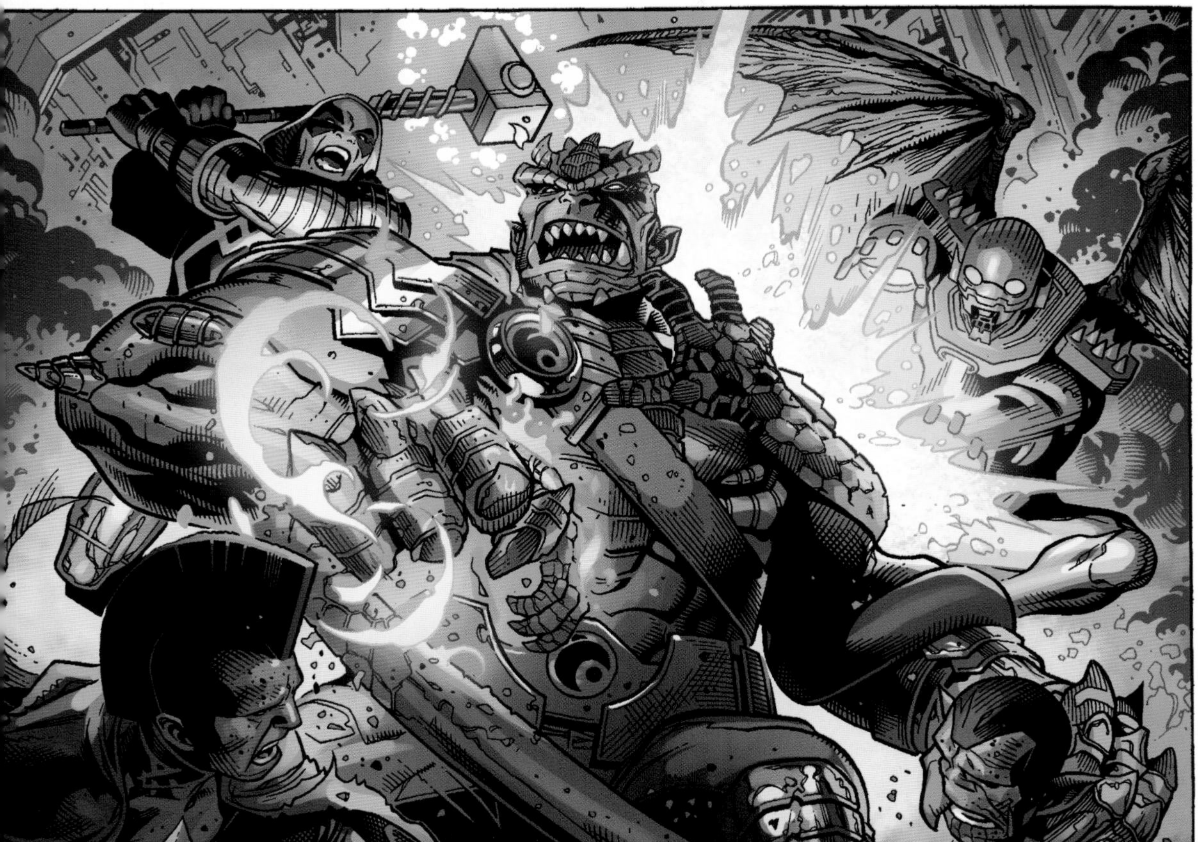

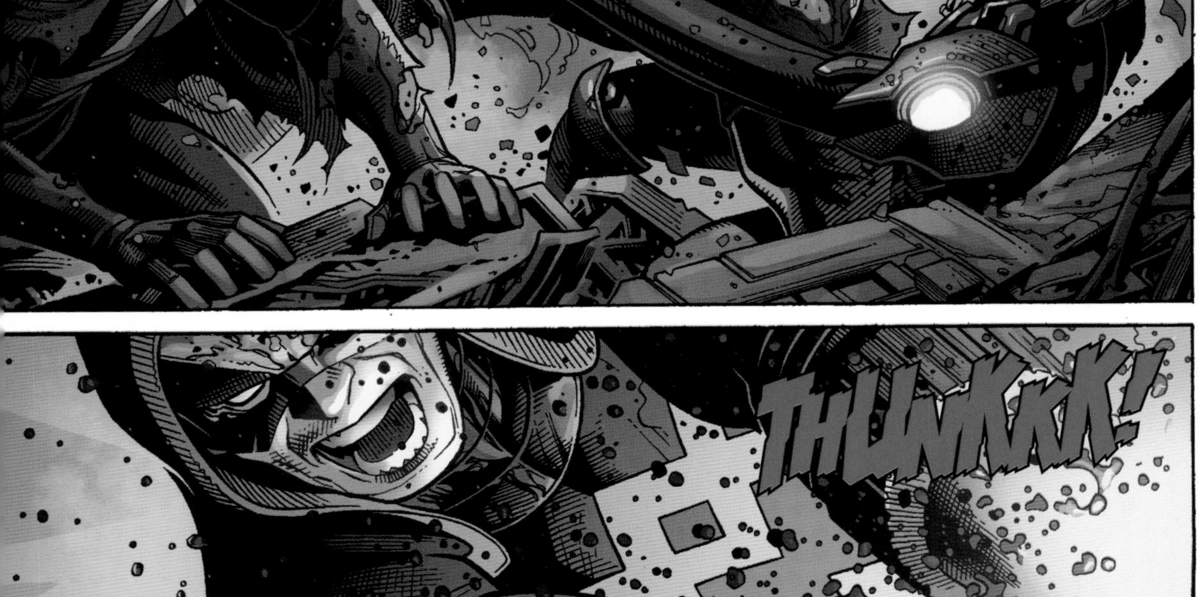
THUNKKK!

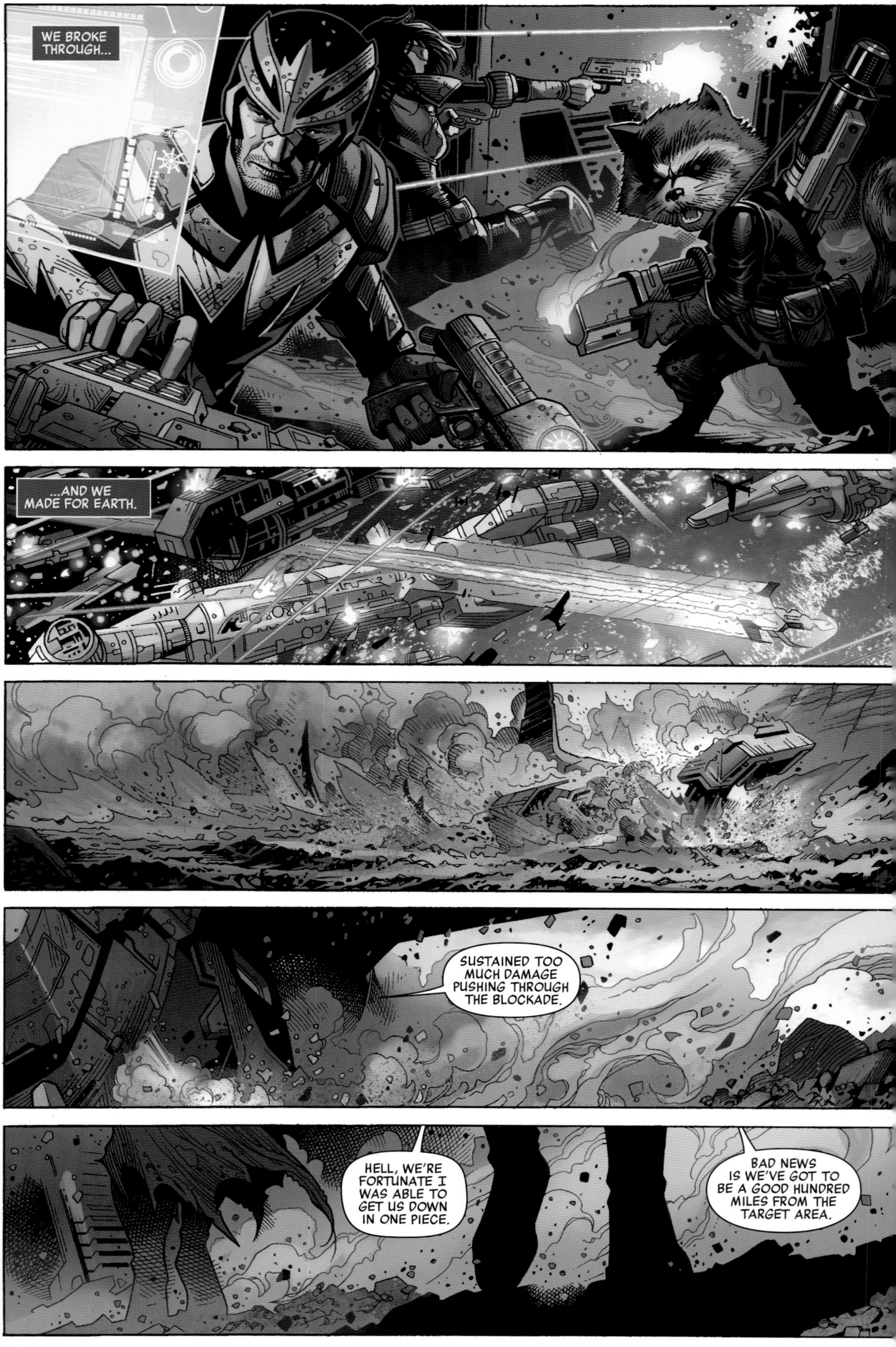
WE BROKE THROUGH...
...AND WE MADE FOR EARTH.
SUSTAINED TOO MUCH DAMAGE PUSHING THROUGH THE BLOCKADE.
HELL, WE'RE FORTUNATE I WAS ABLE TO GET US DOWN IN ONE PIECE.
BAD NEWS IS WE'VE GOT TO BE A GOOD HUNDRED MILES FROM THE TARGET AREA.

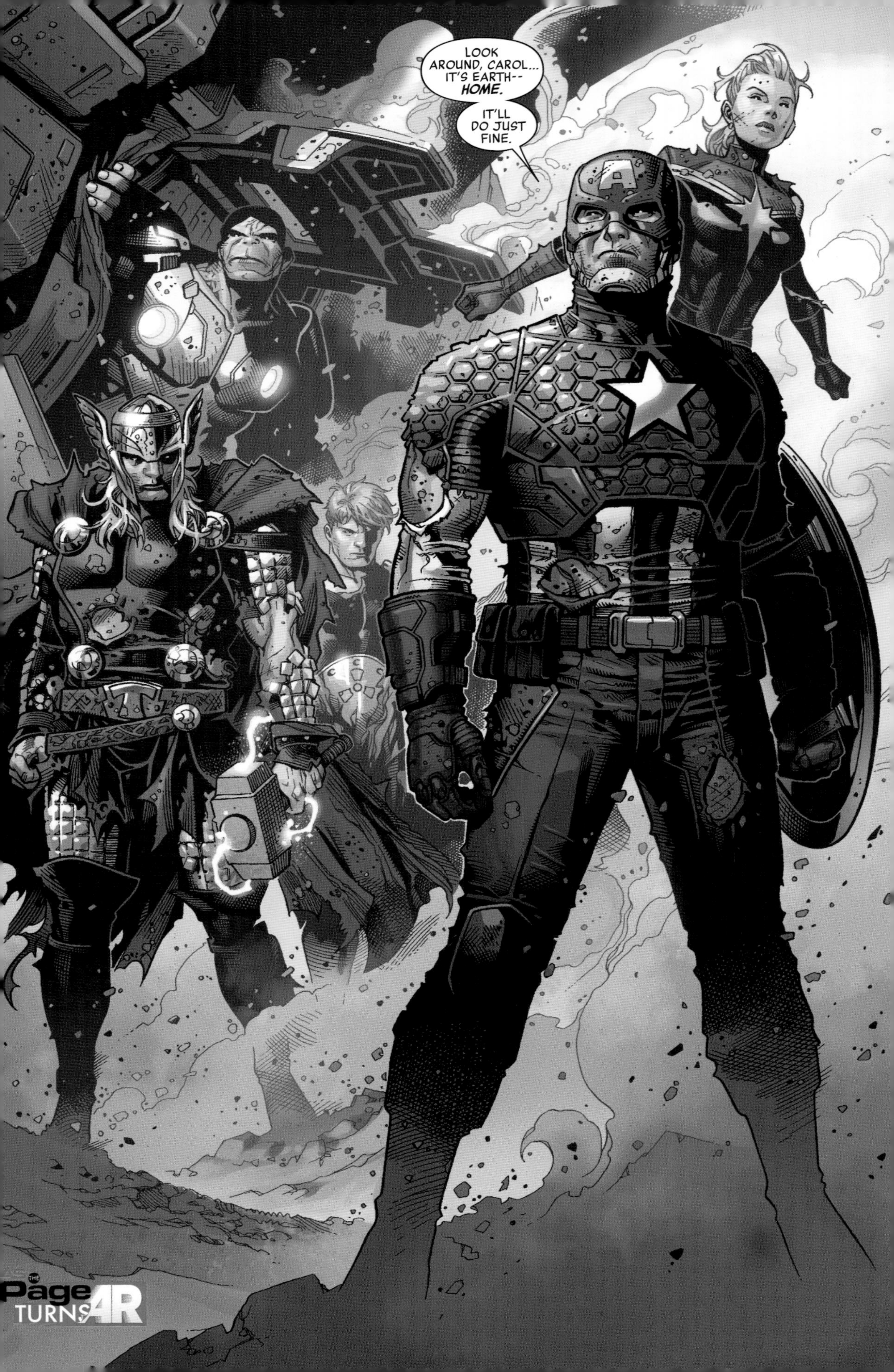
LOOK AROUND, CAROL... IT'S EARTH-- **HOME.**
IT'LL DO JUST FINE.
The Page TURNS AR

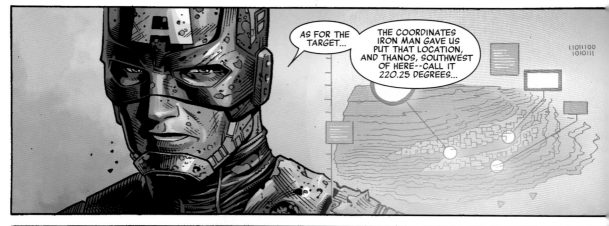

AS FOR THE TARGET...

THE COORDINATES IRON MAN GAVE US PUT THAT LOCATION, AND THANOS, SOUTHWEST OF HERE--CALL IT 220.25 DEGREES...

DISTANCE OF AROUND FIFTY-TWO MILES.

HYPERION?

I SEE IT. APPEARS TO BE AN EXCAVATED BUILDOUT--AN IN-GROUND STRUCTURE.

I'M PICKING UP FIVE LIFE FORMS. ONE IS IN SOME TYPE OF CONTAINMENT FIELD.

THAT WOULD BE THE SON. OKAY...

HULK, KNOCK ON THE FRONT DOOR...SOFTEN 'EM UP--DISTRACT THEM.

WE'LL BE RIGHT BEHIND YOU.

HARNESS YOUR APPETITE, BANNER...

LEAVE SOME FOR THE REST OF US.

HRMPT!

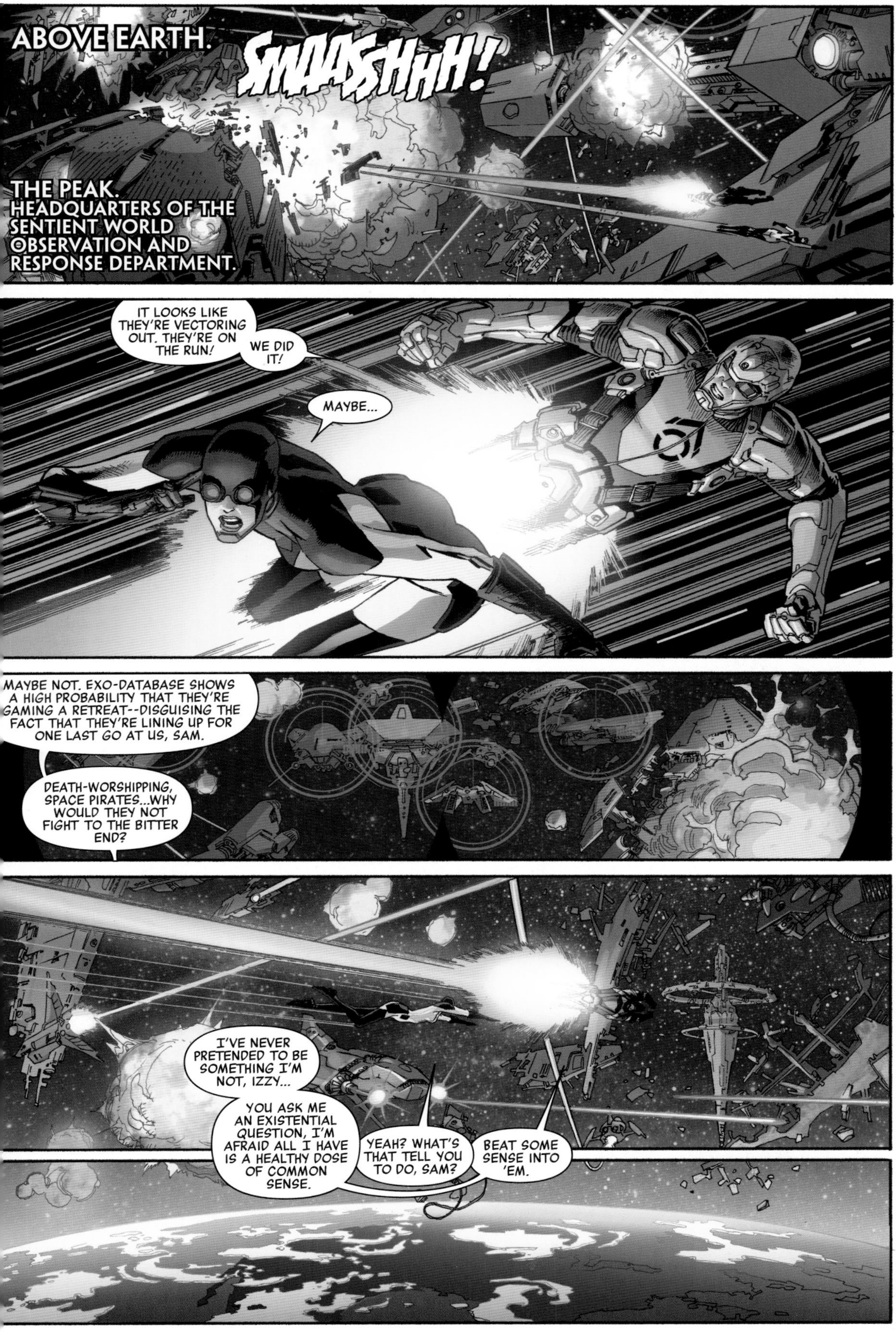
ABOVE EARTH.
SWAASHHH!
THE PEAK.
HEADQUARTERS OF THE SENTIENT WORLD OBSERVATION AND RESPONSE DEPARTMENT.
IT LOOKS LIKE THEY'RE VECTORING OUT. THEY'RE ON THE RUN!
WE DID IT!
MAYBE...
MAYBE NOT. EXO-DATABASE SHOWS A HIGH PROBABILITY THAT THEY'RE GAMING A RETREAT--DISGUISING THE FACT THAT THEY'RE LINING UP FOR ONE LAST GO AT US, SAM.
DEATH-WORSHIPPING, SPACE PIRATES...WHY WOULD THEY NOT FIGHT TO THE BITTER END?
I'VE NEVER PRETENDED TO BE SOMETHING I'M NOT, IZZY...
YOU ASK ME AN EXISTENTIAL QUESTION, I'M AFRAID ALL I HAVE IS A HEALTHY DOSE OF COMMON SENSE.
YEAH? WHAT'S THAT TELL YOU TO DO, SAM?
BEAT SOME SENSE INTO 'EM.

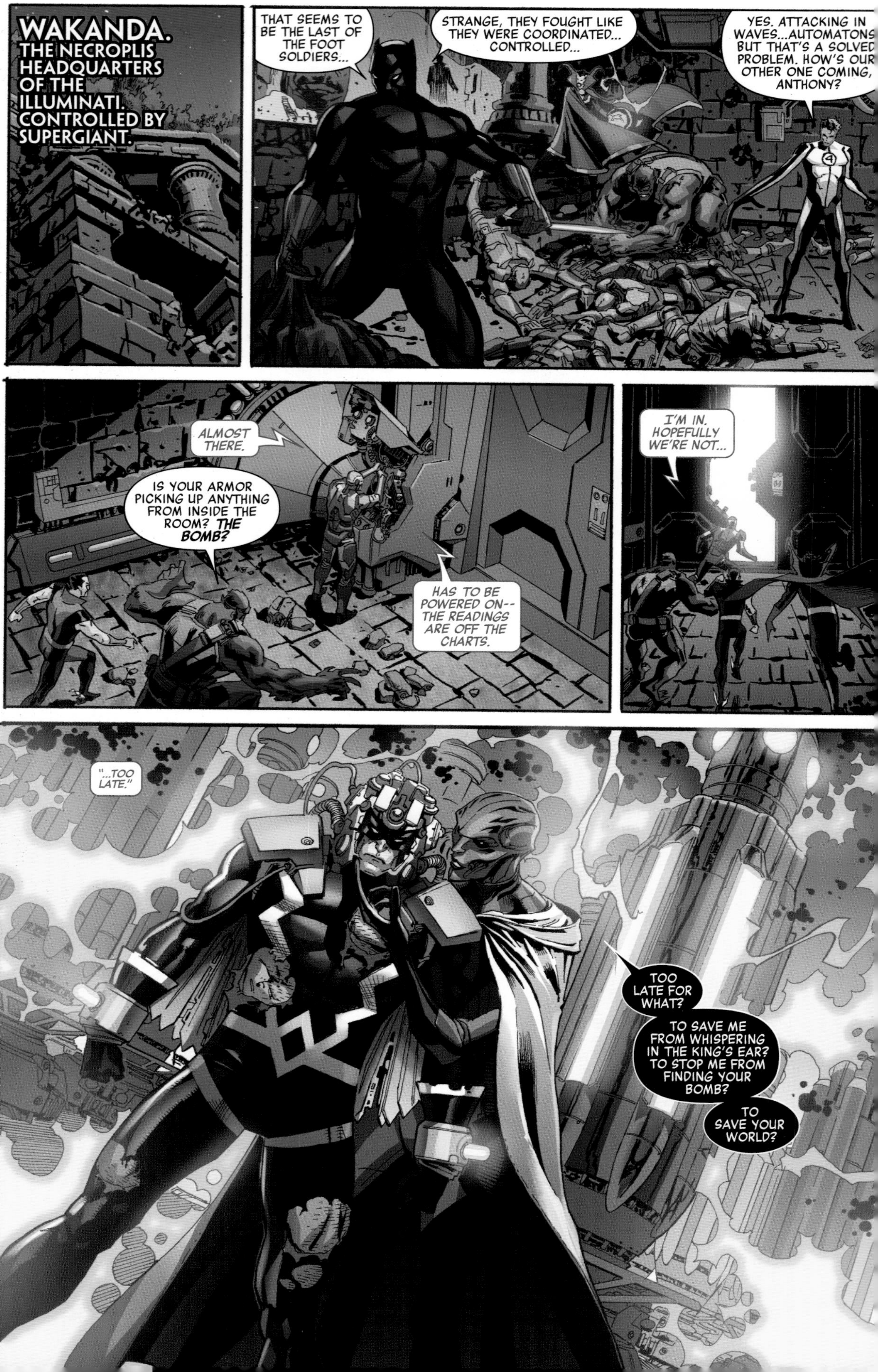
WAKANDA.
THE NECROPLIS HEADQUARTERS OF THE ILLUMINATI. CONTROLLED BY SUPERGIANT.
THAT SEEMS TO BE THE LAST OF THE FOOT SOLDIERS...
STRANGE, THEY FOUGHT LIKE THEY WERE COORDINATED... CONTROLLED...
YES. ATTACKING IN WAVES...AUTOMATONS BUT THAT'S A SOLVED PROBLEM. HOW'S OUR OTHER ONE COMING, ANTHONY?
ALMOST THERE.
IS YOUR ARMOR PICKING UP ANYTHING FROM INSIDE THE ROOM? THE BOMB?
HAS TO BE POWERED ON-- THE READINGS ARE OFF THE CHARTS.
I'M IN. HOPEFULLY WE'RE NOT...
"...TOO LATE."
TOO LATE FOR WHAT?
TO SAVE ME FROM WHISPERING IN THE KING'S EAR? TO STOP ME FROM FINDING YOUR BOMB?
TO SAVE YOUR WORLD?

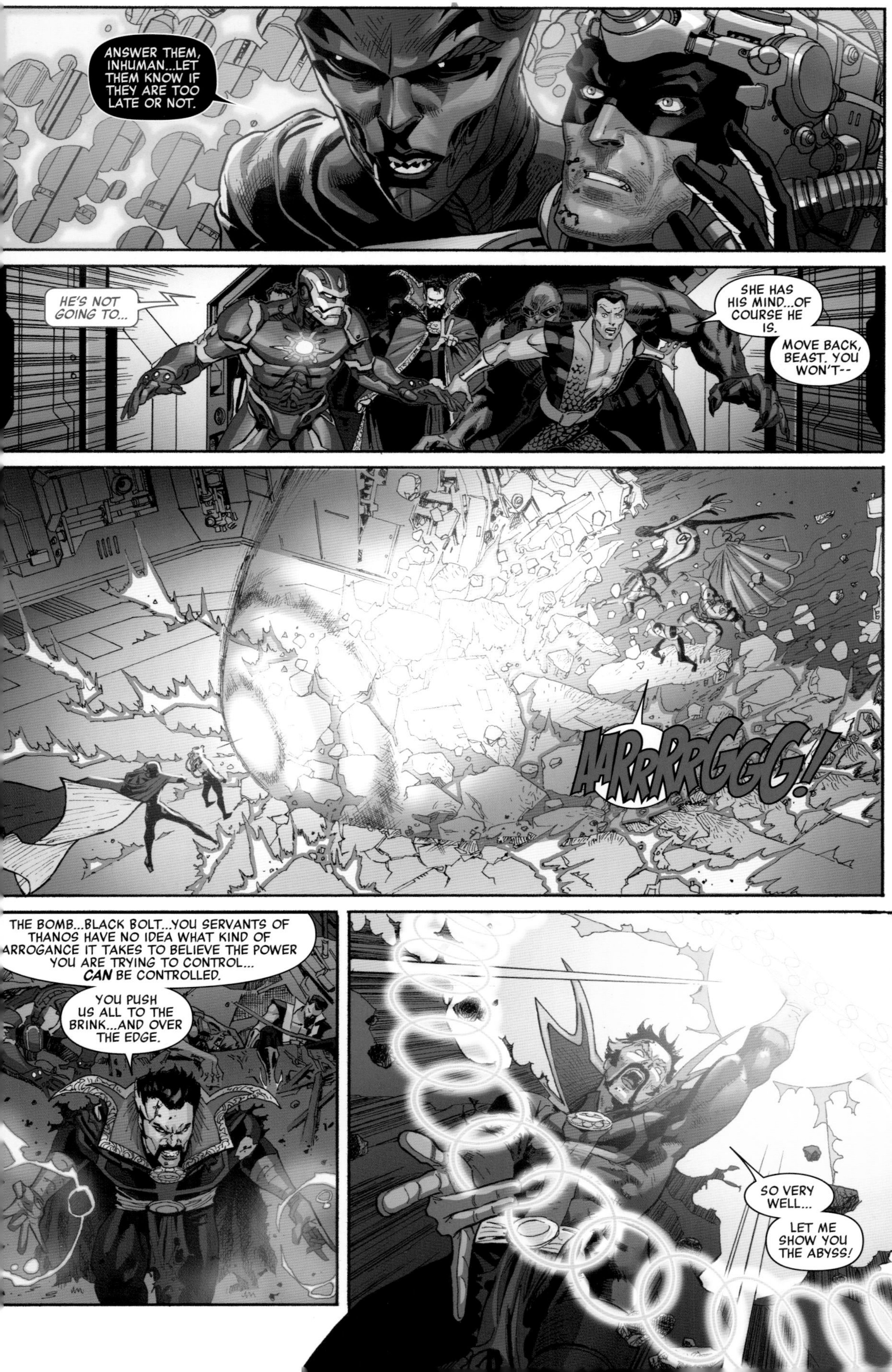
ANSWER THEM, INHUMAN...LET THEM KNOW IF THEY ARE TOO LATE OR NOT.
HE'S NOT GOING TO...
SHE HAS HIS MIND...OF COURSE HE IS.
MOVE BACK, BEAST. YOU WON'T--
AARRRRRGGG!
THE BOMB...BLACK BOLT...YOU SERVANTS OF THANOS HAVE NO IDEA WHAT KIND OF ARROGANCE IT TAKES TO BELIEVE THE POWER YOU ARE TRYING TO CONTROL... CAN BE CONTROLLED.
YOU PUSH US ALL TO THE BRINK...AND OVER THE EDGE.
SO VERY WELL...
LET ME SHOW YOU THE ABYSS!

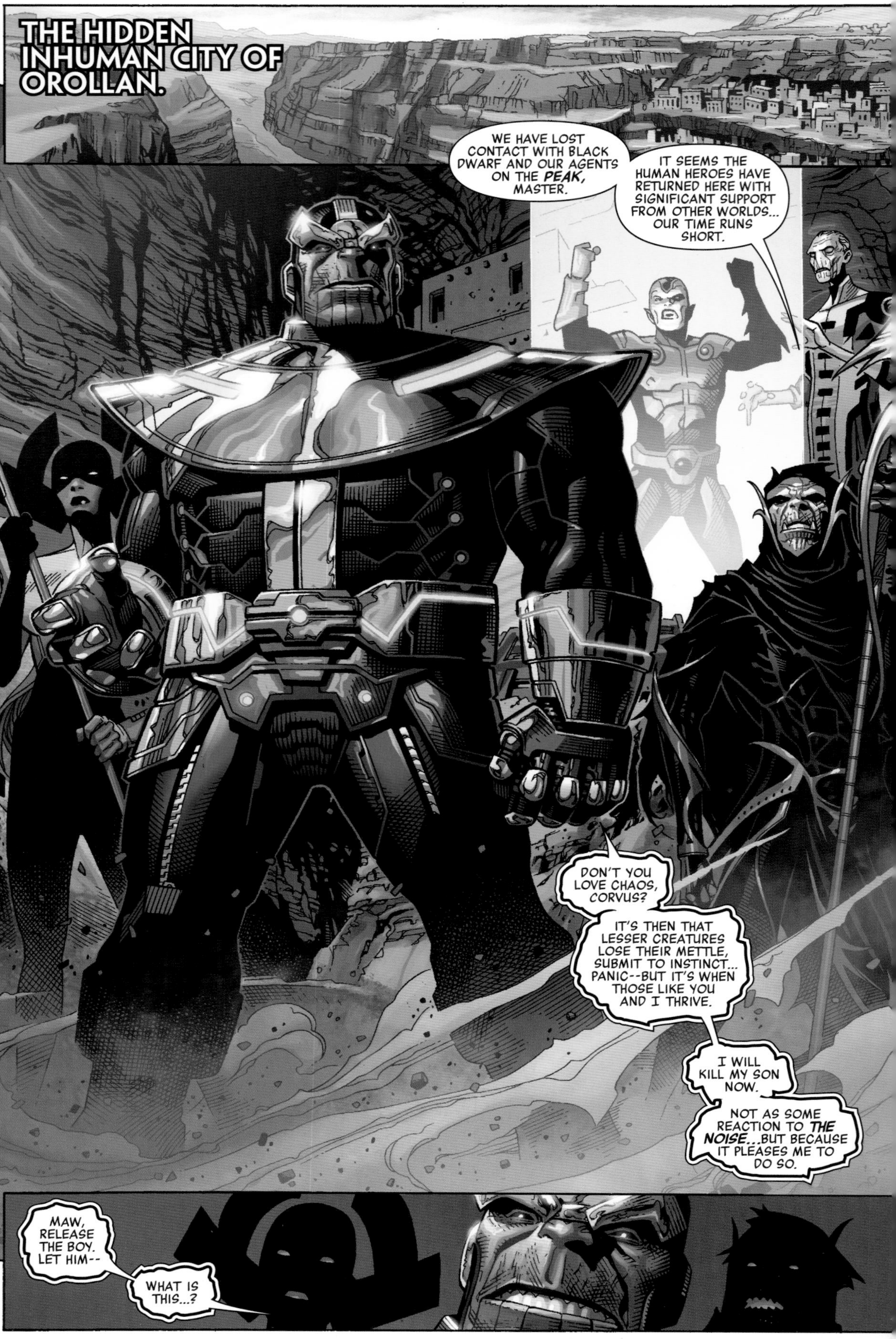
THE HIDDEN INHUMAN CITY OF OROLLAN.
WE HAVE LOST CONTACT WITH BLACK DWARF AND OUR AGENTS ON THE *PEAK,* MASTER.
IT SEEMS THE HUMAN HEROES HAVE RETURNED HERE WITH SIGNIFICANT SUPPORT FROM OTHER WORLDS... OUR TIME RUNS SHORT.
DON'T YOU LOVE CHAOS, CORVUS?
IT'S THEN THAT LESSER CREATURES LOSE THEIR METTLE, SUBMIT TO INSTINCT... PANIC--BUT IT'S WHEN THOSE LIKE YOU AND I THRIVE.
I WILL KILL MY SON NOW.
NOT AS SOME REACTION TO ***THE NOISE...*** BUT BECAUSE IT PLEASES ME TO DO SO.
MAW, RELEASE THE BOY. LET HIM--
WHAT IS THIS...?

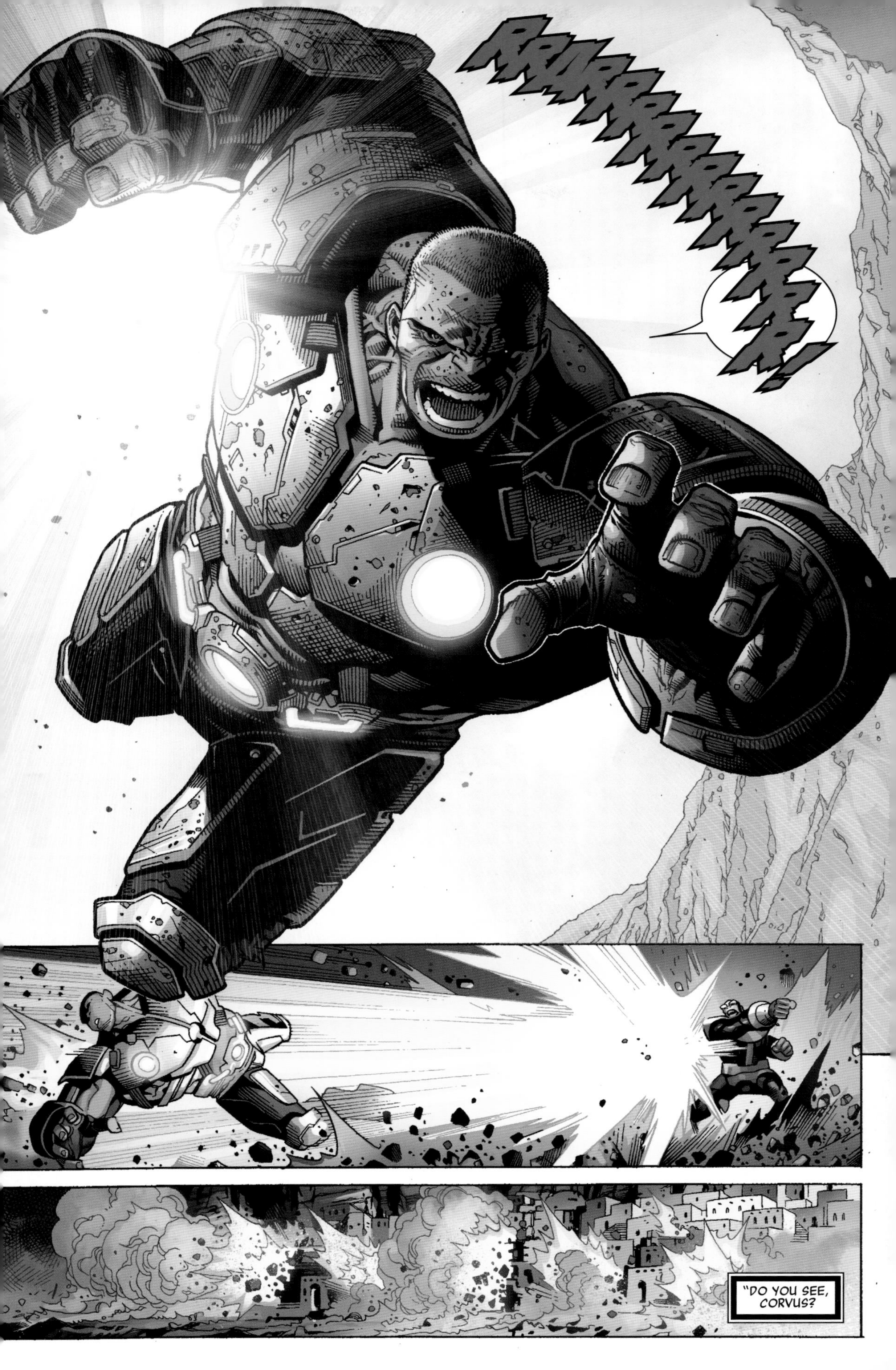
RRRAAARRRRRRRRRRRRR!
"DO YOU SEE, CORVUS?

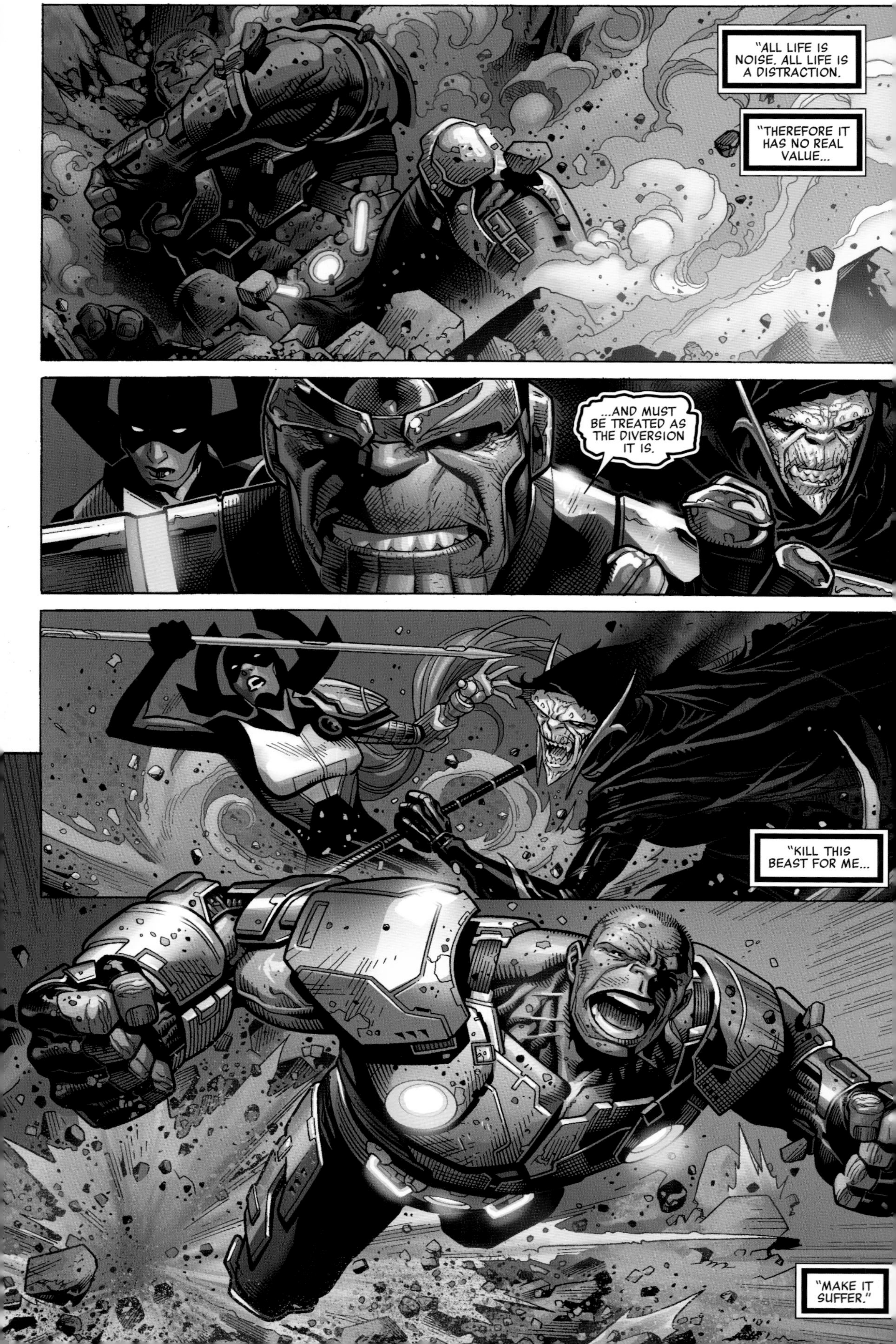
"ALL LIFE IS NOISE. ALL LIFE IS A DISTRACTION.
"THEREFORE IT HAS NO REAL VALUE...
...AND MUST BE TREATED AS THE DIVERSION IT IS.
"KILL THIS BEAST FOR ME...
"MAKE IT SUFFER."

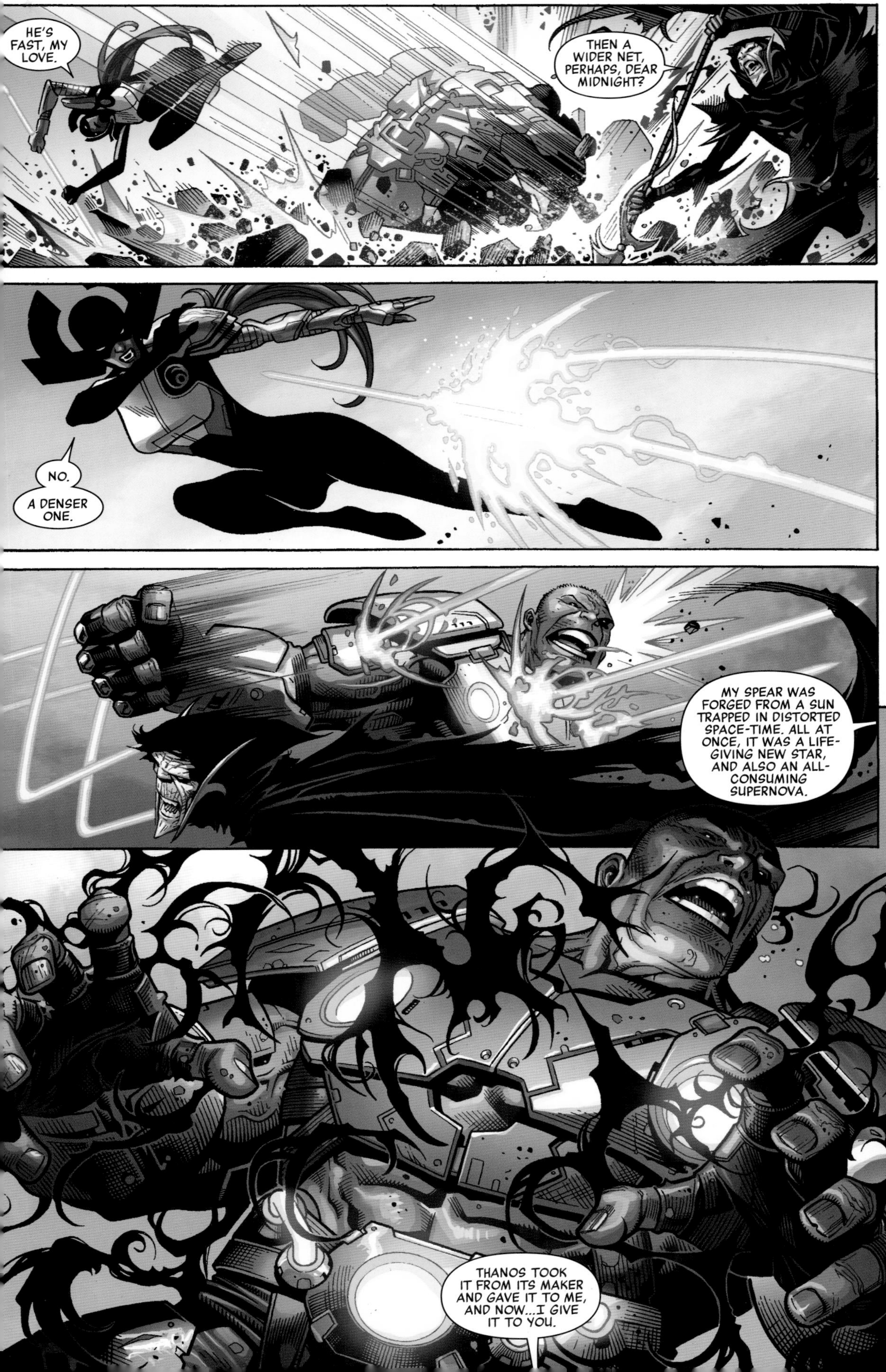
HE'S FAST, MY LOVE.
THEN A WIDER NET, PERHAPS, DEAR MIDNIGHT?
NO.
A DENSER ONE.
MY SPEAR WAS FORGED FROM A SUN TRAPPED IN DISTORTED SPACE-TIME. ALL AT ONCE, IT WAS A LIFE-GIVING NEW STAR, AND ALSO AN ALL-CONSUMING SUPERNOVA.
THANOS TOOK IT FROM ITS MAKER AND GAVE IT TO ME, AND NOW...I GIVE IT TO YOU.

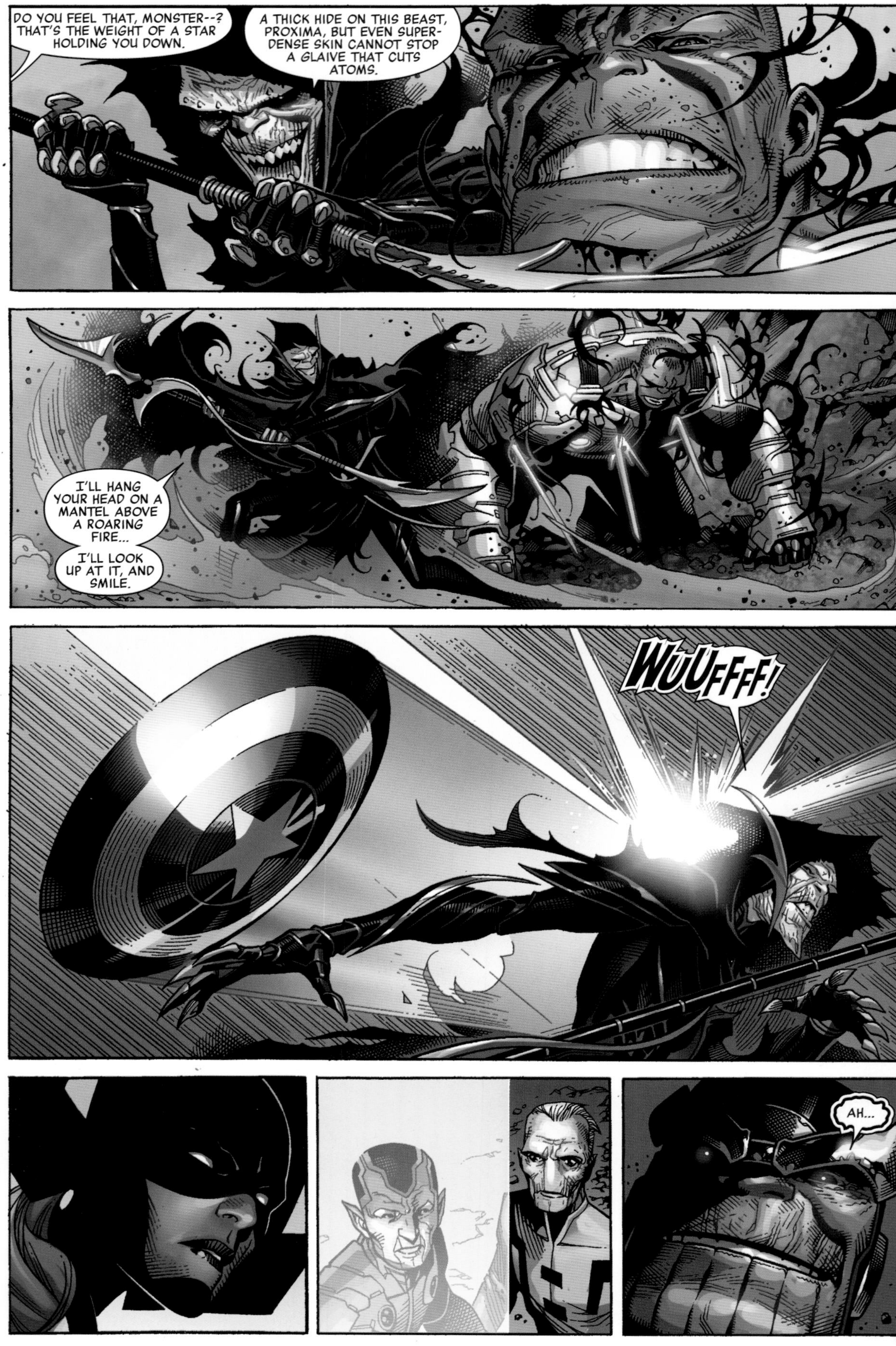
DO YOU FEEL THAT, MONSTER--? THAT'S THE WEIGHT OF A STAR HOLDING YOU DOWN.
A THICK HIDE ON THIS BEAST, PROXIMA, BUT EVEN SUPER-DENSE SKIN CANNOT STOP A GLAIVE THAT CUTS ATOMS.
I'LL HANG YOUR HEAD ON A MANTEL ABOVE A ROARING FIRE...
I'LL LOOK UP AT IT, AND SMILE.
WUUFFFF!
AH...

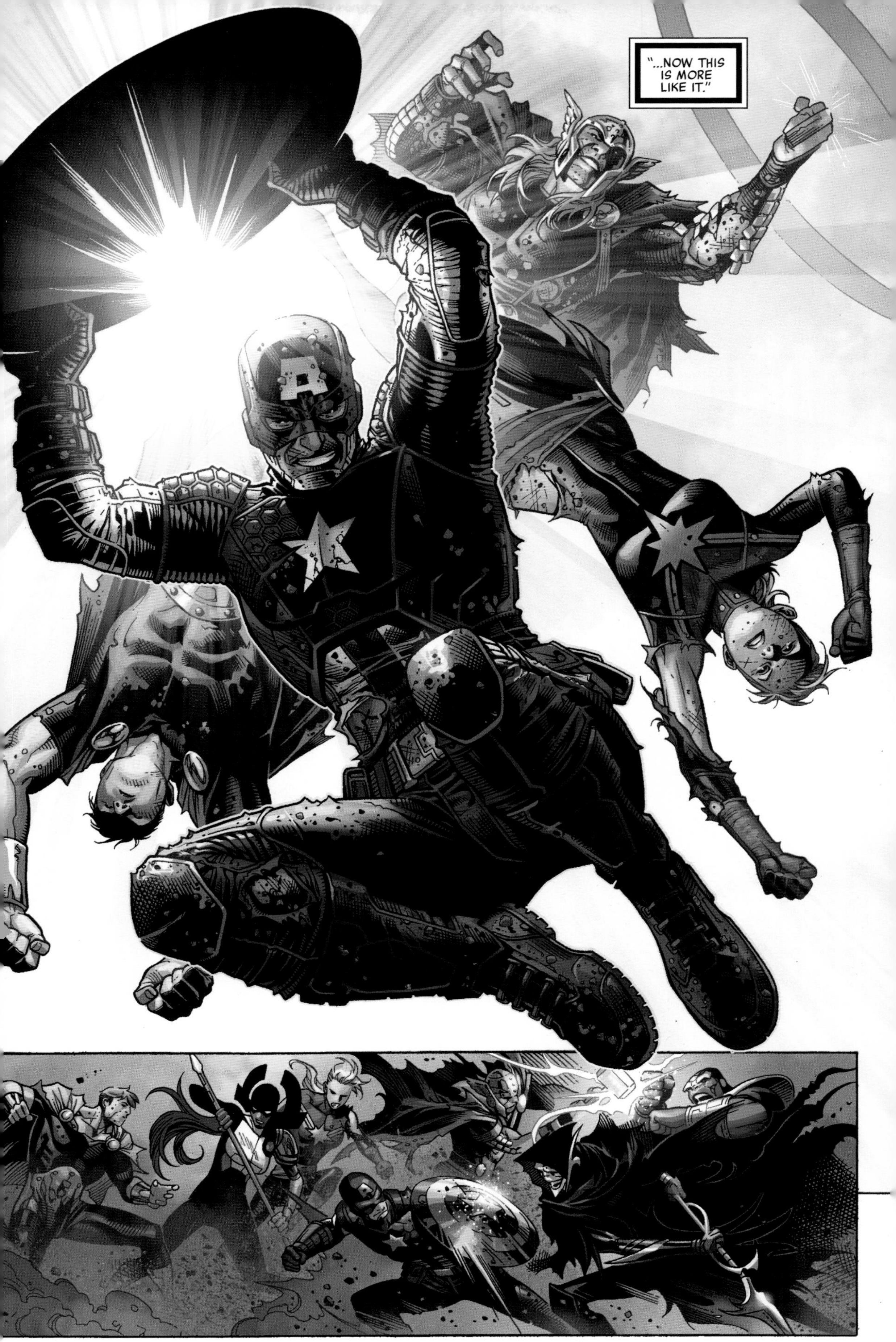
"...NOW THIS IS MORE LIKE IT."

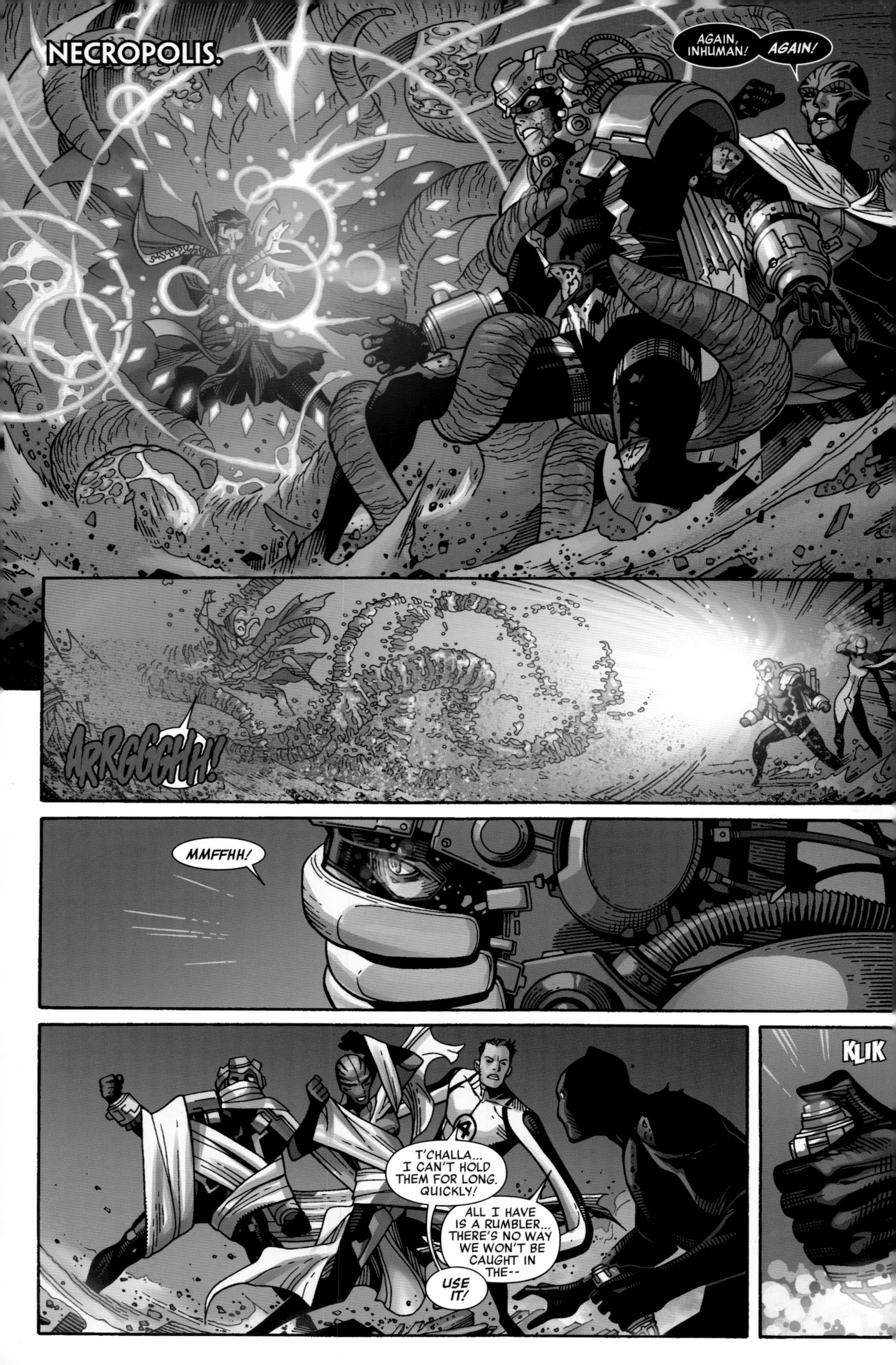
NECROPOLIS.
AGAIN, INHUMAN!
AGAIN!
ARRGGGHH!
MMFFHH!
T'CHALLA... I CAN'T HOLD THEM FOR LONG. QUICKLY!
ALL I HAVE IS A RUMBLER... THERE'S NO WAY WE WON'T BE CAUGHT IN THE--
USE IT!
KLIK

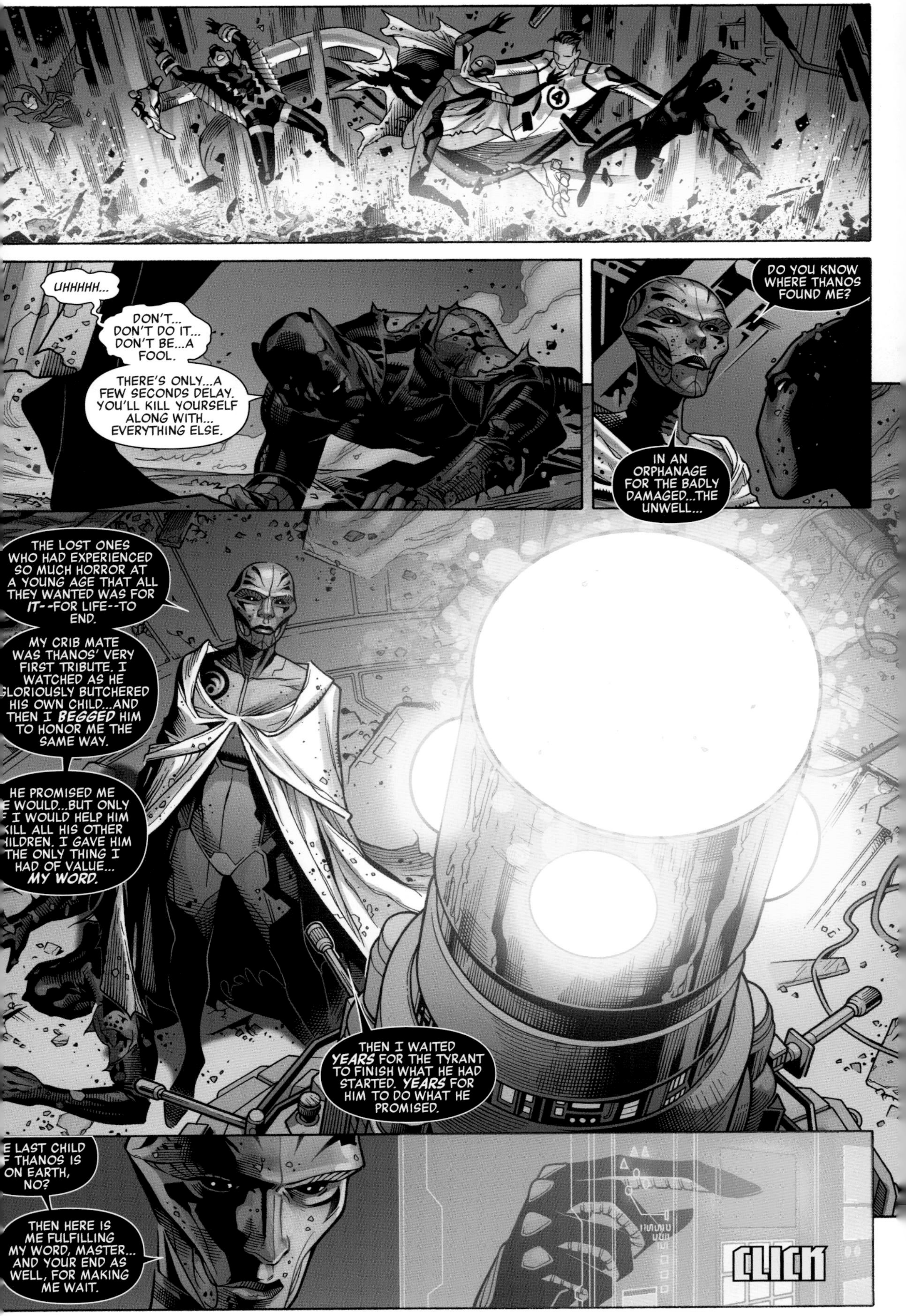
UHHHHH...
DON'T... DON'T DO IT... DON'T BE...A FOOL.
THERE'S ONLY...A FEW SECONDS DELAY. YOU'LL KILL YOURSELF ALONG WITH... EVERYTHING ELSE.
DO YOU KNOW WHERE THANOS FOUND ME?
IN AN ORPHANAGE FOR THE BADLY DAMAGED...THE UNWELL...
THE LOST ONES WHO HAD EXPERIENCED SO MUCH HORROR AT A YOUNG AGE THAT ALL THEY WANTED WAS FOR IT--FOR LIFE--TO END.
MY CRIB MATE WAS THANOS' VERY FIRST TRIBUTE. I WATCHED AS HE GLORIOUSLY BUTCHERED HIS OWN CHILD...AND THEN I BEGGED HIM TO HONOR ME THE SAME WAY.
HE PROMISED ME HE WOULD...BUT ONLY IF I WOULD HELP HIM KILL ALL HIS OTHER CHILDREN. I GAVE HIM THE ONLY THING I HAD OF VALUE... MY WORD.
THEN I WAITED YEARS FOR THE TYRANT TO FINISH WHAT HE HAD STARTED. YEARS FOR HIM TO DO WHAT HE PROMISED.
THE LAST CHILD OF THANOS IS ON EARTH, NO?
THEN HERE IS ME FULFILLING MY WORD, MASTER... AND YOUR END AS WELL, FOR MAKING ME WAIT.
CLICK

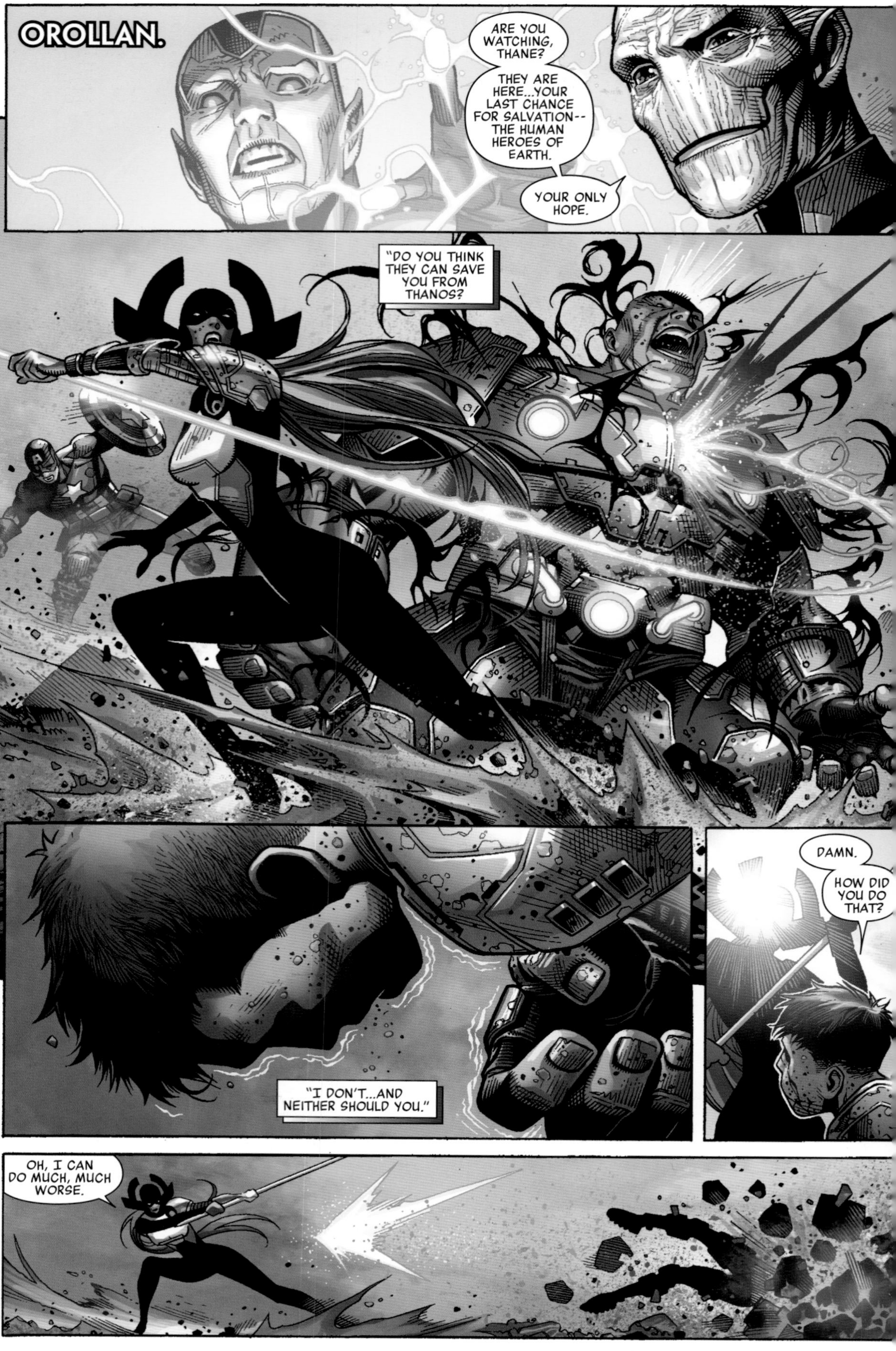
OROLLAN.
ARE YOU WATCHING, THANE?
THEY ARE HERE...YOUR LAST CHANCE FOR SALVATION-- THE HUMAN HEROES OF EARTH.
YOUR ONLY HOPE.
"DO YOU THINK THEY CAN SAVE YOU FROM THANOS?
"I DON'T...AND NEITHER SHOULD YOU."
DAMN.
HOW DID YOU DO THAT?
OH, I CAN DO MUCH, MUCH WORSE.

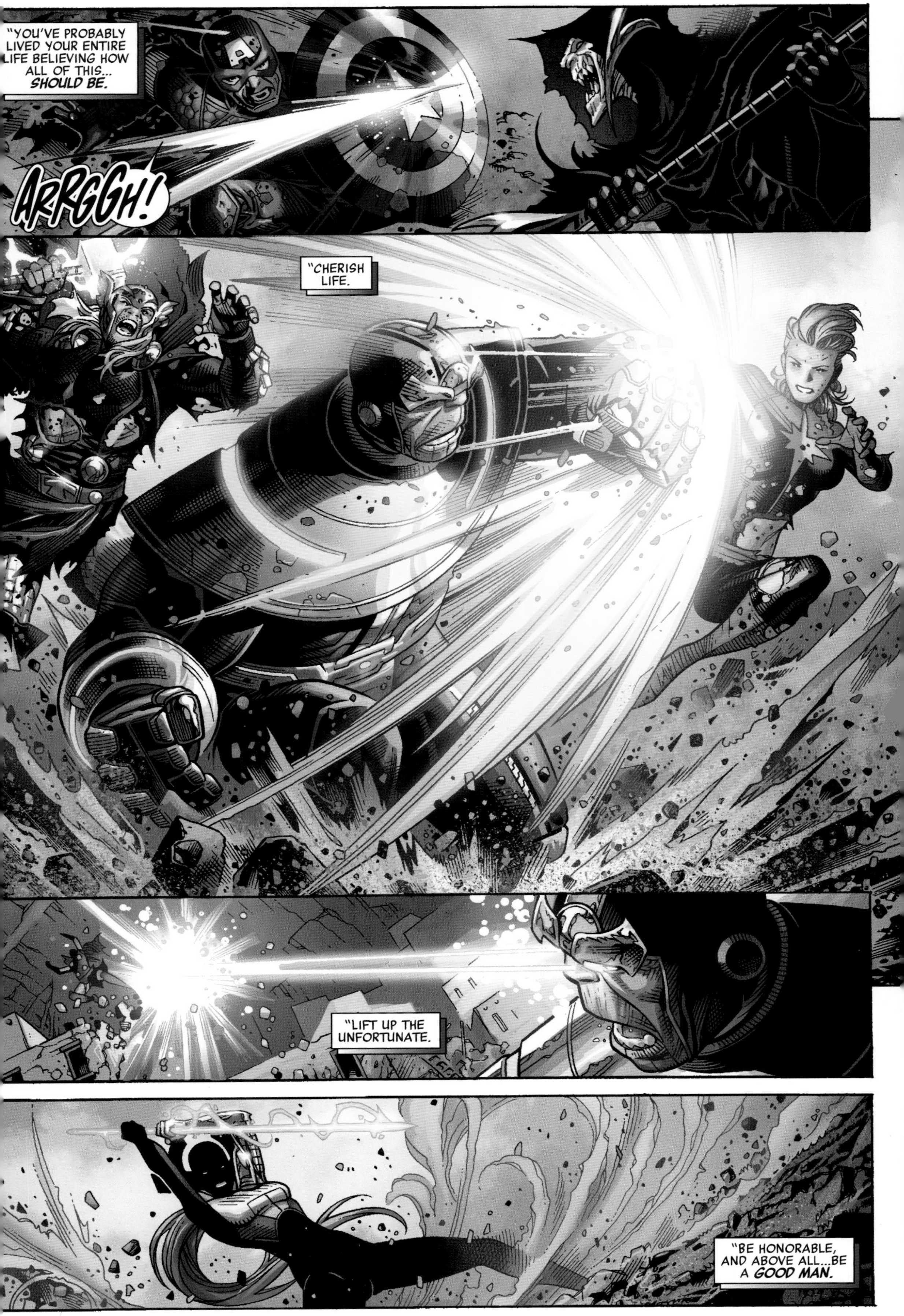
"YOU'VE PROBABLY LIVED YOUR ENTIRE LIFE BELIEVING HOW ALL OF THIS... SHOULD BE.
ARRGGH!
"CHERISH LIFE.
"LIFT UP THE UNFORTUNATE.
"BE HONORABLE, AND ABOVE ALL...BE A GOOD MAN.

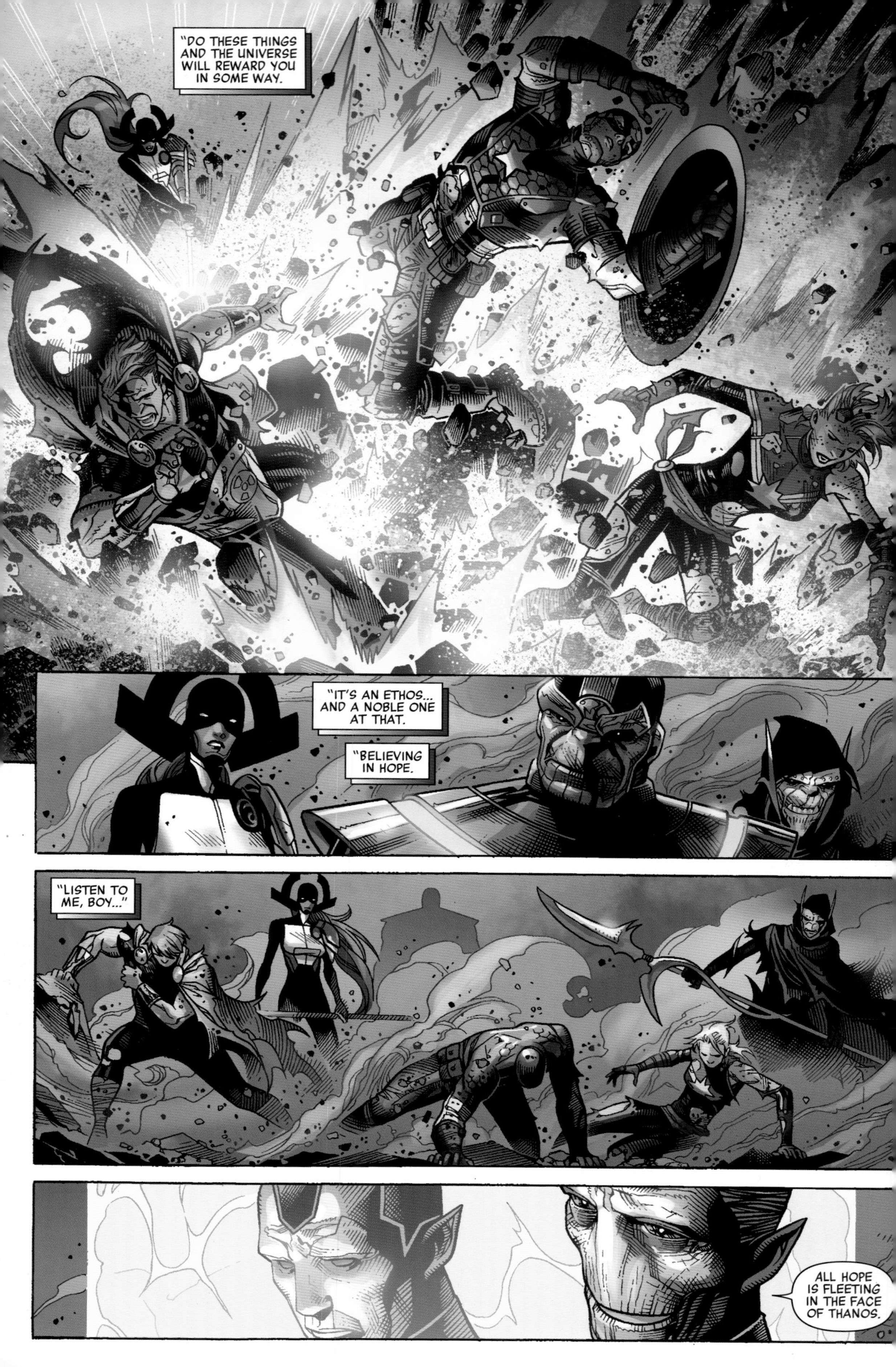
"DO THESE THINGS AND THE UNIVERSE WILL REWARD YOU IN SOME WAY.
"IT'S AN ETHOS... AND A NOBLE ONE AT THAT.
"BELIEVING IN HOPE.
"LISTEN TO ME, BOY..."
ALL HOPE IS FLEETING IN THE FACE OF THANOS.

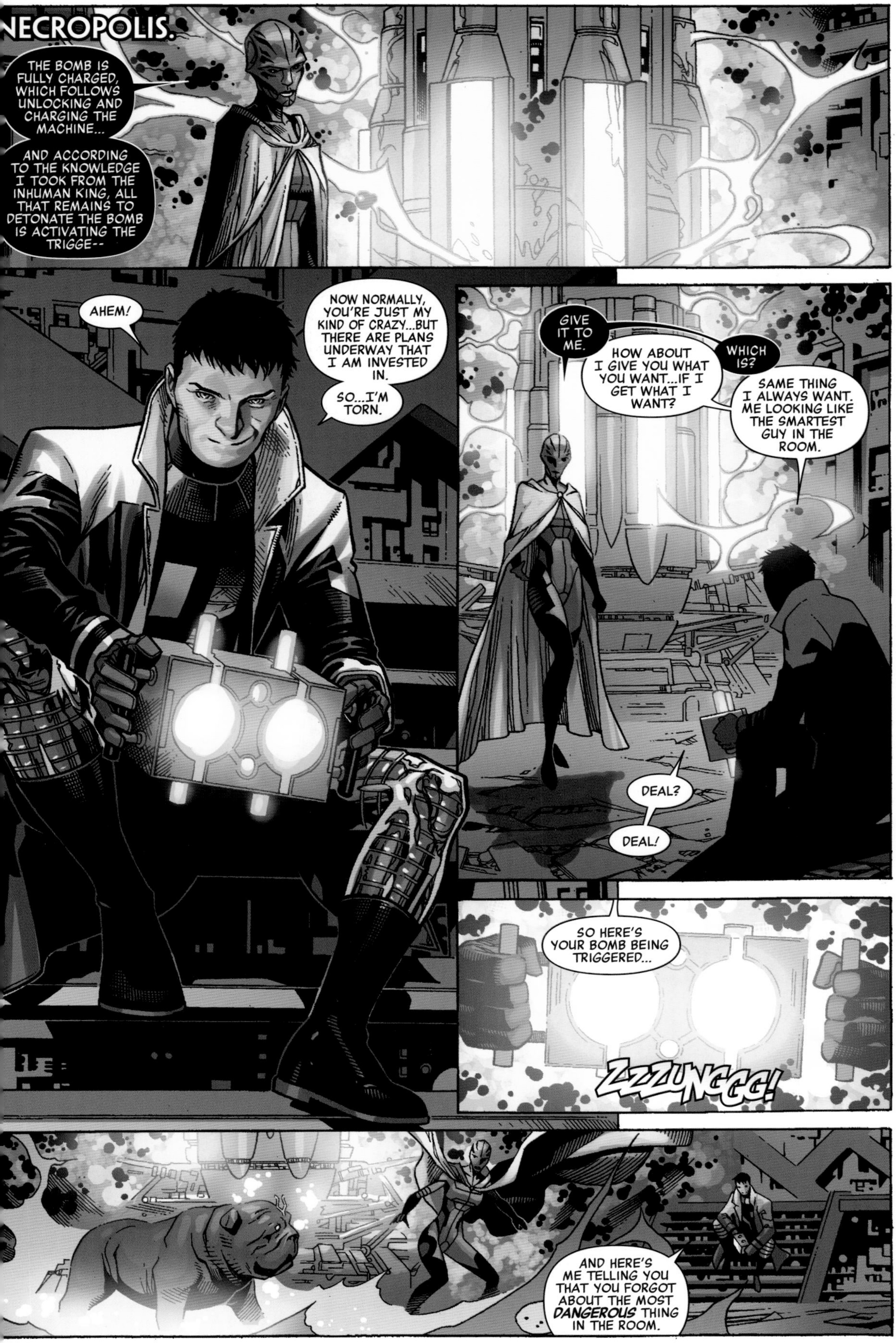
NECROPOLIS.
THE BOMB IS FULLY CHARGED, WHICH FOLLOWS UNLOCKING AND CHARGING THE MACHINE...
AND ACCORDING TO THE KNOWLEDGE I TOOK FROM THE INHUMAN KING, ALL THAT REMAINS TO DETONATE THE BOMB IS ACTIVATING THE TRIGGE--
AHEM!
NOW NORMALLY, YOU'RE JUST MY KIND OF CRAZY...BUT THERE ARE PLANS UNDERWAY THAT I AM INVESTED IN.
SO...I'M TORN.
GIVE IT TO ME.
HOW ABOUT I GIVE YOU WHAT YOU WANT...IF I GET WHAT I WANT?
WHICH IS?
SAME THING I ALWAYS WANT. ME LOOKING LIKE THE SMARTEST GUY IN THE ROOM.
DEAL?
DEAL!
SO HERE'S YOUR BOMB BEING TRIGGERED...
ZZZUNGGG!
AND HERE'S ME TELLING YOU THAT YOU FORGOT ABOUT THE MOST DANGEROUS THING IN THE ROOM.

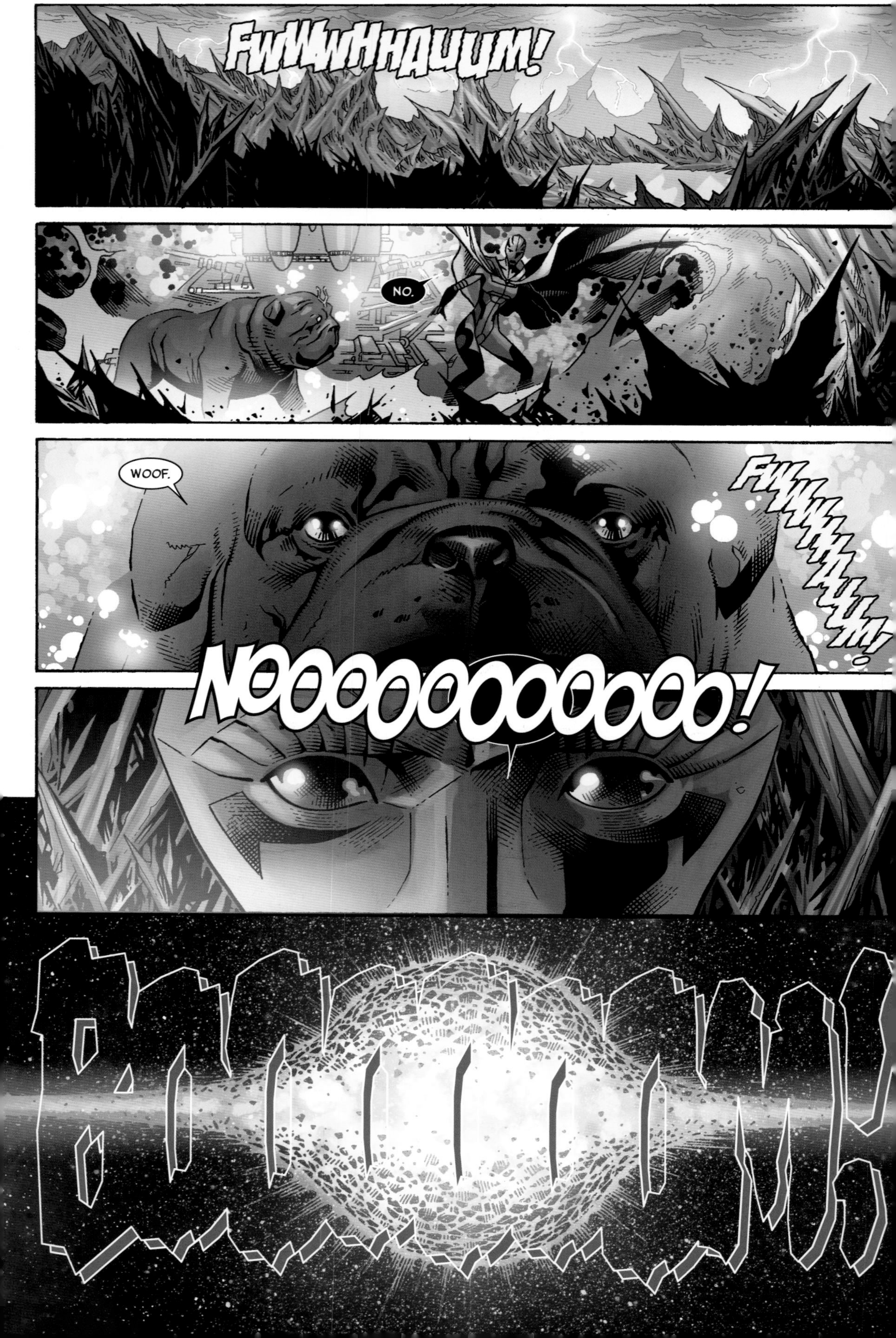
FWWWHHAUUM!
NO.
WOOF.
FWWWHHAUUM!
NOOOOOOOOOOOO!

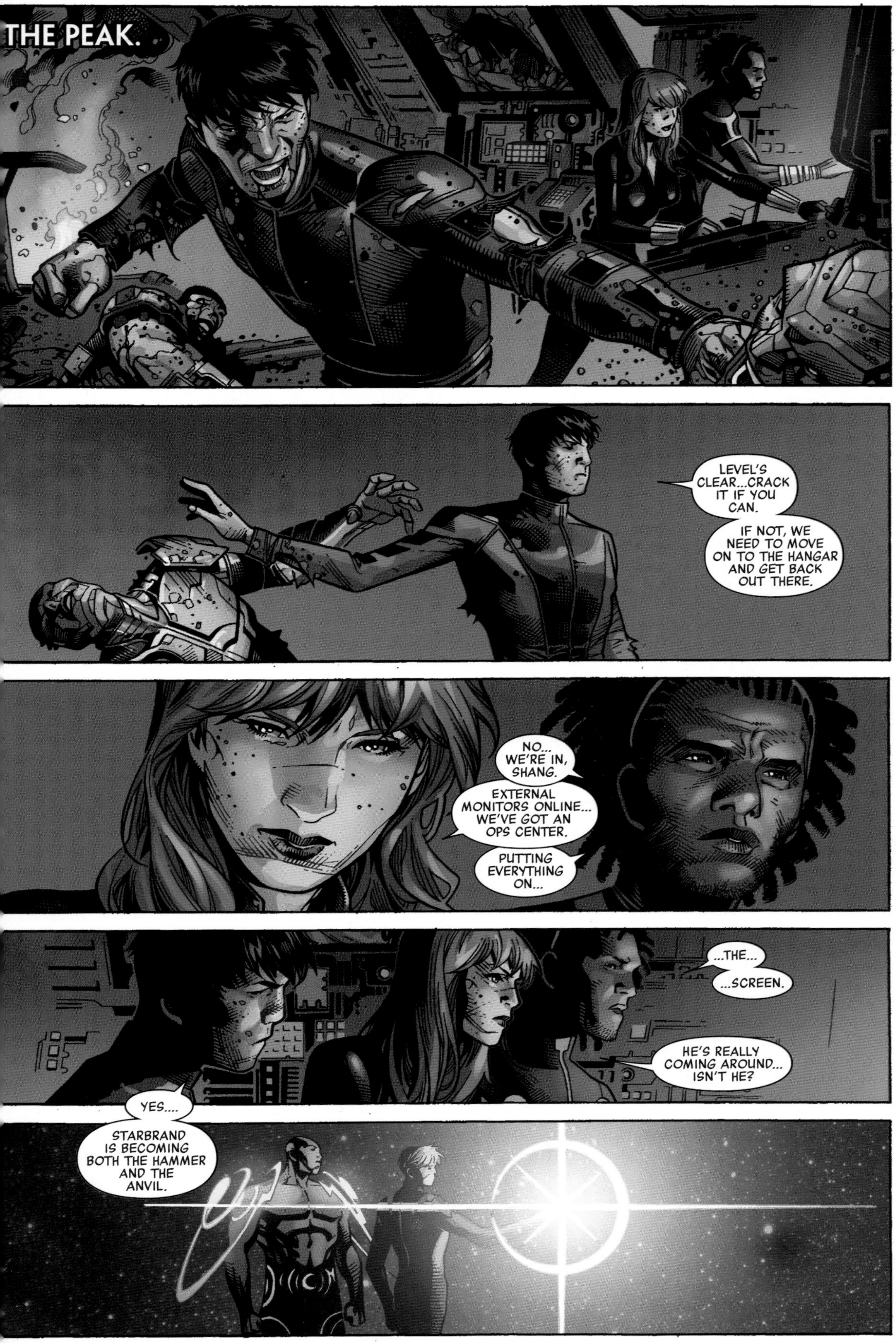
THE PEAK.
LEVEL'S CLEAR...CRACK IT IF YOU CAN.
IF NOT, WE NEED TO MOVE ON TO THE HANGAR AND GET BACK OUT THERE.
NO... WE'RE IN, SHANG.
EXTERNAL MONITORS ONLINE... WE'VE GOT AN OPS CENTER.
PUTTING EVERYTHING ON...
...THE...
...SCREEN.
HE'S REALLY COMING AROUND... ISN'T HE?
YES....
STARBRAND IS BECOMING BOTH THE HAMMER AND THE ANVIL.

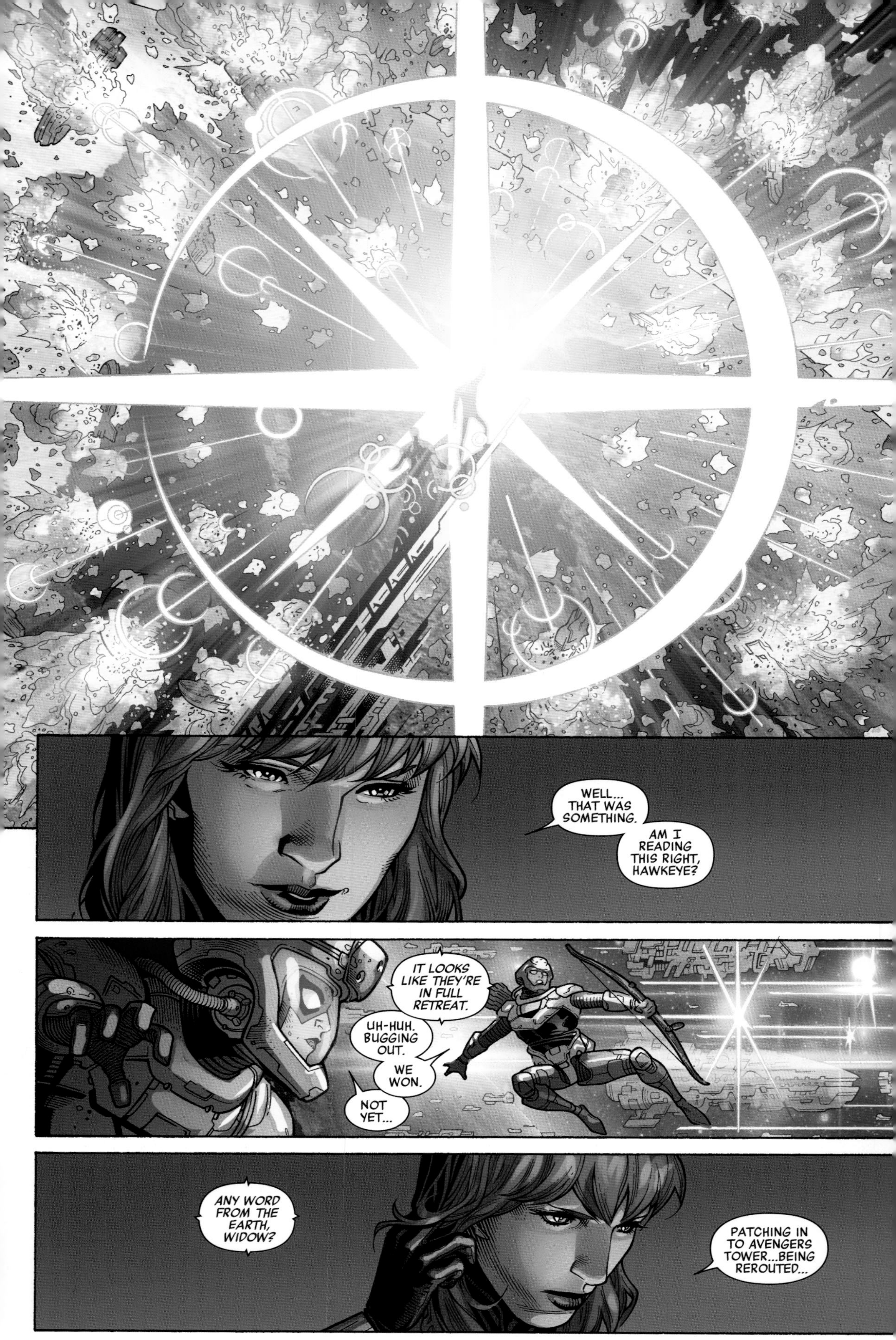
WELL... THAT WAS SOMETHING.
AM I READING THIS RIGHT, HAWKEYE?
IT LOOKS LIKE THEY'RE IN FULL RETREAT.
UH-HUH. BUGGING OUT.
WE WON.
NOT YET...
ANY WORD FROM THE EARTH, WIDOW?
PATCHING IN TO AVENGERS TOWER...BEING REROUTED...

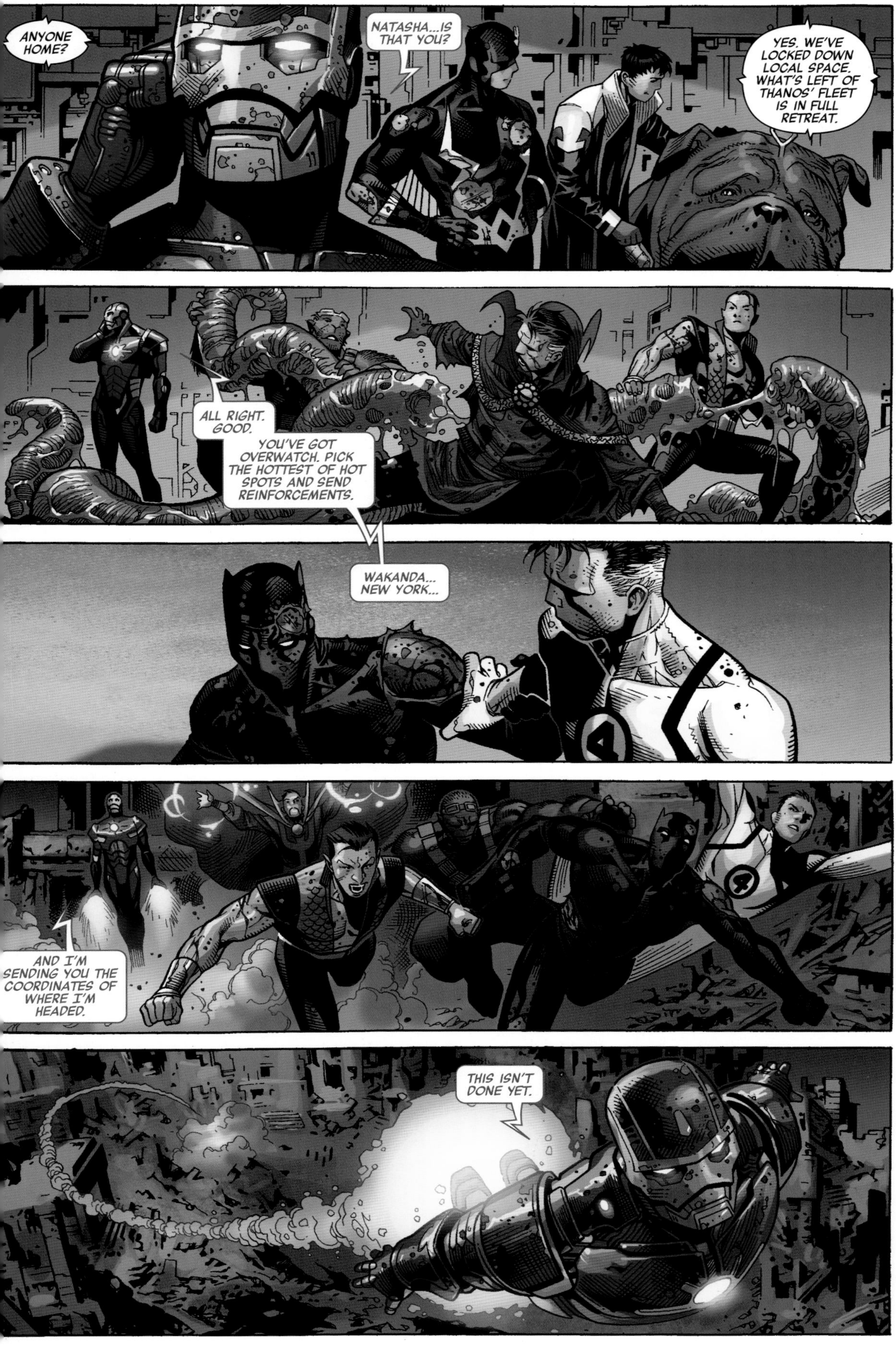
ANYONE HOME?
NATASHA...IS THAT YOU?
YES. WE'VE LOCKED DOWN LOCAL SPACE. WHAT'S LEFT OF THANOS' FLEET IS IN FULL RETREAT.
ALL RIGHT. GOOD.
YOU'VE GOT OVERWATCH. PICK THE HOTTEST OF HOT SPOTS AND SEND REINFORCEMENTS.
WAKANDA... NEW YORK...
AND I'M SENDING YOU THE COORDINATES OF WHERE I'M HEADED.
THIS ISN'T DONE YET.

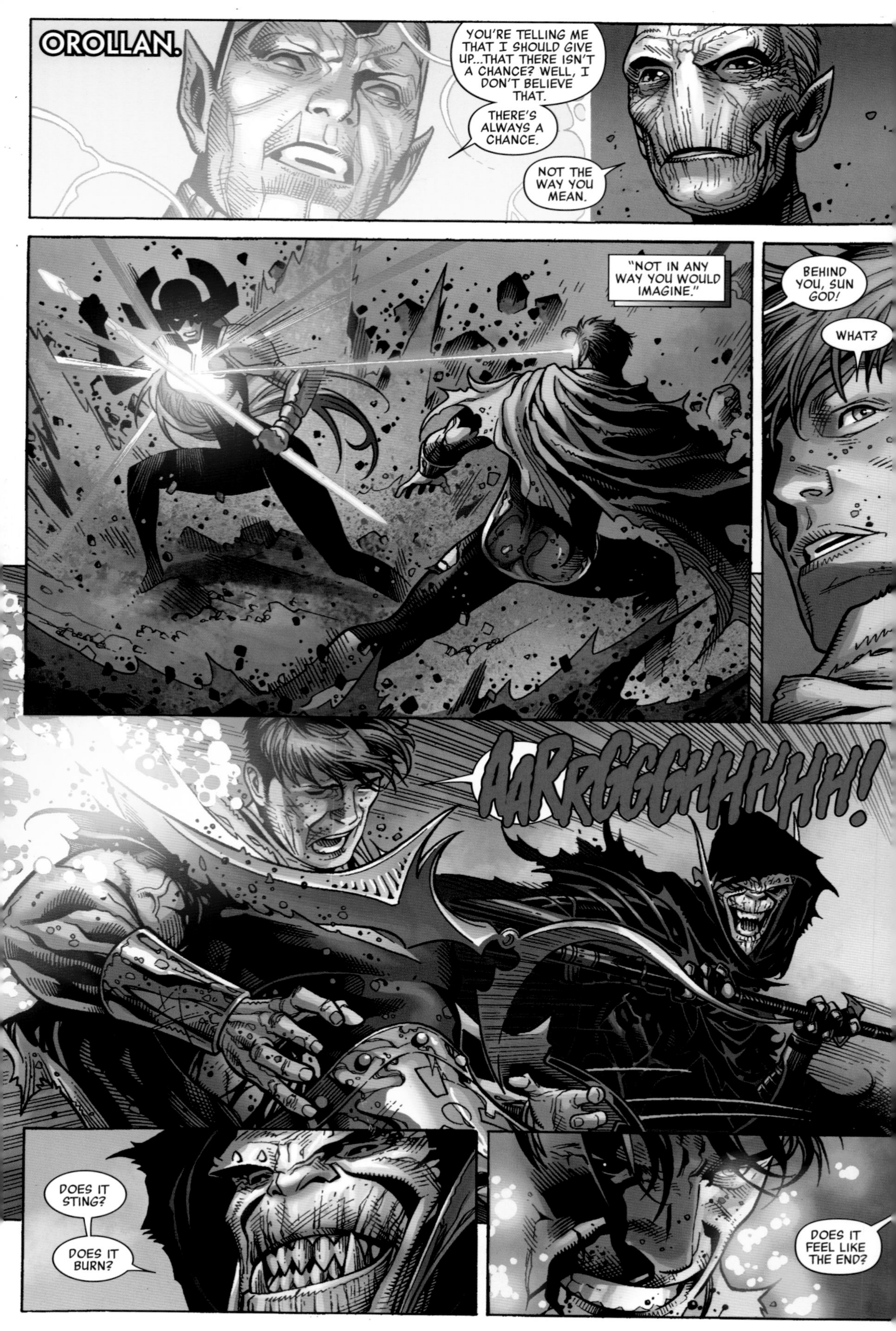

OROLLAN.
YOU'RE TELLING ME THAT I SHOULD GIVE UP...THAT THERE ISN'T A CHANCE? WELL, I DON'T BELIEVE THAT.
THERE'S ALWAYS A CHANCE.
NOT THE WAY YOU MEAN.
"NOT IN ANY WAY YOU WOULD IMAGINE."
BEHIND YOU, SUN GOD!
WHAT?
AARRGGGHHHHHH!
DOES IT STING?
DOES IT BURN?
DOES IT FEEL LIKE THE END?

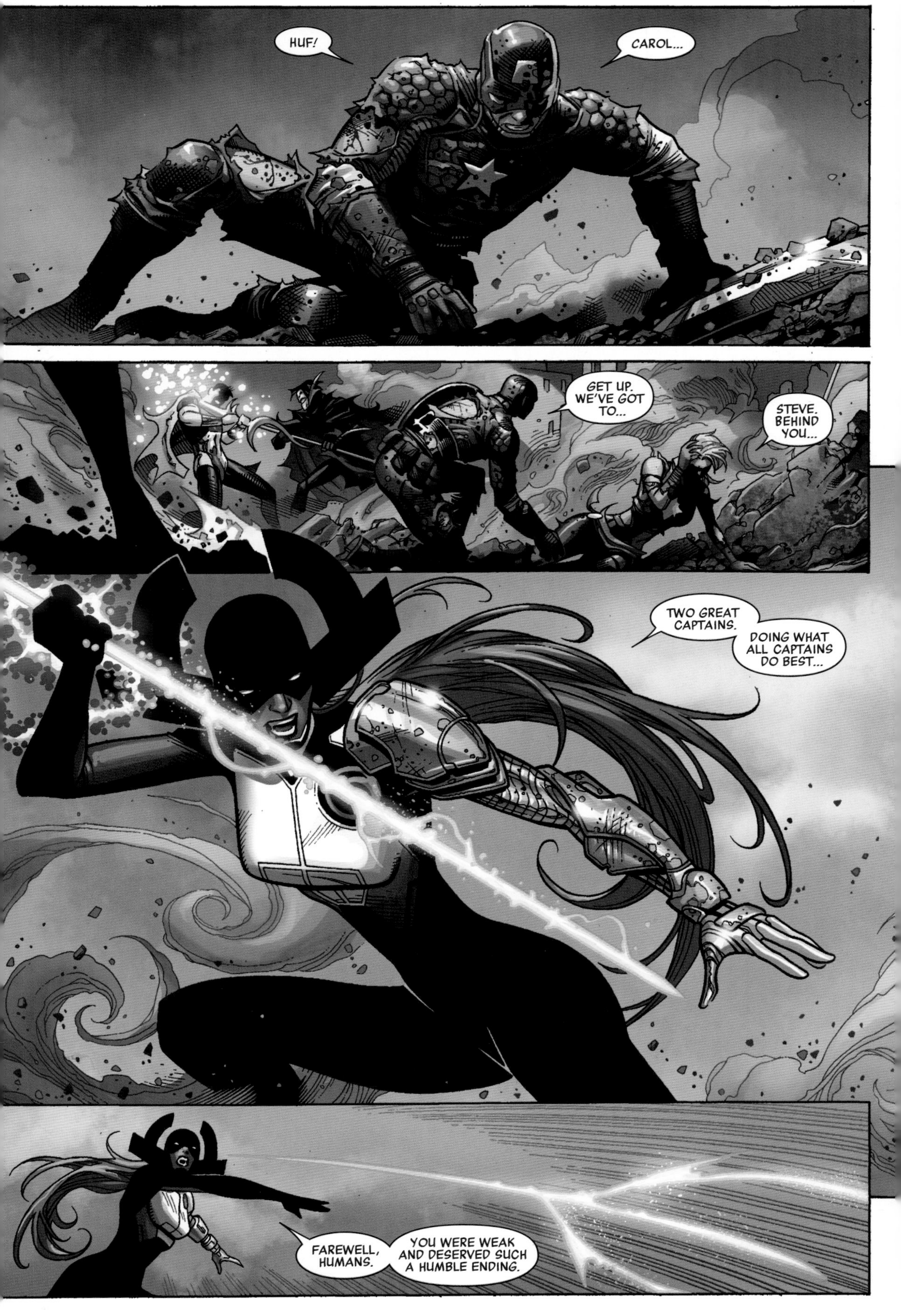
HUF!
CAROL...
GET UP. WE'VE GOT TO...
STEVE. BEHIND YOU...
TWO GREAT CAPTAINS.
DOING WHAT ALL CAPTAINS DO BEST...
FAREWELL, HUMANS.
YOU WERE WEAK AND DESERVED SUCH A HUMBLE ENDING.

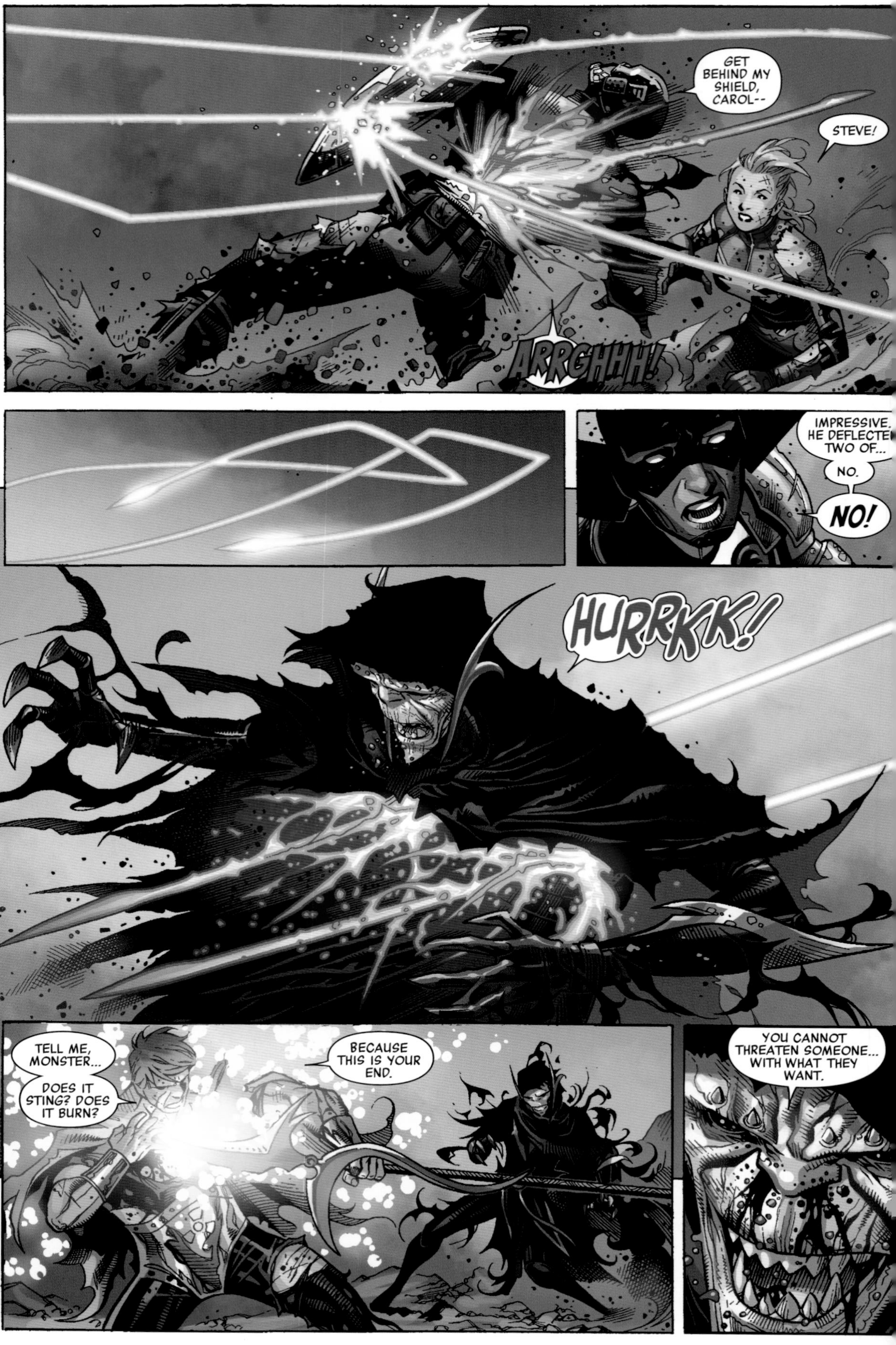
GET BEHIND MY SHIELD, CAROL--
STEVE!
ARRGHHH!
IMPRESSIVE. HE DEFLECTE TWO OF...
NO.
NO!
HURRKK!
TELL ME, MONSTER...
DOES IT STING? DOES IT BURN?
BECAUSE THIS IS YOUR END.
YOU CANNOT THREATEN SOMEONE... WITH WHAT THEY WANT.

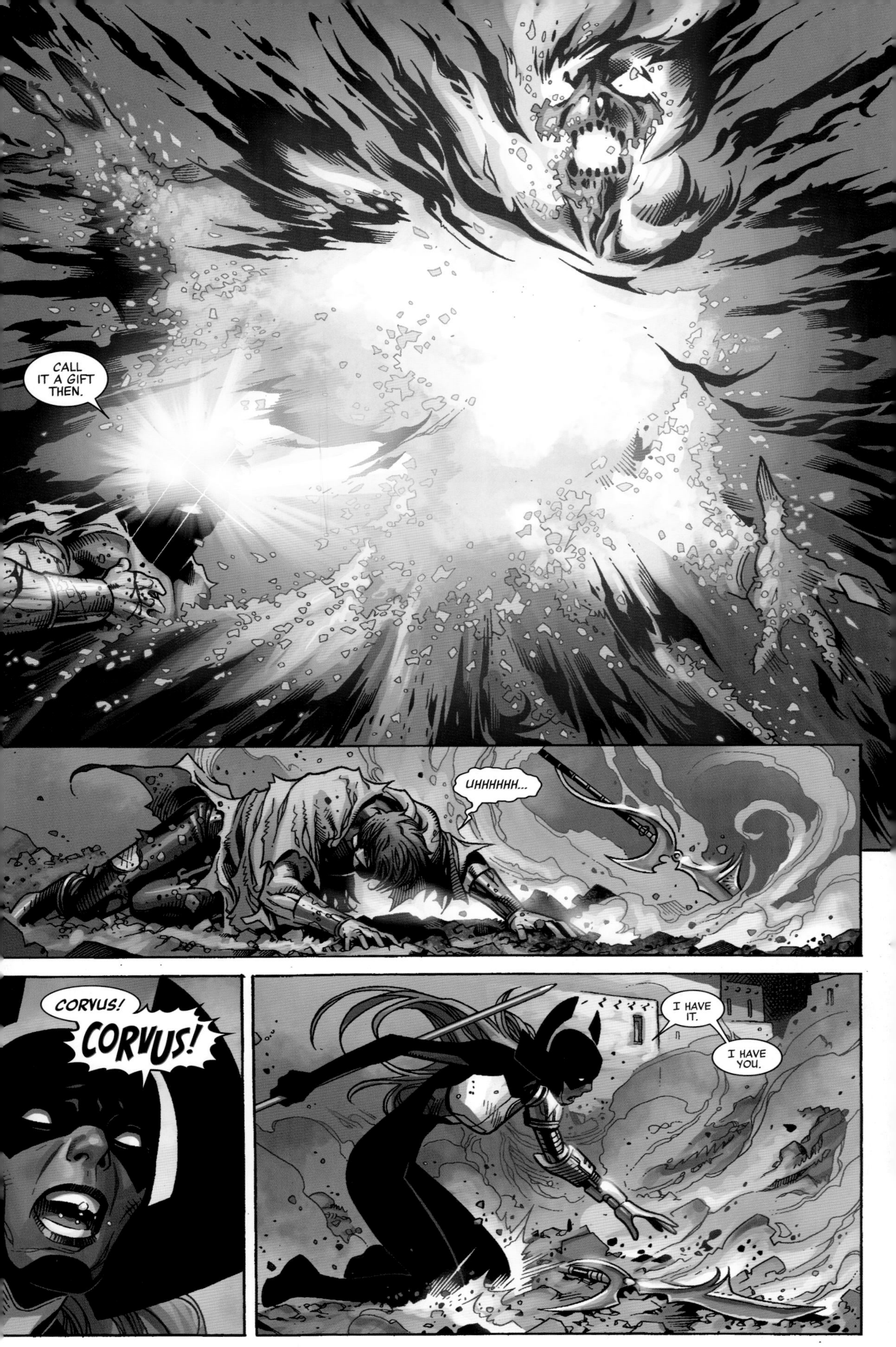
CALL IT A GIFT THEN.
UHHHHHH...
CORVUS!
CORVUS!
I HAVE IT.
I HAVE YOU.

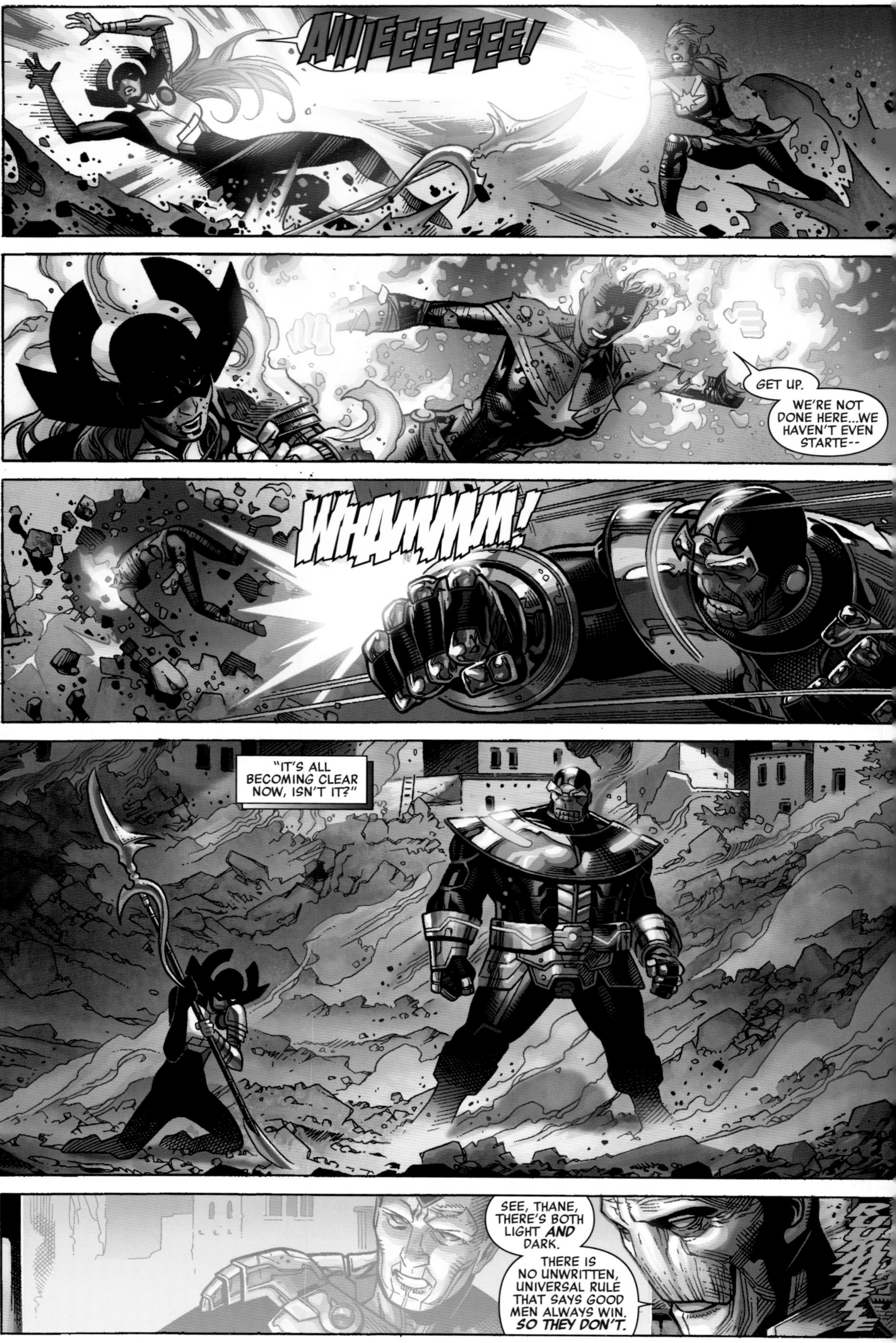
AIIIEEEEEEEE!
GET UP.
WE'RE NOT DONE HERE...WE HAVEN'T EVEN STARTE--
WHAMMMM!
"IT'S ALL BECOMING CLEAR NOW, ISN'T IT?"
SEE, THANE, THERE'S BOTH LIGHT **AND** DARK.
THERE IS NO UNWRITTEN, UNIVERSAL RULE THAT SAYS GOOD MEN ALWAYS WIN. ***SO THEY DON'T.***

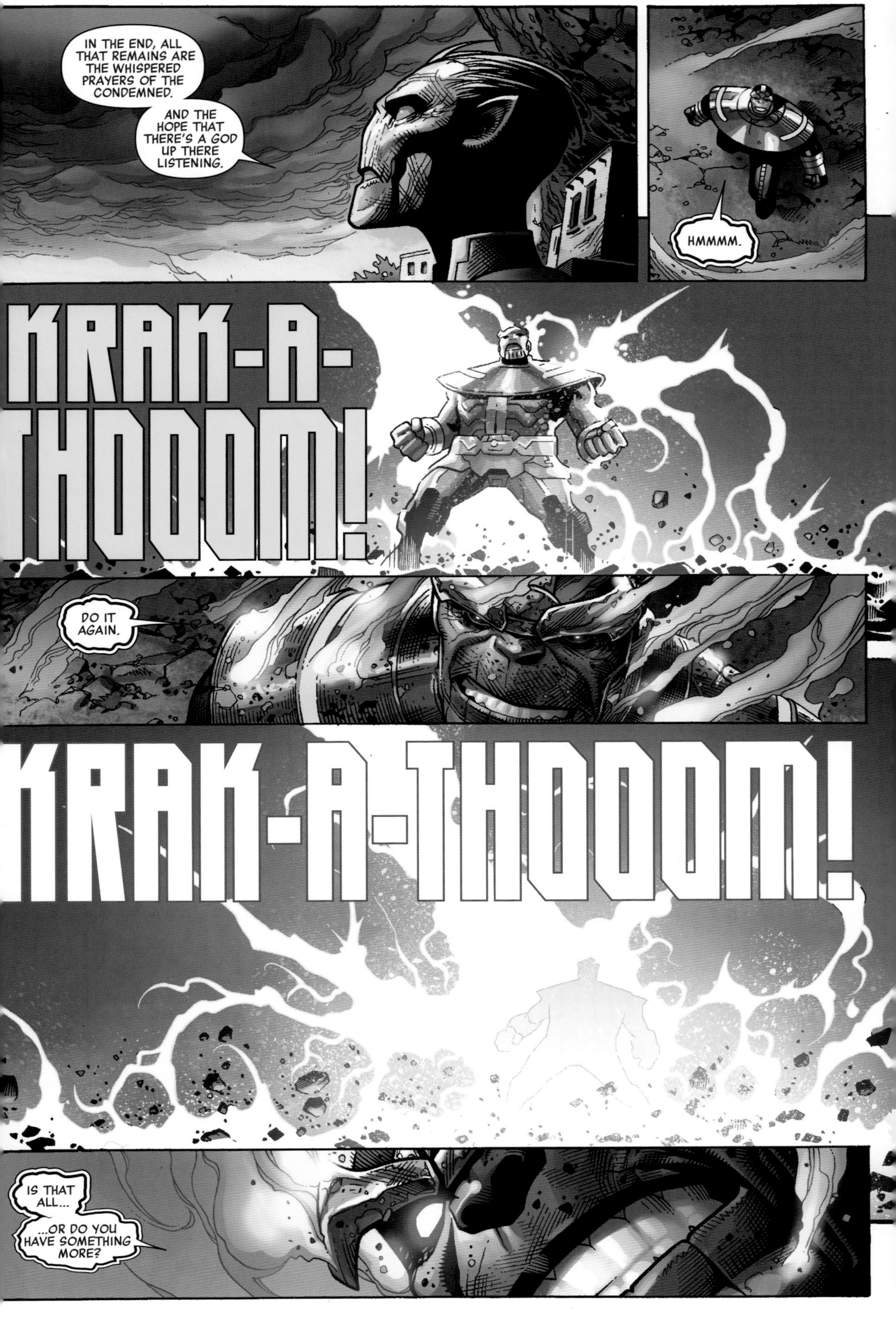
IN THE END, ALL THAT REMAINS ARE THE WHISPERED PRAYERS OF THE CONDEMNED.
AND THE HOPE THAT THERE'S A GOD UP THERE LISTENING.
HMMMM.
KRAK-A-THOOOM!
DO IT AGAIN.
KRAK-A-THOOOM!
IS THAT ALL...
...OR DO YOU HAVE SOMETHING MORE?

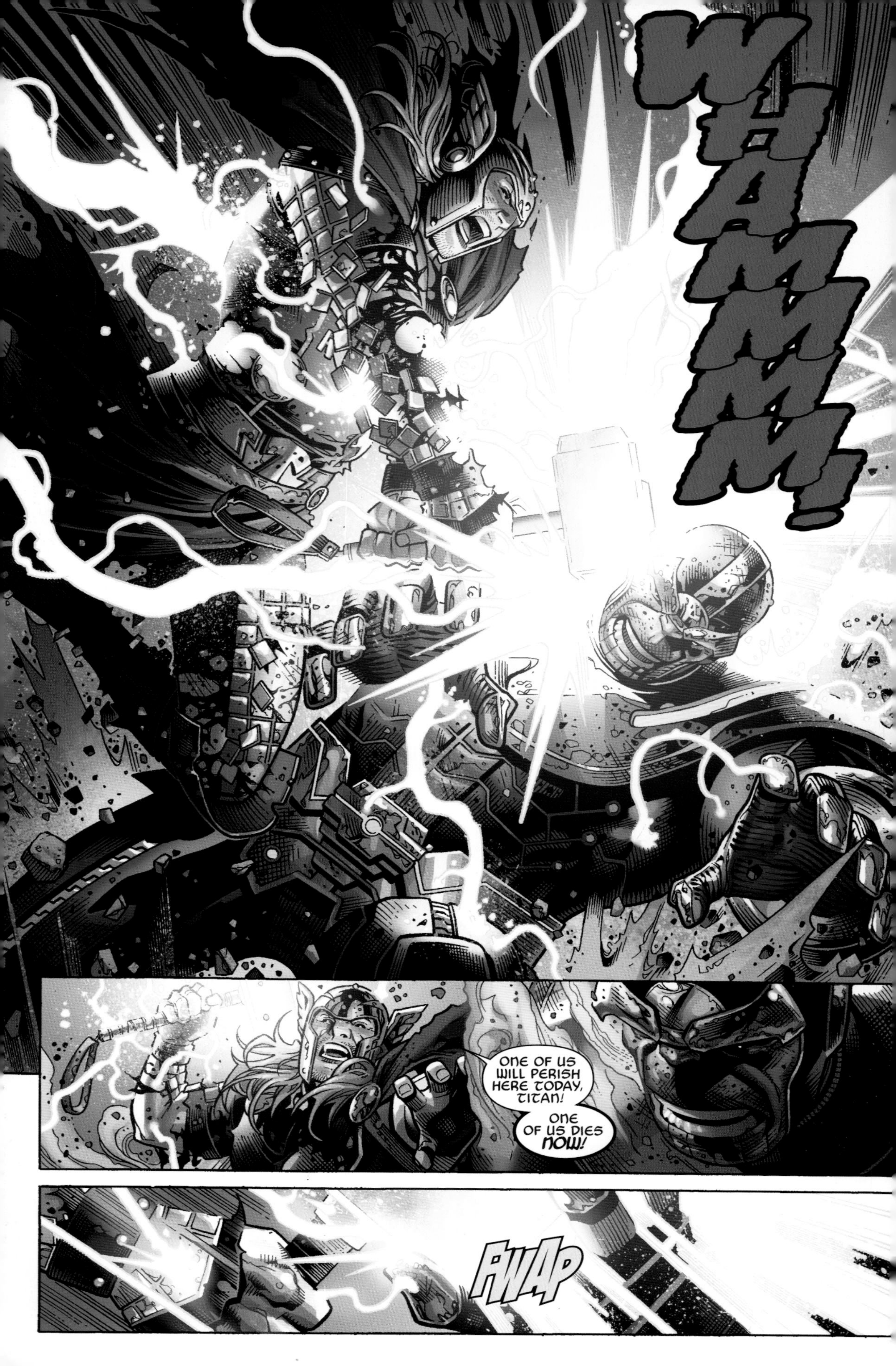
WHAMMM!
ONE OF US WILL PERISH HERE TODAY, TITAN!
ONE OF US DIES NOW!
PWAP

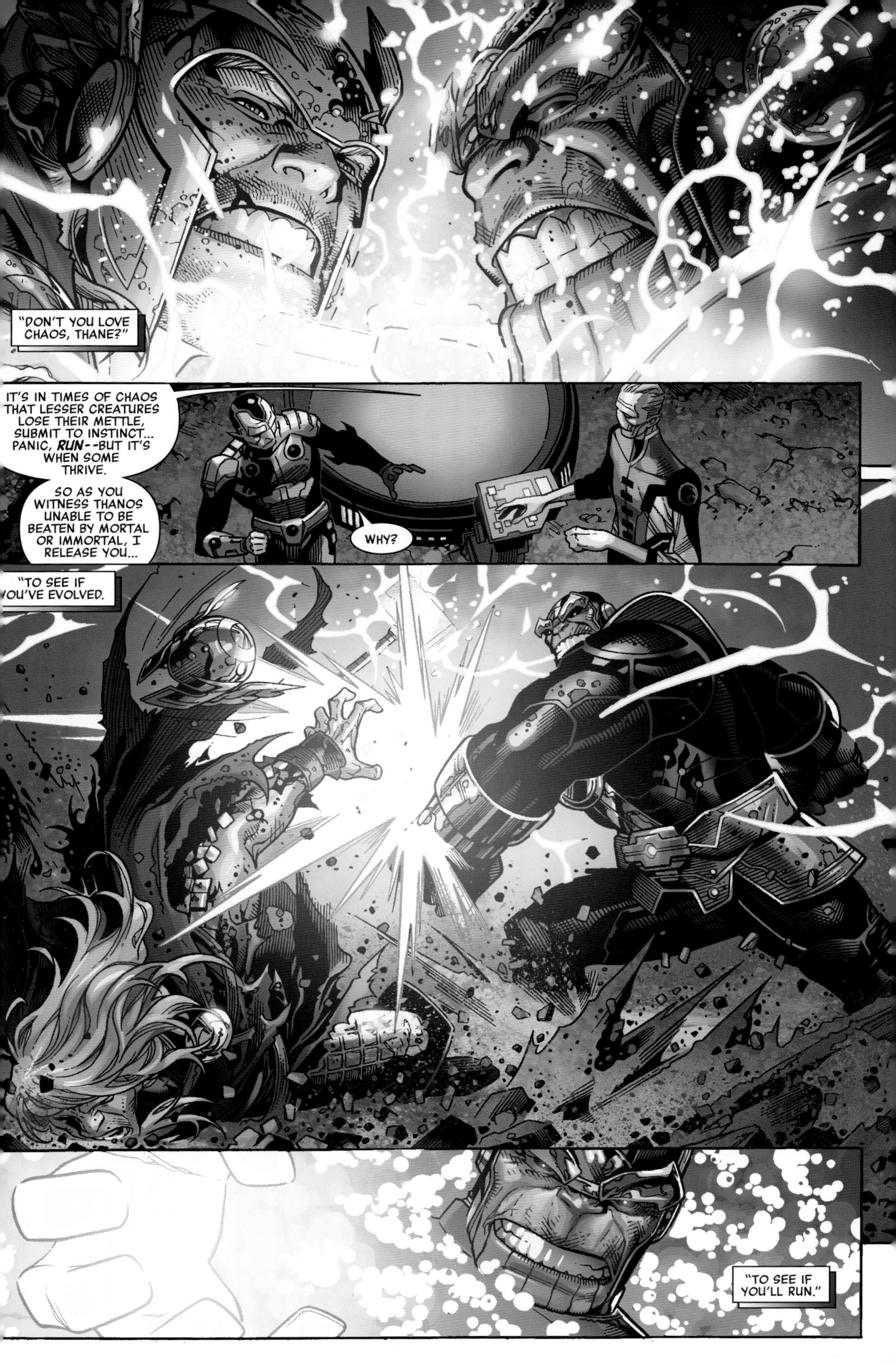
"DON'T YOU LOVE CHAOS, THANE?"
IT'S IN TIMES OF CHAOS THAT LESSER CREATURES LOSE THEIR METTLE, SUBMIT TO INSTINCT... PANIC, RUN--BUT IT'S WHEN SOME THRIVE.
SO AS YOU WITNESS THANOS UNABLE TO BE BEATEN BY MORTAL OR IMMORTAL, I RELEASE YOU...
WHY?
"TO SEE IF YOU'VE EVOLVED.
"TO SEE IF YOU'LL RUN."

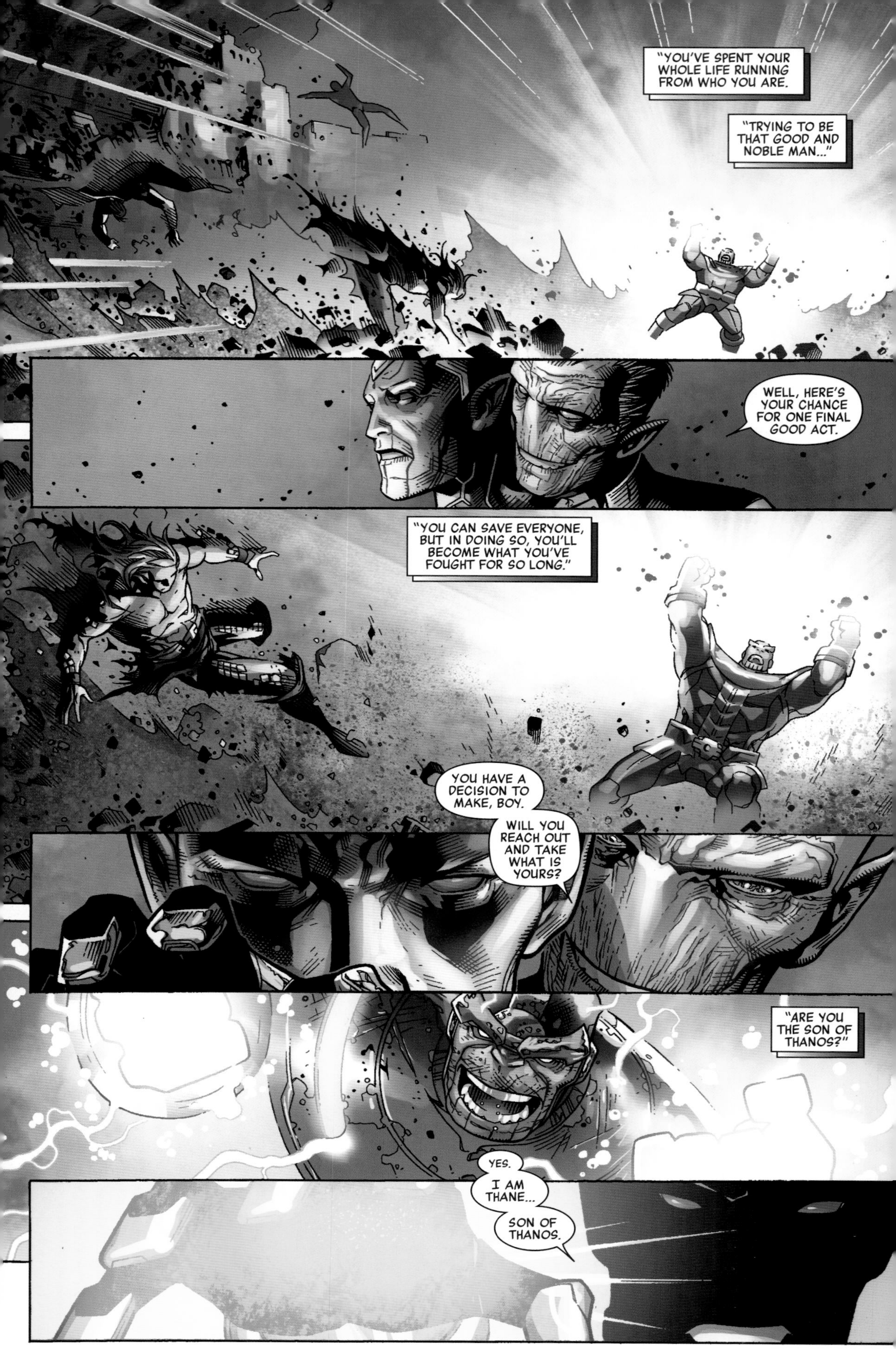
"YOU'VE SPENT YOUR WHOLE LIFE RUNNING FROM WHO YOU ARE.
"TRYING TO BE THAT GOOD AND NOBLE MAN..."
WELL, HERE'S YOUR CHANCE FOR ONE FINAL GOOD ACT.
"YOU CAN SAVE EVERYONE, BUT IN DOING SO, YOU'LL BECOME WHAT YOU'VE FOUGHT FOR SO LONG."
YOU HAVE A DECISION TO MAKE, BOY.
WILL YOU REACH OUT AND TAKE WHAT IS YOURS?
"ARE YOU THE SON OF THANOS?"
YES.
I AM THANE...
SON OF THANOS.

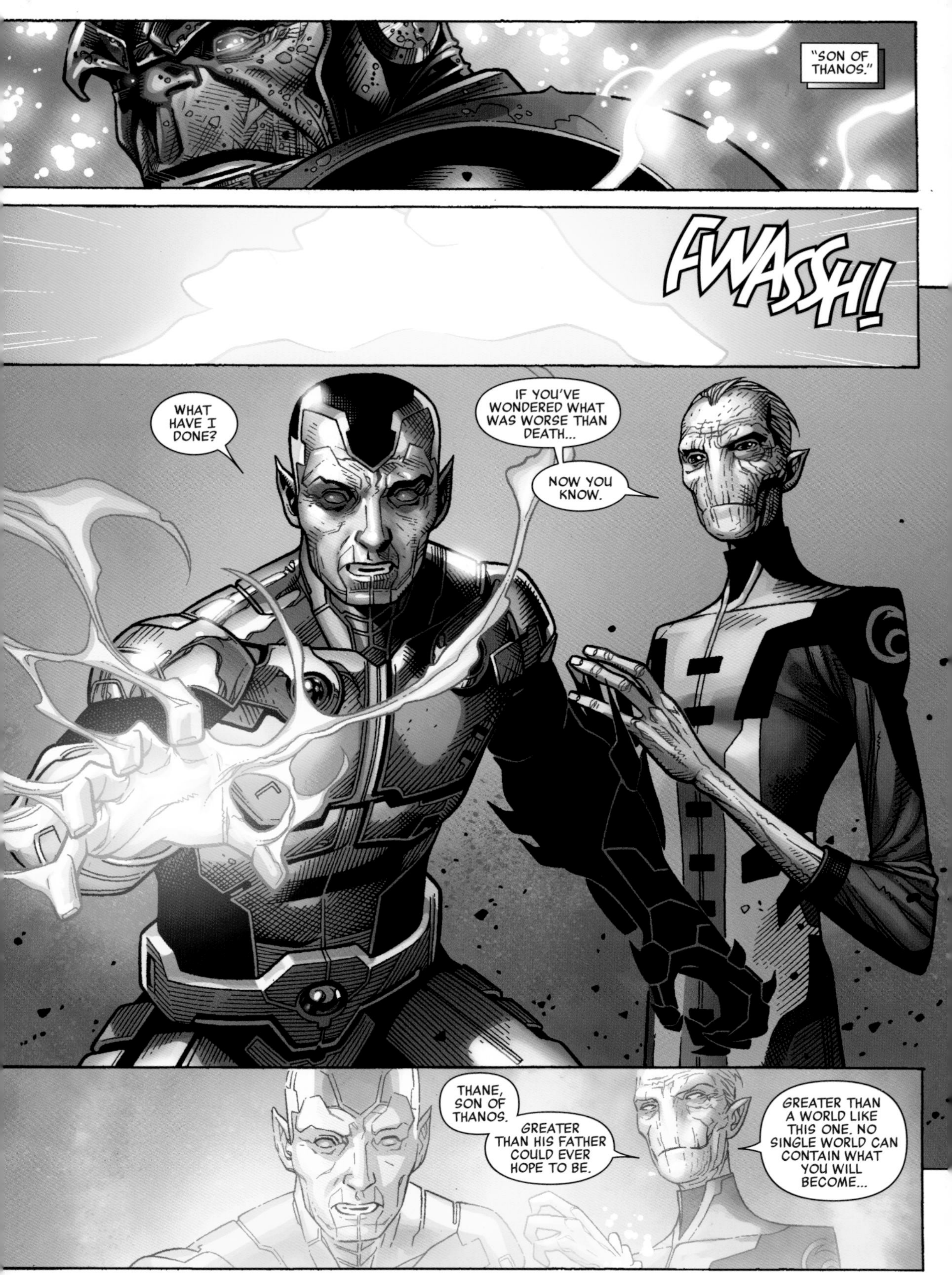
"SON OF THANOS."
FWASSH!
WHAT HAVE I DONE?
IF YOU'VE WONDERED WHAT WAS WORSE THAN DEATH...
NOW YOU KNOW.
THANE, SON OF THANOS.
GREATER THAN HIS FATHER COULD EVER HOPE TO BE.
GREATER THAN A WORLD LIKE THIS ONE. NO SINGLE WORLD CAN CONTAIN WHAT YOU WILL BECOME...

"AFTER ALL...WHAT IS ONE WORLD FOR A MAN THAT COULD HAVE MANY?"

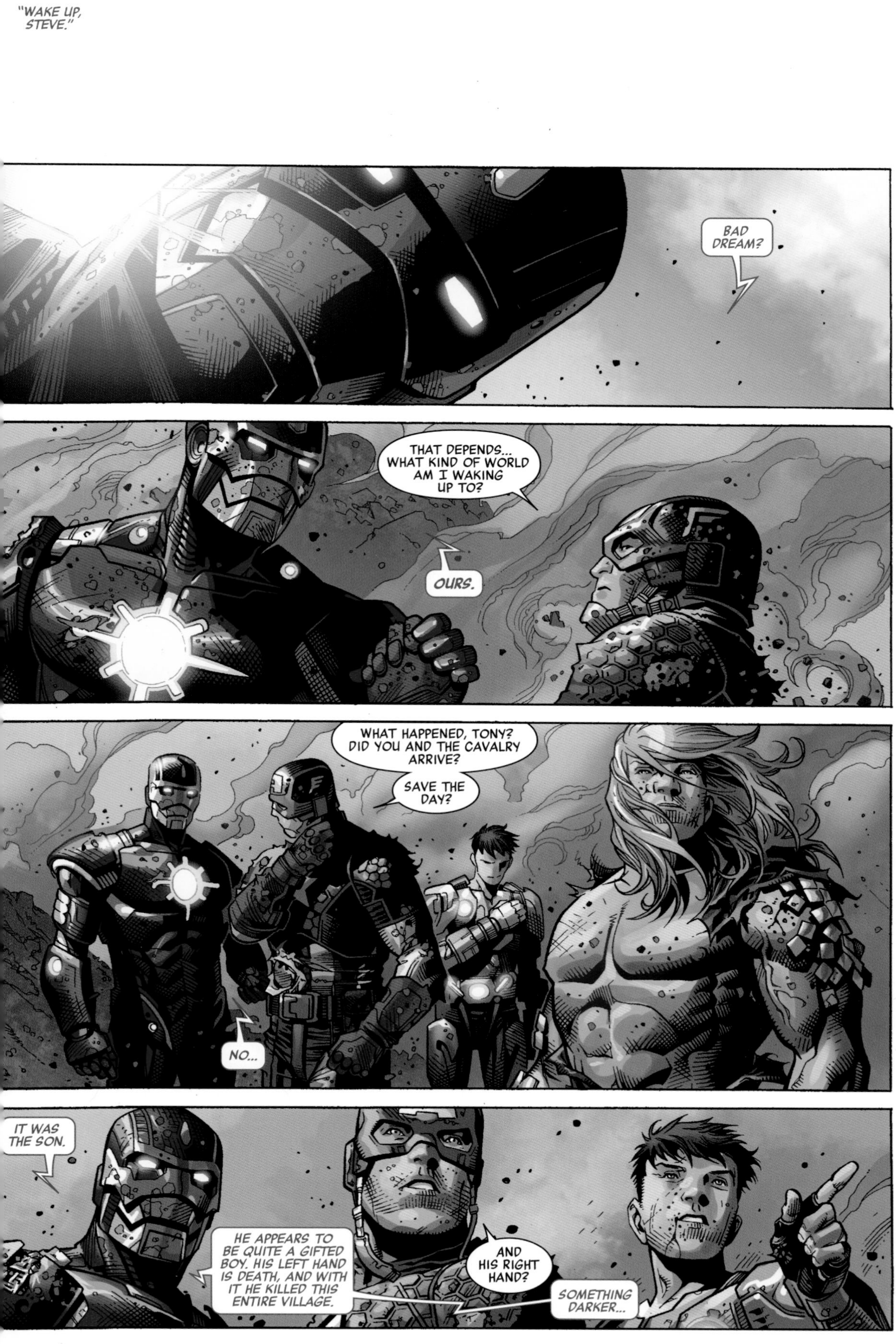
"WAKE UP, STEVE."
BAD DREAM?
THAT DEPENDS... WHAT KIND OF WORLD AM I WAKING UP TO?
OURS.
WHAT HAPPENED, TONY? DID YOU AND THE CAVALRY ARRIVE?
SAVE THE DAY?
NO...
IT WAS THE SON.
HE APPEARS TO BE QUITE A GIFTED BOY. HIS LEFT HAND IS DEATH, AND WITH IT HE KILLED THIS ENTIRE VILLAGE.
AND HIS RIGHT HAND?
SOMETHING DARKER...

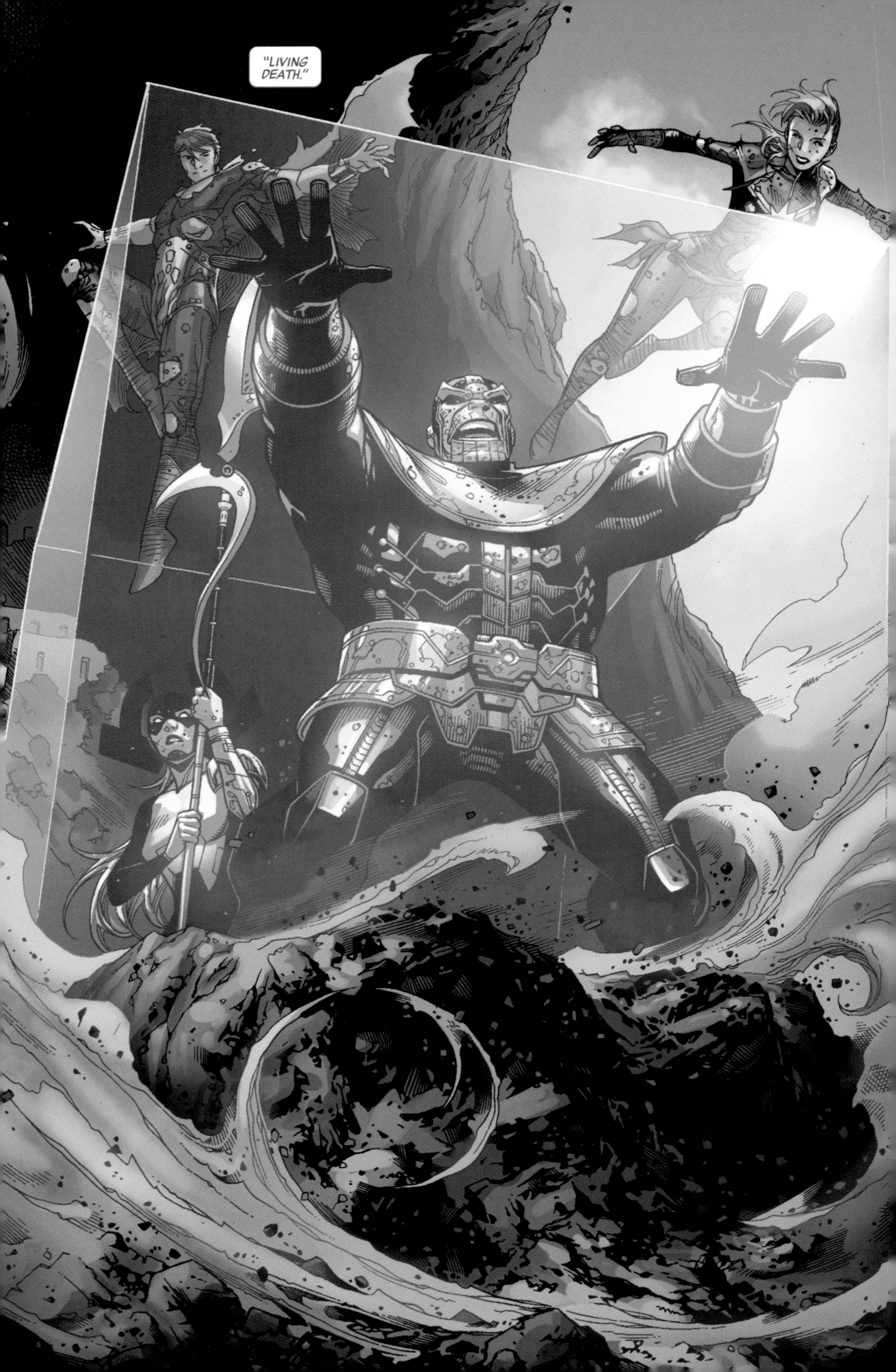
"LIVING DEATH."

EPILOGUE

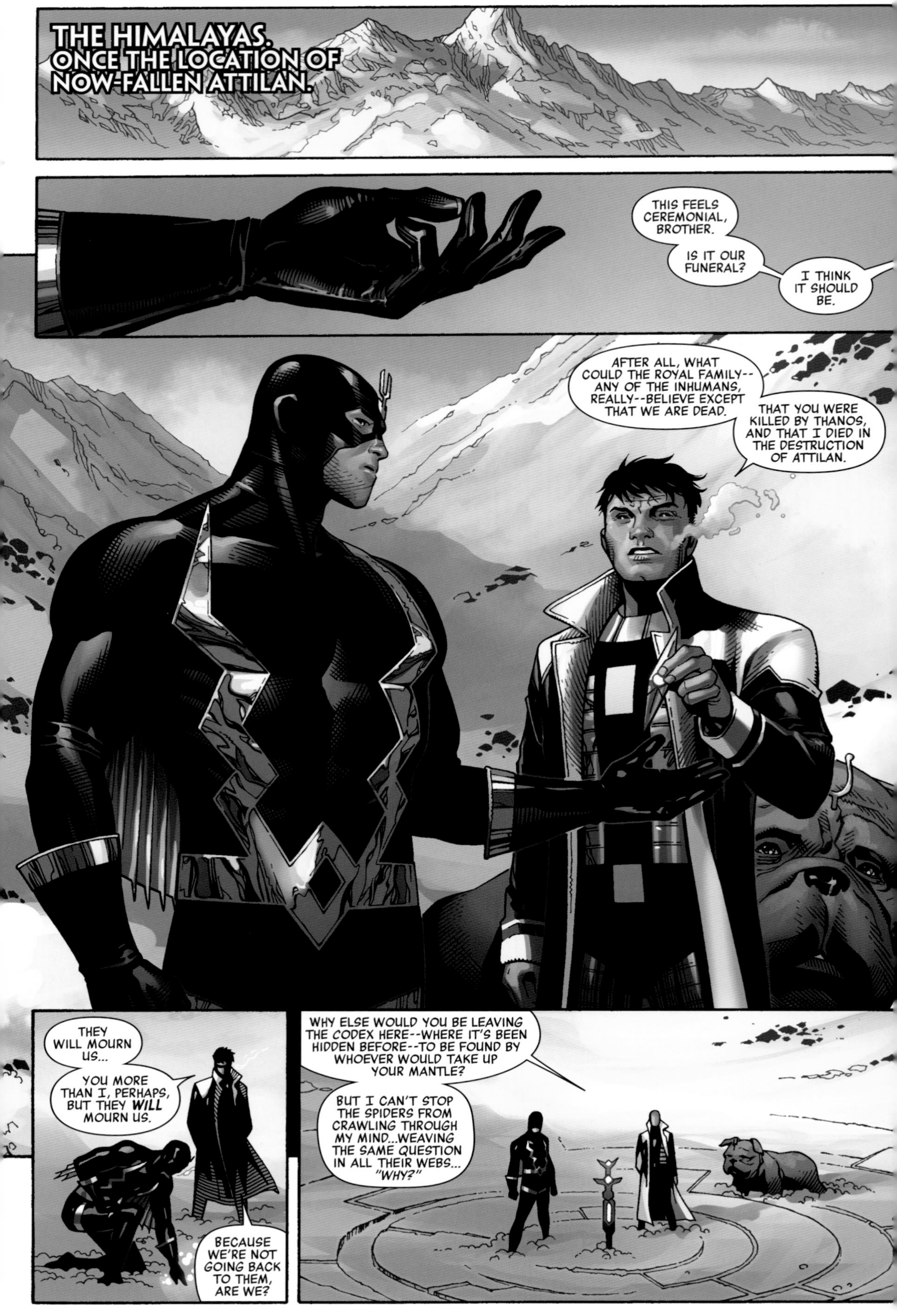
THE HIMALAYAS. ONCE THE LOCATION OF NOW-FALLEN ATTILAN.
THIS FEELS CEREMONIAL, BROTHER.
IS IT OUR FUNERAL?
I THINK IT SHOULD BE.
AFTER ALL, WHAT COULD THE ROYAL FAMILY-- ANY OF THE INHUMANS, REALLY--BELIEVE EXCEPT THAT WE ARE DEAD.
THAT YOU WERE KILLED BY THANOS, AND THAT I DIED IN THE DESTRUCTION OF ATTILAN.
THEY WILL MOURN US...
YOU MORE THAN I, PERHAPS, BUT THEY WILL MOURN US.
BECAUSE WE'RE NOT GOING BACK TO THEM, ARE WE?
WHY ELSE WOULD YOU BE LEAVING THE CODEX HERE--WHERE IT'S BEEN HIDDEN BEFORE--TO BE FOUND BY WHOEVER WOULD TAKE UP YOUR MANTLE?
BUT I CAN'T STOP THE SPIDERS FROM CRAWLING THROUGH MY MIND...WEAVING THE SAME QUESTION IN ALL THEIR WEBS... "WHY?"

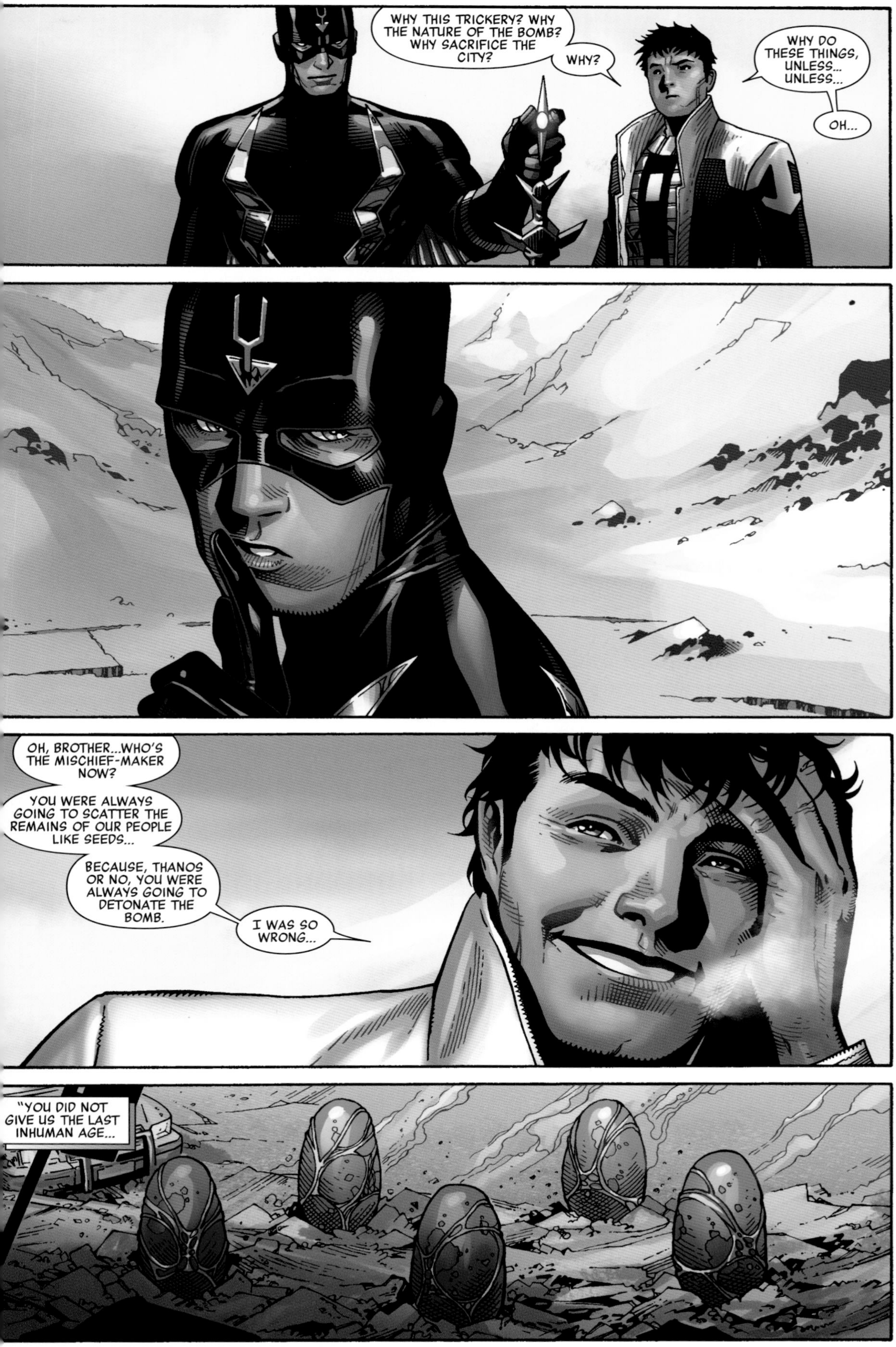
WHY THIS TRICKERY? WHY THE NATURE OF THE BOMB? WHY SACRIFICE THE CITY?
WHY?
WHY DO THESE THINGS, UNLESS... UNLESS...
OH...
OH, BROTHER...WHO'S THE MISCHIEF-MAKER NOW?
YOU WERE ALWAYS GOING TO SCATTER THE REMAINS OF OUR PEOPLE LIKE SEEDS...
BECAUSE, THANOS OR NO, YOU WERE ALWAYS GOING TO DETONATE THE BOMB.
I WAS SO WRONG...
"YOU DID NOT GIVE US THE LAST INHUMAN AGE...

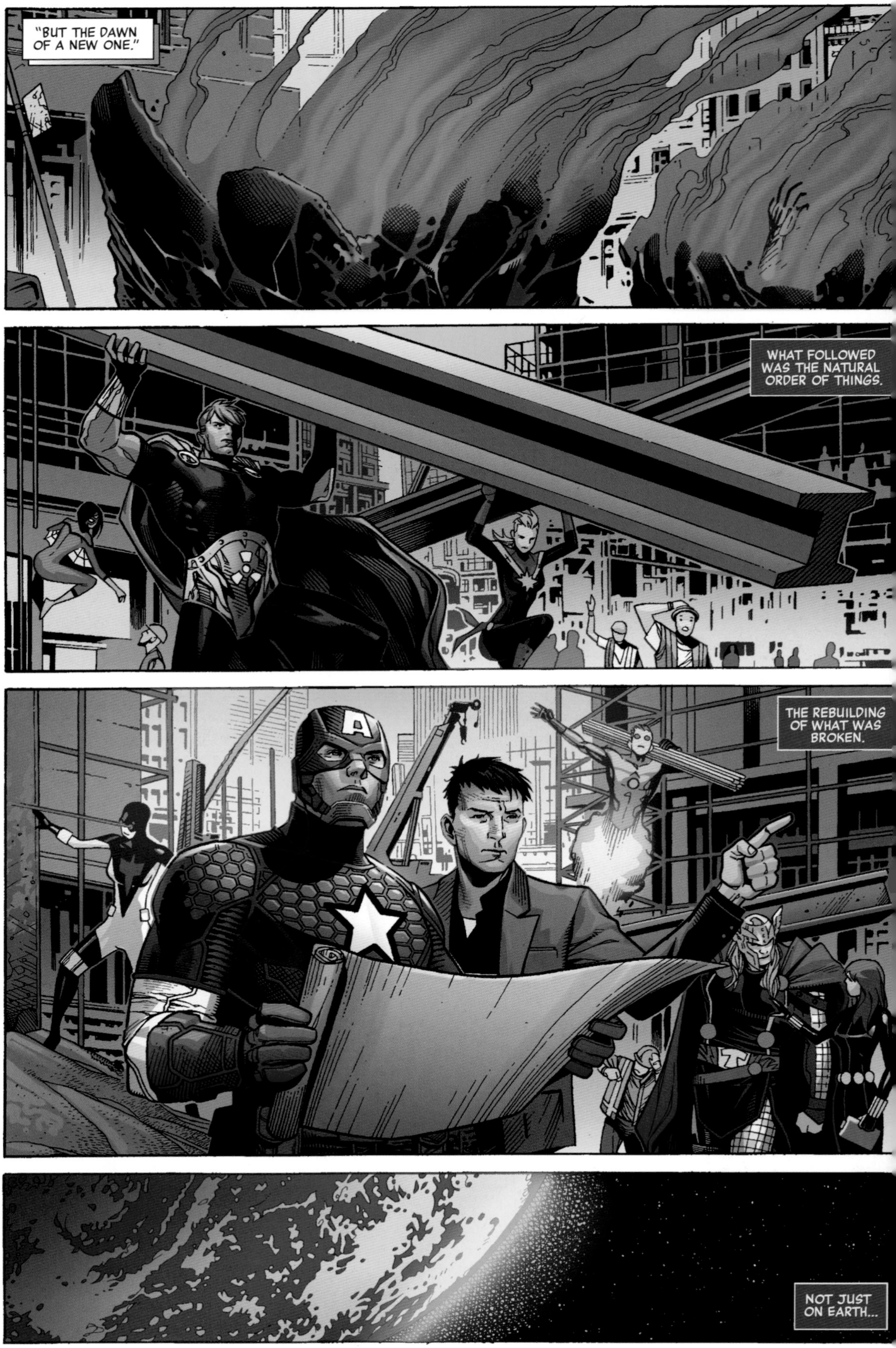
"BUT THE DAWN OF A NEW ONE."
WHAT FOLLOWED WAS THE NATURAL ORDER OF THINGS.
THE REBUILDING OF WHAT WAS BROKEN.
NOT JUST ON EARTH...

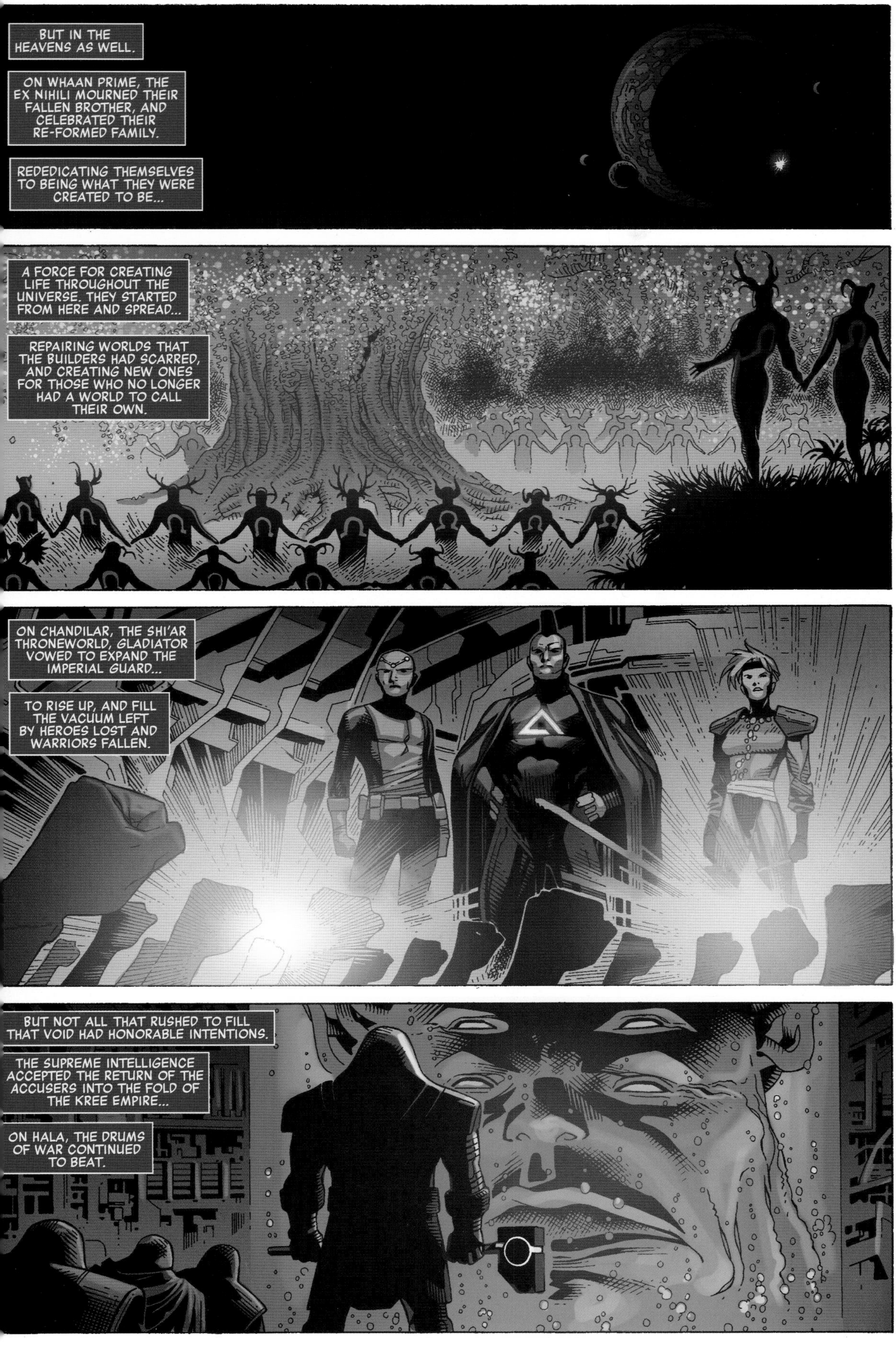
BUT IN THE HEAVENS AS WELL.
ON WHAAN PRIME, THE EX NIHILI MOURNED THEIR FALLEN BROTHER, AND CELEBRATED THEIR RE-FORMED FAMILY.
REDEDICATING THEMSELVES TO BEING WHAT THEY WERE CREATED TO BE...
A FORCE FOR CREATING LIFE THROUGHOUT THE UNIVERSE. THEY STARTED FROM HERE AND SPREAD...
REPAIRING WORLDS THAT THE BUILDERS HAD SCARRED, AND CREATING NEW ONES FOR THOSE WHO NO LONGER HAD A WORLD TO CALL THEIR OWN.
ON CHANDILAR, THE SHI'AR THRONEWORLD, GLADIATOR VOWED TO EXPAND THE IMPERIAL GUARD...
TO RISE UP, AND FILL THE VACUUM LEFT BY HEROES LOST AND WARRIORS FALLEN.
BUT NOT ALL THAT RUSHED TO FILL THAT VOID HAD HONORABLE INTENTIONS.
THE SUPREME INTELLIGENCE ACCEPTED THE RETURN OF THE ACCUSERS INTO THE FOLD OF THE KREE EMPIRE...
ON HALA, THE DRUMS OF WAR CONTINUED TO BEAT.

ON TARNAX II, THE SKRULL EMPIRE WAS OFFICIALLY REBORN WITH THE CROWNING OF EMPEROR KL'RT.

ALL SKRULLS WERE BORN WITH CONQUEST IN THEIR BLOOD, AND EXPANSION WAS THEIR BIRTHRIGHT. IN MANY WAYS, THEY COULD NOT HELP WHAT WOULD FOLLOW.

AS IT WAS WHEN DRONES OF ANNIHILUS CAPTURED THE CONVERTED STARGATES ON PRAXIS-2, LEAVING OPEN A PORTAL BRIDGING THE NEGATIVE ZONE TO THIS UNIVERSE. THE HIGH HOLY DAYS OF THE END TIMES WERE OFFICIALLY UPON US.

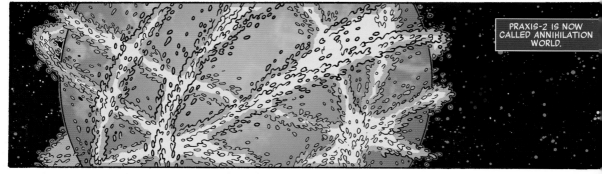

PRAXIS-2 IS NOW CALLED ANNIHILATION WORLD.

AND UNDER THE DISCIPLESHIP OF THE EBONY MAW, THANE, SON OF THANOS, WOULD GROW TO BECOME SOMETHING WORSE THAN HIS FATHER COULD HAVE EVER DREAMED.

A FITTING MATCH FOR WHAT WE LEARNED WAS A DYING UNIVERSE.

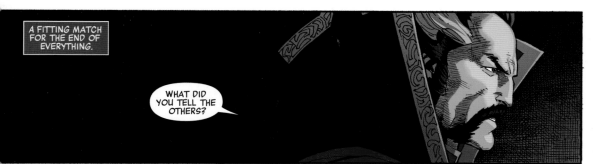

A FITTING MATCH FOR THE END OF EVERYTHING.

WHAT DID YOU TELL THE OTHERS?

THAT I WOULD TAKE CARE OF IT.

AND THEY BELIEVED YOU?

WHY WOULD THEY NOT?

THEY SEE THE WORLD AS THEY WANT IT TO BE...

NOT AS IT IS.

NO NEED TO BE SO FATALISTIC, T'CHALLA. ANTHONY BUILT THIS CURRENT AVENGERS TEAM TO HANDLE THE IMPOSSIBLE...

AND LOOK, THEY DID.

THEY EXIST TO BUILD HOPE SO WE CAN BUILD THE UNTHINKABLE.

YOU KNOW THIS-- DIFFERENT MACHINES ARE OFTEN MADE WITH DIFFERENT TOOLS.

AND CEMETERIES ARE LITTERED WITH DEAD MEN WHO DIED STILL BELIEVING THEY WOULD NOT.

OUR WORLD IS DYING...WHAT ARE WE GOING TO DO ABOUT IT, GENTLEMEN?

WE CONTINUE.

AND THOUGH IT MAY COST US OUR VERY SOULS... WE GATHER THE PROPER TOOLS NECESSARY...

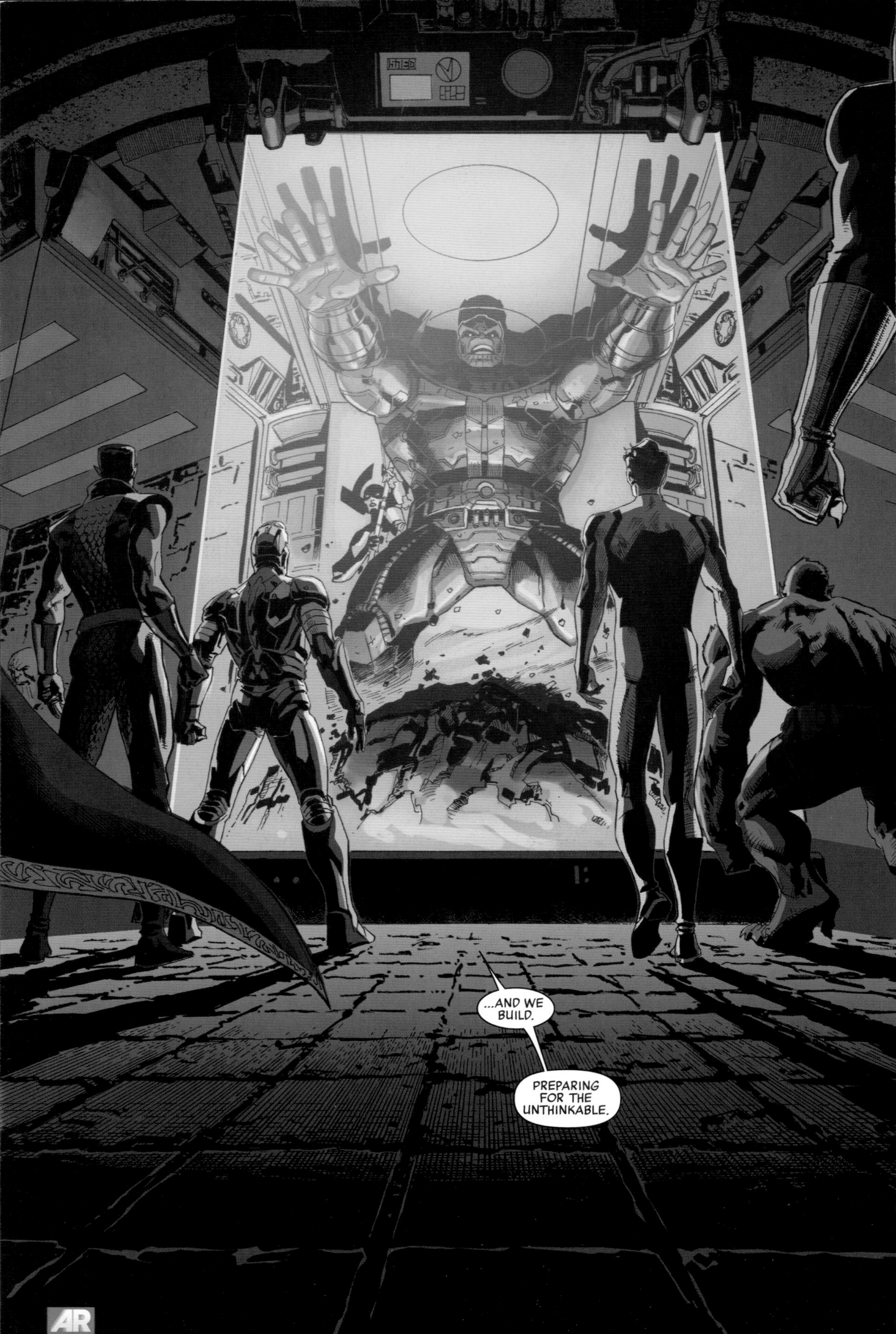
...AND WE BUILD.
PREPARING FOR THE UNTHINKABLE.

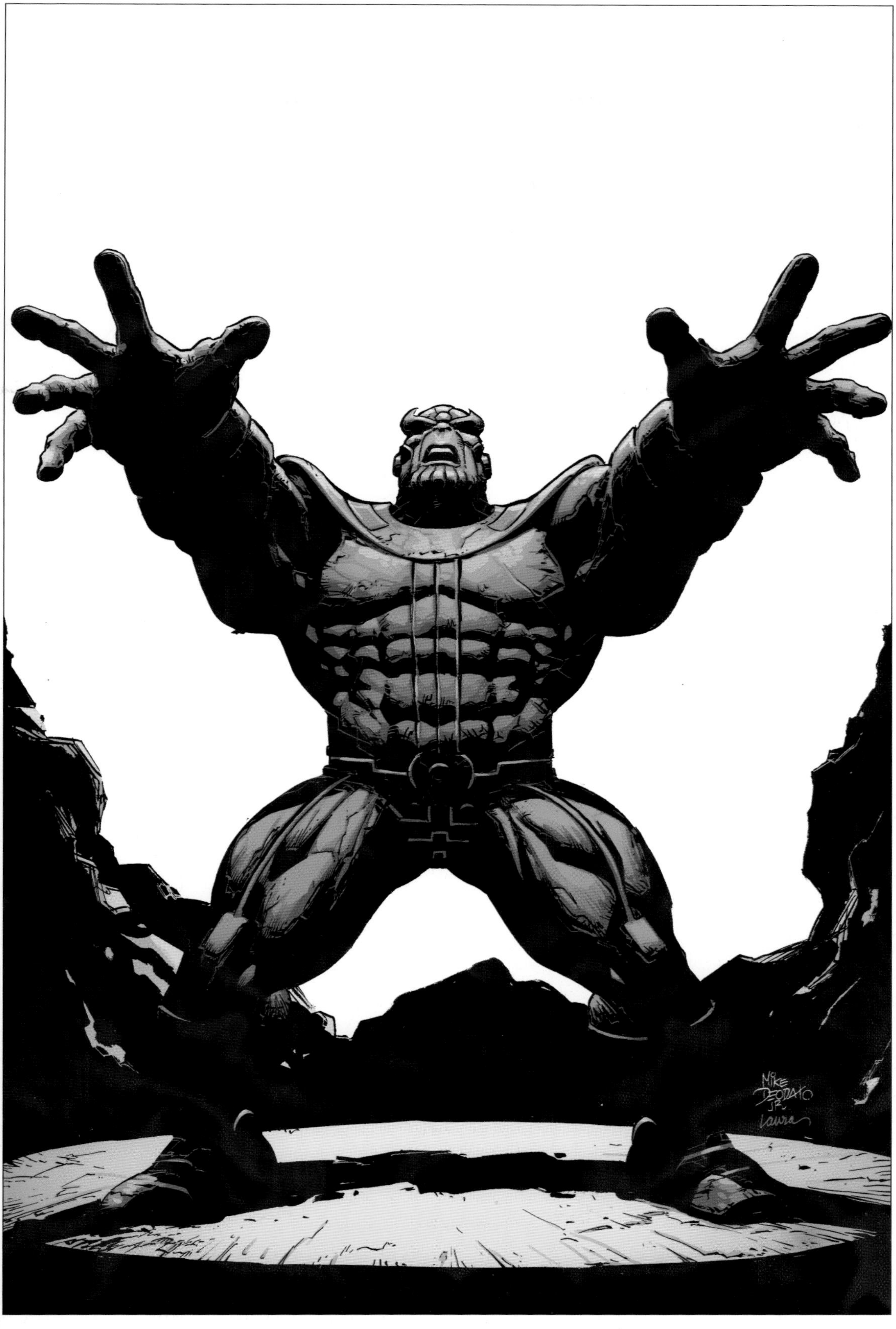

ENDGAME

◆

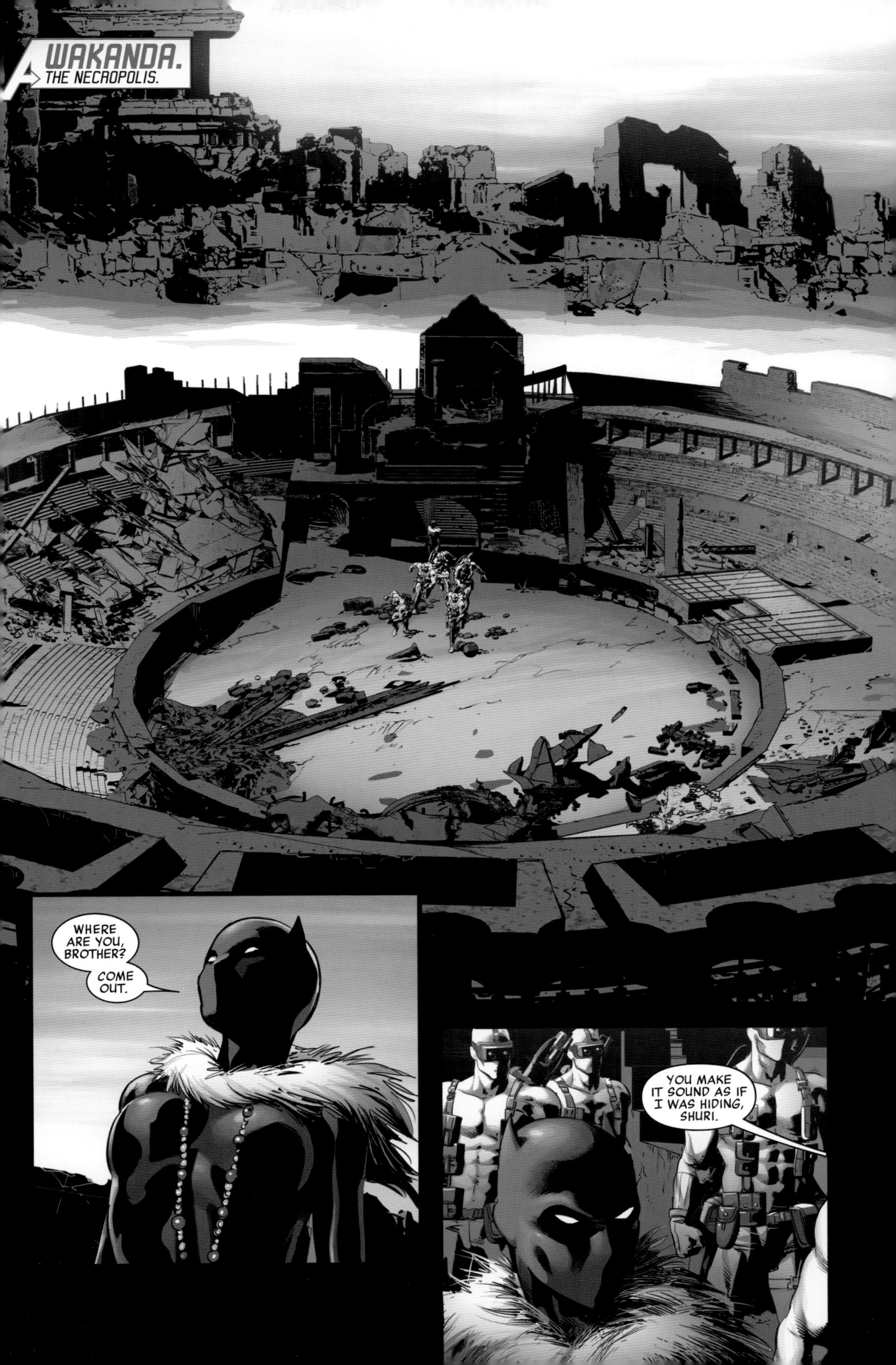
WAKANDA.
THE NECROPOLIS.
WHERE ARE YOU, BROTHER?
COME OUT.
YOU MAKE IT SOUND AS IF I WAS HIDING, SHURI.

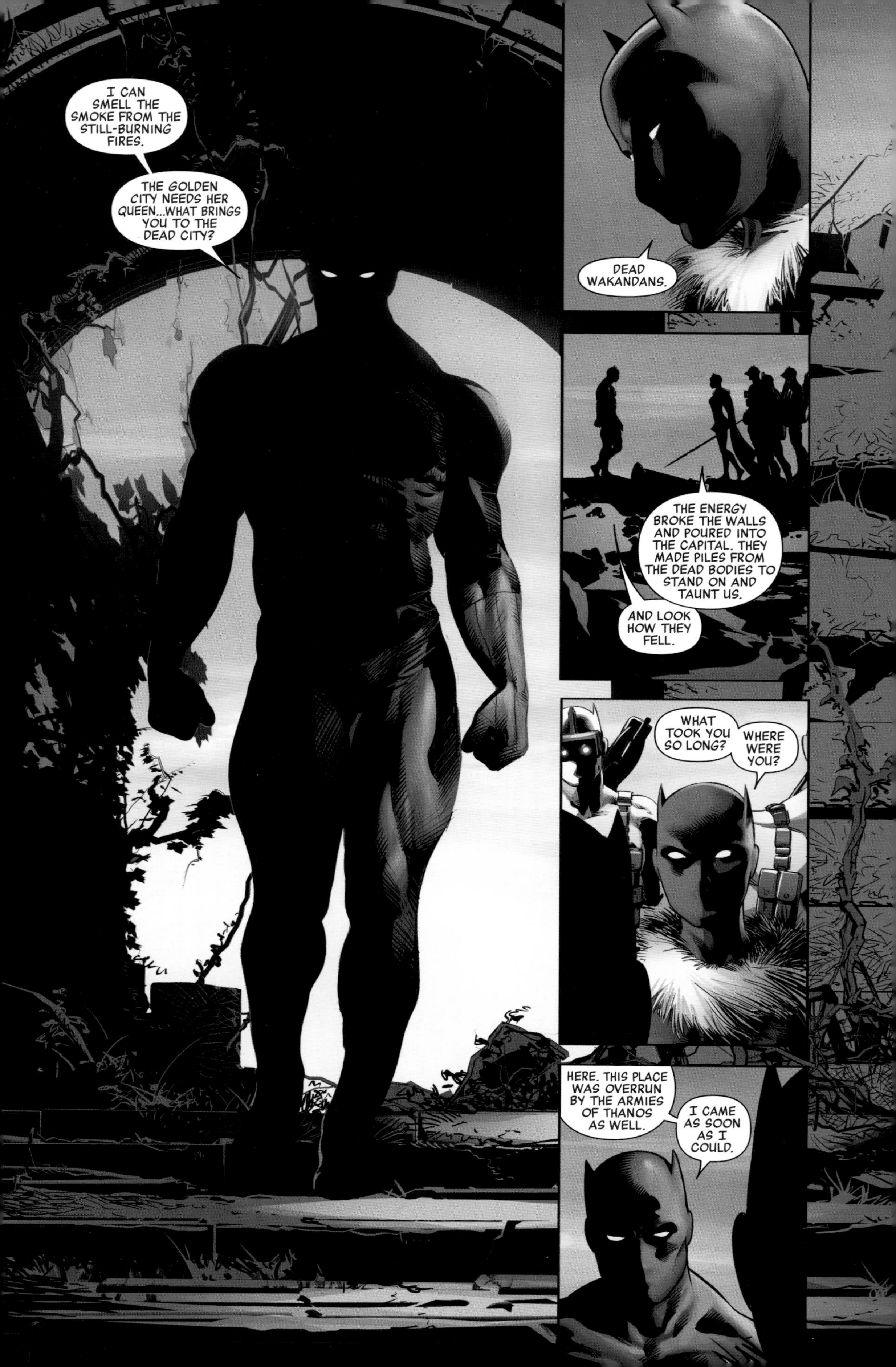
I CAN SMELL THE SMOKE FROM THE STILL-BURNING FIRES.
THE GOLDEN CITY NEEDS HER QUEEN...WHAT BRINGS YOU TO THE DEAD CITY?
DEAD WAKANDANS.
THE ENERGY BROKE THE WALLS AND POURED INTO THE CAPITAL. THEY MADE PILES FROM THE DEAD BODIES TO STAND ON AND TAUNT US.
AND LOOK HOW THEY FELL.
WHAT TOOK YOU SO LONG?
WHERE WERE YOU?
HERE. THIS PLACE WAS OVERRUN BY THE ARMIES OF THANOS AS WELL.
I CAME AS SOON AS I COULD.

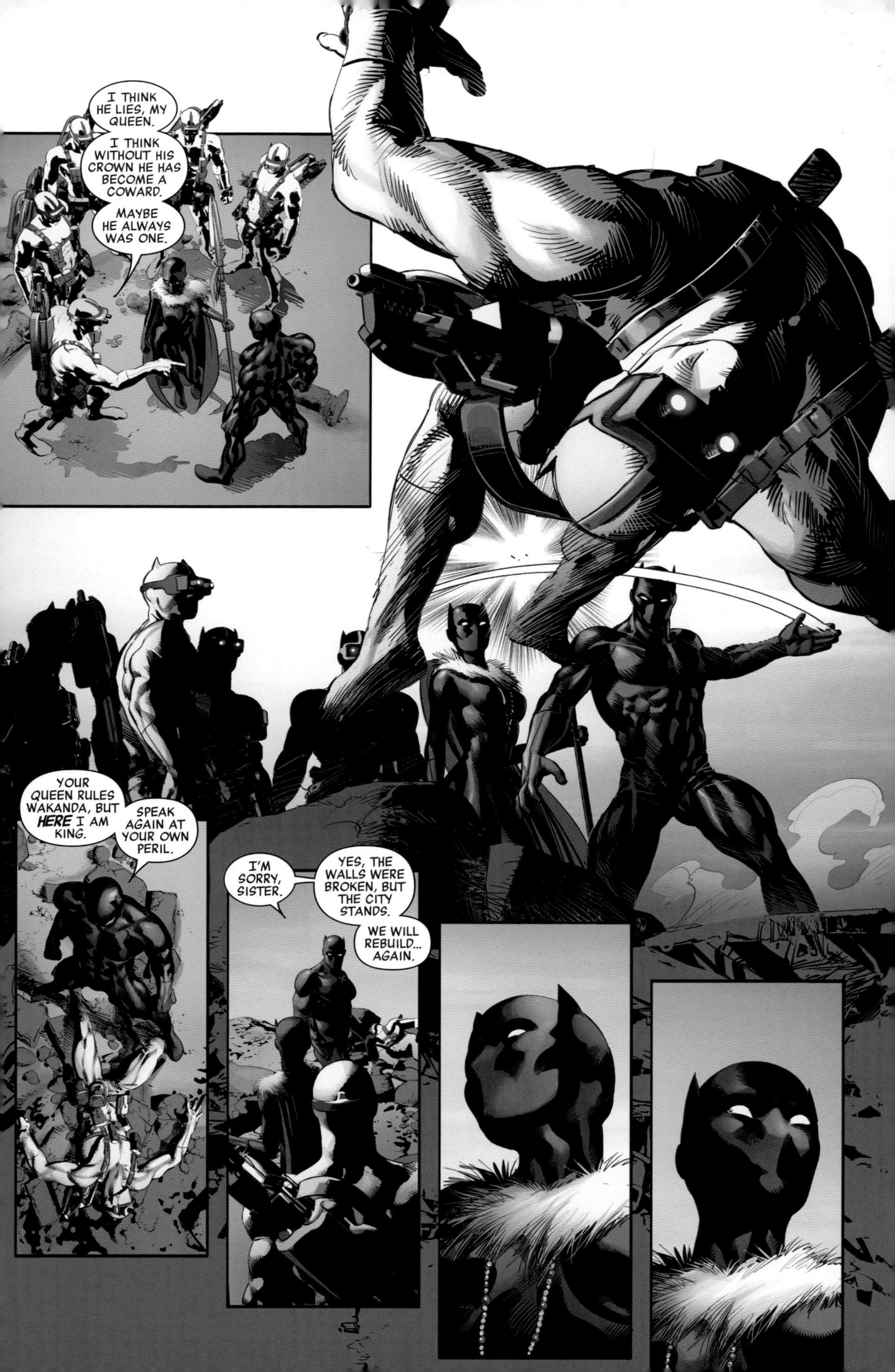
I THINK HE LIES, MY QUEEN.
I THINK WITHOUT HIS CROWN HE HAS BECOME A COWARD.
MAYBE HE ALWAYS WAS ONE.
YOUR QUEEN RULES WAKANDA, BUT HERE I AM KING.
SPEAK AGAIN AT YOUR OWN PERIL.
I'M SORRY, SISTER.
YES, THE WALLS WERE BROKEN, BUT THE CITY STANDS.
WE WILL REBUILD... AGAIN.

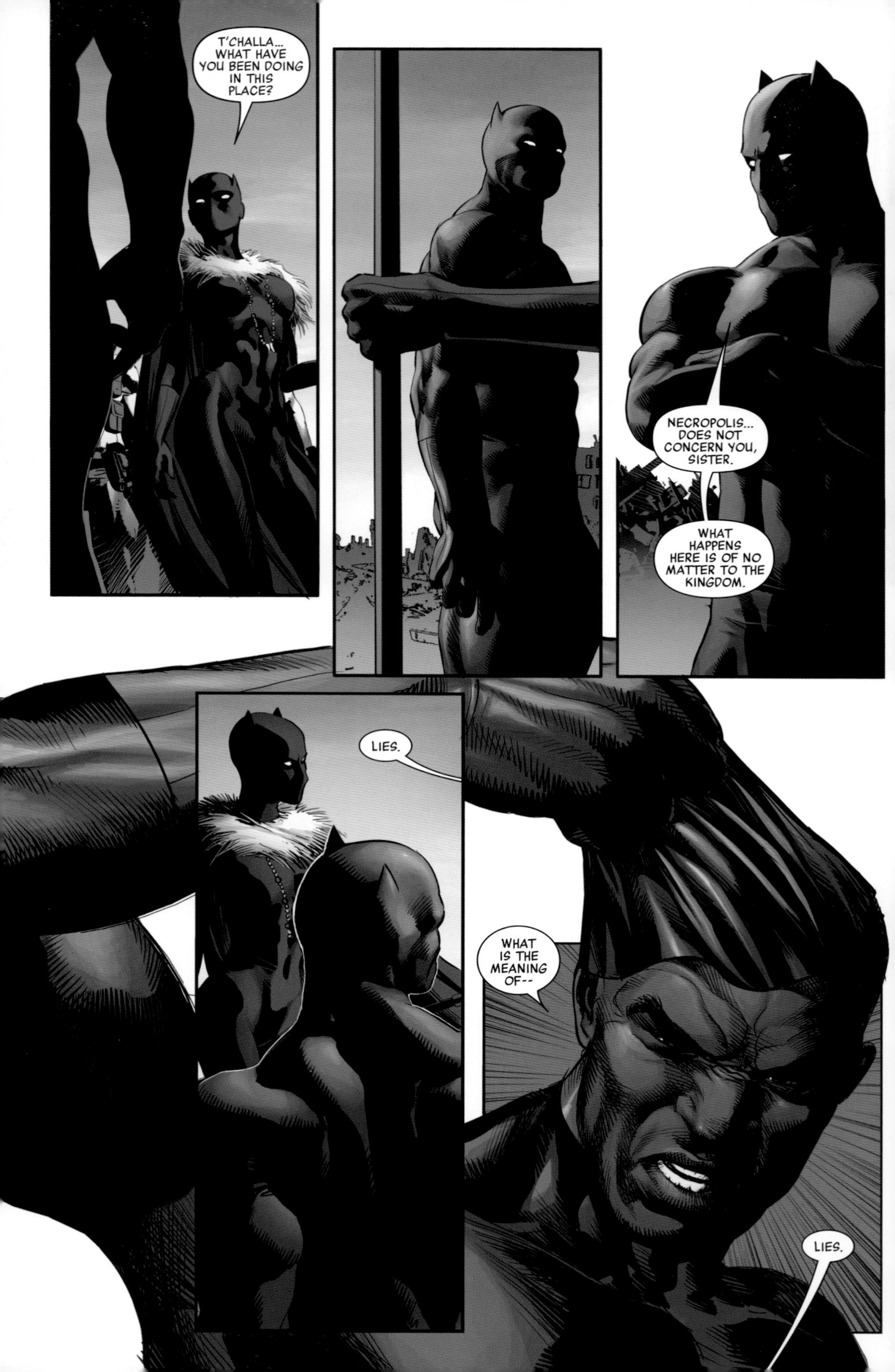
T'CHALLA... WHAT HAVE YOU BEEN DOING IN THIS PLACE?
NECROPOLIS... DOES NOT CONCERN YOU, SISTER.
WHAT HAPPENS HERE IS OF NO MATTER TO THE KINGDOM.
LIES.
WHAT IS THE MEANING OF--
LIES.

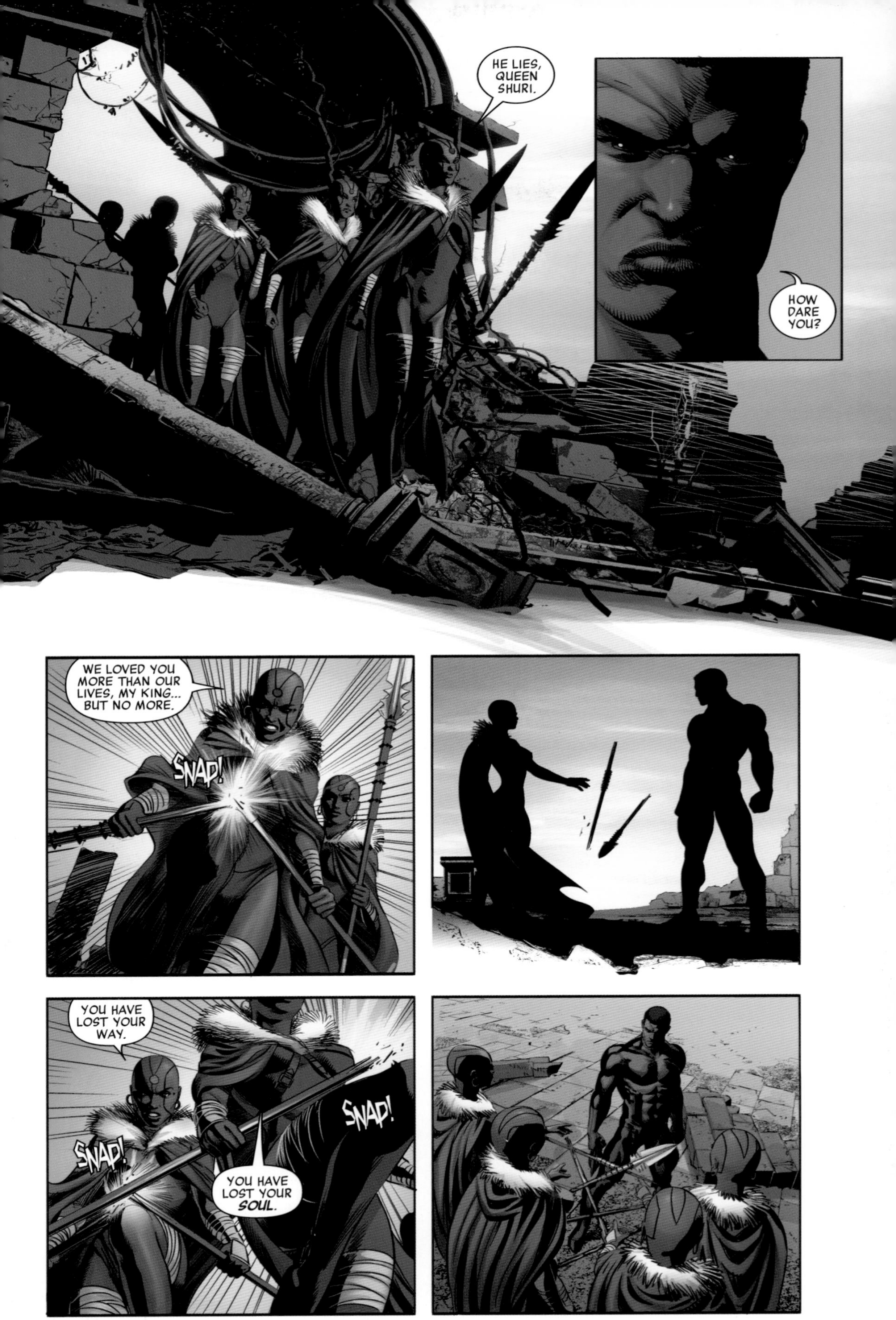
HE LIES, QUEEN SHURI.
HOW DARE YOU?
WE LOVED YOU MORE THAN OUR LIVES, MY KING... BUT NO MORE.
SNAP!
YOU HAVE LOST YOUR WAY.
SNAP!
SNAP!
YOU HAVE LOST YOUR SOUL.

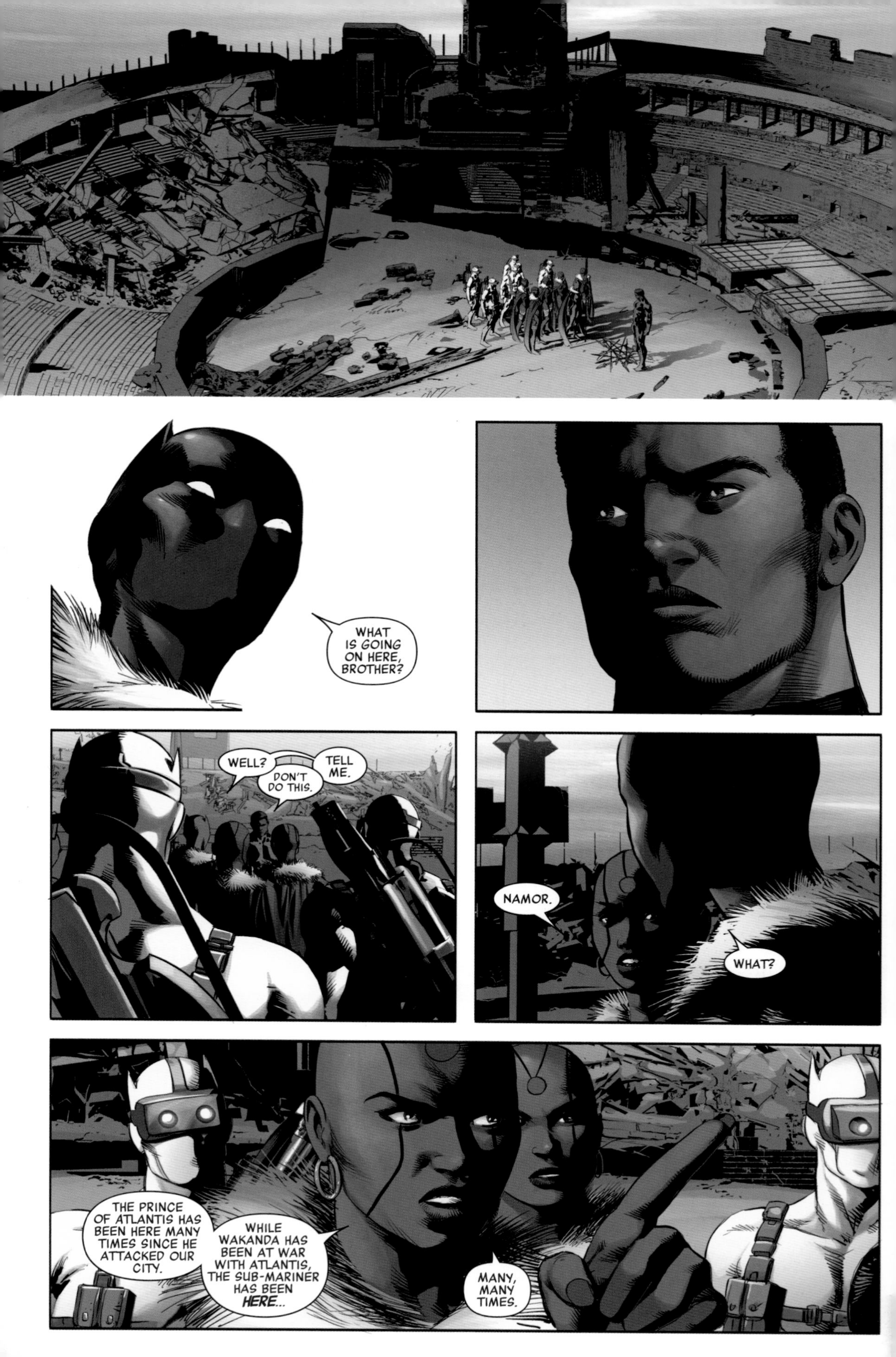
WHAT IS GOING ON HERE, BROTHER?
WELL?
DON'T DO THIS.
TELL ME.
NAMOR.
WHAT?
THE PRINCE OF ATLANTIS HAS BEEN HERE MANY TIMES SINCE HE ATTACKED OUR CITY.
WHILE WAKANDA HAS BEEN AT WAR WITH ATLANTIS, THE SUB-MARINER HAS BEEN *HERE*...
MANY, MANY TIMES.

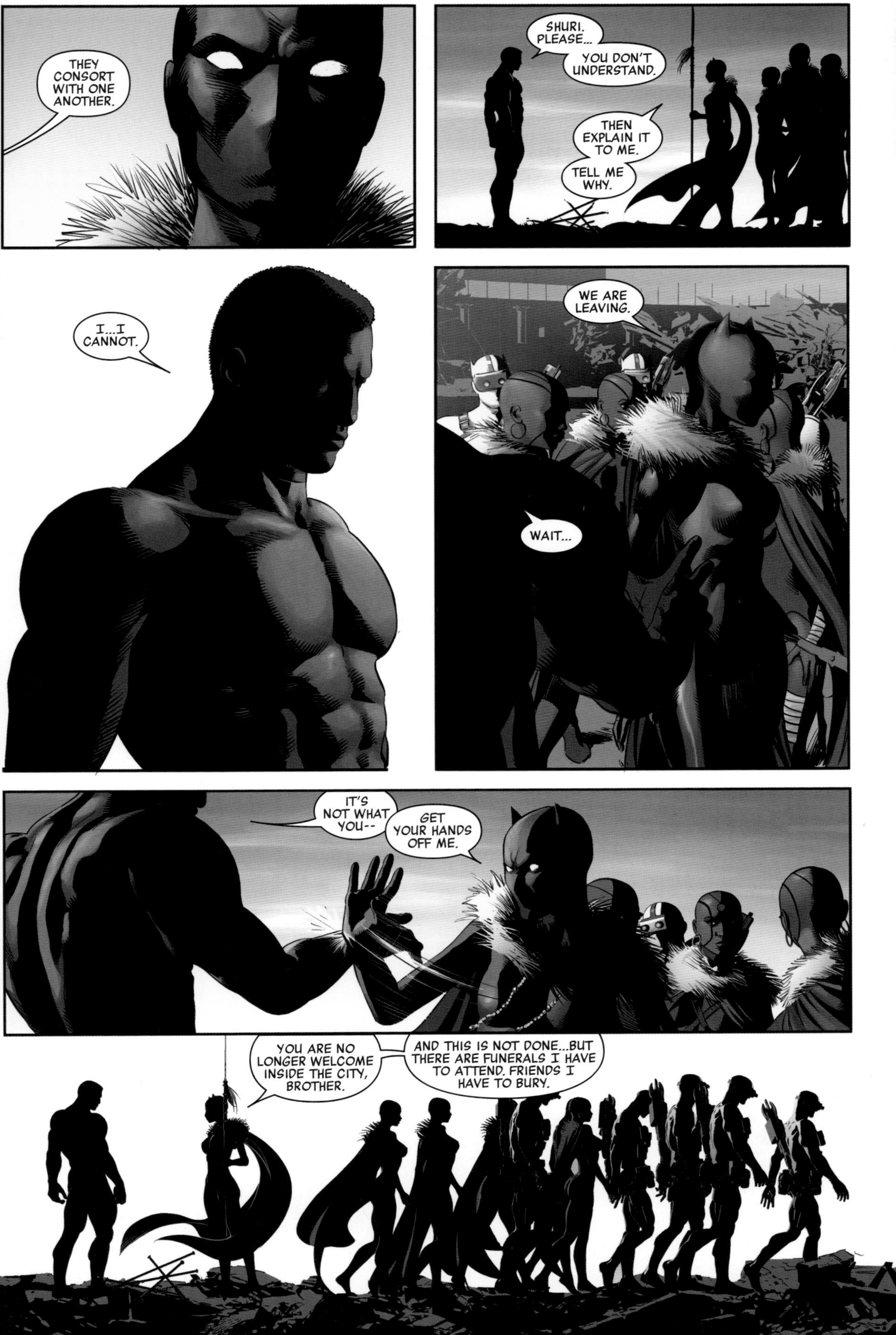
THEY CONSORT WITH ONE ANOTHER.
SHURI. PLEASE...
YOU DON'T UNDERSTAND.
THEN EXPLAIN IT TO ME.
TELL ME WHY.
I...I CANNOT.
WE ARE LEAVING.
WAIT...
IT'S NOT WHAT YOU--
GET YOUR HANDS OFF ME.
YOU ARE NO LONGER WELCOME INSIDE THE CITY, BROTHER.
AND THIS IS NOT DONE...BUT THERE ARE FUNERALS I HAVE TO ATTEND. FRIENDS I HAVE TO BURY.

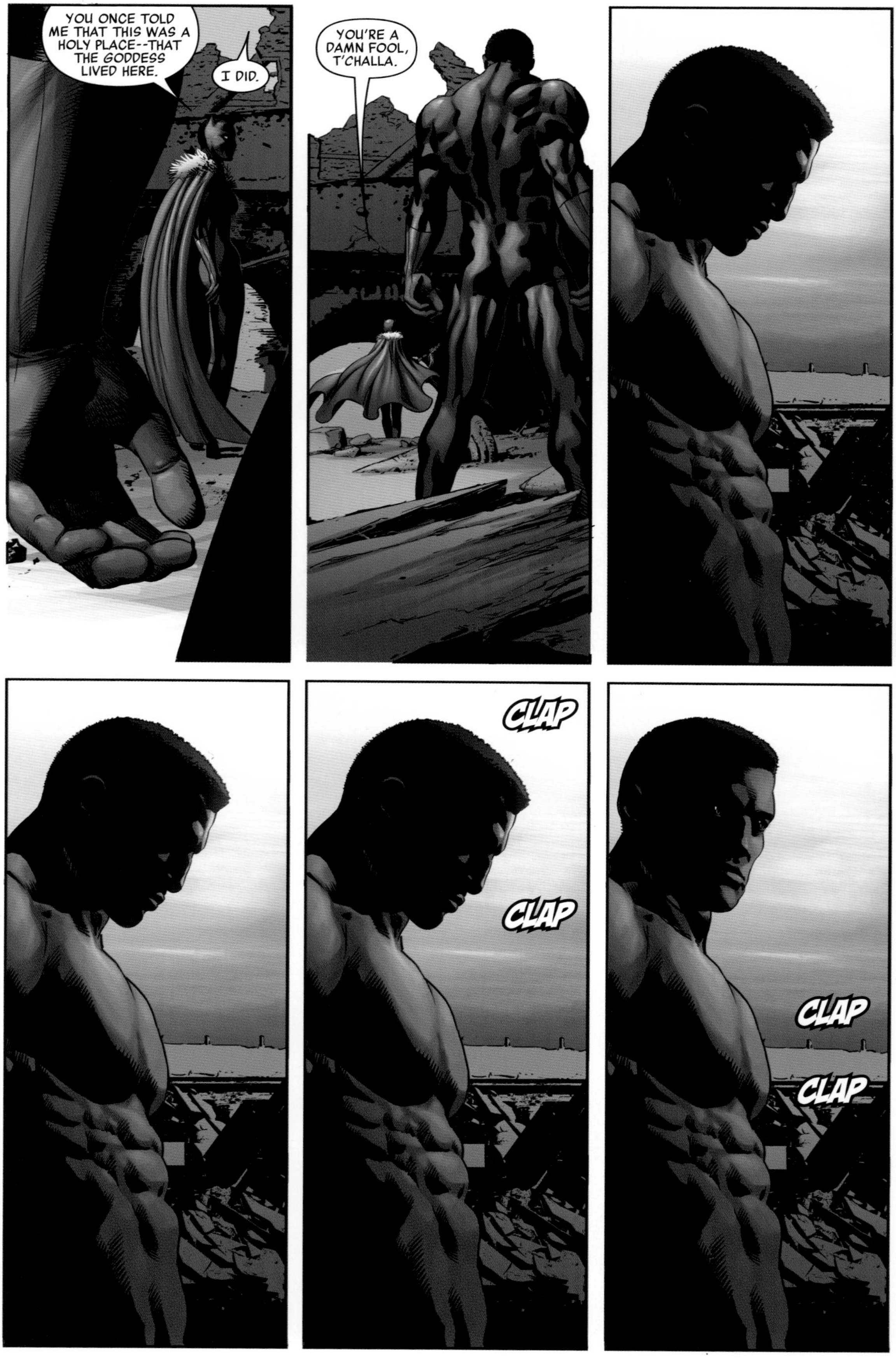
YOU ONCE TOLD ME THAT THIS WAS A HOLY PLACE--THAT THE GODDESS LIVED HERE.
I DID.
YOU'RE A DAMN FOOL, T'CHALLA.
CLAP
CLAP
CLAP
CLAP

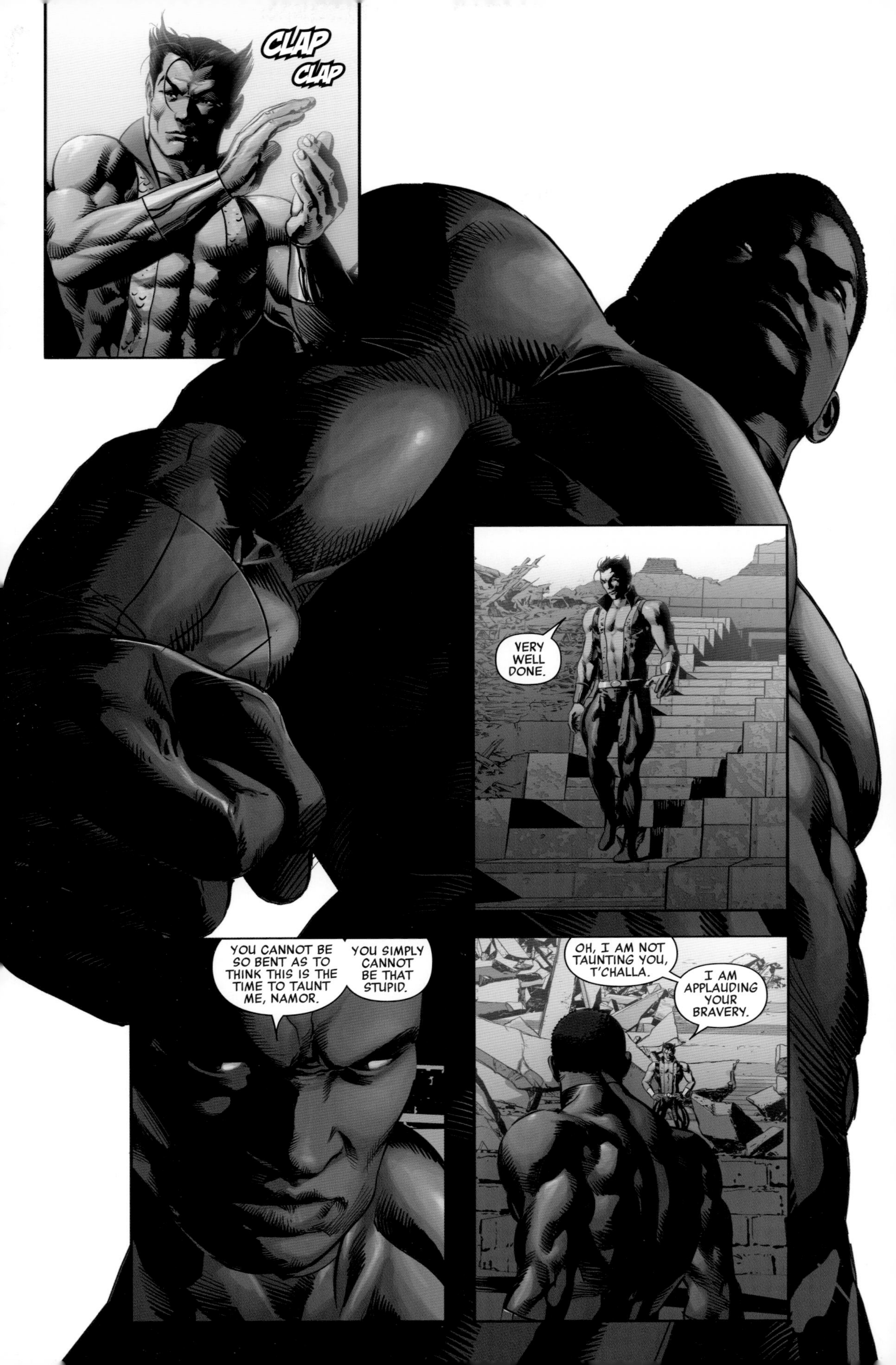
CLAP
CLAP
VERY WELL DONE.
YOU CANNOT BE SO BENT AS TO THINK THIS IS THE TIME TO TAUNT ME, NAMOR.
YOU SIMPLY CANNOT BE THAT STUPID.
OH, I AM NOT TAUNTING YOU, T'CHALLA.
I AM APPLAUDING YOUR BRAVERY.

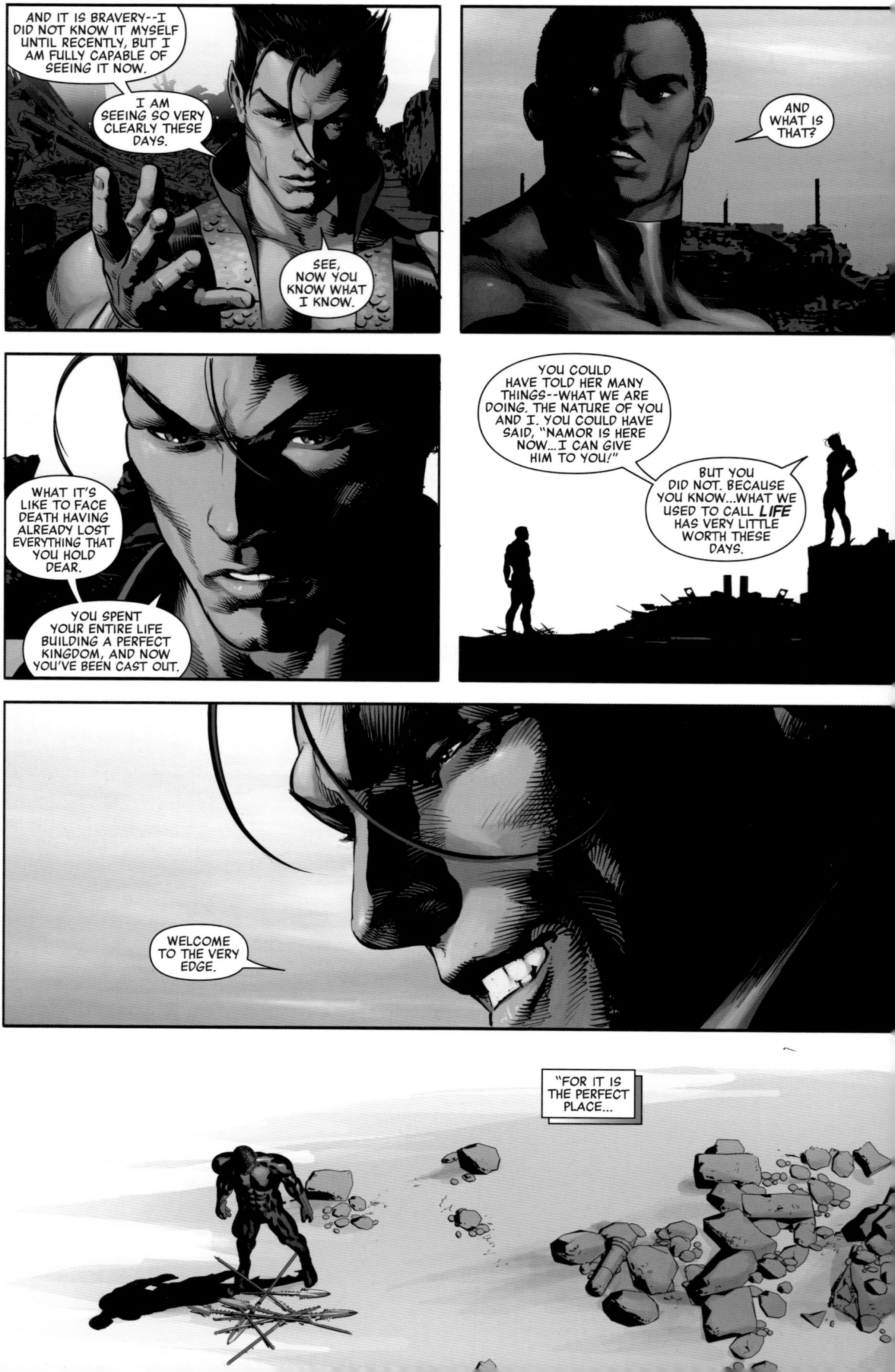
AND IT IS BRAVERY--I DID NOT KNOW IT MYSELF UNTIL RECENTLY, BUT I AM FULLY CAPABLE OF SEEING IT NOW.
I AM SEEING SO VERY CLEARLY THESE DAYS.
SEE, NOW YOU KNOW WHAT I KNOW.
AND WHAT IS THAT?
WHAT IT'S LIKE TO FACE DEATH HAVING ALREADY LOST EVERYTHING THAT YOU HOLD DEAR.
YOU SPENT YOUR ENTIRE LIFE BUILDING A PERFECT KINGDOM, AND NOW YOU'VE BEEN CAST OUT.
YOU COULD HAVE TOLD HER MANY THINGS--WHAT WE ARE DOING. THE NATURE OF YOU AND I. YOU COULD HAVE SAID, "NAMOR IS HERE NOW...I CAN GIVE HIM TO YOU!"
BUT YOU DID NOT. BECAUSE YOU KNOW...WHAT WE USED TO CALL LIFE HAS VERY LITTLE WORTH THESE DAYS.
WELCOME TO THE VERY EDGE.
"FOR IT IS THE PERFECT PLACE...

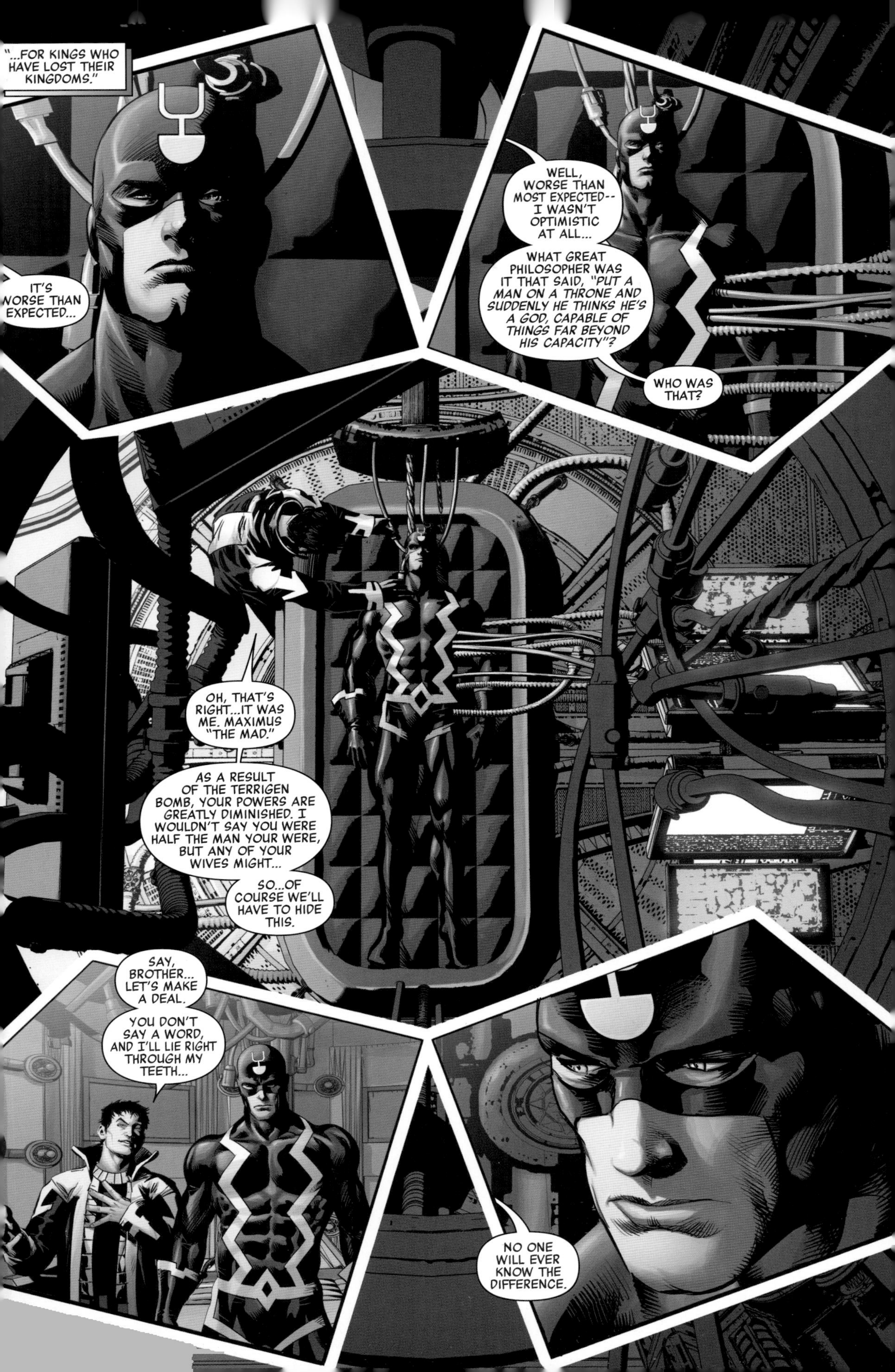
"...FOR KINGS WHO HAVE LOST THEIR KINGDOMS."
IT'S WORSE THAN EXPECTED...
WELL, WORSE THAN MOST EXPECTED-- I WASN'T OPTIMISTIC AT ALL...
WHAT GREAT PHILOSOPHER WAS IT THAT SAID, "PUT A MAN ON A THRONE AND SUDDENLY HE THINKS HE'S A GOD, CAPABLE OF THINGS FAR BEYOND HIS CAPACITY"?
WHO WAS THAT?
OH, THAT'S RIGHT...IT WAS ME. MAXIMUS "THE MAD."
AS A RESULT OF THE TERRIGEN BOMB, YOUR POWERS ARE GREATLY DIMINISHED. I WOULDN'T SAY YOU WERE HALF THE MAN YOUR WERE, BUT ANY OF YOUR WIVES MIGHT...
SO...OF COURSE WE'LL HAVE TO HIDE THIS.
SAY, BROTHER... LET'S MAKE A DEAL.
YOU DON'T SAY A WORD, AND I'LL LIE RIGHT THROUGH MY TEETH...
NO ONE WILL EVER KNOW THE DIFFERENCE.

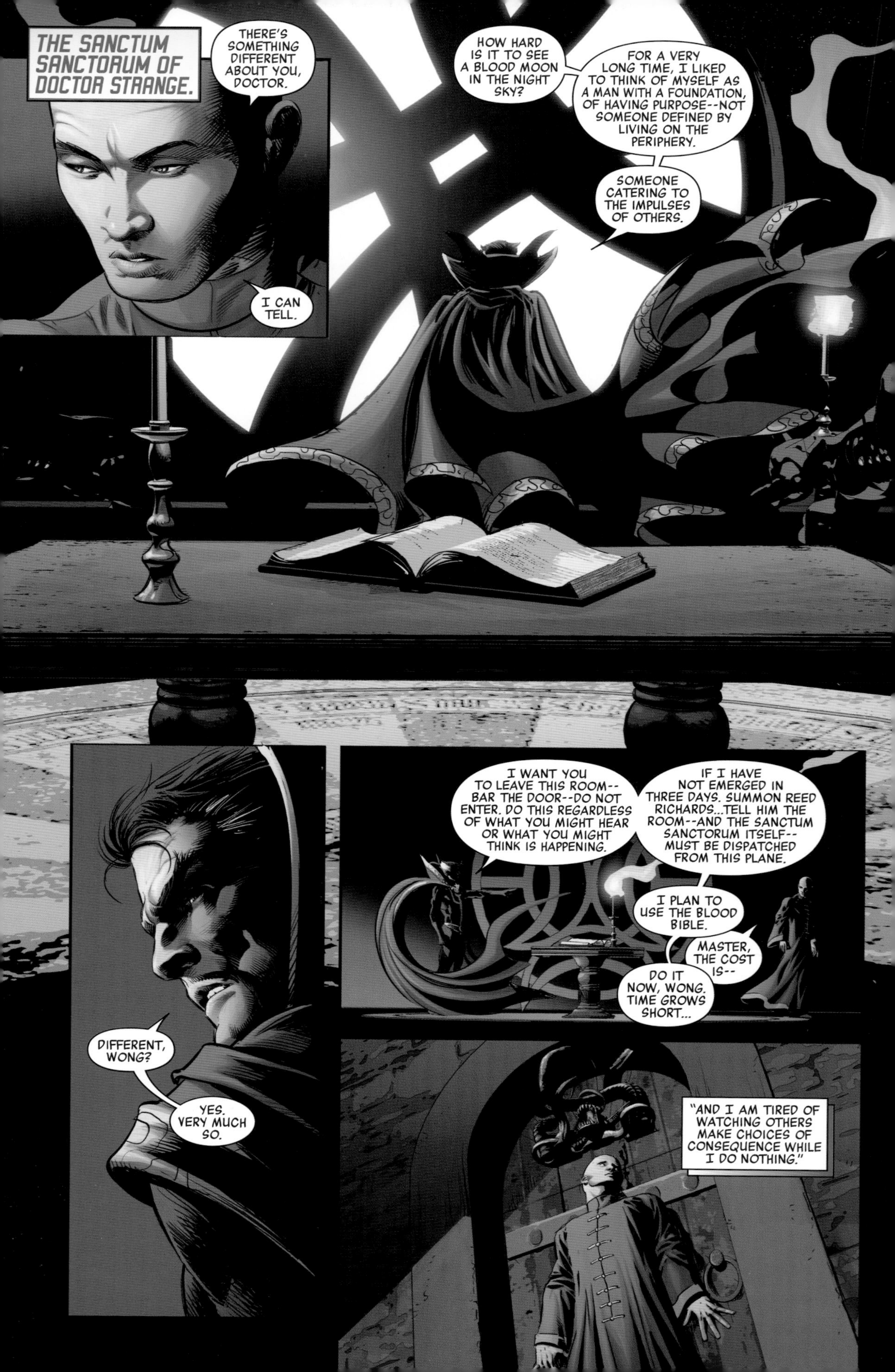

THE SANCTUM SANCTORUM OF DOCTOR STRANGE.
THERE'S SOMETHING DIFFERENT ABOUT YOU, DOCTOR.
I CAN TELL.
HOW HARD IS IT TO SEE A BLOOD MOON IN THE NIGHT SKY?
FOR A VERY LONG TIME, I LIKED TO THINK OF MYSELF AS A MAN WITH A FOUNDATION, OF HAVING PURPOSE--NOT SOMEONE DEFINED BY LIVING ON THE PERIPHERY.
SOMEONE CATERING TO THE IMPULSES OF OTHERS.
DIFFERENT, WONG?
YES. VERY MUCH SO.
I WANT YOU TO LEAVE THIS ROOM--BAR THE DOOR--DO NOT ENTER. DO THIS REGARDLESS OF WHAT YOU MIGHT HEAR OR WHAT YOU MIGHT THINK IS HAPPENING.
IF I HAVE NOT EMERGED IN THREE DAYS. SUMMON REED RICHARDS...TELL HIM THE ROOM--AND THE SANCTUM SANCTORUM ITSELF--MUST BE DISPATCHED FROM THIS PLANE.
I PLAN TO USE THE BLOOD BIBLE.
MASTER, THE COST IS--
DO IT NOW, WONG. TIME GROWS SHORT...
"AND I AM TIRED OF WATCHING OTHERS MAKE CHOICES OF CONSEQUENCE WHILE I DO NOTHING."

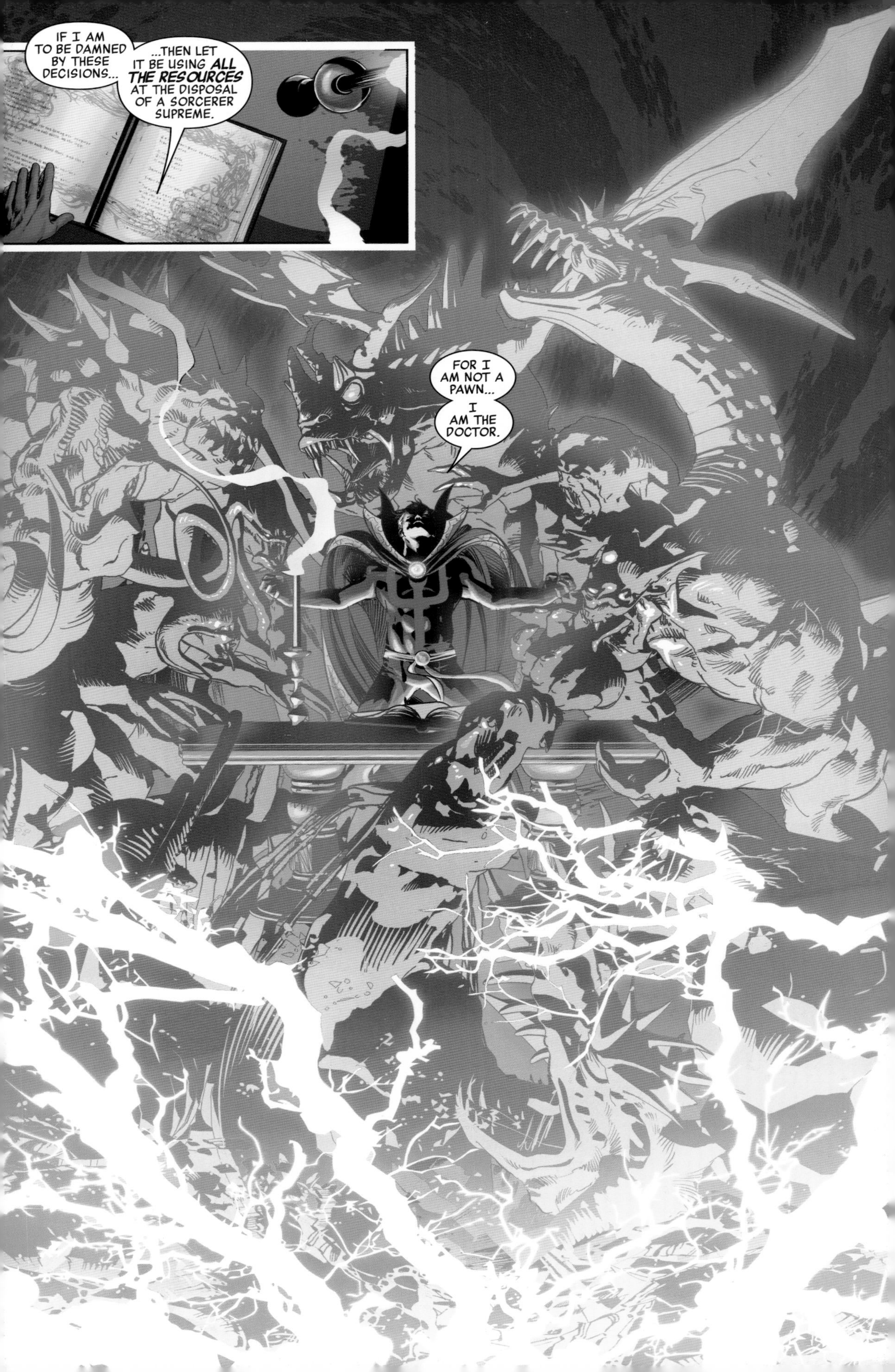
IF I AM TO BE DAMNED BY THESE DECISIONS...
...THEN LET IT BE USING ALL THE RESOURCES AT THE DISPOSAL OF A SORCERER SUPREME.
FOR I AM NOT A PAWN...
I AM THE DOCTOR.

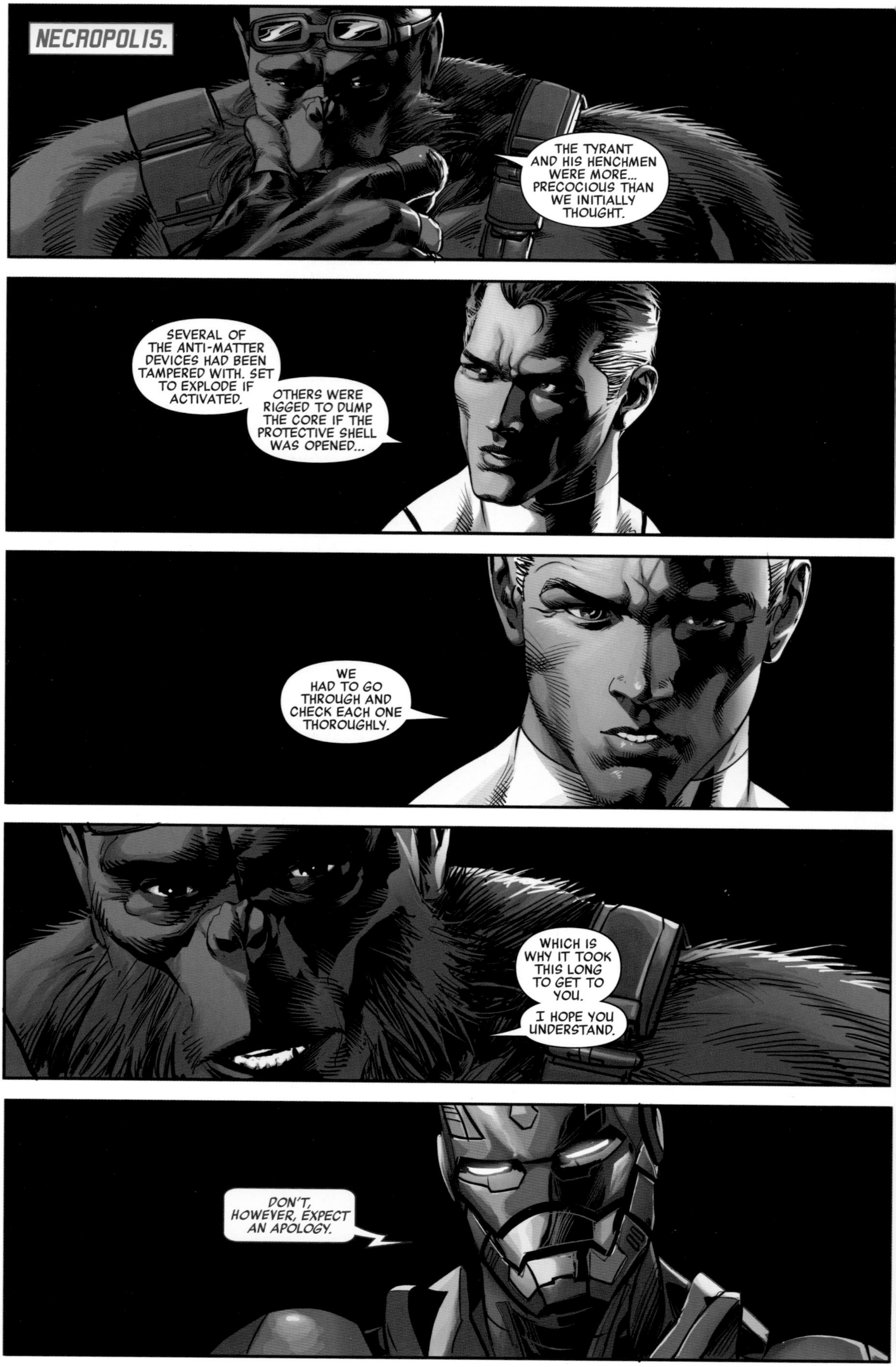
NECROPOLIS.
THE TYRANT AND HIS HENCHMEN WERE MORE... PRECOCIOUS THAN WE INITIALLY THOUGHT.
SEVERAL OF THE ANTI-MATTER DEVICES HAD BEEN TAMPERED WITH. SET TO EXPLODE IF ACTIVATED.
OTHERS WERE RIGGED TO DUMP THE CORE IF THE PROTECTIVE SHELL WAS OPENED...
WE HAD TO GO THROUGH AND CHECK EACH ONE THOROUGHLY.
WHICH IS WHY IT TOOK THIS LONG TO GET TO YOU.
I HOPE YOU UNDERSTAND.
DON'T, HOWEVER, EXPECT AN APOLOGY.

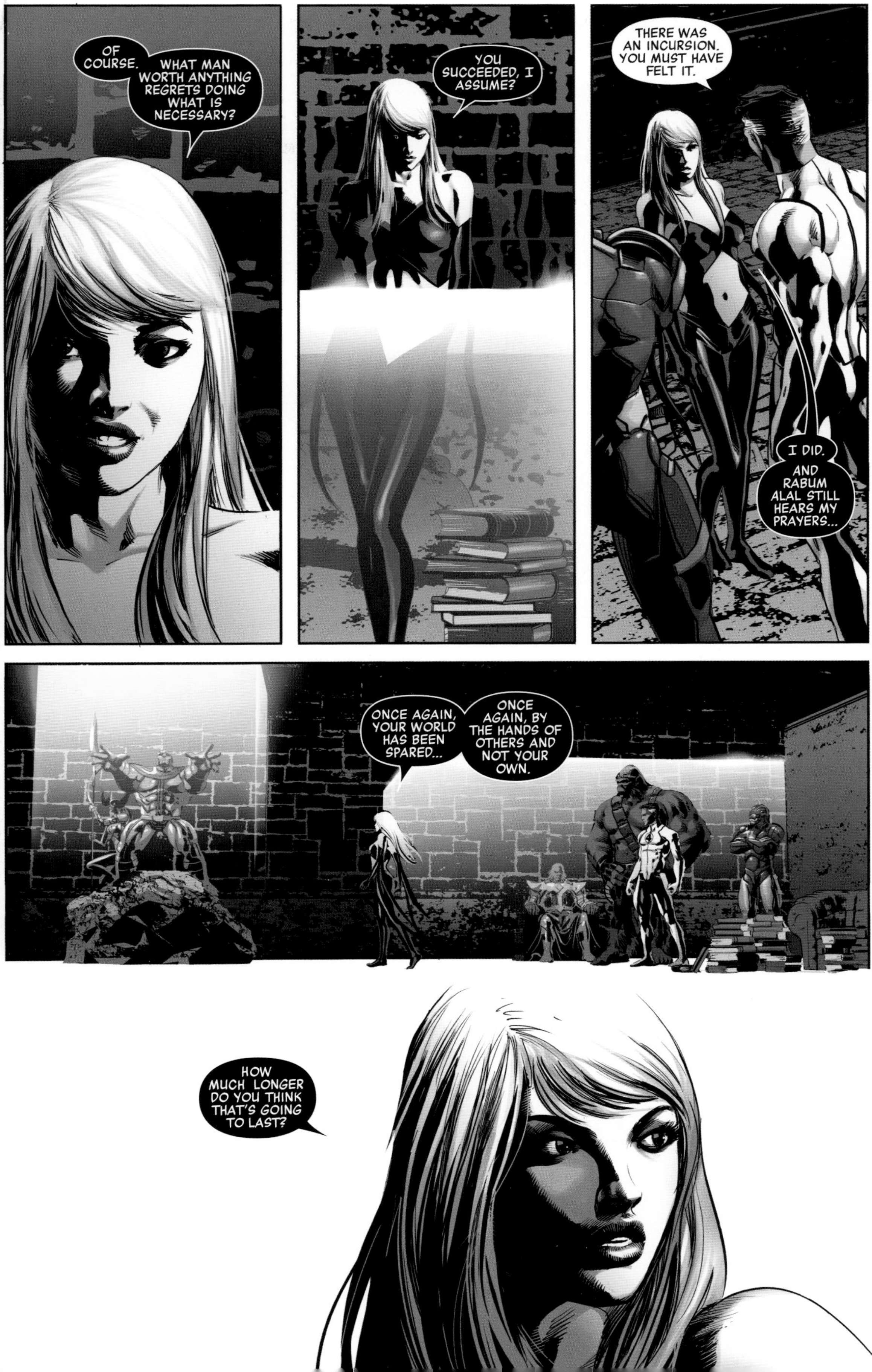
OF COURSE.
WHAT MAN WORTH ANYTHING REGRETS DOING WHAT IS NECESSARY?
YOU SUCCEEDED, I ASSUME?
THERE WAS AN INCURSION. YOU MUST HAVE FELT IT.
I DID.
AND RABUM ALAL STILL HEARS MY PRAYERS...
ONCE AGAIN, YOUR WORLD HAS BEEN SPARED...
ONCE AGAIN, BY THE HANDS OF OTHERS AND NOT YOUR OWN.
HOW MUCH LONGER DO YOU THINK THAT'S GOING TO LAST?

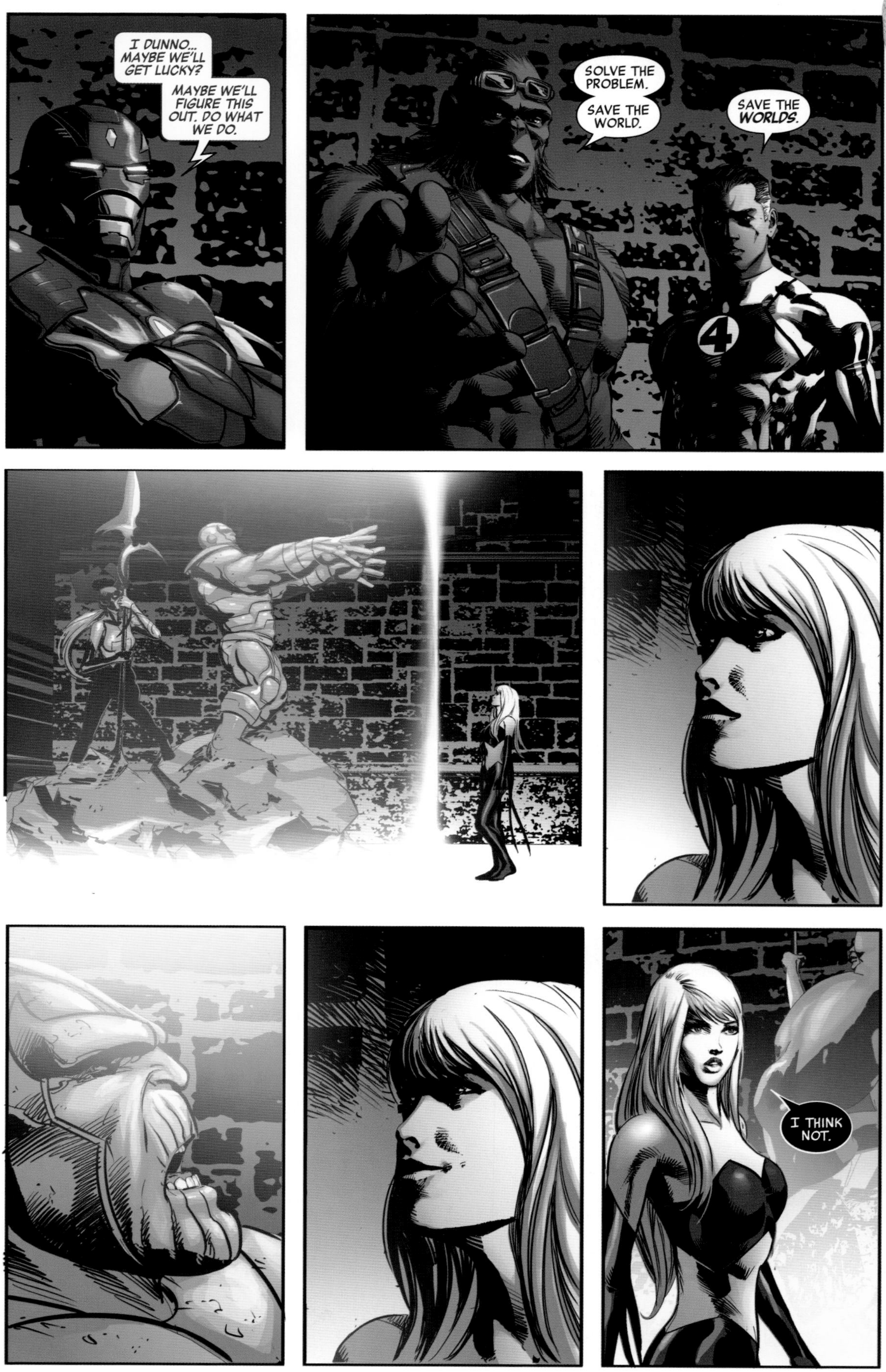
I DUNNO... MAYBE WE'LL GET LUCKY?
MAYBE WE'LL FIGURE THIS OUT. DO WHAT WE DO.
SOLVE THE PROBLEM.
SAVE THE WORLD.
SAVE THE *WORLDS*.
I THINK NOT.

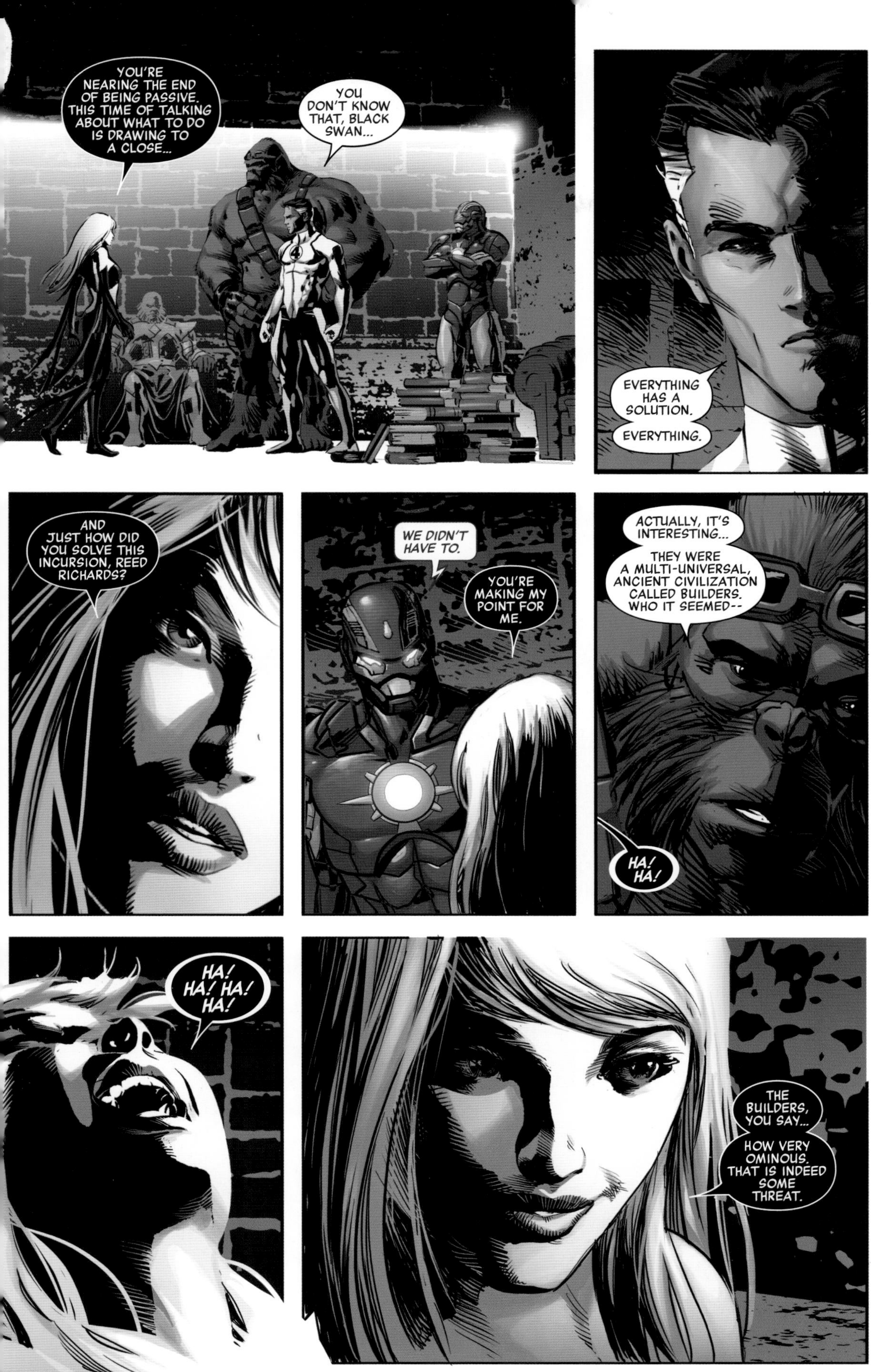
YOU'RE NEARING THE END OF BEING PASSIVE. THIS TIME OF TALKING ABOUT WHAT TO DO IS DRAWING TO A CLOSE...
YOU DON'T KNOW THAT, BLACK SWAN...
EVERYTHING HAS A SOLUTION.
EVERYTHING.
AND JUST HOW DID YOU SOLVE THIS INCURSION, REED RICHARDS?
WE DIDN'T HAVE TO.
YOU'RE MAKING MY POINT FOR ME.
ACTUALLY, IT'S INTERESTING...
THEY WERE A MULTI-UNIVERSAL, ANCIENT CIVILIZATION CALLED BUILDERS. WHO IT SEEMED--
HA! HA!
HA! HA! HA! HA!
THE BUILDERS, YOU SAY...
HOW VERY OMINOUS. THAT IS INDEED SOME THREAT.

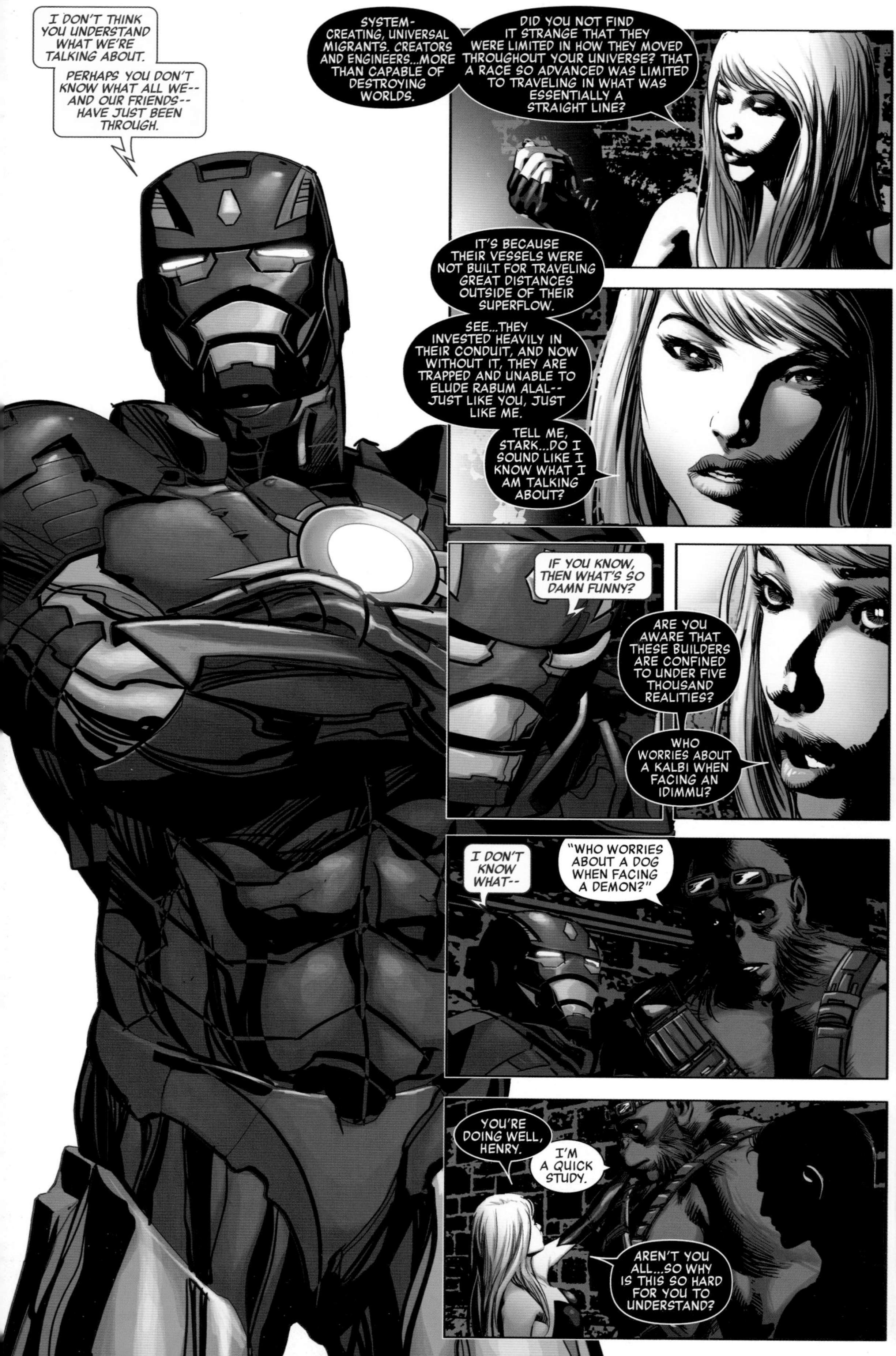
I DON'T THINK YOU UNDERSTAND WHAT WE'RE TALKING ABOUT.
PERHAPS YOU DON'T KNOW WHAT ALL WE-- AND OUR FRIENDS-- HAVE JUST BEEN THROUGH.
SYSTEM-CREATING, UNIVERSAL MIGRANTS. CREATORS AND ENGINEERS...MORE THAN CAPABLE OF DESTROYING WORLDS.
DID YOU NOT FIND IT STRANGE THAT THEY WERE LIMITED IN HOW THEY MOVED THROUGHOUT YOUR UNIVERSE? THAT A RACE SO ADVANCED WAS LIMITED TO TRAVELING IN WHAT WAS ESSENTIALLY A STRAIGHT LINE?
IT'S BECAUSE THEIR VESSELS WERE NOT BUILT FOR TRAVELING GREAT DISTANCES OUTSIDE OF THEIR SUPERFLOW.
SEE...THEY INVESTED HEAVILY IN THEIR CONDUIT, AND NOW WITHOUT IT, THEY ARE TRAPPED AND UNABLE TO ELUDE RABUM ALAL-- JUST LIKE YOU, JUST LIKE ME.
TELL ME, STARK...DO I SOUND LIKE I KNOW WHAT I AM TALKING ABOUT?
IF YOU KNOW, THEN WHAT'S SO DAMN FUNNY?
ARE YOU AWARE THAT THESE BUILDERS ARE CONFINED TO UNDER FIVE THOUSAND REALITIES?
WHO WORRIES ABOUT A KALBI WHEN FACING AN IDIMMU?
I DON'T KNOW WHAT--
"WHO WORRIES ABOUT A DOG WHEN FACING A DEMON?"
YOU'RE DOING WELL, HENRY.
I'M A QUICK STUDY.
AREN'T YOU ALL...SO WHY IS THIS SO HARD FOR YOU TO UNDERSTAND?

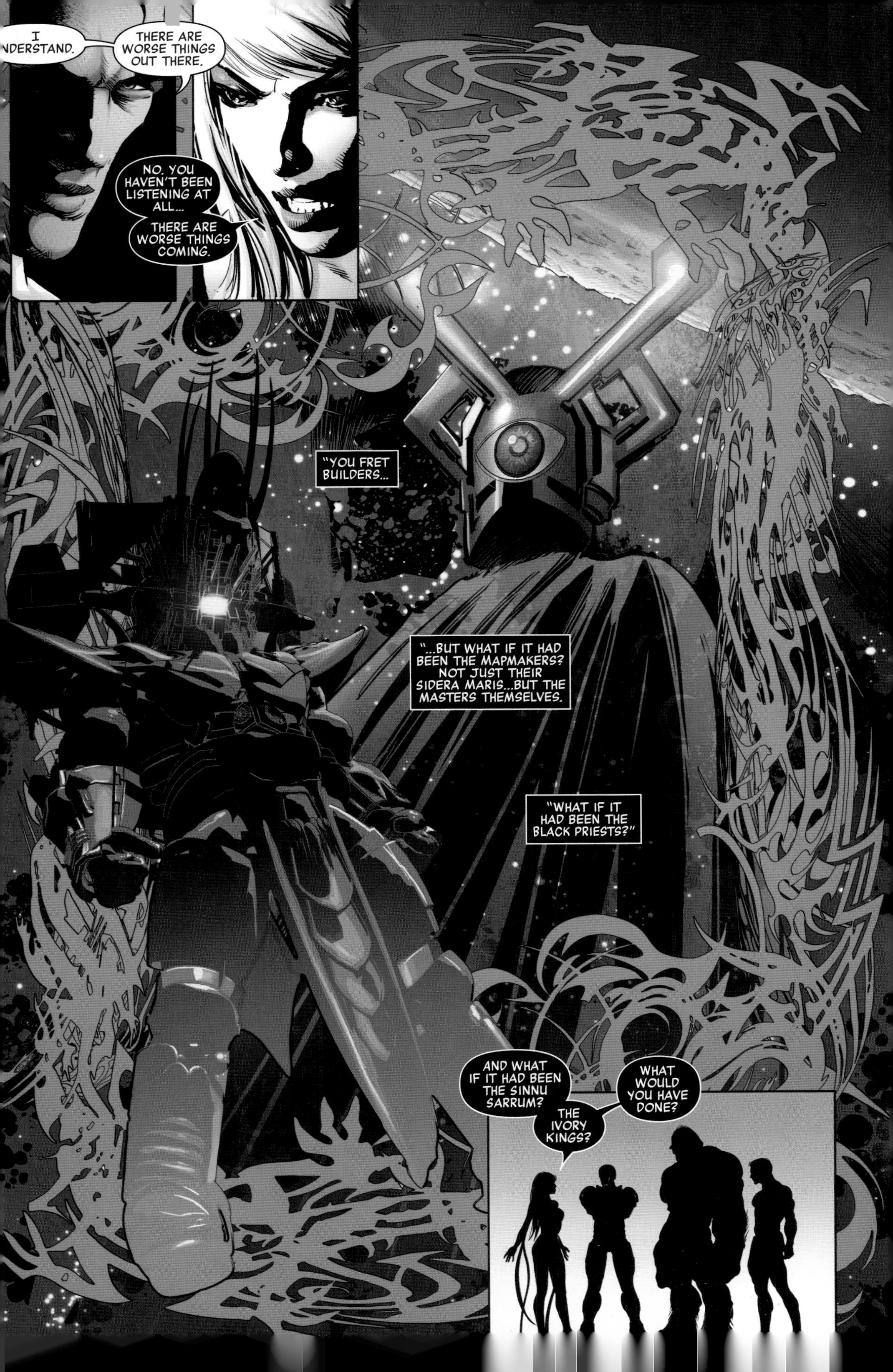
I
NDERSTAND.
THERE ARE
WORSE THINGS
OUT THERE.
NO. YOU
HAVEN'T BEEN
LISTENING AT
ALL...
THERE ARE
WORSE THINGS
COMING.
"YOU FRET
BUILDERS...
"...BUT WHAT IF IT HAD
BEEN THE MAPMAKERS?
NOT JUST THEIR
SIDERA MARIS...BUT THE
MASTERS THEMSELVES.
"WHAT IF IT
HAD BEEN THE
BLACK PRIESTS?"
AND WHAT
IF IT HAD BEEN
THE SINNU
SARRUM?
THE
IVORY
KINGS?
WHAT
WOULD
YOU HAVE
DONE?

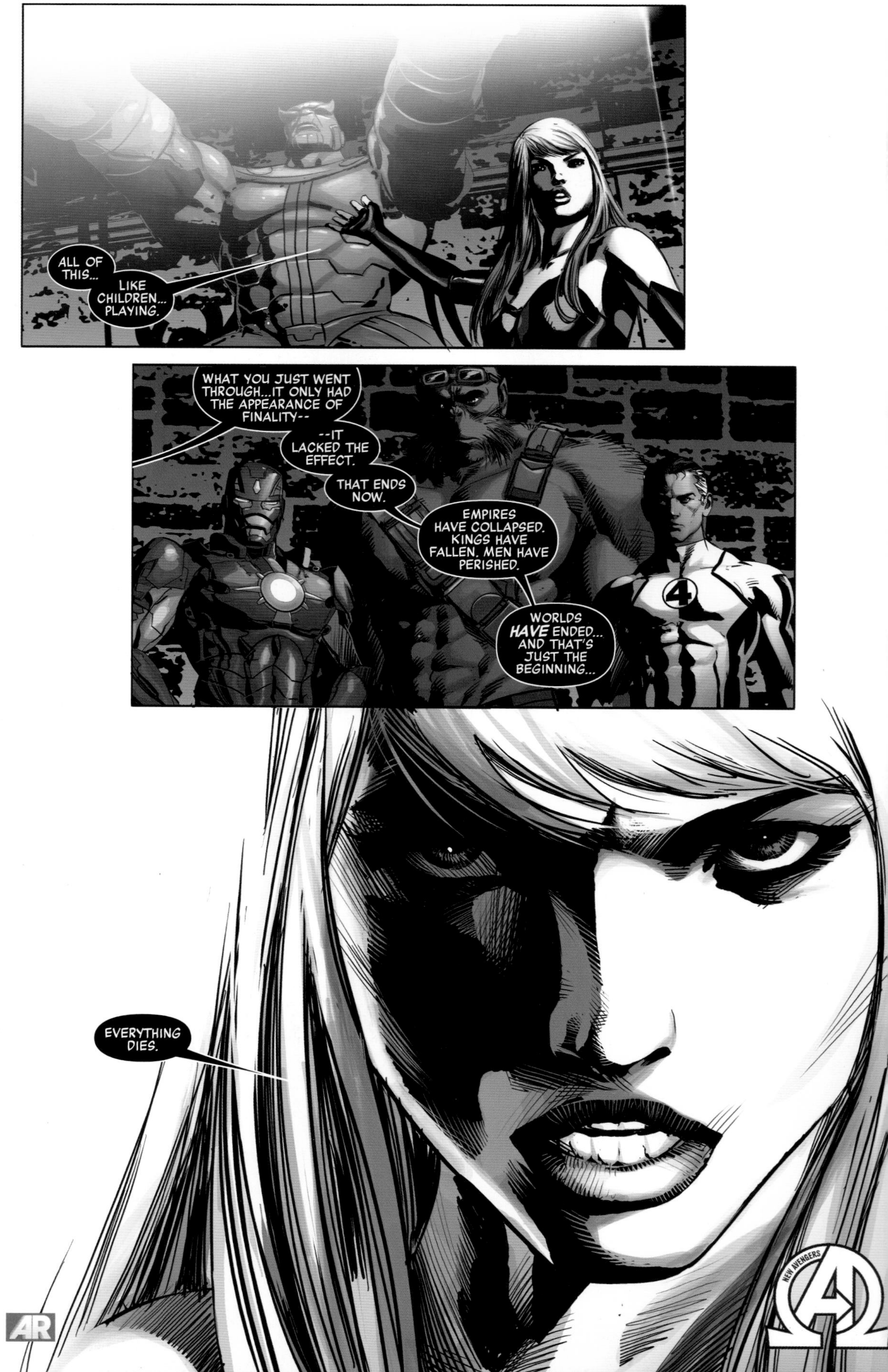
ALL OF THIS...
LIKE CHILDREN... PLAYING.
WHAT YOU JUST WENT THROUGH...IT ONLY HAD THE APPEARANCE OF FINALITY--
--IT LACKED THE EFFECT.
THAT ENDS NOW.
EMPIRES HAVE COLLAPSED. KINGS HAVE FALLEN. MEN HAVE PERISHED.
WORLDS HAVE ENDED... AND THAT'S JUST THE BEGINNING...
EVERYTHING DIES.
NEW AVENGERS
AR

INFINITY™ Variant Cover Gallery

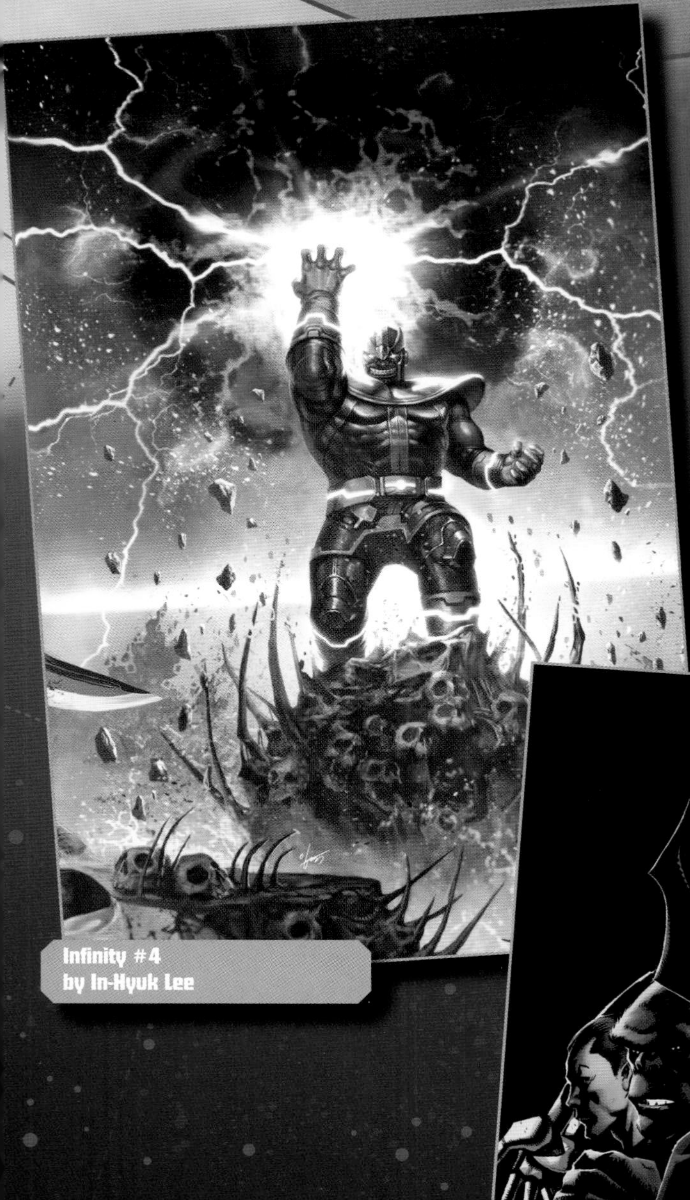

Infinity #4
by In-Hyuk Lee

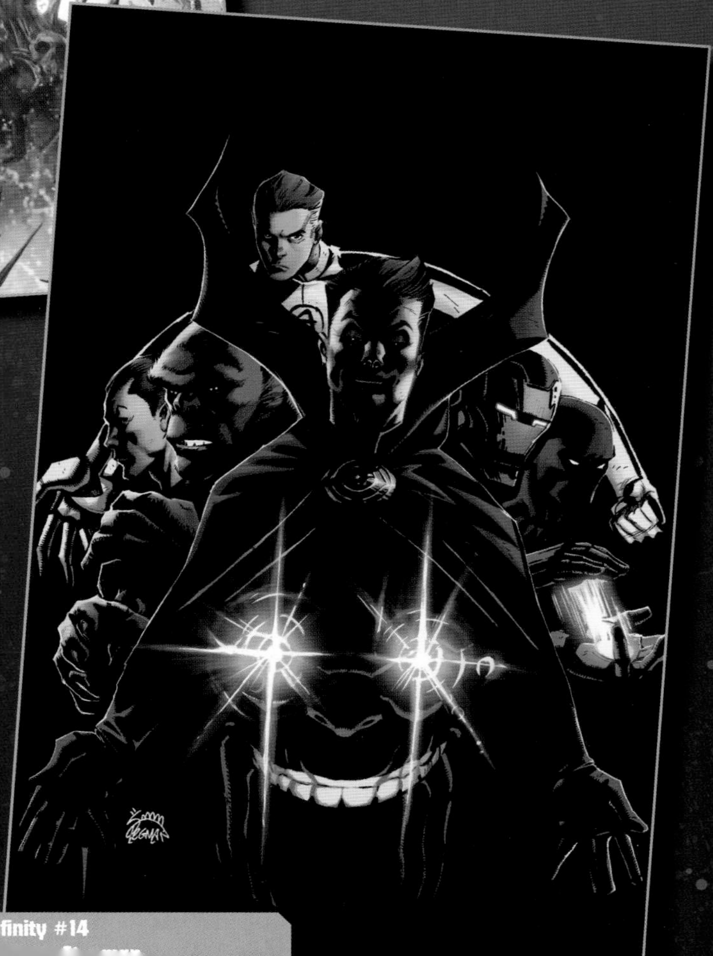

Infinity #14

ng

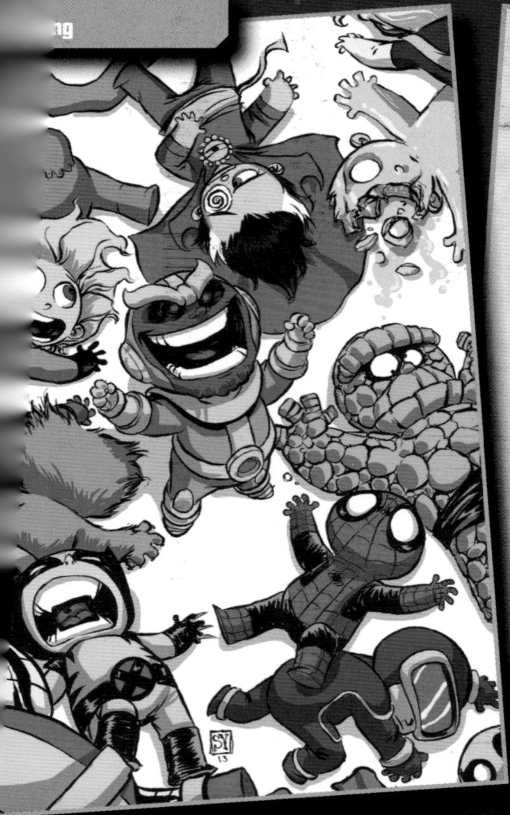

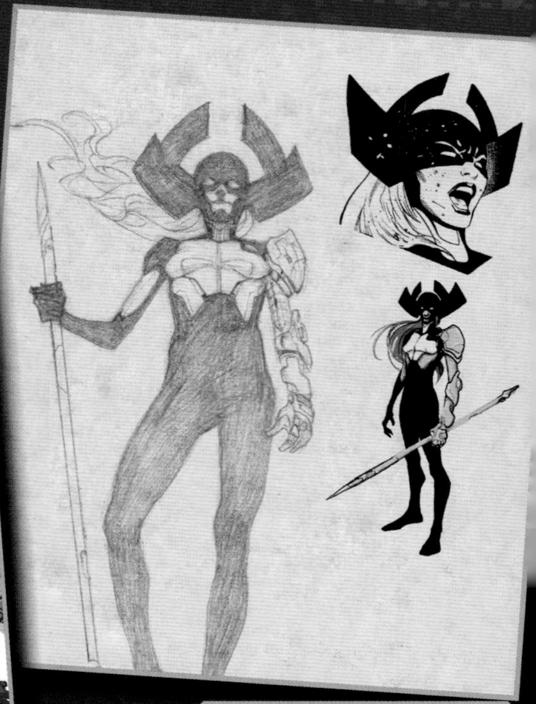

Infinity #5
by Jerome Opeña

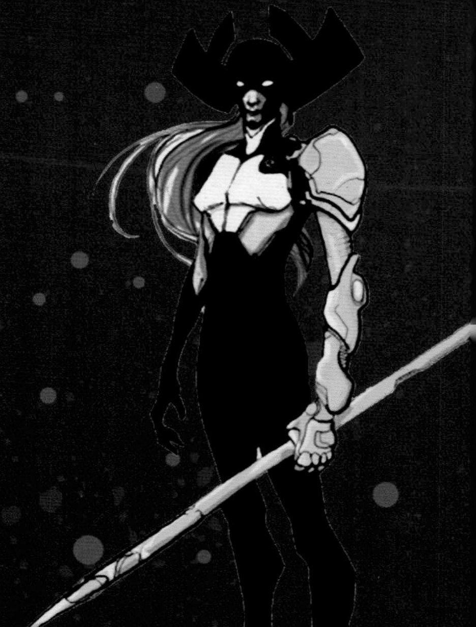

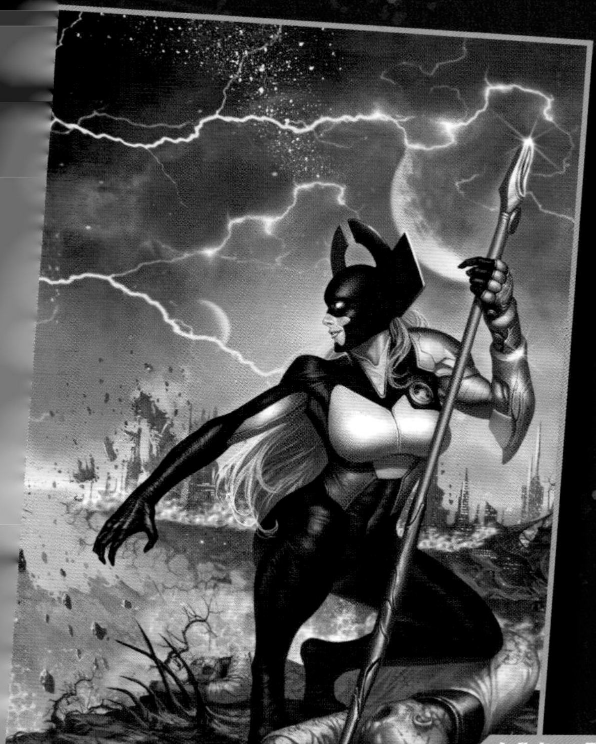

Infinity #5
by In-Hyuk Lee

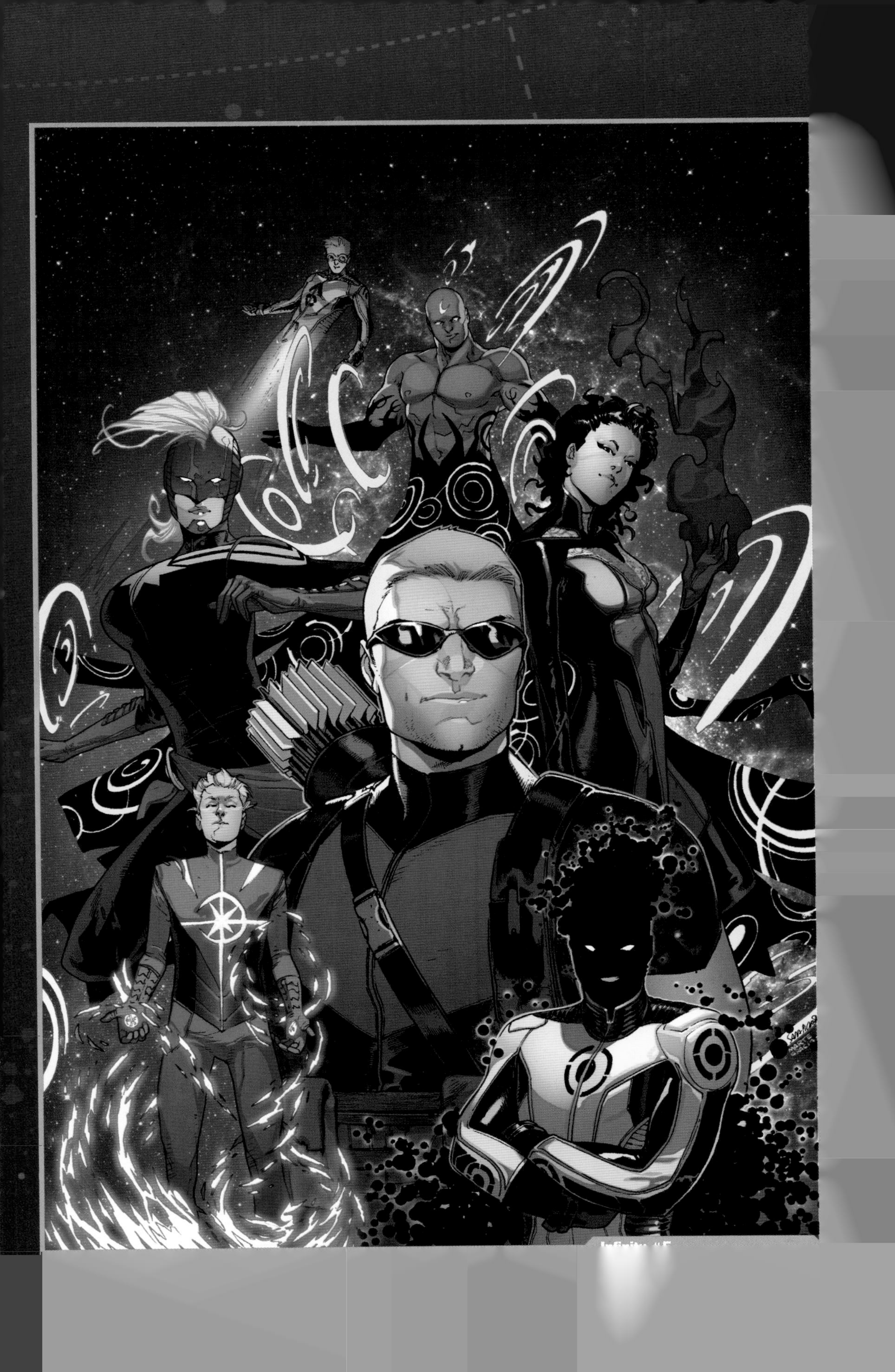

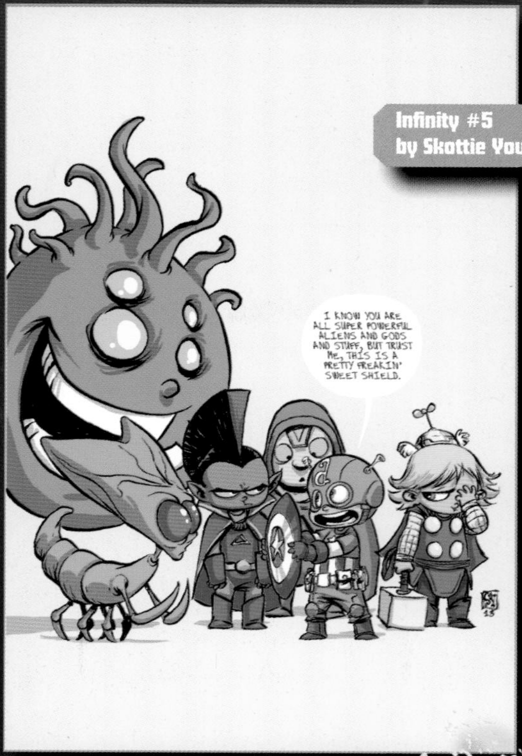
I KNOW YOU ARE ALL SUPER POWERFUL ALIENS AND GODS AND STUFF, BUT TRUST ME, THIS IS A PRETTY FREAKIN' SWEET SHIELD.

Infinity #5
by Skottie Young

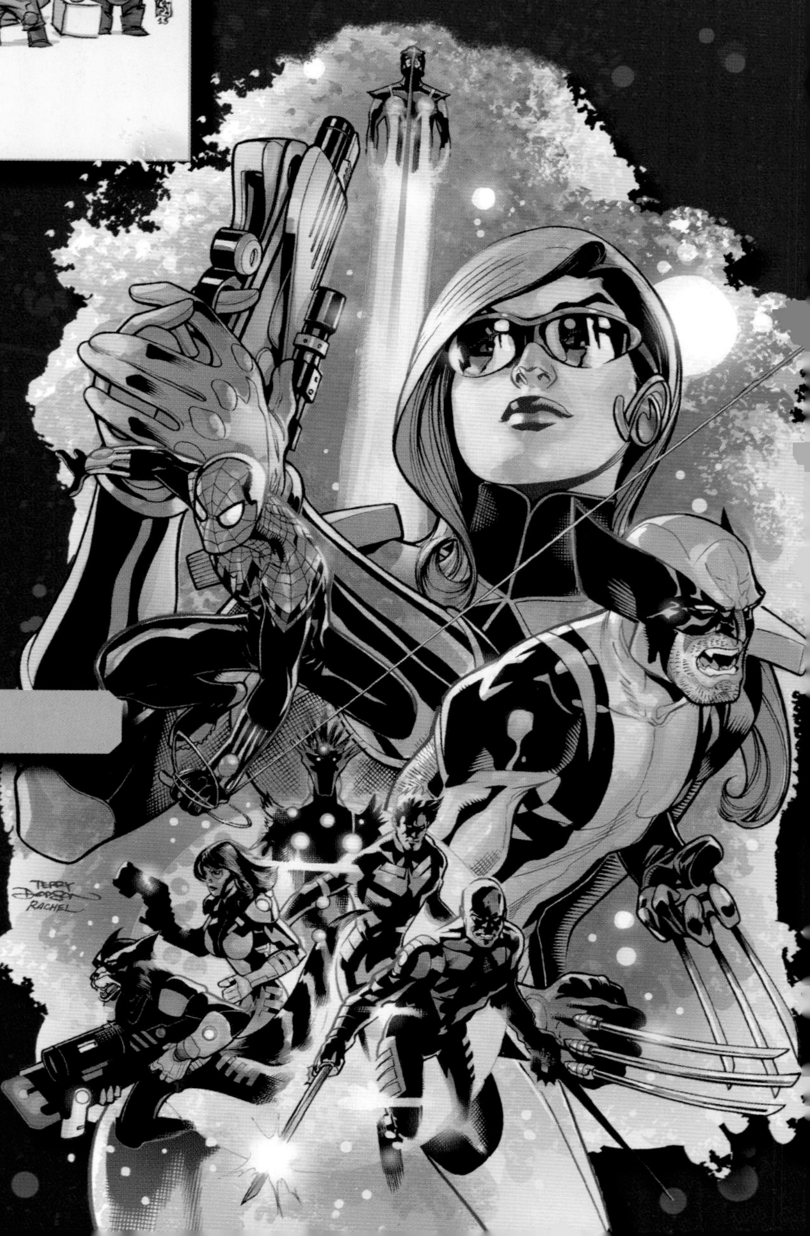
TERRY DODSON RACHEL

Infinity #6
by Terry Dodson

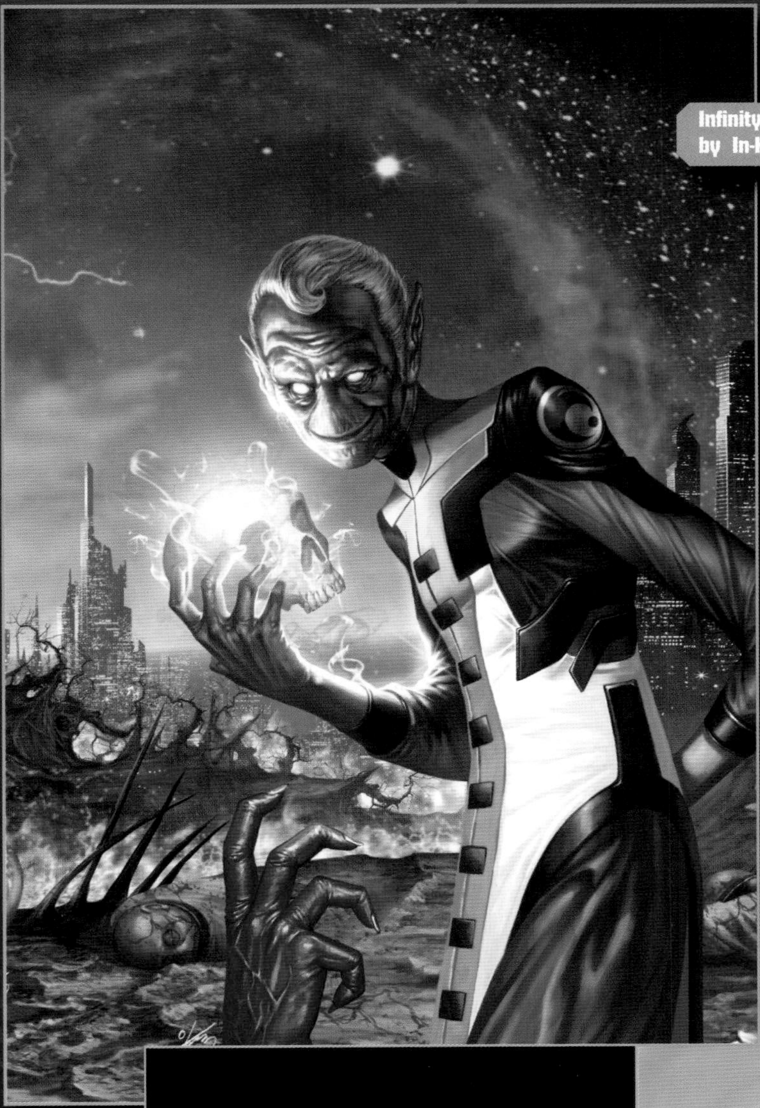

Infinity #6
by In-Hyuk Lee

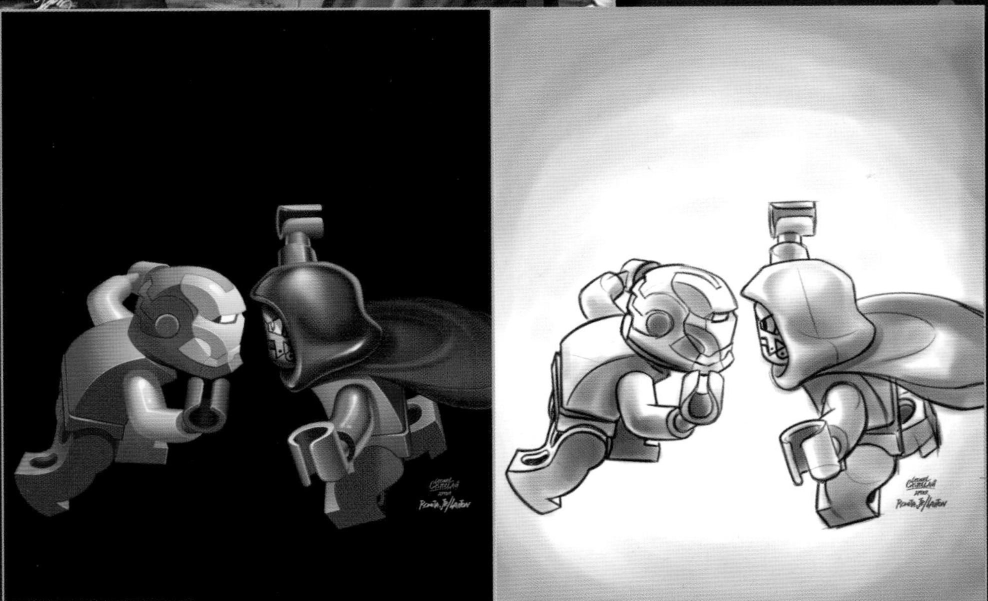

New Avengers #11

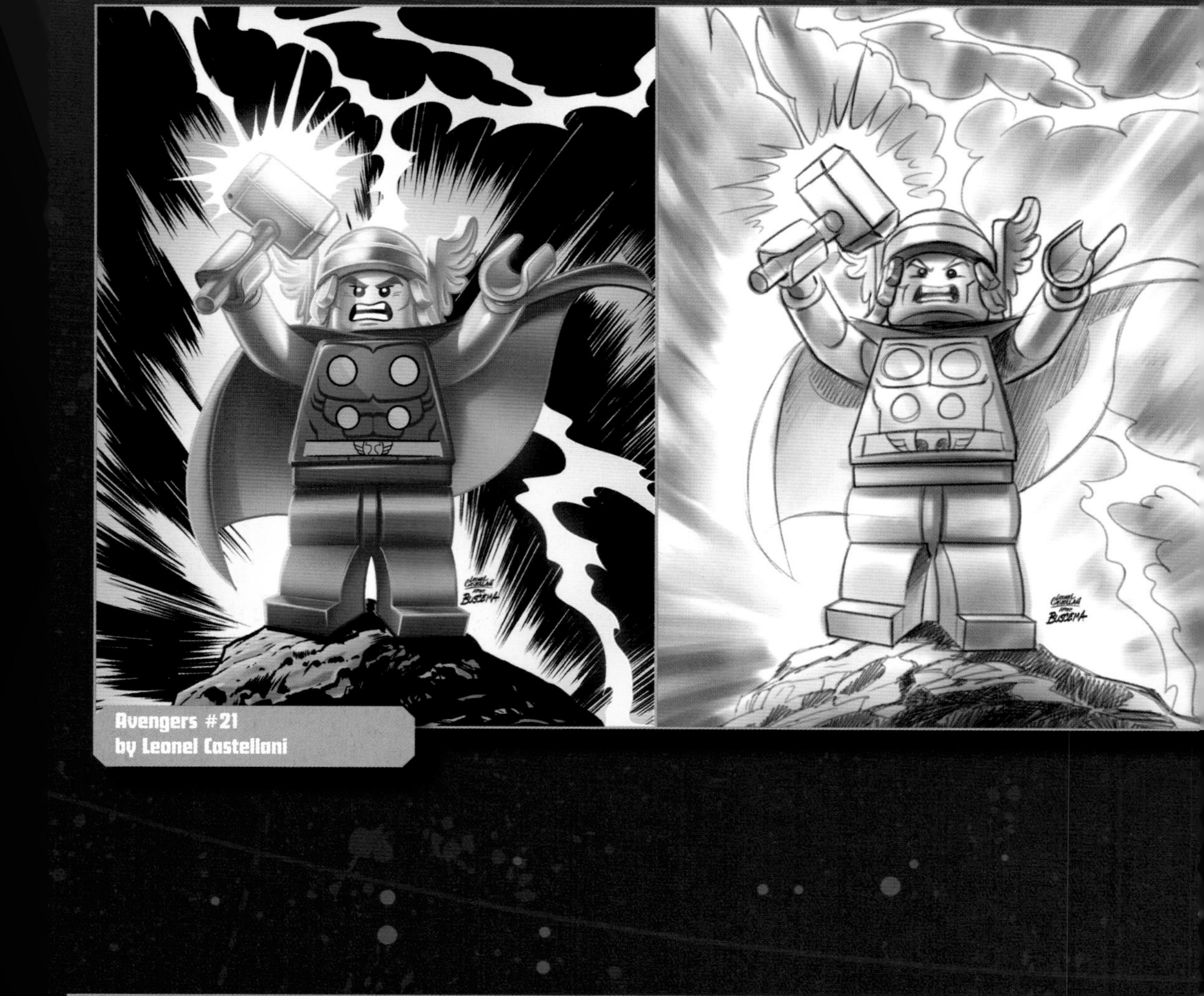

Avengers #21
by Leonel Castellani

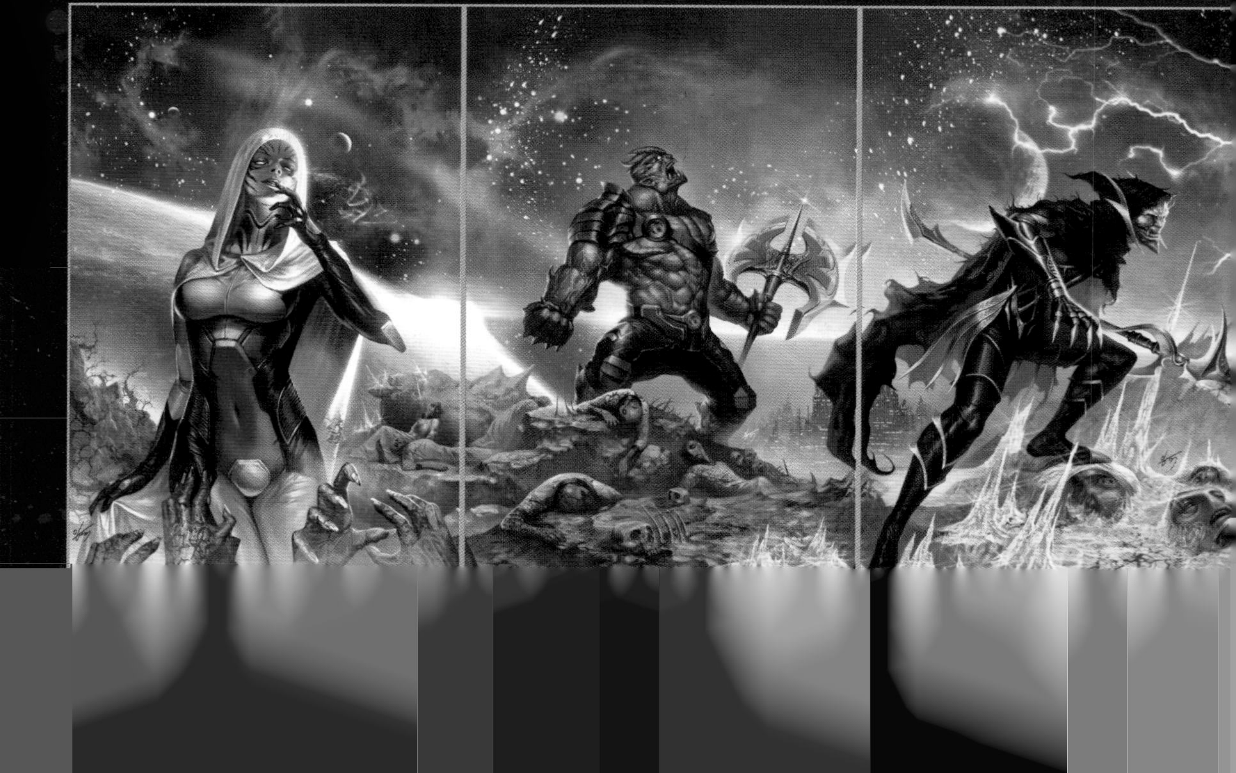

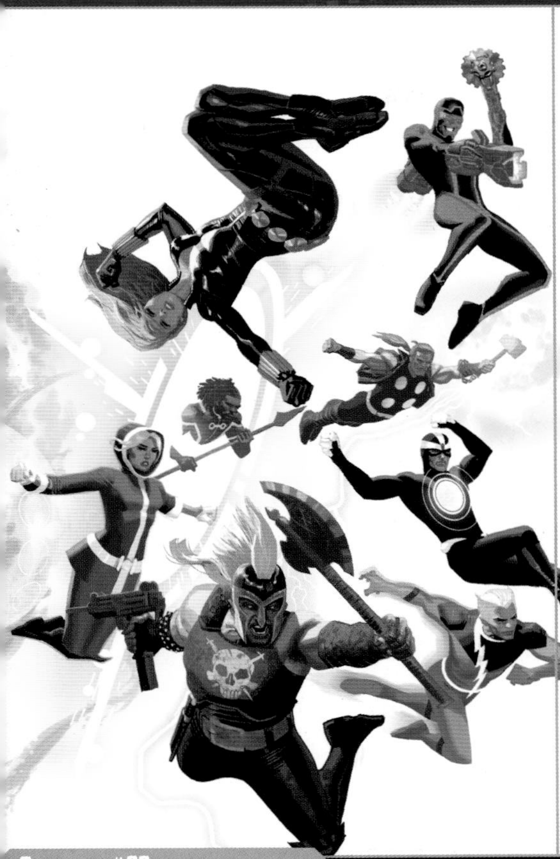

Avengers #22
by Daniel Acuña

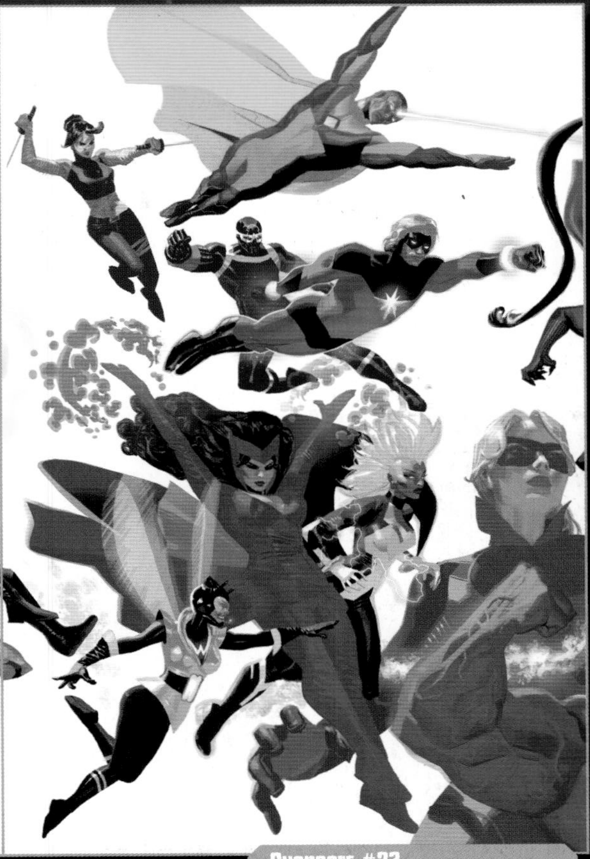

Avengers #23
by Daniel Acuña

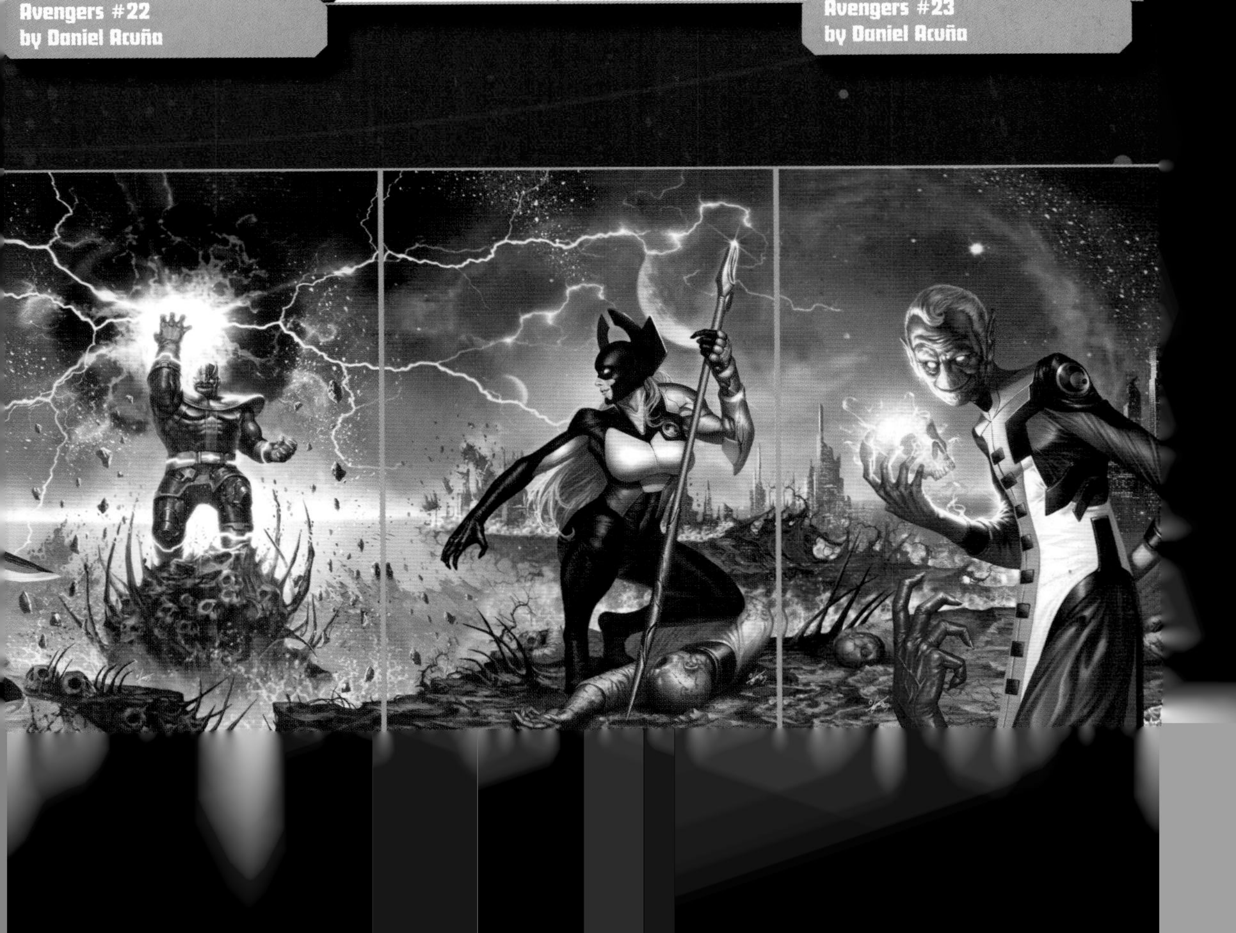

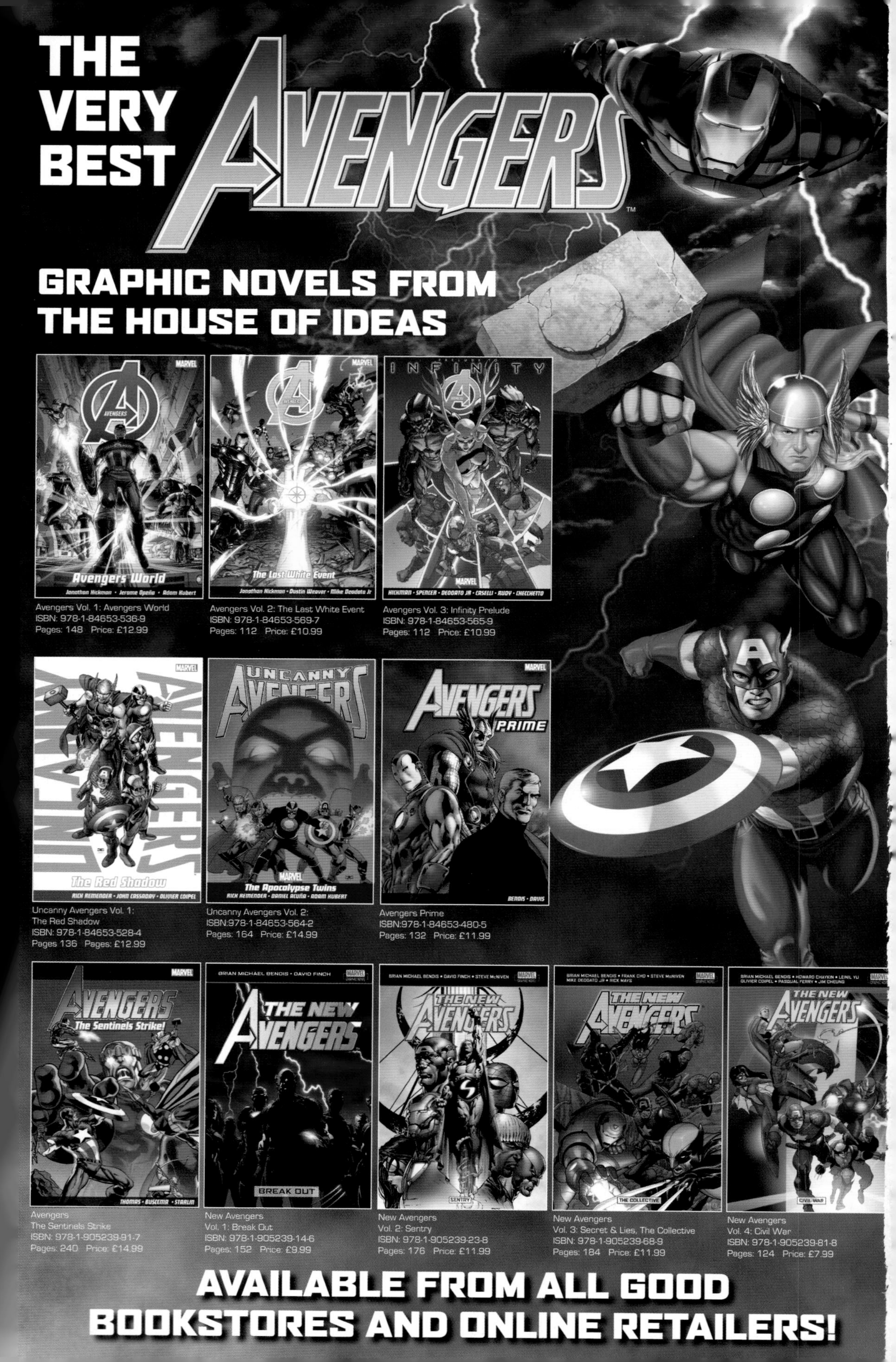
THE VERY BEST
AVENGERS
GRAPHIC NOVELS FROM THE HOUSE OF IDEAS
Avengers World
Jonathan Hickman • Jerome Opeña • Adam Kubert
Avengers Vol. 1: Avengers World
ISBN: 978-1-84653-536-9
Pages: 148 Price: £12.99
The Last White Event
Jonathan Hickman • Dustin Weaver • Mike Deodato Jr
Avengers Vol. 2: The Last White Event
ISBN: 978-1-84653-569-7
Pages: 112 Price: £10.99
INFINITY
Hickman • Spencer • Deodato Jr • Caselli • Rudy • Checchetto
Avengers Vol. 3: Infinity Prelude
ISBN: 978-1-84653-565-9
Pages: 112 Price: £10.99
The Red Shadow
Rick Remender • John Cassaday • Olivier Coipel
Uncanny Avengers Vol. 1:
The Red Shadow
ISBN: 978-1-84653-528-4
Pages 136 Pages: £12.99
Uncanny Avengers
The Apocalypse Twins
Rick Remender • Daniel Acuña • Adam Kubert
Uncanny Avengers Vol. 2:
ISBN:978-1-84653-564-2
Pages: 164 Price: £14.99
Avengers Prime
Bendis • Davis
Avengers Prime
ISBN:978-1-84653-480-5
Pages: 132 Price: £11.99
Avengers
The Sentinels Strike!
Thomas • Buscema • Starlin
Avengers
The Sentinels Strike
ISBN: 978-1-905239-91-7
Pages: 240 Price: £14.99
Brian Michael Bendis • David Finch
The New Avengers
Break Out
New Avengers
Vol. 1: Break Out
ISBN: 978-1-905239-14-6
Pages: 152 Price: £9.99
Brian Michael Bendis • David Finch • Steve McNiven
The New Avengers
Sentry
New Avengers
Vol. 2: Sentry
ISBN: 978-1-905239-23-8
Pages: 176 Price: £11.99
Brian Michael Bendis • Frank Cho • Steve McNiven
Mike Deodato Jr • Rick Mays
The New Avengers
The Collective
New Avengers
Vol. 3: Secret & Lies, The Collective
ISBN: 978-1-905239-68-9
Pages: 184 Price: £11.99
Brian Michael Bendis • Howard Chaykin • Leinil Yu
Olivier Coipel • Pasqual Ferry • Jim Cheung
The New Avengers
Civil War
New Avengers
Vol. 4: Civil War
ISBN: 978-1-905239-81-8
Pages: 124 Price: £7.99
AVAILABLE FROM ALL GOOD BOOKSTORES AND ONLINE RETAILERS!